DIVIDED

PLANET

THE ECOLOGY OF
RICH AND POOR

Tom Athanasiou

The University of Georgia Press

Athens and London

Published in 1998 by the University of Georgia Press

Athens, Georgia 30602

© 1996 by Tom Athanasiou

The paper in this book meets the guidelines for
permanence and durability of the Committee on
Production Guidelines for Book Longevity of the
Council on Library Resources.

Printed in the United States of America

02 01 00 99 98   P   5 4 3 2 1

Library of Congress Cataloging in Publication Data

Athanasiou, Tom.

Divided planet : the ecology of rich and poor / Tom Athanasiou.

p.   cm.

Originally published: Boston : Little, Brown and Co., 1996.

Includes bibliographical references (p.   ) and index.

ISBN 0-8203-2007-2 (pbk. : alk. paper)

1. Environmentalism. 2. Environmental degradation—Political
aspects. 3. Environmental degradation—Economic aspects.
I. Title.

GE195.A85   1998

363.7—dc21   97-30503

British Library Cataloging in Publication Data available

TO MURRAY, *who got me thinking*

In the coming world order, there will be winners and there will be losers. The losers will outnumber the winners by an unimaginable factor.

— JACQUES ATTALI,
founding president of the European Bank for
Reconstruction and Development, 1991

Contents

Acknowledgments

I owe many thanks, the greatest to the people who read and criticized my early drafts. More than once, I felt I was verging on friend abuse by asking people to review texts that were too rough by half. Given an infinite amount of time, I would have made fewer demands, but, then, there is not an infinite amount of time.

Writing this, I'm amazed by how many people have helped me. I will, however, single out two for special thanks. Andrea Torrice is the first. *Divided Planet*, and the pains of its birth, figured larger in her life than, I think, she would have wished. Joe Spieler, too, though he will be bemused to find himself in this paragraph, has been more than an agent. He has also been a coach, and even a father confessor. I hope he takes real satisfaction in the final result.

I owe special thanks as well to the movement institutions that have supported me in the course of *Divided Planet*'s long gestation. First among these is the Blue Mountain Center, which allowed me to retreat to its Adirondack silences not once but three times. To Blue Mountain's director, Harriet Barlow, and to Shiela Kinney, Ben Shrader, and the rest of its staff, I am grateful far beyond words. And there is the Berkeley-based International Rivers Network, a small but sophisticated outfit to which I wish boundless success, as long as that success entails no loss of conviviality. Writing a book can be a lonely undertaking, and IRN's staff, and especially Juliette Majot, allowed me to know myself as part of the movement, and not merely as a loose cannon on its decks. Without the ideas and contacts she so freely offered me, this book would certainly be far less satisfactory.

Thanks, too, to Food First, The Institute for Food and Development Policy, in Oakland, California, an outfit that had me, briefly, as a "visiting scholar," or at least as the occupant of the room designated for that exalted office. Food First was a pathbreaker among U.S. green organizations. May it play the same role again! Finally, I want to thank the staff of Berkeley's Nautilus Institute for Security and Sustainable Development — Peter Hayes and Paula Fomby, to be sure, and of course Lyuba Zarsky, my favorite economist, but especially Rachel Sommerville, who among much else is quite a gifted and fine-spirited reader.

There are many others to thank. The people who submitted to my interviews are really the ones who made this book possible, but I will not thank them here — their names are all in the notes. Jim Silberman, my editor at Little, Brown, is a meticulous gentleman of the old school; I was lucky to have him, and I know it. Peggy Leith Anderson, my copy editor, then startled me again with her precision and care. Judy Levine, Jane Staw, and Dan Gorden, each in their own way, helped me believe I could perhaps write well enough to pull this off. Marcy Darnovsky read more than her share of my half-raw prose, as did Blair Sandler, who worked hard to help me distill a critique of green economics that made sense. Cynthia Kaufman, Chris Carlsson, and Richard Grossman all tried to save me from my ecumenism, and though they failed, they did help suppress the optimism to which I somehow remain vulnerable. John Gershman and John Sundman both took the time to give me close, complete readings and detailed feedback. I needed it badly. Sundman, moreover, tried his best to disagree with me. Matt Holdreith helped me to see the ironies of humility. Elinor Nauen is a fine editor, and a hoot. Ralph Ostermann, Lenore Goldman, Tomasz Terlecki, David Gorden, and Margaret Bowman all went out of their way to help me make sense of events in the former Soviet bloc. Bill Walker, Elena Eger, Vicot Menotti, David Helvarg, Paul Hawken, Josh Karliner, Ian McWilliam, Owen Lamers, Paddy McCully, Beth Burrows, Bruce Rich, R. Dennis Hayes, Claire Greensfelder, Ron Davis, and Cal Broomhead all helped me bring one or another element of the sprawling movement mosaic into focus. The members of the Lorax Group likewise helped me keep my head screwed on straight, or at least firmly. Ward Bell and John Markoff both reminded me of the virtues of balance and judiciousness, and Ward, in particular, helped me see their limits.

TOM ATHANASIOU (toma@igc.apc.org)
San Francisco, October 1995

DIVIDED

PLANET

ONE

Where Are We Now?

The suicidal mentality of those in power is absolutely terrifying.

— UN staffer, off the record.

Divided Planet has a simple premise — environmentalism is only now reaching its political maturity. Its childhood heroes are, if not broken, at least diminished by a sense of high stakes and ramifying agendas. Past enthusiasms offer little solace, and before the challenges of Asia and Africa, of the oceans and the air, past victories seem only the slightest prelude. Faith in solar democracy, easy reform, deep ecology, and simple utopias of all kinds has faded year by year. The greens need enthusiasm, but they need all the powers of adulthood besides, and they know it.

This claim has many corollaries. Twilly Cannon, a former director of Greenpeace USA's Action Resources, gave me one of the most important. According to Cannon, the environmental movement is reaching the end of its "alert function." The alarm has been rung, and heard. "We now know that the world is burning. The question is how to put out the fire." It won't be easy, for "direct action, which works as a fire alarm, doesn't always work so well to put the fire out."[1]

In fact, nothing works so well, at least not yet. The future, to be sure, will be new, but we can't know just how. What we do know is that in the short time since the fall of the Berlin Wall, the currents of history have swept us quickly into deep, turbulent waters. Asian capitalism is booming, and its boom is an ecological catastrophe. The United States, or at least its electorate, is lurching wildly, and flirting with an inchoate, right-wing populism that does not admire environmentalism. Everywhere, greens strain to reinvent themselves, to announce their projects and intuitions as the keys to the future, but in this they are hardly alone. Free traders and arms traders, nationalists and knaves, everyone wants the future. The greens, obviously, are not ready.

In the East, the former "communist" lands, the lands where the old left utopia died, mafias of all varieties now conspire with *biznesmeni* and disappointed commissars to shape a future that will quite likely be as bitter as the past. Here, as everywhere, the market flaunts its victories — love and forests are both freely available to those with cash. Here, to state the obvious, concern with environmental protection is a luxury few can afford.

In the West, home of modern environmentalism, the times have also changed. The West German Green Party proves the point. The Greens were once "wise children," born, as Frieder Wolf, a pillar of the party's "center left," told me, to announce a new politics.[2] Recent time, though, has seen these children age beyond their years. Germany's 1990 election, its first as a reunified nation, found the Greens disoriented amidst the euphoria. Unwilling to celebrate West Germany's annexation of the East, insistent on a "third way" they could only dimly articulate, the Greens fell hard.

That, too, was the old days. Since 1990 the masses of post–Cold War politics have shifted and shifted again. The German Greens, merged with the peace and environment activists of East Germany's Alliance 90, have even enjoyed a comeback. In 1994 they won 10.1 percent in the European Parliamentary elections and 7 percent in Germany itself, and they've replaced the Free Democrats as Germany's pivotal third party. Good news, all of this, though evidence as much of disgust with politics as usual as of any rising ecological spirit. Green politics is back, but curiously, its significance is unclear. The certainties of the past are almost an embarrassment.

Around the world, history is a dark blur. The wild optimism of the falling Wall can scarcely even be remembered. Who still imagines that the East can "leapfrog" the West and rebuild on the basis of new green technologies? No one. This once common dream has withdrawn into a sour realism. Roger Manser, the British author of *Failed Transitions* — a rare study of social and environmental destruction in the East *after* the collapse of the old regime — was only stating the obvious when he told me that "the key to the East lies in the West. A sustainable restructuring must take place here first."[3]

He could as well have been speaking of the South — the former "Third World." In the South, too, changes in the West are the keys to a better future. In the South, too, often terrifying facts of life make the best argument for fundamental global change. Yet, such change remains merely a possibility, merely a promise. Nineteen eighty-nine's hope that the collapse of the Cold War system would bring the "real issues" to the surface proved to be quite without foundation. The German political ecologist Wolfgang Sachs put it well. It was "as if a barrier broke and nothing came through."[4] Nothing but hopelessness, fear, xenophobia, and the sense of a halting, inexorable decline.

In 1990 Greenpeace USA could raise big and easy money with mailing lists bought from such green stalwarts as the Victoria's Secret lingerie company. Those days are history. The terrifying new economy, the confusion of the post–Cold War world, the tiresome certainties of the old-line environmental groups, the well-funded "grassroots" anti-environmental movement, the sophistication of the "greenwashing" services available in the public relations marketplace, the aggressive promotion of a new genre of optimistic volumes that deny the existence of any environmental emergency — all combine to define a new regime. When Greenpeace USA stood against the Persian Gulf War, its more pragmatic staffers worried that they would pay for their principles — for insisting that beneath the fine rhetoric of peacekeeping there was only an old-fashioned oil war — in smaller donations and scaled-back campaign budgets. And Greenpeace's income did drop, though only in part because of its antiwar stance. The deeper problem is that green fund-raising is no longer the cherry-pick it was in the easy-living 1980s.

The salad days of the old environmentalism ended with the shallow enthusiasms of 1990's Earth Day. In 1991 the "recession," as it was called, hit even middle-of-the-road environmental groups like the Natural Resources Defense Council, World Wildlife Fund, National Wildlife Federation, and Sierra Club, and uncounted smaller outfits besides.[5] Many were forced to major cutbacks, and not for the last time. The immediate problem was economic insecurity, but as notable is the fact that corporations are nowadays donating far less money to environmental groups and have become far more conscious of the influence they purchase with their tax-deductible grants. *O'Dwyer's PR Services Report*, an insider's newsletter serving the U.S. public relations industry, puts the new situation bluntly: "Cash-rich companies are funding hard-up environmental groups in the belief [that] the imprimatur of activists will go a long way in improving their reputation among environmentally aware consumers."[6]

The bottom line, said Bill Walker, then a self-described "Greenpeace media doctor," is that "Greenwashing is working. People really seem to think that Exxon is cleaning up its act."[7] They get plenty of help. The election of the Clinton-Gore administration saw millions of Americans conclude that good times had come for the environment, and mainstream greens, flush with their new access to the offices of power, did little to disturb this illusion. Meanwhile, of course, the antigreen right enjoyed the solaces (and fund-raising advantages) of opposition. As in the early 1980s, when environmentalists found that James Watt, the rabidly antigreen millenarian Christian whom Ronald Reagan appointed as his secretary of the interior, was their perfect fund-raising icon, so now the antienvironmental "wise use" movement campaigned against Al Gore, whom they accused of being a "radical environmentalist."[8] The *Financial Times* captured the new mood perfectly just before the 1994 U.S. midterm elections that swept the Republicans back into power. In an article that began by discussing Greenpeace's financial crisis, the *Financial Times* was quick to claim that the environmental problems of the bad old days had been solved, and that, "to some extent," Greenpeace "has campaigned itself out of a job." The real question was if, with only "technical" problems remaining, "environmentalists were now in danger of extinction."[9]

Greenwashing, in which images of change substitute for and exaggerate change itself, joins an impressive antigreen arsenal that already boasts capital flight, whereby companies large and small flee regions and nations with strong environmental or labor laws; fake "scientific studies" designed to delegitimate grassroots challenges; lobbying of various kinds; smear campaigns that paint greens as "doomsters" and even "terrorists"; harassment legal and illegal; violence; shifting of blame from polluters to "individuals"; and even the direct corporate support of antienvironmental groups. Such groups will flourish in the next few decades, for two reasons. The first reflects a danger visible around the world — hard-right movements bloom when conditions worsen, for they offer at least the bitter comforts of resentment. The second reason is more specific to the battlegrounds of ecology: antienvironmental groups — which, according to Ron Arnold, a leader of the wise-use movement, aim "to destroy the environmental movement, once and for all"[10] — are remarkably well funded and supported. As *The Greenpeace Guide to Anti-Environmental Organizations*,[11] a catalog of antigreen groups from the Abundant Wildlife Society of North America to the Yellow Ribbon Coalition, amply demonstrates, there's lots of corporate money sloshing around this particular "social movement."

The old environmentalism has hit its limits. The fine promises of 1992's Earth Summit have almost everywhere been forgotten, or at least pushed aside. In the United States, ecology in the large sense has vanished from the political foreground, and the environmental establishment, if not always the green grass roots, is everywhere in retreat.[12] California, the bellwether that so often marks emerging trends, testifies to the new reality. According to Sam Schuchat, executive director of the state's League of Conservation Voters, 1993 saw so many antienvironmental bills in the legislative hopper that "all it took to be rated as a green legislator was to vote no."[13] Al Gore must have noticed the trend. As U.S. vice president, he quickly showed himself to be cut of altogether thinner cloth than the liberal idealist who, as a senator, wrote *Earth in the Balance*.[14] Bill Clinton likewise learned fast. If he had any big green ideas when entering office, he lost them early, after his halfhearted attempt to pass an almost insignificant tax on nonrenewable forms of energy was rudely clobbered by fossil-fuel lobbyists. It was a pathetic spectacle that showed exactly where environmental forces fit into the larger political landscape. Green taxes are chief among the policy prescriptions of the green mainstream, yet even this tiny levy was far beyond the limits of the politically acceptable.

Greenhouse policy is a telling measure of our paralysis. Details vary, but the overall pattern is all too stable. To see it, keep your attention on the bottom line, the "immediate reduction in global man-made carbon dioxide emissions by 60 to 80%" that the UN's expert scientific panel on climate change insists is necessary to slow global warming — the "greenhouse effect" — and prevent a climatic catastrophe.[15] Nowhere will politicians even talk of reductions on this scale, and their reticence should be absolutely no surprise. The daily lifestyle of the average U.S. or European citizen yields nearly one hundred times as much carbon dioxide as that of the average black African, and thus — in anything like an equitable scenario — a huge portion of this reduction would have to come in the North. Americans would need to cut their emissions by 95 percent; the British by 91 percent.[16] Obviously, it's not going to happen anytime soon. Press this point with the friends of "political realism" and you see an increasingly familiar response — embarrassment and resignation.

So, how to proceed? There is, first, no shortage of either good ideas or shared vision. Among grassroots activists, an international consensus is forming about where we must go, and why, and about what must take place before there can be any honest hope of arriving in time. Alabama's antitoxics organizers, the Chipco tree-huggers of India's highlands, and a good fraction of the staff (if not always the executives) of mainstream American environmental groups agree on the need for democratic renewal and a grassroots redefinition of "sustainable development" — as principles in themselves and as preconditions for a transition to an ecologically stable society. On the technical side, the menu of alternatives, from ancient forms of agricultural forestry to new hybrid solar-hydrogen energy systems, is now so impressive as to make it obvious that lack of options is not what impedes progress. At the policy level, too, a rough consensus is in place. New ideas emerge from time to time — global taxation of the arms trade is a recent example[17] — but they do not emerge to stand alone. An endless stream of books, reports, and newsletters long ago sketched out the general features of a new, green "policy regime."

Nineteen ninety-two's Earth Summit, in Rio, a dismal anticlimax, paradoxically reinforced this agreement. Its preparatory conferences ran for over two years, and at them officials and activists from more than a hundred countries on all six inhabited continents exchanged words, drinks, and position papers — and watched each other operate. The general level of political sophistication, already high in 1990, increased significantly and, more important, spread to dozens of new networks and tens of thousands of new activists. The drafting of the pre-Summit *Agenda Ya Wananchi*, a "citizens' action plan for the 1990s," exemplified the best of this frenetic consultation. *Ya Wananchi* (Swahili for "children of the earth") is a remarkable document. Finalized in Paris in late 1991 by activists from more than 160 countries, it is uneven and incomplete, and yet, in vision and realism, vastly superior to anything contrived by the Summit's official government negotiators.

Further, and like all the other products of this long, difficult international conversation — "alternative treaties," information networks, and schemes of all variety — it is as noteworthy for the hard-won sympathies and pixilated late-night sessions that fed its common understandings as it is for the startling degree of consensus it reveals.[18]

"Suddenly," *Ya Wananchi* begins, "it is like the birth of a new Earth." Indeed it is, though only now, years after the fall of the East, is the shape of the new earth becoming clear. The sense of decisive globalization — economic, political, cultural, and of course ecological — has become pervasive. There is a widely shared feeling of common peril and a rising, inclusive sense of a tightly wound political and environmental crisis. Moreover, the "social issues" are everywhere seeping up through the floors of old-school environmentalism. The need for "justice" and "equality" haunts the green movement. Those who seek to avoid it, to advocate "nature protection" in any simple manner, seem atavistic even to themselves. Ten years ago, only a few isolated radicals saw the Third World's crushing international debt as a green issue. Today, it is well known as a key link in the fiscal chains strangling the world's ecosystems. Likewise, land reform, women's rights, world trade, consumerism, technology, poverty, and immigration are widely recognized as environmental issues. There is a common sense of a new holism in which the ambit of green politics expands to include the entire cultural and institutional nexus of environmental degradation, to become a "social ecology" more fully realized than any even suspected during the long chill of the Cold War.

The stakes were clear at the Earth Summit, at least to those who would admit them. Others, choosing to ignore the big picture, had no trouble doing so — there were lots of distractions. There were, in fact, lots of conferences. First was the official, governmental, side of the Summit, the United Nations Conference on Environment and Development, UNCED ("unsaid"), a politicians' extravaganza and world-historic media event (perhaps eight thousand reporters in all). Miles away, along a freeway newly built to protect the international masses from the danger and squalid realities of Rio de Janeiro's slums, were the sweltering green-and-white tents of the Global Forum, which hosted dozens of nongovernmental conclaves of all varieties. Farther away still was the Earth Parliament, a global summit of indigenous peoples.

The Earth Summit was, as Noel Brown of the UN Environment Program put it, an "environmental *Rashomon*," in which each could see just what he or she wished.[19] Nevertheless, it somehow remained a single event, complex but integral. Rio was a snapshot of the global movement in all its fantastic confusion and glory. It was a stupendous waste of time and money, a "long flatulence," a sprawling day-care center for environmental wanna-bes, the occasion for "the highest level international policy centered mumbo-jumbo you can imagine,"[20] a defining moment in the evolution of greenwashing. All this is true. And yet, if only by dint of the sheer volume of its hype and the scale of its circumstances, it still marks the morning of Day Two in the story of environmentalism.

Note, then, the Summit's official products — the UN's toothless new Commission on Sustainable Development; weak and deeply flawed climate and biodiversity treaties; the hundreds of vague, still unfunded pages of Agenda 21 (the encyclopedic master treaty); the World Bank's new Global Environment Facility, which is helping it to purchase environmental legitimacy and position itself as the fiscal agent for the brave green world of the twenty-first century. A focus on official outcomes at least allows an unambiguous judgment of the Summit: it was a failure.

But such a focus may fail to capture the Summit's real significance. First, and despite the apologetic intention with which these words are usually offered, Rio was a rallying ground, not a final destination. The forces that made the Summit necessary roil now as they did in mid-1992, and they will not calm soon. As James MacNeill, former secretary-general of the Brundtland Commission (famous for *Our Common Future*,[21] the report that thrust "sustainable development" into our common library of political clichés), put it at the start of the Summit, "The days of Sunday School environmental politics are over. Now that we have brought development into the center of the environmental debate, we face a series of hard-fought battles."[22]

Just how hard-fought can be inferred from the sweep of the emerging movement agenda. Wangari Maathai, feminist, human-rights campaigner, and founder of the Kenyan Greenbelt Movement, sketched out its terms, when — on behalf of the world's activists — she addressed the official UNCED plenary. In naming the "issues vital to building environmentally sound and socially equitable societies," she

provided as fine a statement of the task before us as we will find for
some time:

- eliminating poverty
- fair and environmentally sound trade
- reversal of the net flow of resources from South to North
- clear recognition of the responsibilities of business and
  industry
- changes in wasteful patterns of consumption
- internalization of the environmental and social costs of
  natural resource use
- equitable access to environmentally sound technology and
  its benefits
- redirection of military expenditures to environmental and
  social goals, and
- democratization of local, national, and international political institutions and decision-making structures.[23]

It is a daunting list, made all the more so by the chasm that separates
it in content and spirit from the official treaties, a chasm so wide that,
even had the Summit gone very well, the gap would not have much
narrowed. And the Summit did *not* go well. The United States and its
allies insisted on cutting all carbon dioxide targets and timetables from
the climate treaty. The biodiversity treaty spends as much time on "intellectual property rights" as on protecting threatened species. The forestry talks focused narrowly on the South, as if only its forests needed
protection, as if they could be saved without likewise saving the forests of the North. The master treaty, Agenda 21, so often hyped as an
environmental Magna Carta, somehow manages to omit any discussion of greening the international trade system, or disarmament, or
any means by which global inequity might actually be significantly
reduced.

Greenpeace summed up the situation. The day after George Bush's
flat-footed, no-problems speech to the UNCED plenary, seven Greenpeace climbers defied Rio's lockdown security and, under cover of
darkness, scaled its landmark Sugarloaf Mountain. Rappelling down

its sheer face at the crack of dawn, they unfurled a fourteen-thousand-square-foot banner on which was pictured only a giant image of the home planet and a single word: SOLD.

Language Trouble

Words serve us poorly. If we seek to understand our present, unenviable position, they serve us particularly poorly. The language of environmental politics is confused, contested, heavy with the equivocations of long, bitter debates. Where are we? Where have we come from? Are these waters into which we have wandered as deep as they seem?

Where are we? If we are readers of this book, most likely in "the North," the "industrial world," in the "developed world" among the planet's "rich." Each term tells its own lies. The most obvious is that "the North" is no simple geographical territory. How can it be when it includes Japan, Australia, South Africa? When it is generally synonymous with "the West"? More curiously, if we are the "rich" (as we certainly are from the point of view of, say, a Bangladeshi peasant), why are so many desperate poor among us? If we are "developed," what are our cousins in "the South"? "Underdeveloped"? "Developing"? "Underdeveloping"?

Environmentalists have traditionally avoided these confusions in favor of those offered by dividing the world into "industrialized" and "nonindustrialized" camps. Their intention in this has been to name something fundamental, and to swim against the tide of Cold War ideology by stressing similarities between "the East" (the old "communist" lands) and "the West," rather than the differences. This strategy, unfortunately, has never been as successful as its partisans imagined. Industrialism, as a notion, is simply too abstract, too bleached of content to explain all that is asked of it. Each pattern of "industrial" destruction (compare the nuclear wastelands of Ukraine to the oil-sodden bayous of Louisiana) has its specific qualities and causes. Overlarge generalities in the end explain too much, and thus nothing at all.

Names conceal as they reveal — not only "industrialism" but "gigantism," "rationality," "technology," "greed," "human nature," "capitalism," and "patriarchy" have all found favor as ultimate explanations, as charms against confusion. The green movement writhes with such abstractions, each with advocates eager to offer its partial truth as *the* essential cause of the crisis. This might be for the good were it not that abstract explanations, lacking specificity, leave us open to absurd, apolitical solutions. Wendell Berry, the Kentucky horse farmer whose elegiac essays have taught so many to know the "expectations of the land," offers hope only in old-fashioned values and a return to "settled communities."[24] Christopher Manes, Earth First! bad boy and author of *Green Rage: Radical Environmentalism and the Unmaking of Civilization,* goes even further and claims hope only in the "Pleistocene Mind."[25] Bill McKibben, in his much-admired *The End of Nature,* sets out to write a requiem for nature primeval, and ends by imagining a future in which we find ourselves alone, with only the plants and animals we have chosen to save, on a desiccated and meaningless world.[26]

Ultimately, each of us must judge the matter alone, but it would help if we could at least talk to one another. Unfortunately, we share no adequate language, or even an understanding of the words we do hold in common. Talk of the "free world" has faded into the "free trade" utopia of the post–Cold War world, but this is only the latest in a long series of odd linguistic slippages. Was that really "communism" that just crashed in Russia, and what responsibility does "the left," the anti-totalitarian left in particular, have for its infamies? What is "development," anyway, and what, really, is "the economy"? When did "the jungle" become "the rain forest," and why? Is there even a "crisis," and if so, is it "ecological"?

I believe there is an ecological crisis, and that it is deadly real, but though I'll cite plenty of evidence, I'll not try to "prove" the point. Specialists have written far more authoritatively than can I about the state of the air, the forests, and the seas. I take up the different task of arguing that the ecological crisis, though inescapably a crisis of "nature," is not natural in any simple way. The oil and water wars of the Middle East, the toxic wastelands of the U.S.-Mexico borderlands, the clouds of carbon dioxide projected to rise from Northern cities and from the copycat industrialization now sweeping the South — all these mark the time passed since "ecology," once a specialized branch of biology, came to denote a less distinct, more encompassing fear.

This shift of meaning came, notably, during the Cold War, when "the evil empire" could still plausibly be claimed a threat to "the free world." With the planet torn between two nuclear-armed camps, ecology was a cosmopolitan tonic, a symbol of planetary unity. Its icon was the "whole Earth," hanging small and vulnerable in a deep, gorgeous, sterile sky. Today that moment has passed. The realities of globalization, long hidden by East-West shadowplay, are becoming clear. In the West anticommunism was once the irreducible measure of rectitude and right thinking; today's orthodoxy is "free markets," and its dominion spans the world. Yet as productivity keeps rising, as each is forced to compete against every other, it is not at all clear that free trade and ever-increasing productivity are unsullied blessings. Globally, the economy is doing well, but the same cannot be said of the people. Millions fear, with justification, that they will never be secure again. New and terrifying and diffuse kinds of war are emerging, yet the arms industries continue pumping out ever-deadlier weapons. The world is of a small and single piece, and the field of meanings that adhere to the word "ecology" is slowly, dramatically shifting.

The meaning of "Cold War" is likewise contested, as is the significance of its end. Here, the collapse of communism is called "the victory of the West," or "the revolutions of 1989." In the East one hears little of victory or revolution, and instead of "the changes," or "the turn." These are more judicious terms, but they are deliberately, almost self-consciously vague — too vague to explain, for example, why outside small green circles, fear for "the economy" so easily displaced fear for "the ecology." In early 1993, thinking "the turn" a curious phrase, I asked Friedrich Heilman, long an Eastern peace activist and then a member of the national executive committee of the (unified) German Green Party, if "the restoration" might not be more precise. He replied, after some equivocation, that it is "just the right word, but we can't use it, because it was a part of the official language." How was it used? "Actually, it was used correctly," to imply the mending of preexisting, broken ties. "For example, our schoolbooks told us of 'the restoration' of the ties between the Nazi war machine and the rest of the Western war machine after the end of World War II."[27]

Words echo in so many ways. In Russia, "restoration" easily implies the return of the czar. Even geography is a problem. My aging map says "Eastern Europe," but the citizens of the region prefer "Central Europe," no doubt because it better expresses their hope that, when the "changes" subside, they will find themselves in Europe, in the West, among the elect. Still, we must have maps, and so I will follow common usage and call the poor, indebted, population-booming regions of the world "the South," and the rich, demographically stable regions "the North." These are deeply unsatisfactory terms. They exclude the East; they obscure newly industrialized enclaves like Taiwan and Indonesia, and hide distinctions between large developing countries like India and Brazil, which dump ever more carbon into the air, and "victim states" like Bangladesh and the Maldives, which see global warming as a real threat to their existence. Further, North and South are often taken to denote "rich" and "poor," and this is so misleading as to be dangerous — Southern elites consume, as they pollute, at well above middle-class Northern levels. Still, the war between rich and poor will be a major fact of future history and will have strong racial and regional overtones. "North" and "South" have at least the virtue of reminding us of this.

In the South, "environmental protection" is of a single piece with survival and "justice"; its Northern definition as "nature protection" is commonly rejected as naive or worse. In the East, ecology has fallen far down the social agenda, a victim of the restoration's cruelties and, paradoxically, of the relative openness that has deprived environmentalism of its earlier role as a shelter for opposition. In the North, new generations of green and antigreen politicians are on the scene, and environment is a factor in geopolitics (and geo-economics) as never before. Here, too, words are contested. Dana Alston, speaking at 1991's People of Color Environmental Leadership Summit, declared that "we refuse narrow definitions."[28] She spoke for thousands of grassroots "environmental" activists, many of whom, though active in public health and toxics campaigns, refuse to identify themselves as greens of any stripe. Everywhere, there are currents and countercurrents, and while even the conservative *National Review* tells us that "environmentalism is no longer a cult issue,"[29] neither does it hold center stage. Everywhere, its meaning is confused and in transition.

Given all this, does it still make sense to speak of an environmental "movement"? Perhaps not, but I will nevertheless do so, if only as an act of faith and a way of naming the hundreds of thousands of organizations — Southern self-help groups and Northern think tanks — that around the planet treat ecology, economic development, and social change as elements of a single complex tendency.[30] Usually, too, I will treat "environmental" and "green" as synonyms, though there are many among us who see "green" as denoting only environmentalism's scruffy shock troops — Earth First! and Green Party activists, Greenpeace canvassers, aggressive teenage vegetarians — and having little to do with the professionalist eco-management institutes now proliferating in the North. The feeling is mutual. The Group of Ten (an elite conclave of managers from "the majors," the largest, most mainstream environmental groups) was officially dissolved in 1990,[31] but the name persists, and is the basis for "gang of ten," a term of endearment often employed by green radicals, who take the majors to embody a conformist, technocratic politics disengaged from and even hostile to the "grass roots."

What's in a name? Often, a great deal. Today, after our "victory" in the century-long war against "communism," we may see how automatic, how studied, our own vagueness has become. In the offices of Washington's environmental establishment, you need merely speak about "the movement" to see, by grimace and gesture, that the term engenders a palpable discomfort. The preferred euphemism seems to be "environmental community," an outstanding example, if ever there was one, of sanitized language in the service of political obscurity.

There is confusion in abundance here, and no end of irony. Tani Adams, former coordinator of Greenpeace International's Latin American networks, told me that within Greenpeace "radicals" are most often taken to be the "direct-action folks,"[32] a deceptive usage that is unlikely to help us pioneer a new and more expansive green politics. Certainly such narrow usage wasn't much help in Germany in the early 1980s — in fact, it helped propel the Green Party into a sterile, interminable, and destructive debate defined by radical environmentalist "fundamentalism" on the one side and disoriented "realism" on the other.

That debate is over, but it would not serve us to forget it. The early West German Greens were pioneers, and their mistakes were significant. They were playing, as we still do today, within an environmentalism that invented itself — its philosophies, tactics, issues, and languages — during a century in which politics was defined by "business" on one side and the "Red threat" on the other. Northern greens still almost instinctively avoid the taint of the left, though if without its verve and history they can never hope to see the democratic rebirth upon which their own dreams, too, depend. This we know as "realism," a distemper that extends far beyond 1980s-trained environmental lawyers afraid of pinko notions like "environmental movement." Witness an event that took place just before the Earth Summit, when Greenpeace's German, Dutch, and British offices (the "G-3") refused to distribute copies of *Beyond UNCED*, a fine pamphlet produced for the Rio gathering by Greenpeace USA and Greenpeace Latin America. The G-3, it turned out, strongly objected to its use of "leftist" terms like "social equity" and even "democracy."[33]

When I asked Paul Hohnen, head of Greenpeace International's political unit, about the flap, he downplayed it — "*Beyond UNCED* was published, after all." He then appealed to Greenpeace's canvassers, who "can't be expected to go door-to-door raising money for a socialist organization."[34] Obviously, this is true, though I had asked him about "social equity," not "socialism." Are we now to be so terrified of redbaiting that we accept even "equity" as a suspect goal? How far shall we go, how confused shall we become, in search of language designed to avoid the never-ceasing charge that environmentalists are only watermelons, "green on the outside but red on the inside?" In the age of appearances, this is not a trivial question.

Discretion, of course, has its advantages, as do open-mindedness and the embrace of real change. The Filipino movement, once defined as much by the doctrinaire rigidity of its Maoist guerrillas as by the venality of the Marcos dictatorship they fought against, now enfolds those guerrillas, mellowed by time, in coalition with church-based reformers and even odd birds like Maximo "Junie" Kalaw, former playboy, big-game hunter, and human potential enthusiast. In 1993, speaking to a conference of Filipino and U.S. activists, Junie spoke of the "new paradigms" that define organizing in his strained country. Amidst highly charged talk about "freedom from debt" and saving the last shards of the rain forests, these words seemed strange, but there can be no doubt that the political culture that supports today's fluid, democratic opposition is a happy advance over the past.

"New paradigm" thinking, unfortunately, is not always so fruitful. In the new East, very old paradigms best explain the direction of events. The old regime, after all, was brought down by a social implosion in which freedom, long imagined and desperately sought, was confused with better cars, blonder cigarettes, and all the other mass-marketed and free-traded products of the West's consumer utopia. Is it any wonder, then, that the dream of building a more humane and greener capitalism upon the Eastern ruins, a dream once widespread among both communist reformers and capitalist idealists, has quickly and ignobly been pushed aside by the imperatives of surviving "real" capitalism? Do we need new paradigms to understand why?

Today, in contrast to two decades ago, most greens do not automatically assume the protection of nature to take precedence over human livelihood, rights, and survival. In Latin American "popular organizations" and U.S. "citizens groups," there are few unalloyed environmentalists, yet these are still, irreducibly, environmental groups, linked by the logic of their project — protecting humans and the lands in which they live — to even the most gray-suited environmental lobbyists. This is a new time in the story of green politics, and how we name and understand it will play a key role in defining it.

The greenwashers have noticed this, as is made all too clear by the sorts of "nongovernmental organizations" (NGOs) now showing their colors. NGO, a bit of United Nations lingo that has ramified like a fungus in the damp, is now used to lump the most radical Brazilian land-rights groups together with conservative U.S. green lobbyists. Even indigenous groups ("Indians") are sometimes called NGOs, though they often reject the term, occasionally with considerable heat, as it explicitly denies their status as "nations." Moreover, at Rio, NGO was used to name the World Bank, the Kuwaiti Ministry of Information, the International Chamber of Commerce, the Business Council for Sustainable Development, the American Nuclear Society, and even Petrobras, the Brazilian state oil company whose toxic dumping made it unwise to swim on the very beaches that, spreading out from the tents of the NGO Global Forum, became, in the world's press photos, synonymous with the sexier side of saving the earth.

Which brings us to the lexicon of economics, so thick with the habits of ideology that it makes environmental language seem a model of clarity. Just about everyone with any power today, to give one obvious example, is in favor of "free trade," though such a thing has never really existed outside the capitalist imagination. Somehow, this does not stop "free trade" from being asserted as the sign of all that is good in geo-economics, as "protectionism" designates all that is bad.

"Free trade" is not part of the traditional green agenda, yet this only marks the distance crossed in recent years. Trade, in fact, may be the single most important "social-ecological" issue, for what it really signifies is globalization, and the restructuring of markets, all markets, in everything from redwood to tuna fish to human labor. Even a word as routine as "price" is deeply marked, for it somehow manages to imply rational economic judgments, when in reality prices are irreducibly political, expressing as they do myriads of decisions about what will be made, and where, and how.

We can measure our predicament by the fact that "capitalism" itself — the proper name for the now global economic system — is a suspect term, at least if used critically. *Forbes* and *Fortune* may celebrate the dynamism and fecundity of the market unchained, but one need only suggest that economics as we know it is basic to the dark drift of planetary events to be immediately painted as a leftist atavism, a child unable to face necessity.

"Progress," the longtime companion to "capitalism," also deserves mention here, for it has always been first to stand and defend "the economy" from the pessimists who dog its heels. As a call for optimism, though, "progress" has lost its once-mythic power. Greens are still attacked as antitechnology Luddites, but when Ross Perot, who made his fortune in computers, is similarly cursed (for his opposition to "free trade"),[35] the frail state of the technological religion, and the defensiveness of its ministers, is obvious. Today, one must be brash to the point of recklessness to assume the perpetual "improvement" that has so long been claimed as the reward of industrial enlightenment. The arguments for disillusion run from Auschwitz to Chernobyl to Bosnia, and will not end soon.

And there is "development," which, it seems, is what remains once the vapors of progress have boiled away. It, too, is a term in crisis. Where once "development" implied to the world's poor the means by which they would "catch up with the West," its pretensions have shrunk to "not falling altogether apart." There are, of course, those who remain loyal to "development," but they are yesterday's men, marketeers and self-interested optimists who claim, against all evidence, to be realists. "Development," as both word and idea, has been ceded to a discredited, though still living past.

"Sustainable development," that favorite incantation of the eco-politician, is nowadays more often spoken as a matter of delicacy than with any honest intention. Around the world, PR specialists by the thousands work to refine its usage, and to paint their clients in the earth tones appropriate to the day's mood. Thus, the World Bank's notorious Tropical Forest Action Plan was offered to the world as the centerpiece of a comprehensive set of environmental reforms, and as a plan for saving the rain forests. In practice, the TFAP meant financing for large-scale commercial logging, but this didn't keep the Bank's managers from calling it "sustainable logging."[36] That was 1987, and such terms were signs of things to come. Today, in the South, "reforestation" often means the eviction of local people from forests slated to be clear-cut and sold, and then converted to monoculture tree plantations.

The truth of "development" is found elsewhere — in older terms like "economic liberalization" (which seems to mean nothing so much as planetary deregulation), or in the bloodless syllables of "structural adjustment," a term used to bear the bad news about lower expectations, falling environmental standards, the dismantling of the welfare state, and all the other dark realities of life in the late twentieth century. In 1962 Eugene Banks, the World Bank's third president, speaking of such old words, summed up the official position on language as follows:

> We attach . . . a lot of conditions to our loans. I need hardly say that we would never get away with this if we did not bend every effort to render the language of economics as morally antiseptic as the language the weather forecaster uses in giving tomorrow's prediction. We look on ourselves as technicians or artisans. Words like "savings" and "investment," "efficiency," and "productivity" are tools of our trade.[37]

Looking Backward

Standard histories of U.S. "environmentalism" trace its origins to the days of John Muir and his fellow, late-nineteenth-century, Progressive-era "preservationists" — larger-than-life heroes who fought to protect "wilderness" against all comers. The typical focus of the story is the confrontation between Muir and his "conservationist" foes, an altogether modern lot who spoke for the "scientific" management of "natural resources." In this oft-told tale, Earth Day 1970 marked the shift from a bygone epoch during which nature was considered to be separate from everyday life to the more complex and, it is implied, more enlightened environmentalism of the present day.

This standard history, though, is peculiarly selective. In fact, says Robert Gottlieb, a green historian who has dug far deeper than most of his fellows, Progressive-era environmentalism included not only the preservationists, but also

> the female-led municipal housekeeping movement, which focused on issues like sanitation, public health, and food and nutrition; the muckraker-inspired urban reform organizations and settlement houses, which led the push for better housing, for new regulatory agencies such as the Food and Drug Administration, and for improving the harsh conditions of industrial labor; and the "sewer" socialists, who helped revolutionize municipal governance over the urban environment.[38]

The systematic omission of this other, socially oriented and largely urban ecology movement from the common histories of environmentalism is deeply misleading. Marcy Darnovsky, an activist and analyst who has closely examined dozens of such histories, argues that its absence suggests "that those who take up similar issues today are latecomers to, or even interlopers in, environmental politics."[39] The narrow frame of the standard history creates an illusion in which today's intermittent sense of a broader agenda seems more unusual, and more unprecedented, than it actually is. Are the "social issues" now churning green politics — from "justice" to militarism — recent arrivals, or have they been with us all along? The answer makes a difference, for it tells us if we are discovering new lands, or only, finally, belatedly, regaining lost ground.

The official history of environmentalism has been sanitized to a surprising degree. We've all heard of Rachel Carson's *Silent Spring*, but how many of us know that the chemical industry flacks of her day charged that her book was a communist plot to destroy U.S. agriculture? We remember her warnings of chemical dangers to birds and wildlife, but do we also recall her discussion of the origins of pesticides in the World War II search for new, more deadly chemical weapons, or the parallels she drew between chemical toxins and nuclear fallout, or her claims for the inseparability of public health and environmental protection?[40]

The political tone of Earth Day 1970 has likewise been lost in the haze. If we know Earth Day's origins at all, it is by way of today's bland annual ritual. The imagined continuity can be misleading. Peter Bahouth, then with Greenpeace USA, spoke at 1990's major Earth Day rally. He remembers "about four hundred calls for individual responsibility and green consumerism, and hardly a word about production or the corporations."[41] By the time Earth Day 1995 was being prepared, its official prospectus offered potential corporate underwriters "very special business building and marketing opportunities," and were it not for the brief clarity that followed November's elections, the twenty-fifth Earth Day would have been almost entirely bleached of critical political content.[42] Earth Day 1970 was a child of braver times, and was intolerant of both commercialism and loose, forgiving rhetoric. Here, for example, is a fragment of the speech Denis Hayes, a key organizer of both events, delivered back at the main 1970 rally:

> I suspect that the politicians and businessmen who are jumping on the environmental bandwagon don't have the slightest idea of what they are getting into. They are talking about filters on smokestacks while we are challenging corporate irresponsibility. . . . Our country is stealing from poorer nations and from generations yet unborn. . . . We're spending insanely large sums on military hardware instead of eliminating hunger and poverty. We squander our resources on moon dust while people live in wretched housing. We still waste lives and money on a war that we should never have entered and which we should get out of immediately.[43]

Those were the days of *The Closing Circle* and *The Limits to Growth*, days that passed like any others. The urgency of discovery soon faded, and the news media, confused by an increasingly complex debate between industry and environmentalists, began to avoid dramatic reports of imminent and extreme danger. Ecological crisis faded from the media foreground. Time passed, and just because it did, *Limits* came to seem overstated and the limits to growth themselves much further away than had been supposed.

In the summer of 1974, I went to Vermont to attend Murray Bookchin's first Social Ecology Institute. Bookchin, whose *Our Synthetic Environment*[44] preceded even Carson's *Silent Spring*, is the grand old man of radical ecology. By the end of the summer, I knew I'd been naive in my sense of the ecological crisis. I'd read the literature too eagerly and expected—even desired—a sudden catastrophe that would not likely come. I had failed to reckon the uneven distribution of the suffering, or to consider humanity's almost boundless, and easily manipulated, capacity for amnesia, adaptation, and denial. I had imagined collapse where there would be a slow, unfair deterioration.

The radical green movements of the 1970s and 1980s began that same summer—with the antinuclear movement. I was at the Social Ecology Institute when someone rushed in to announce that Sam Lovejoy had toppled a weather tower at a nearby powerplant construction site, that he had then hitchhiked to the police station, turned himself in, and issued a call for more resistance. It was the birth of the Clamshell Alliance and of American mass disobedience to what the German writer Robert Jungk has called *die atomstadt*—the atomic state. The protesters eventually numbered in the tens of thousands.

The battle dragged on for years, and, amazingly, the antinuke forces were winning. Widespread resistance and escalating capital costs were killing nuclear power — first in Europe and the United States and then in the Third World. Antinuke activists could have felt euphoric, but euphoria was rare. In the United States, the cold silence of the 1980s was beginning. President Carter's Council on Environmental Quality published *The Global 2000 Report*, but the policy offensive that had been planned to accompany it died a sudden death when Ronald Reagan won the 1980 election. Jimmy Carter's solar panels were torn from the White House roof, and the report's warning that the next century would be "more crowded, more polluted, less stable ecologically, and more vulnerable to disruption" was largely ignored.[45]

The reckoning, though, continued its slow approach, as is easily shown with a look back at *Global 2000*'s predictions. Written in 1980, it foresaw a population increase of 2.25 billion over the next twenty-five years. By 1990 the global population had in fact risen by 840 million, and almost a billion more are expected in the 1990s — just about right. *Global 2000* also predicted that, largely because of deforestation, 20 percent of all species extant in the 1980s would vanish by the turn of the millennium. With deforestation rates now far higher than in 1980, and replacement forests, attractive though they may be, often far less biodiverse than were their primeval predecessors, the story has not appreciably changed — perhaps one hundred species vanish every day, and *Global 2000*'s estimate of 20 percent loss remains as good as any other.[46] Further, with the Earth Summit's failure to contrive even a shadow of a meaningful forestry treaty, and all the myriad incentives for deforestation in continued, almost unobstructed operation, there is no real reason to think that green pessimists will be mistaken in their prediction of more or less total loss of the tropical rain forests, and their species, by the middle of the next century.[47]

But *Global 2000* was wrong, too, in an important way. It predicted, as did most futurist prognostications of the 1970s and 1980s, that 2000 would see sharply higher energy prices. This actually would have been good news, because even slightly higher prices would make solar power and other renewable energy sources undeniably competitive. But as we know, this was not to be. In fact, it now seems that fossil-fuel prices will long remain too low to provide an adequate incentive for reduced consumption. As the Worldwatch Institute's chief energy analyst, Christopher Flavin, told me in 1991, just after the Persian Gulf War, everyone in Washington had gotten the message, if only "subliminally" — "We'd rather fight than switch."[48]

Step back to 1984, George Orwell's year, when a Union Carbide pesticide plant in Bhopal, India, was torn by what was at the time the single worst industrial accident on record. Union Carbide held the title for only two years, however, for in 1986 the meltdown at the Chernobyl nuclear plant set the benchmark by which all localized man-made disasters will long be measured. In 1987 scientists, after thirteen years of effort and the appearance of the Antarctic ozone hole, were finally able to prove, even to Du Pont, that chlorofluorocarbons were destroying the earth's atmospheric ozone layer. The Montreal Protocol on Substances That Deplete the Ozone Layer was signed that same year, though new evidence immediately showed it to be painfully inadequate. In 1988 there was an intense North American drought and summer heat wave, and a spike of greenhouse fear. In 1989 the collapse of the Iron Curtain regimes brought welcome good news, though the joy was short-lived as the extent of the political, economic, and ecological dilapidation of the East came to be widely appreciated. Then came the Exxon *Valdez* spill, by no means a record as these things go, but notable for its stark images of oil-sodden Alaska coastlines, and for the attention it momentarily focused on the ecological downside of the oil economy. Earth Day 1990, an international benchmark in its own right, was soured by cascades of misleading ads by companies both tiny and transnational claiming themselves among the earth's most loyal friends; "greenwashing" entered the environmental lexicon.

Nineteen ninety-one brought us the Gulf War and the consequent human and ecological catastrophe in the Persian Gulf. It was also the year the German Greens, long an inspiration to environmentalists around the world, became, to use their own vivid term, and for better or for worse, a "stinknormal" player in the coalition politics of the modern German state. It was the year that millions of people in the North began to finally admit that the new world economy would not be a particularly pleasant one; the year ecology became, again, one crisis among many; the year we learned that even over the temperate midlatitudes (including the United States and Europe), the ozone shield was decaying fast; the year that Europe began to look to the East with fear instead of schadenfreude; the year the Bush administration was forced to admit that greenhouse warming was "a problem"; the year a cyclone washed through the crowded Bangladeshi floodplain and, coming on the heels of famine in Africa and the scattering of the Kurds, finally produced the "disaster fatigue" that international relief officials had been fearing for years.[49]

Then came the big year, 1992, the year the Earth Summit put ecological crisis and the fate of the South on the public political agenda and simultaneously made it clear that we should not look to politicians to save the planet. Nineteen ninety-two: the year the battle over the North American Free Trade Agreement (NAFTA) began at earnest, and finally pulled world trade into the central currents of the environmental debate; the year the opening protocols of the Climate Change Convention (pitiful though they were) were signed; the year of strained celebrations of Columbus's arrival in the "New World"; the year the battle against the World Bank began to heat up, and Al Gore — but not his green agenda — was elected to executive office. Nineteen ninety-two: the year that set a disappointed tone for the rest of "the crucial decade."

In 1993 environmentalists, hungover from the frenetic optimism of the Earth Summit, began to admit that the Clinton-Gore administration, too, was a very mixed bag. Nineteen ninety-three saw the euphoria over the West's Cold War victory fade into a gray anxiety, as a seemingly endless series of international political crises rose to seize the headlines. It saw "overpopulation" — a polite term generally taken to mean a pressing surplus of nonwhite poor — return to the foreground of environmentalist rhetoric. And in October, months after the devastating midwestern floods of the summer past, it finally saw the *New York Times* speculate mildly on the possibility that these floods were linked to "a relatively persistent change in the climate."[50]

The New Year's Day rebellion by the Mexican "Zapatistas" against "free trade" and dismal, hopeless poverty started 1994 with a flourish. Ecology, bound to the NAFTA debate with a thousand tangled cords, was bound as well to the long Latin American struggle for land and justice. Soon came the UN Population Summit, the unhappy fiftieth anniversary of the World Bank and International Monetary Fund, and the founding of the crucial, and startlingly undemocratic, World Trade Organization. In November, in the U.S. midterm elections, the far right rode its "Contract with America" into sudden, undeniable prominence, and swore to a profoundly antienvironmental campaign against "unfunded mandates" and "takings" of "private property" — rhetoric that hapless liberals had only days before dismissed as the stuff of an unimportant political fringe. In December the Mexican economy, so long the poster child of the neoliberal development model, went into free fall.

Then came 1995, and years beyond both anticlimax and watershed. In Berlin the climate negotiations began again at earnest and saw testy delegates, harassed by reporters and activists from around the world, declare momentous victory when in fact they managed only enough agreement to keep negotiations from collapsing. The accuracy of global climate models is improving with surprising speed,[51] and each year the claim that global warming is only doomster speculation is less plausible than the last; yet that claim is still repeated, and still reported, and among nonspecialists, it may actually hold greater sway than five years ago. The pattern is visible everywhere — denial, hope for the indefinite "containment" of worsening problems, and plenty of brave rhetoric, but barely a hint of action. The weather is becoming measurably more violent and unstable, and in 1995, with a landmark UN report on the state of climate science, the likely consequences of global warming have been clearly set out — judging, for example, by current best projections of sea level increase, most of the beaches on the East Coast of the United States could be washed away in a mere twenty-five years.[52] Still, with oil, gas, and coal providing 90 percent of the world's energy, a rapid shift to alternatives is almost unthinkable. So it is everywhere. Science improves and the economy grows, but the world brims with the bitter, the frustrated, and the disinherited. What must be done is not done. Politicians fiddle at the expansion of a global trading system that, as structured, will predictably make matters worse. The transnationals continue to evolve into true planetary corporations outside all regulatory control. Social and ecological pressures slowly build.

What will happen now, as the South continues its impossible "development," as so much of the world is stripped of its forests and its wildlife; as the majority of the world's ocean fisheries sink into decline and the irrigation civilizations that feed the world begin to teeter at the brink of a catastrophic water crisis; as the world's politicians confront not only a disordered new terrain but a thin and warming sky?

In 1962 Rachel Carson dedicated *Silent Spring* to the "host of people" who are "even now fighting the thousands of small battles that in the end will bring victory for sanity and common sense in our accommodation to the world that surrounds us."[53] She was an optimist when she wrote those words, and her optimism no doubt sustained her in her work. A similar optimism moved thousands of others to join the fledgling ecology movement, and in so doing helped set the stage we occupy today. It did not, however, make Carson much of a prophet, at least not yet.

The use of DDT was banned in the United States in 1972, and Carson gets a full share of the credit. Still, it was a small victory. Neither DDT's production nor its export was ever prohibited, and today it is in use all over the world. Figure in all its cousins, and pesticide sales are dozens of times higher than they were in 1962. Each year organochlorine pesticides kill thousands of farm laborers and injure millions more.[54] And for the record, spring is now a more silent season than it was back in

1962. Some species are doing well, but around the world, 70 percent of all bird populations are declining, often precipitously.[55] The causes of this decline, moreover, are accelerating—birds are suffering pesticide poisoning and habitat loss, both here in the North and in the South, where great numbers of migratory birds fly in the winter.

This loss of habitat, commonly named deforestation, cannot be understood without shifting from birds themselves to the systems of cash, power, and trade that are the economic metabolism of the modern world. It is that simple. The armies and plantations of the South return to us as thinning flocks and seas of immigrants, and they will do so for a long time, certainly for as long as we prefer corrupt and optimistic fantasies — about, for example, the likely effects of "free trade" on Mexican peasants — to an honest appraisal of the world we have inherited from the Cold Warriors.

The Hangover

In Prague in May of 1990, with the nonviolent Velvet Revolution fresh in the air and hope for the future high, I found I could again believe in green politics. I was in the streetside café of the art nouveau Hotel Europa, talking with Vladimir, an animated if bitter young Czech physician. We were talking politics, and Vlad was confirming what I already knew — that the ecological devastation suffered by Eastern Europe under the communists had helped catalyze its revolutions. I will not forget his summation: "In the face of any argument, any ideology, one could simply say, 'This is the water you have given us. This is the air.' It was definitive. There was nothing they could say. Everyone knew it was true. Everyone knew that the system just didn't work."

The system just didn't work; that was the decisive matter. Statist communism could not often deliver the goods, and even when it could it exacted a price, in dignity and destruction, that was stunningly high. At the same time, environmentalism was usually not seen by the authorities as subversive. Thus it played a key role in the revolutions of the East, providing arenas for protest — from 1960s Moscow student groups fighting for nature preserves to 1980s East European oppositionists campaigning against the damming of the Danube — that were immensely popular, relatively safe, and able in the end to build to more than a simple environmentalism. Like their comrades in the West, Eastern greens usually got their start campaigning for purely ecological issues such as nature conservation, and while they stuck to these issues they were usually tolerated. When, however, they came to expand their agendas, and to oppose the gigantic maldevelopments of communist industrialism, they quickly found themselves cast as subversives and opponents of "progress," and descended into underground streams that surfaced only with glasnost.

Now the Berlin Wall had fallen. Like many others, I tried to be helpful, to interrupt bright conversational optimism with muted warnings about Western political and economic realities. But in those few vivid days, with the scent of emancipation thick and sweet, realism was not welcome. Vlad spoke for millions of his countrymen when he insisted that Czechoslovakia would soon become the "Sweden of Central Europe." It was an unlikely, even ridiculous hope, and it has passed away. Today even President Vaclav Havel — the dissident Czech playwright whose stand for "the truth" once symbolized the Velvet Revolution — is a pathetic shadow of a younger and more heroic figure, and "the truth," interpreted by the new *nomenklatura*, is that capitalist reconstruction demands priority over all else. In 1992 Havel went so far as to grudgingly support, as a sop to Slovakian nationalism, the ecologically and politically disastrous, and economically absurd, Gabcikovo Dam on the Danube. It did not slow the breakup of his country into two states, but it was a step in his reeducation — by 1994, Havel was touring the world as a high-tone representative of the Czech Republic's arms industry.[56]

Today (though one does not learn this without leaving the tourist-thick prosperity of Prague's city center) the Czech future looks as much like Mexico's capitalist primitivism as it does Sweden's fading social democracy. The ruling fears are political and economic, not ecologic, and austerity — for the many if not for the flashiest and most newsworthy — is widely accepted as the only open road. In Prague, as elsewhere in Europe, the "strong ministries" — Finance, Industry, and Privatization — long ago sealed their decisive ascendancy over the Ministry of Environment.

In the West, the home of the modern ecology movement, the mood is not much brighter. Environmental dilapidation is visible on all sides, and persistent rumors of terrible invisible catastrophes — mass extinc-

tions, ozone depletion, greenhouse warming — create a grim background to the now daily reports of political and economic upheaval.
Stories of even more brutal ecological destruction in the fallen East fail
to inspire confidence in the future; at this point we know too much
about our own problems to gloat long or easily. As the American nov-
elist Norman Rush put it, "Capitalism and socialism both have their
contradictions, and it may turn out that socialism's contradictions just
happened to be fatal first."[57] One thing is certain — little has occurred
in all the whirl of the last years to challenge the belief, long a defining
tenet of green radicalism, that communism and capitalism have more
in common than either is eager to admit.

Most discussions of the environmental catastrophe in the East still
recall nothing so much as the Manichaean days of the Cold War, when
we wore white hats and the Soviets wore black. The 1992 book *Ecocide in
the USSR*, by Murray Feshbach and Alfred Friendly, Jr.,[58] is a fine example, not because of the tale it tells but because of the way it tells it. It
does not even suggest all the ways in which West European industry, in
particular, was the quiet beneficiary of Eastern ecocide,[59] nor does it
mention the present, or the future. Here again there is only the part of
the story we already know, where ecological disaster in the East is cited
to prove the superiority of the West; where, like the Gulag, Bohemia's
withered forests and Chernobyl's radioactive suburbs are offered as the
inevitable results of "socialist economics and central planning." This
they may even be, but still this moral is incomplete, and dangerously so.
The destruction the East suffered under the old regime is fact. But how,
in this Cold War frame, shall we understand the infamies of the new?

Little is known about nature protection in the old East, and almost
nothing about the environmental degradation now ravaging the region. The new destruction is less flattering to the West, for it comes as
an aspect of privatization, open borders, and reconstruction. Nor is
there much notice paid to the uncomfortable fact that ecological destruction in the East was long known, and long ignored, by Western
governments more worried by their own green protest movements
than by environmental depredation in enemy lands. It was the West
European ecology movement that did the most, before Chernobyl, to
alert the world to the nuclear catastrophe looming in the East, and to
sound the alarm on the East's primitive, leaking toxic dumps. Even at
the time, this was not welcome news, for these dumps were not only

familiar to the West, they were routinely used by the West, before the change, as elements of a quiet and very lucrative international trade in Western toxic wastes, a trade that continues unabated to this day.[60]

Like so many Cold War stories, ecocide in the East is true but not the whole truth. First, the East, though it suffers some of the worst localized ecological "hot spots" on the planet, does not, in this, exemplify the greatest ecological dangers, which are global, gradual, and diffuse. Second, the opportunity now being squandered in the East, and the lessons that it speaks to those who will attend to it, are extremely depressing. The East is in no position to finance or guide its own ecological reconstruction — how could it be, given the severity of its hangover? — and yet the West's hands, visible and invisible, have been neither firm nor helpful. Its private investments have aimed exclusively at securing immediate economic advantage, and the policies of Western governments have been cobbled together out of ideology and reflex, with scarcely any thought to rational, long-term self-interest. Besides, the reigning "Wild West" investment climate hardly encourages the growth of effective ecological protection regimes. The details are worse than most people can easily imagine, as when transnational firms like Weyerhauser and Hyundai learn to play impoverished local and national politicians off against each other in their quest for cheap and unregulated access to Siberian forests.

The victory of the West only confirms the overall sense of inevitability. There will be a global corporate future — McDonald's in Moscow is proof enough of this. But what is most notable about this strange victory is that it finds us in the West bereft of optimism, and for such good reasons. Bright scenarios can always be contrived, but the "recession," the Gulf War, the portent of Bosnia, periodic disasters in Africa, the sense of a wild economic dynamism untempered by care and safety nets, all dampen the post–Cold War celebration. And always there is ecology — occluded by daily events yet adding its special part to the gloom. If the green Jeremiahs are right — if industrialism, consumerism, and uncontained, hegemonic economism are in fact eroding the ecological substrata of society — then the exhaustion that came at last to Soviet communism, or Stalinism, or communist state capitalism, or whatever it was, pursues us, the victors, as well.

The collapse of the Cold War's global order — the Cold War system — is a rare and precious opportunity. But the hope for a sudden postcommunist era of peace and renewal, which once filled all but the most hardened of realists, has faded into an indistinct past. Matters must somehow change, but we are oppressed by the inability to imagine, let alone create, workable transitions. It is not only that in the East an opportunity for new departures is being squandered, it is that there seems to be no way *not* to squander it. Without excusing Western politicians and businessmen for their shortsighted realism, it must be said that with the exception of rare dissidents the citizens of the East wanted nothing but to join the West as quickly as possible. This was most poignantly obvious in Germany in 1990, where the (Western) Green Party was ridiculed — and trounced — for opposing rapid unification. Frieder Wolf told me that the Western Greens had acted in solidarity with the East German opposition, for a "third way," and from an "economic common sense" that told them that a rush to unification would destroy the East German economy. In early 1993, with millions of Germans having come to regret "the annexation" of the East, Wolf was not above a bit of philosophical self-congratulation. "We were right, of course, but the question remains, was there any other possibility?"[61]

Borderlands

Few places are as unappreciated in their oddity as borders, and few borders are as odd as those on the western extreme of the U.S.-Mexico frontier. Long before NAFTA, this was another country, a borderland that was neither Mexican nor American, but both, and neither. Stand in the endangered Tijuana estuary, which lies within the United States but drains a largely Mexican watershed, and look across the rising desert mesas, and the situation emerges with a rare clarity. There is, first of all, the sharp line of the rusted border fence, and the glint of traffic on the Mexican-side frontier road. But the strongest impression is of a shabby and irregular urban mass, encrusting the border-side Mexican hills and pressing hard against that thin brown line. Looking east, there are ranks of mesas, split by the meandering fence. To its south, the sprawl of Tijuana; to its north, the dusty green of the damaged desert hillsides that are the southern extent of San Diego County.

There are few roads on the American side, and those swarm with the light-green vans and trucks of the Border Patrol. On the southern edge of the estuary, though, along the base of the frontier highlands, a rough road runs to the small, almost desolate state park that marks the border's intersection with the Pacific Ocean. In 1992 the fence stopped abruptly at the beach. On any given day, standing on a rise above it, only a few dozen feet from an idling Border Patrol cruiser, a Mexican crowd could be seen, talking, barbecuing, lounging, and spilling just over the borderline, waiting for darkness and a chance to cross into the estuary and, beyond it, north. Today that crowd is gone, for in 1992 the state Coastal Commission finally granted the Immigration and Naturalization Service permission to extend its fence across the beach and into the ocean. It stretches out 340 feet, on pilings spaced to allow the sands to pursue their natural flows, far enough that, even at low tide, the water is eight feet deep.

The fence is a monument to pragmatism, and to the militarization of the border. It is built from modular, Vietnam-era, army-surplus airplane landing pads that the Border Patrol has converted to civilian use. Though it is easy to hop, it is backed by an ever more intensive array of searchlights and surveillance systems.[62] And the fence does draw the line. Beyond it is the estuary, full of footprints pointed north, lost shoes, paths into the southern suburbs of San Diego.

The estuary is tiny (about twenty-four thousand acres), fragile, and beautiful. It contains a good number of now rare habitats, and supports a range of plant and animal communities — and birds by the score, including great egrets, blue herons, least terns, and the endangered clapper rail. I asked Jim King, a calm, sad man from the state Coastal Conservancy, if fleeing "illegals" do much damage to the estuary itself. "No, not really — they don't want to get wet." Sometimes, though, they have no choice — as at "underwear point," at the northern end of the reserve, where ambitious Latinos shed their pants to wade through sloughs heavy with invertebrates and pickleweed.

The estuary is endangered. California has lost 91 percent of its original wetlands, more than any other state, and this small island of tidal habitat is among the little that remains. The real threat, however, comes not from the illegals, or even from the Border Patrol, though it is their constant war of position that lends the area its tense, militarized air. It comes, rather, from what Jim, with impressive understatement, called "bad land-use practices." To the north lies San Diego, and then Los

Angeles, that paradigm of real estate and automobile culture run amok. To the south, restrained only by the geopolitical forcefield of the borderline, lies Tijuana, with its unreckoned population and its raw hillsides from which flow rivers of untreated, nauseating, indeterminately toxic sewage, twelve million gallons of it on an average day. It is this sewage, along with the sheets of siltation washing down from the disturbed soils of a disturbed watershed, which most immediately threatens the estuary.

Twenty years ago, Tijuana and San Diego were both towns, and the border between them, as a friend told me with unconscious nostalgia, was "European" in character. Back then, it was not so strange for a San Diegan to drive down to Mexico to pick up some pastries for breakfast. By the 1990s, matters had changed. Partly in response to the deterrent of the new border fence, such a drive would take you past large illuminated signs alerting drivers to the panicked men, women, and children who could be wandering on the freeway, to a chronically backlogged border checkpoint where in the late 1980s illegals had begun, after grouping to a critical mass, rushing onto the road and fleeing north, in desperate search of a wall to climb, a subdevelopment into which to vanish.

NAFTA will not change this, for while it will increasingly open the border to the movement of things — to trade and to capital — it will not open it to people.[63] In fact, Mexico's post-NAFTA plunge into low-intensity civil war has only sharpened efforts to seal the frontier. Note well, then, that walls and armed patrols do not altogether deter the hopeful. Unlike the Iron Curtain that once divided Europe, this wall is only an aggravation. It halts some seekers, but others climb it, or burrow beneath it, or evade it altogether. The Iron Curtain worked better, but this was only because they shot at you for trying to cross, and they shot to kill. The most extreme of California's anti-immigrant groups want such a "lethal force" policy adopted on the U.S.-Mexico border,[64] but this, we may hope, will never be tolerated, not even by the terrified citizens of some future America.

The Iron Curtain is gone, but in a certain sign of the times, an anxious German government has replaced it with tough new immigration laws, and with a new "electronic curtain" — infrared motion detectors and rapid-deployment police units — along its long Eastern border.[65] In the early 1990s, most of Germany's illegals were Gypsies, a clever, persecuted people quick to seize opportunity. But the citizens of the

Balkans threaten, and the nightmare scenario is *Russians,* millions of Russians fleeing hyperinflation or civil war, or simply chasing the dream of the West. You can see their scouts in Polish parks, huddled on benches with piles of worn luggage, flat broke and looking it.

The Russian hordes will almost certainly never arrive. Rarely do events as closely imagined as the collapse of the former Soviet bloc unfold in just the manner that is anticipated. Still, *something* unpleasant is likely. Given the weight of history in this tragic region, given its extraordinary levels of unemployment, given the shortsightedness of Western policy toward the East, and what Wolfgang Sachs called the "Mexification of the Eastern frontier,"[66] we can be confident that the future warrants no easy confidence. We can also be sure that the electronic curtain will be made quite as invisible as possible, and will garner far less bad press than its "iron" predecessor.

There is much talk these days of "Fortress Europe," but the name is a delusion — as much of a delusion as the U.S.-Mexico border fence. The illegals hop fences into San Diego, cross central Europe by train and bus, ride boats onto Spanish beaches, make their way overland to the new South Africa, enter the closest promised land through a thousand semipermeable frontiers. They are the tide that will not abate, the mass-produced products of their time, the children of local poverty and planetary TV, of corporate "outsourcing," postcolonial chaos, foreign aid, international debt, free trade, religious fanaticism, environmental destruction, and all the other tender mercies of this peculiar world. They are the not-so-secret side effects of the new economy, and of the old economies that laid its foundations.[67]

What does all this have to do with ecology? Better to ask what it has to do with the future. Better to ask if this fragile civilization could survive the "great migration"[68] that many now fear lies near ahead. Better to ask how environmentalism itself will emerge from a time in which "nativists" (as they are so politely called) have picked up its rhetoric and ambitious politicians are rushing to blame illegal immigrants for state fiscal crises,[69] invoking "overpopulation" as the motor of immigration[70] and appealing to the anxious workers of the North with calls to "save jobs for Americans" (or Frenchmen, or Austrians, or Australians, or Germans). Better to ask about a future in which xenophobia has become an organized tendency within the environmental movement.[71]

Europe's post-Wall neofascist redux is a warning, as is the rising power, and right-wing tilt, of the anti-immigrant lobby in the United States. People when afraid and confused have a demonstrated tendency to blame the weak rather than the strong — a serious problem, since fear and confusion will be in no short supply. Globalization, rationalization, and automation have already made a huge portion of the world's people quite economically superfluous, and there is no good reason to think — given the logic of planetary economic competition and the power of the free trade lobby — that the many losers will soon be welcomed into the bosom of prosperity. In the Third World, joblessness and misery are already far worse than even the unemployed of the North can easily imagine, and are getting worse.[72] In the North, the sense of a long slide in living standards that economic growth somehow does nothing to assuage, the fear that we will never again see anything like "full employment,"[73] and the confused awareness of a beating sea of "alien" immigrants have already become new corrosives, as if more were needed, in the fraying fabrics of our democracies.[74]

Jacques Attali, a French Cold War socialist, man of letters, and the founding president of the European Bank for Reconstruction and Development, imagines the future thus:

> In restless despair, the hopeless masses of the periphery will witness the spectacle of another hemisphere's wealth. Particularly in those regions of the South that are geographically contiguous and culturally linked to the North — places such as Mexico, Central America, or North Africa — millions of people will be tempted and enraged by the constant stimulation of wants that can't be satisfied. And they will know that the prosperity that is not theirs partly comes at the cost of their well-being and at the price of their environment's degradation. With no future of their own in an age of air travel and telecommunications, the terminally impoverished will look for one in the North as economic refugees and migrants on an unprecedented scale.[75]

This is remarkable prose, coming from a politician, and its warning is altogether too plausible to ignore. Moreover, it casts the new immigration into its proper light as the last green issue, the product of a divided, degraded, and yet highly integrated world, the ready-made target for those seeking scapegoats rather than solutions. "Population" is not the cause of "immigration" (that honor must go to the economic and technological forces that are "shrinking" the planet),[76] but in both, the knots of social-ecological politics are tightly bound indeed, and resist disentanglement. To even have a hope, one must be willing to face political-economic realities as large as they are unpleasant, and to draw difficult conclusions.

Why did Edward Abbey, once the wise and lucid author of *Desert Solitaire,* come to rail so intemperately against Latino immigrants, to blame them for everything from "mass unemployment" and "an overloaded welfare system," to "rotting cities" and "a poisoned environment"?[77] Why did Dave Foreman, a founder of Earth First!, defend him? Why does the simpleminded notion that there are just too many people, and that overpopulation is the ultimate root of the ecological crisis, seem such a self-evident truth to so many Northern environmentalists?

These questions are not as difficult as they may seem. We are not, after all, always brave enough to face terrifying truths square on. Overpopulation, like poverty, is less cause than consequence, but this is a large point with no end of uncomfortable corollaries. If current patterns of consumption do not change, the 57 million Northerners born in the 1990s will pollute more than the 911 million Southerners;[78] and yet, somehow, even greens who know as much fall back on Malthusian habits of mind. There is at least one unflattering reason why — without the strength to see that the global economic system, in daily, routine operation, gives us billions of poor as automatically as it destroys their environments, it is comforting to blame those poor for their own predicaments, and even for trying to escape them.[79] We all fear automation, and sense the emergence of a society that does not need us, and wonder how our children, if not we ourselves, will make a living. It is natural, I suppose, to turn away from such fear. Optimism is one possibility; another is to follow Garrett Hardin, ecology's original dark knight, now an old man who thinks his time has come round at last, and to imagine a future in which we "seal the borders" and let "the wretched nations" of the earth "go up in flames."[80]

The alternative to fear and loathing is a hope real and justifiable enough to hold our attention, and our belief. It is a commonplace of green radicalism that such a hope demands a vast renewal, a move toward economic democracy on a global scale. Too bad that these days it's so easy to conclude that democratic renewal, let alone ecological renewal, is just not in the cards. Too bad it's so hard to imagine putting a "preventive migration policy" into practice, so hard to imagine creating a world in which people everywhere can make decent lives for themselves without becoming nomads. The problem, as German essayist and longtime political ecologist Hans Magnus Enzensberger points out, is that to have a chance of success such a migration policy would have to "remove the gap between rich and poor countries, or at least reduce it considerably."[81] Such is possible, and even necessary, but it is hardly the direction of history.

A Poverty of Riches

The world may be going to hell, but there's lots
of really neat stuff you can buy!

— Review of *Wired* magazine,
somewhere on the Internet, late 1993

In 1978, when Vaclav Havel argued that the Eastern regimes were "built on foundations laid by the historical encounter between dictatorship and the consumer society," he was not going out on a limb. Communism's loyalists always saw it as a better, fairer road to industrialization, and to a good life defined by material comfort and a universal culture of mass-produced happiness. Its objects of personal aspiration — cars, refrigerators, jeans, TVs — were the same as those in the West. That they were only available to the few was a serious problem, one that eventually brought the whole edifice tumbling down, but this only proves the power of the consumption culture. There is, as former Brazilian secretary of the environment José Lutzenburger once put it, something in consumerism that seems a "messianic religion," and the people of the East had long ago heard its call. Their lands had long ago, in Havel's 1978 words, "ceased to be a kind of enclave, isolated from the rest of the developed world and immune to processes occurring in it."[82]

Havel, for a time, was as popular among Western idea makers as he was among his own countrymen. Few in the West, though, read his work with special care. Havel the anticommunist hero spoke, as was widely noted, for freedom and dignity, and for "the power of the powerless," but he also argued that "the greyness and the emptiness" of life in the East was "only an inflated caricature of modern life in general." Today, with Havel sunk into the mire of realpolitik, it is well to remember this earlier man, a voice of the East bloc's radical underground who spoke for a "third way," and for the "desperate and, given the turmoil the world is in, fading voice of the ecological movement"; the man who once asked his countrymen, "Do we not in fact stand (although, in the external measures of civilization, we are far behind) as a kind of warning to the West, revealing to it its own latent tendencies?"[83]

Is the East in some strange, paradoxical manner a warning to the West? It's an easy notion to dismiss, but given the dilapidated condition of our own democracies, and given particularly our own helplessness before the same imperious globalization, the same mass-produced consumption culture now battering the East, it bears thought. East Europe may no longer be a "post-totalitarian" society, but it is hardly without masters. First among these is the consumer society, the American Dream — as universal today in Moscow (remember, it's a dream) as in Anytown, U.S.A.

That American Dream, just what does it mean? This may be the most important ecological question of all. With the people of the East, and the South, struggling up the consumption ladder, and most of them falling off, it is too late for greens to honestly seek hope in "voluntary simplicity." Over a billion people lack regular access to safe drinking water. But how many of them, if they had the choice, would prefer Cola-Cola?

In these matters, precision is elusive. The desire for a good life, for security, opportunity, pleasure, comfort, dignity, is not easily separated from the globally marketed dreams that draw humanity each year more desperately into the culture of possession. Everywhere, comfort and affluence are besieged by spreading seas of deprivation. Sometimes the deprivation is absolute, a true poverty, sometimes it is only relative to an industrially cultivated desire. The crucial point is that it is no longer possible to draw a distinct line between the two. In the cities of the United States, where few civic spaces remain open to public culture, teenagers pace and circle in the malls, surrounded by tantalizing displays, by their own longings come back to them as fashions and commodities. In all but the very poorest regions, there are at least the televisions, blaring out the dream. Watch a few thousand commercials, and know that hundreds of millions of other people, all around the earth, are watching them with you, and it is easy to suspect that something fundamental must eventually give.[84]

In *How Much Is Enough? The Consumer Society and the Future of the Earth,* the Worldwatch Institute's Alan Durning argues that globally the population divides into three "consumption classes" — "consumers," the "middle class," and "the poor." In 1992 there were 1.1 billion poor and 1.1 billion consumers, with 3.3 million members of the global middle class between them. Durning's definition of these classes is anything but abstract. Take food. Consumers eat lots of meat and processed, overpackaged foods, and drink strange, sweet concoctions, mostly from disposable containers. The middle class eats a diet based on grains and clean water. The poor aspire to the middle-class diet but find inadequate grains and unclean water. Or take transportation. Consumers own the vast bulk of the private autos and airplanes, while the middle class travels by bus, rail, and bicycle. The poor generally walk.[85]

Consumers, however, do not always experience themselves as such. When, in Bucharest in the spring of 1993, I told Horatio, a charming cynic who had studied microbiology but was making his way in the new world as "a driver," that he was in the world's upper class (he has a car, albeit a sloppy one, eats meat regularly, and, though the pipes in his apartment tower produce water only irregularly, we were drinking Stolichnaya vodka), he was quite uncharacteristically surprised. In fact, he thought I was having him on. Speaking to an American who was soon flying off to Prague, he did not "feel" rich.

"Consumption class" is the very model of a modern political idea. In sharp contrast to the traditional left notion of class, which focuses on ownership, and specifically, ownership of the means of production, the focus here is on eating, drinking, and driving. If ever there was a conceptual revolution, a paradigm shift, this is it. Why did it occur? What does it portend? These are not simple questions. I called Alan Durning, in part to congratulate him for the power and simplicity of his notion of consumption class, but when I asked him how he would change *How Much Is Enough?*, he said that he would leave the idea out altogether, because "Americans hate being told they are rich."[86]

This is no surprise, for few people feel rich, or even satisfied. But why not? It's a tough question, though one could hardly know this from the green literature, which almost always treats the mania for acquisition as "addiction," and counterposes it to the odd notion of "authentic needs," with which we have somehow lost touch. This was Al Gore's strategy in *Earth in the Balance*, a book that contains so many pages on consumption as addiction that it almost calls for a twelve-step program to save the planet.[87] He is perhaps forbidden by his vocation from honest talk about needs and their manufacture. But what about the rest of us? Why do we still take comfort in the guilty image of ourselves as profligate consumers? Consider, for a moment, these words, taken from the original introduction to *Fifty Simple Things You Can Do to Save the Earth*: "Institutions alone can never solve the problems that accumulate from the seemingly inconsequential actions of millions of individuals. My trash, your use of inefficient cars, someone else's water use — all make the planet less livable for the children of today and tomorrow."[88]

It's the emphasis here that's odd. Certainly we bear responsibility for our actions, but this hardly means that we should turn our sight from "institutions" and attend to our trash. Yet many of us welcome invitations to do just this. Why? Is it because we can imagine changes in individual consumption, while production seems altogether beyond our reach? If so, it must be said that to count on such changes alone is to indulge an absurd illusion. Billions of "individuals" around the world want nothing more than to join us in our "seemingly inconsequential actions," and are unmoved by the piety of affluent Northern greens who, with breathtaking excess, have gone so far as to glorify "ragpickers, scavengers, and shoeshine boys" as heroes of simple living and ecological revolution.[89]

It is curious that we often imagine significant changes in individual consumption patterns coming more easily than larger social transformations, for the evidence argues that the opposite is more likely. The history of voluntary simplicity movements is anything but encouraging,[90] and we should not imagine that this will suddenly change. In 1994 a major study of U.S. attitudes toward population and consumption highlighted the public secret here — Americans "cherish the ability to consume more than people elsewhere, and many perceive their ability to consume at high levels as an earned privilege."[91] This is the reality, and it is social, cultural, political — not individual.

Fortunately there is nuance here. These same U.S. voters "recoiled" at the thought of "reducing real comforts in their lives," and, contrary to the primitivism that haunts green culture, it is just not necessary that they do so — not, that is, if "comfort" can be redefined. Besides, the costs of consumerism are visible as never before, and many of the people who see them are not content to blame the individual. Greens increasingly speak not for a culture of austerity but for a politics of sufficiency. The longing for a decent standard of living is not identical to consumerism, and though telling the one from the other can be almost impossibly difficult, we must learn to appreciate the distinction. Southern activists, wearied unto death by ritual invocations of "overpopulation" as the cause of the environmental crisis, respond that "overconsumption in the North" is the real problem. It's not that simple, of course, but this argument, and its new familiarity, is a real step forward.

Facing the facts will be extremely painful. In consumption cultures, success, contentment, and celebration are all expressed in acquisition. Nor is it obvious how to distinguish overconsumption from consumption proper. Even the terms, as commonly understood, are problems. "Overconsumption" is often taken as the equivalent of "individual overconsumption," as if individual responsibility were the only issue here. The notion of overconsumption can be expanded to include advertising and the manufacture of desire, but even this obvious move is resisted. Changing the focus to production, Durning told me, "just lets us off the hook."

There is a terrible truth in this. The cities of Eastern Europe are clotting with traffic, and no amount of analysis about the defunding of public transportation, however fair it may be, will negate the fact that *people want cars,* as they want beef, TV, and, finally, riches. This is simply true. The Japanese are launching a major burger chain in China — three thousand "Mos Burger" outlets to start.[92] The obvious green question is, where will the beef come from? The less obvious question is, where will the desire for the beef come from? We may answer it with thoughtful reflections on the history of needs and status,[93] and on the appropriation of that history by capitalist marketeers, but is this sufficient? Is there, particularly, a danger that, in focusing on the marketeers, we will conveniently let ourselves, and millions of aspirants in nations like China, "off the hook"?

Perhaps, but if consumerism is to be understood, there is no choice but to closely scrutinize the manufacture of needs. The size of the advertising industry alone proves the point. That it is a key industry is well known, though its size — $256 billion in 1990, globally, up from

$39 billion in 1950 — can still surprise, as can the fact that the industry is growing far faster in the South than in its Northern heartland,[94] and simply because the market in the North is closer to saturation. The standard American teenager watches twenty thousand TV commercials a year, which comes to hundreds of thousands by the time he or she leaves high school. Worse, this fact no longer outrages us.[95]

Alan Durning tells us that "advertisements increasingly resemble dreams," and that brand identification is "much akin to the role of myth in traditional societies."[96] These comments explain less than they seem to. They bear upon marketing's devices, but not its goals. To understand the "messianic religion" of consumerism, one must eventually turn to production, to the profits that are the goal of production, to the never-ending effort to ensure that there are customers in profusion, to the matter that maverick American sociologist Thorstein Veblen described back in 1923, when he wrote that "the fabrication of customers can now be carried on as a routine operation, quite in the spirit of the mechanical industries and with much the same degree of assurance as regards the quality, rate and volume of output."[97]

The next time you find yourself staring, irritated, at a television commercial, realize that the pitch you are watching is only half of a clever two-sided transaction. The other half is that you (or, more precisely, your attention) are being sold to an advertiser. And, in truth, there is no mystery here, no surprise. Advertising is now seen as entirely "natural," as are its consequences. It is crucial to the dynamism of the economy and as every recession proves once again, the economy *must* expand. But though we usually see this as an *extensive* process, one that takes place "out there" somewhere, in "markets," that is only the beginning. Economic expansion is an *intensive* process as well, an expansion into life, culture, and the mind.

Americans, who have come to view shopping as a primary cultural activity, spend, on average, about six hours shopping each week. This is more time than Russians spent in the late 1980s, when Soviet shopping queues were world famous.[98]

Globalization

Just after World War II, with Europe in ruins and the whole world staggering into a new age, the Allies set out to create an unprecedented set of global institutions. The United Nations, the International Monetary Fund (IMF), the World Bank, the General Agreement on Tariffs and Trade (GATT) — all hail from the late 1940s.

The primary goal of this institution building, according to economic analyst Robert Kuttner, was to prevent the reemergence of the "chaotic economic conditions" that many saw as the ultimate cause of the two world wars, and in so doing to prevent a third. It was, unfortunately, a goal that was soon forgotten in the postwar battle for economic and geopolitical position, and in the "de facto military Keynesianism of the Cold War,"[99] which provided both the sketch of an industrial policy and lots of R&D cash, and asked in return only that military priorities be served.

Half a century later, we may justifiably ask, did all this "reluctant statecraft" succeed? If we accept that, in Kuttner's words, its purpose was "to allow for domestic planning and full employment within each nation and to avoid the instability created by a global system driven by purely market forces,"[100] the answer is clear enough. It was a failure. True, there was not another world war, but neither was there peace, or the preparation for peace. Instead, there was the Cold War, proxy wars both violent and "low intensity" throughout the Third World, the institutionalization of the modern arms trade, the emergence of Eisenhower's "military-industrial complex." And there was the pathetic futurism of MAD, of "mutual assured destruction." Claims for the military stability of the Cold War world devolve not to political institutions but to the balance of terror.

As for the avoidance of economic chaos, geopolitical conflict, and war, it would today — with the world fracturing into competing economic blocs and nations everywhere seeking prosperity in exports, with poverty at terrifying levels and economists groping even to locate the ecological crisis on their charts — be quite an extraordinary act of bravado to embrace the legacy of the last fifty years.

From the perspective of the new world disorder, with economic, political, and ecological chaos all competing for our scant time and attention, with "globalization" become a euphemism for a commercial imperative unbuffered by ethical skepticism, care for the weak and vulnerable, environmental protection, or even democracy, the schemes of the post–World War II geopoliticians do not seem to have worn well at all.

The IMF, originally envisioned by John Maynard Keynes as a guarantor of free and fair trade and of global monetary liquidity, has become instead the most vilified of international institutions. The problem is that, these days, liquidity often means austerity, and the IMF, by its eagerness to be the planet's chief enforcer of austerity and "structural adjustment," has cast itself less as a planetary credit union than as the administrator of an international debtor's prison.

The consequences of the IMF's policies — excoriated for years by Southern politicians and development activists, and more recently by environmentalists — seemingly remained unknown to Western political elites until early 1993, when, anxious about possible chaos in the former Soviet Union, they ordered the IMF to loosen its aid (loan) criteria, at least for Russia. It didn't. IMF technocrats aren't in the habit of taking orders from politicians, and the politicians didn't really push for a new policy. "Shock therapy" came after all, as slashed safety nets, open borders, and breakneck privatization, and these are still the official religion. Besides, "the institutions," as the *Financial Times* put it in early 1993, "must think about life after Russian reform" when considering special deals for Russia's president, Boris Yeltsin. They must, in particular, take into account that "other, often poorer, [IMF and World Bank] members in Latin America and Africa" might demand the same consideration.[101]

The winds changed a bit in December of 1993, when Vladimir Zhirinovsky, a "nationalist" (fascist) promising to "raise Russia from her knees," took 23 percent of the Russian vote (the highest fraction won by any party) — and a full third of the armed forces vote![102] Suddenly, safety nets were in rhetorical vogue, and there was even talk that, as a "senior official of one multilateral agency" put it, "shock therapy" might be less than a "coherent road map for reform."[103] Such a map, it should be said, is far more likely to come from activist think tanks than from the IMF, which resists reform with all the zealotry of power and belief. The Russian crisis was still echoing when, in its 1994 report, the IMF argued for deregulation, wage reductions, and social security cutbacks as a solution to the Western jobs crisis — shock therapy, but this time for *Western* Europe![104] As for the environment, the IMF has thus far been altogether unwilling to see that draconian austerity measures have heavy ecological costs, and it is not clear that it ever will.[105]

The World Bank, for its part, has drifted so far from its original mandate as an agent of postwar European reconstruction that today it is the largest single purveyor of the "development" model that has razed the social and ecological foundations of the nonindustrial world. Economists and politicians tell its story in terms of loans, projects, and "consultations," but activists see instead phalanxes of social-ecological disasters — gigantic dams and power plants, export-facilitating deep-water ports, "green revolution" plantations, rain forest roads and "forestry projects," destroyed villages and displaced peasants by the million.[106] Nor is the Bank's history alone at issue here. In mid-1994, with the Bank under rising criticism and its image-conscious managers arguing that they had turned over a new leaf,[107] the Bank's ongoing projects were, by its own calculations, forcing the "involuntary re-settlement" of more than two million people.[108]

None of this is accidental. Despite overwhelming evidence that small, community-based projects are by far the most likely to benefit the poor,[109] and despite even real changes of policy, the Bank's manag-ers retain their traditional bias toward industrial gigantism. No doubt their official religion of "development" plays a large part in their loy-alty to the old ways, but this is only a partial explanation. The Bank is a bureaucracy above all else, and there is no mystery why it designs its projects and policies with scant input from the people in poor coun-tries who will be most affected by them, or why its constructions tend toward the monumental. Mega-projects are bureaucratically convivial, for despite irritating differences in local cultures and ecologies, they always make similar, convenient demands.[110] Big projects mean big money, and big money has a logic all its own. "The Bank's $25 billion annual lending," according to Bruce Rich, director of the U.S.-based Environmental Defense Fund's International Project, is "a global po-litical patronage machine without precedent in world history."[111]

All the Bank's promiscuous construction has unfortunately failed to achieve its aggressively advertised goal of sharply reducing poverty. It has, however, moved greens of all shades and origins to take a hard look at "development," and for this we may be grateful. The Bank, too, has changed in recent years. Waking to find itself one of the world's most hated institutions, it has, at least in its many public pronounce-ments, launched major efforts to fund "sustainable" models of devel-opment, and — again — to reduce poverty. Given the grim state of the world, it's hard to maintain skepticism in the face of such a wonderful offer; too bad there are so many good reasons to do just that.

And there is GATT, which seeks to govern international trade, and thus to set the fundamental terms of global integration. Trade is the economic baseline of both ecological destruction and, potentially, environmental protection, and the ground upon which a long series of key social-ecological battles will be fought. This became clear in the NAFTA and GATT fights of the early 1990s, and in 1994's transformation of GATT into the officially celebrated, highly secretive, and profoundly undemocratic World Trade Organization (WTO). The die has now been cast. The WTO, and its extension of GATT's free-trade regime into new areas as wildly diverse as agriculture, intellectual property, health and safety, and services, will be the scene of key trade-versus-environment battles. Are the environmental majors serious about saving the earth? Is business? Look not to their ad campaigns but to their strategies in the WTO's quiet byzantine maneuverings.

It should be said that "free trade" is a colossal misnomer. GATT/WTO and NAFTA are both *managed* trade agreements, and bad ones at that. Walter Russell Mead, a senior analyst with the New York–based World Policy Institute, put this well: "They lower some barriers to trade, keep others high, and contain vast and lucrative loopholes that benefit interest groups who were successful at lobbying powerful elected officials."[112]

The trade battles will not be over soon. How can they be when they involve matters fundamental to shifting patterns of global economic power? What is key from the environmental point of view, though, is that they *also* involve matters fundamental to ecological protection. The details are many but the point clear — we can already look back to the trade-and-the-environment debate of the early 1990s as a watershed on the green movement's long road to political maturity.

And how can one sum up the United Nations, the most public and the most disappointing of the post–World War II institutions? During the Cold War, it became a bad joke, but is there now hope? Perhaps, but the UN is neither effective nor democratic, and after the dismemberment of Bosnia, it is clear that these two goals will not be easily brought together. The problem is not limited to peacekeeping — it's easy to suspect that many of the UN's official goals are, intentionally or by default, designed more for public admiration than success. Again and again, there is the stark mismatch between goals and the resources allocated to their fulfillment. The World Health Organization, for example, has as its official goal "Health for All by the Year 2000," but a ridiculously tiny budget with which to pursue it. Even the Security Council, with its putative goal of keeping the peace, lacks the legitimacy, the power, and the will to do so, though this fact is obscured by periodic resort to American and European military forces. The United Nations is now fifty years old, but it has never been given the means to accomplish its public goals, or even to make peace. This could change, of course, but it will not change easily.

History can be instructive. Today, with global institution building again on the agenda, and instability replacing communism as the ruling geopolitical fear, it particularly rewards attention. In debates about the greening of trade, the restructuring of the UN, and the need for new global political institutions, and especially in the rapidity with which "environmental diplomacy" is emerging as a viable career path for ambitious politicians, we can see the outline of another wave of political globalization, one that will take the concerns of the post–World War II era as only part of a far larger and still emerging agenda. We are usually, in this process, invited to see only hope. And there is hope, and possibility. But there is also, as after World War II, abundant justification for skepticism, and a deafening dissonance between rhetoric and reality.

A sense of reckoning is large, but denial and gridlock only thicken. Corporations have become planetary in their operations and outlook, but the political apparatus — the state — remains national in its orientation, and is declining in power. This development, in the rare cases when it is seriously discussed, is treated as more or less inevitable, and yet it may be catastrophic. Nations already besieged by global cash flows and corporations they can barely hope to control will have no great inclination to cede additional power to any multinational authority, including those dreamt of by the eco-diplomats.

In early 1994 Herman Daly, perhaps the world's most influential green economist, decided that six years in the strange obscurity of the World Bank's Environment Department was enough. In his farewell lecture to Bank staff, he made exactly this point. "To globalize the economy by erasure of national boundaries through free trade, free capital mobility, and free, or at least uncontrolled migration, is to wound fatally the major unit of community capable of carrying out any policies for the common good." This is only the truth, and just the problem. Internationalism is being thrust upon us, but it must not be taken as it is being offered. Dreams of globalization are everywhere, but which of them offers an alternative to the "despotic internationalism"[113] of the actually emerging world — an internationalism which, in Daly's words, weakens "national and subnational communities, while strengthening the relative power of transnational corporations"?[114]

Globalization and its dilemmas are fundamental to our age. It is a word proper to a time that has added "ecological security" and "geo-ecology" to the political lexicon, in which East and West are obsolete categories, in which the brutality of the planet's harsh divide into rich and poor has become unavoidable. It names this time of global markets and global warming, this time in which, despite rising awareness, occasional victory, and now backlash against environmentalism, not a single major trend in global ecological degradation has been reversed.

Childhood's End

In the meantime, environmentalism is changing. It has already shed much of its middle-class veneer, and if it is to succeed, it must lose a good deal more. The "social issues," justice first among them, figure large in its future. Even angry Southern activists know of the enclaves of desperate poverty that pepper the North, almost as mirrors of the islands of affluence in the South. There is much talk of "the South within the North and the North within the South," and a bitter new awareness of class — of the division between rich and poor — as a fundamental ecological issue.

Not that all those who see themselves as environmentalists have awakened to the full extent of the coming reckoning, or even begun to understand the links between ecological crisis and economic globalization. But a large minority have, and many others have their suspicions. The turning point is difficult to pin down. Was it the opening of the East, and the growing sense that victory would not be altogether sweet? Was it the Gulf War — the first ever in which military ecocide was widely reported, and widely denounced, even before the shooting had stopped? Was it an echo of a recession that, in a manner unique since the Great Depression, was seen as a portent of permanent economic polarization? In any case, a new wind is blowing. The far right knows it, for, frustrated by the loss of their beloved "evil empire," its spokesmen have searched for new enemies, and found not only illegal immigrants and the other usual suspects, but also, as a logging company flack put it during the California timber wars, "all environmentalists," because they embrace "some form of left-wing radical collectivism" and are, as a result, "the greatest threat to you, to me, to our communities, to our state, and to our nation."[115] Economists know it, for the odd abstraction that is their science is besieged by a rising school of green neo-Keynesians who insist that, come what may, the ecosystem will not support indefinite economic growth. Politicians know it, for their driest debates — about intellectual property rights, the world trading system, the management of Third World debt — are now minutely scrutinized by people throughout the world who see their lives and life around them as endangered by an economy that has become, in Wendell Berry's felicitous phrase, "too economic."

We may at last be turning the curve that long seemed to be just ahead. In the East, environmentalism, like other forms of basic human sympathy, breeds profound doubt about the terms of the reconstruction. In the South, and among poor people's movements in the North, the demands of ecology and of community development are visibly converging. In the North, ecology threads through political questions of all variety; social justice, the drawdown of the military economy, the globalization of the economy, all are green issues. In the United States, ecology helps to mark the often obscure border between the Republican school of planetary neoliberalism and the vaguely greener globalism of the Democrats. A weird mix of right-wing pundits make their careers by attacking greens as reds in disguise.

So it can be said that ecology is assuming shapes most environmentalists never expected. The new ecology is unabashedly political, economically and technologically sophisticated, insistent about justice, intolerant of old simplicities, full of startling and dangerous questions. How could it be otherwise? With the fogs of the Cold War lifting, ruin appears everywhere, and everywhere there is the suspicion that nature cannot be saved without saving democracy as well. In Africa, where only strong communities can hope to protect the remaining trees, the Greenbelt Movement faces constant and sometimes brutal state repression.[116] In the United States, matters are not so extreme, but here, too, it is difficult to argue that democracy is doing well, or that the environment has much chance without its renewal. Change comes when it must, and according to veteran investigative reporter Mark Dowie, it is grassroots activism and not lobbying that provides the muscle. He argues, in fact, that the environmental mainstream is "courting irrelevance," and that, absent real democratic renewal, the majors will "continue their evolution towards a weak and superfluous interest group, absorbing almost 90 percent of the contributed environmental dollar and doing less and less with it to protect the environment."[117]

The sense of new times is palpable, if hard to focus. Look back, then, on the faded avant-garde of 1980s environmentalism. Earth First! is the best example, for it was an almost ideal product of its times. An anarchic radicalization of the American wilderness movement, Earth First! was angry, rebellious, funny, and media-wise enough to invent forms of activism appropriate to a time in which Ronald Reagan was president and James Watt in charge of the national forests. Unfortunately, its apostles often knew the roots of ecological crisis in terms so abstract and politically sanitized — "industrialism" and "technology" — that they were doomed to serious disorientation. They made a fetish of wilderness, and many of them saw "humanity," and especially the breeding poor, as the engine of ecological destruction. It was a tidy Malthusian resolution, appropriate to a movement which, following the main currents of Cold War ideology, rejected left analysis out of hand. When, in the late 1980s, Northern California Earth Firsters broke the mold by asking commonsense questions about the corporations that were razing the old-growth forests, the end of an era had come.

In the ancient days of the early 1980s, the West German Greens never tired of insisting that they were "neither right nor left but out front." Today the striking thing about this slogan is how stale and even absurd it seems. The green movement has faced our real conditions of life to just the extent that it has rethought traditional left issues — the global polarization of wealth, the need to regulate the market in general and planetary corporations in particular, the need for a new and "unalienated" technology, an end to racism, and so on. Its flirtations with right-wing politics[118] have been decidedly less productive.

The childhood of green politics is over, but that childhood has not been left behind. Today, as years ago, there is back-to-the-landism, UN politicking, technological alternativism, cultural revolt, legislative and regulatory horse-trading, and all the other variations on the still-ramifying environmental theme. The big difference now is that there is a corps of veterans who have reflected upon their failures and are willing to admit — over beers if not always in fund-raising letters — that they were naive to believe that the old questions about justice, power, and emancipation could be put off while the earth was saved.

The social issues will not be denied. The question is how they will be understood. It is common these days to hear that the Third World poor, desperate for fuel and livelihood, often have no choice but to strip the trees, no choice but to bear large families as personal social security systems. This is hard-won knowledge, but it is only a beginning. What is needed, in the face of the xenophobia and ecological deterioration that will frame our futures, is a deeper, more visceral understanding of desperation and choicelessness.

It is folly to expect that changes large and significant enough to ground a new hope will grow smoothly from initiatives in the dominant institutions. In a world where oil, arms, and cocaine are among the most profitable of all globally traded commodities, where the "poor" number well over a billion and slavery in all its forms — child labor, debt bondage, and even chattel slavery, the actual ownership of one person by another — is returning,[119] where unemployment has become, according to Dominique Moise, deputy director of the French Institute of International Relations, "the biggest security problem facing the Western world today,"[120] it is folly to expect environmentalism to remain aloof from fundamental social questions. It is folly to believe that a realistic environment and development agenda, one that seeks peace rather than new kinds of war, will not be compelled to take up the unfinished business of the old left movement.[121]

In the South, socialism — Marxism-Leninism, Maoism, and Sandinismo all — was always less important as ideology than as an alternative development model, a path (so it was hoped) to social justice and dignity. It didn't work out that way, but there is no reason to think that the much-advertised death of communism has eliminated the longing for justice and dignity. Indeed, the standard measure of justice seems to have shrunk as the decades have passed, at least judging by the facts of global income distribution.

Nowadays it is public knowledge that in the United States, the rich are getting richer and the poor poorer. Not so well known is that the

same pattern holds at the global level, and to an even greater and cru-
eler extent. It's not simply that the world's people are arrayed between
the consumer class and the extreme poor, it is that, according to the
United Nations Development Program, the distance between the two
extremes doubled between 1960 and 1989, by which time the richest
fifth of the world's people received 82.7 percent of the world's total income and the poorest fifth received only 1.4 percent — a ratio of 60 to
1![122] Even these figures conceal the scale of the injustice, for they are
based on average per capita incomes *within* countries. Forget borders
altogether and directly compare the richest and poorest 20 percent of
all the world's people, and the income differential rises to at least 150
to 1.

It is common knowledge among greens that the North, with a fourth
of the world's people, consumes 70 percent of the world's energy, 75 percent of its metals, 85 percent of its wood, and 60 percent of its food.
What is too often news is that in the 1980s the situation dramatically
worsened for the world's poor. During that "lost decade" of Southern
development, the real wages of the poorest fell around the world. In
Latin America the lowest nonagricultural wages fell 41 percent between 1981 and 1987. In Africa indicators of social welfare such as nutrition and access to doctors sank below their levels in colonial times.[123]
By 1990 over 1.3 billion people lacked access to safe drinking water,
880 million adults could not read or write, 770 million had insufficient
food for an active working life, and over a billion lacked even the most
rudimentary necessities. Today, as then, an estimated 13–18 million
people, mostly children, die from hunger and poverty each year. That
is about 40,000 people per day, or 1,700 people an hour.[124]

Something fundamental is wrong here, and has been for a long time.
Demographer Paul Bairoch contrasted the relative wealth of the "presently developed" and "presently less developed" countries, that is, the
capitalist and noncapitalist worlds, in the 1750s and again in the 1980s.
In the 1750s, living standards in what we today call the North were
not notably higher than those in the South, a fact that runs so sharply
against received wisdom that it is difficult for us even to imagine. Over
the next 230 years, the average citizen of the capitalist world grew to
be eight times richer than one in the noncapitalist world, and contrary
to all the tales told by the friends of "progress," this "improvement"
has not always been by virtue of the North's technological and cultural

innovations. The less-flattering and, according to Robert Heilbroner, "more important" side of the story, "was the drainage of wealth from the underdeveloped Periphery to the developed Center — a capitalist version of the much-older imperialist exploitation of the weak by the strong."[125]

We must return again to some ancient battlegrounds. The ecosystem as we know it cannot be saved while the poor people of the South are left to make their way along the paths of a haphazard and unjust development. The alternative, of course, is "sustainable development," but how, in rural societies where the rich own most of the agricultural land, can "sustainable development" be more than a cynical slogan? In Guatemala 2 percent of the population owns 63 percent of the good land, while in El Salvador that same 2 percent claims 60 percent. In Zimbabwe white farmers, less than 1 percent of the population, command 39 percent of the land. In the Philippines the statistics are less dramatic, but nevertheless 3 percent of landowners control a quarter of the country, most of the good farmland is given over to export crops, and 60 percent of rural families are either landless or own too little land to feed themselves.[126] In Brazil 0.8 percent of the landowners own 43 percent of the land.[127] Given all this, is it a surprise that peasants migrate into rain forests or onto fragile uplands? Only to those who blame the poor for their poverty. In fact, governments often promote rain forest colonizations as "a convenient safety valve for land hunger and social discontent."[128]

Land reform is just one example, but it serves to illustrate a difficult history with which greens must inevitably come to terms. Land reform has long been a "pinko" demand, and greens cannot hope to take it up without reckoning with its past. This won't be easy, for in most of the world, status and wealth have long been rooted in sharply inequitable patterns of land ownership. Still, change is possible, if only because it is necessary. With superpower conflict largely out of the way, land redistribution and other old "radical reforms" can at least be taken directly, rather than as battles in the great East-West confrontation.

The future is again open. Today realism as well as radicalism tells us that the social-ecological crisis demands new agendas. There is hope in this, as there is in the fact that alternatives by the score remain attractive and plausible. No natural law requires that the global military budget continue to consume almost a trillion dollars a year. The Earth

Summit treaties could be fleshed out into the basis of a global New Deal. Sustainable development could become something more than a catchphrase. The South could be freed from its burden of odious debt, and even escape the crushing poverty that is the immediate, if not ultimate, cause of so much devastation. Women throughout the world could win the security and respect they need to control their childbearing. "Progress" and "modernization" could be redefined. The air, seas, and forests could be protected by new treaties. These treaties could even be enforced.

In the autumn of 1989, with the wilting heat wave and greenhouse fear of the previous summer still vivid memories, *Scientific American* published a special issue entitled "Managing Planet Earth." In it, Stephen H. Schneider, a noted climatologist at the National Center for Atmospheric Research, offered an optimism as extreme as any doomsayer's despair. Arguing that the developed world would have to "invest hundreds of billions of dollars every year for many decades, both at home and in financial and technical assistance to developing nations, to achieve a stabilized and sustainable world," Schneider insisted that this was nevertheless a realistic prospect and reminded us that "not long ago a massive disengagement of NATO and Warsaw Pact forces in Europe also seemed inconceivable."[129] This disengagement, of course, is now old news; so what, then, about those "hundreds of billions of dollars every year for many decades" that must be invested in laying the foundations of a sustainable economy? Will we see them allocated anytime soon?

This is an odd and bitter moment. The last decade has brought changes larger than any we expected, changes we have yet to digest. Yet these are nothing compared to the changes needed for "sustainability," and, knowing this, we may find despair seeming all too reasonable. Still, Schneider is right — with the fall of the East in recent memory, only fools can be certain that other, equally unreckoned changes are not also gathering, waiting only for their own moment.

Apocalyptics

A permanent modern scenario: apocalypse looms, and it doesn't occur. . . .
Apocalypse has become an event that is happening, and not happening. It
may be that some of the most feared events, like those involving the irrepa-
rable ruin of the environment, have already happened. But we don't know
it yet, because the standards have changed. Or because we do not have the
right indexes for measuring the catastrophe. Or simply because this is a
catastrophe in slow motion.

— Susan Sontag[1]

I make a distinction between optimism and pessimism on the one hand,
having to do with the betting man's expectation based on evidence; and on
the other hand, hope and despair, the existential/religious attitude one im-
poses on the situation. I think one can be hopeful and still pretty
pessimistic.

— Herman Daly[2]

In 1990, not so very long ago, Washington's Worldwatch Institute
gave us forty years — not forty years until "the end," but forty years
to make the transition to an "environmentally stable society." Worldwatch's president, Lester R. Brown, spelled out the consequences of
failure in cool, unambiguous terms: "If we have not succeeded by then,
environmental deterioration and economic decline are likely to be
feeding on each other, pulling us into a downward spiral of social
disintegration."[3]

Forty years. It's an odd, precise figure, just the sort usually discounted as apocalyptic excess. Brown, in fact, is high on the list of

greens whom cornucopians and other assorted optimists love to deride as professional pessimists. Nevertheless, Brown's warning warrants serious consideration. It is, first, a subtle, modern one, for he attends closely to the deadly feedback between ecological deterioration and economic inflexibility. The elements of his projected catastrophe — desertification, rising human population, political instability, famine, mass extinction, deforestation, pollution, and global warming, just for starters — have become depressingly familiar, as has the weight and inertia of the global economy.

Worldwatch is no millenarian cult. Its annual *State of the World* reports — like that which issued the forty-year warning — have become the planet's semiofficial environmental annual reports, and are translated into dozens of languages. Further, Worldwatch's forty-year figure is based in large degree on precise quantitative measures of the earth's "vital signs" — continued loss of topsoils and forests, rising population and carbon dioxide levels, falling per capita agricultural productivity, eroding genetic diversity, dying lakes, reefs, and rivers. There is almost no end to the grim data.

It gets worse. *Beyond the Limits,* by the authors of 1972's eco-blockbuster *The Limits to Growth,* argues in precise numerical detail that in the two decades since *Limits* was first published, and "in spite of the world's improved technologies, the greater awareness, the stronger environmental policies, many resource and pollution flows had grown beyond their sustainable limits." At this point, if we hope to avoid "an uncontrolled decline in per capita food output, energy use, and industrial production," we must not only find a way of eliminating poverty, but of doing so "while the human material economy contracts."[4] It will be a hard sell, and we do not have forever.

Not all greens think the clock is set for 2030, but the early 1990s saw a remarkable number of environmentalists declare that the 1990s would be the pivot of future history. The World Resources Institute, no hotbed of radical environmental pessimism, published a book entitled *The Crucial Decade.* Anita Gorden and David Suzuki, in *It's a Matter of Survival,* insisted that the 1990s must be "a turning point for human civilization." They gave us fifty years, and Harvard University Press published their call to arms.[5] Mostafa K. Tolba, head of the UN Environment Program, agreed, as did Jacques Cousteau, the dean of the oceans, who told us we only had ten years left to "get it." San Francisco's Earth Island Institute actually counts down the years remaining in the "crucial decade" on the opening page of its monthly journal.[6]

What are we to make of such rhetoric? Have greens, as even sympathetic critics now eagerly charge, come to fetishize pessimism and doomsaying? Are greens, especially radical greens, unable to tolerate good news? Is environmentalism too often an apocalyptic cult? I do not think so, and this despite the fact that some greens have been expecting the end for a long, long time. Back in 1990, Mike Roselle, a cofounder of Earth First!, told me, "Hell, I thought we had ten years left in 1980."[7] He was not alone in this fear, but neither — and this is an important point — was he happy about it.

Fear informs everything that greens say and do. Beneath their love of wilderness, solar power, and whole food, beneath their hopes for regulatory and legislative innovation, there is fear. It is fundamental to green culture, to the apocalyptic temptations that mark green culture, and to our common predicament. The ecological crisis is real, but it is also gradual in its evolution, and it does not find us — rich and poor, black and white — equally prepared for its depredations. Greens know they are right, and can be almost crushed by that knowledge. They long for movement and resolution, and this, it seems, is a weakness. As the right wing settles into a long, dirty campaign against environmentalism, among its prominent weapons is a snide dismissal, a feigned ironic certainty that strong environmental warnings are only apocalyptic fearmongering or, worse, a neobolshevik tree-hugging hysteria. It is as if science itself — long an ally of business as usual but now, as ecology, become inconvenient — can simply be ignored.

But it cannot be ignored. It is a matter not of opinion but of incessant and terrible fact that we are living in a time of slow biophysical cataclysm. Today's species extinction rates, hundreds or perhaps thousands of times greater than those typical of the last 600 million years, demonstrate this well enough. What is far less obvious is that this is, finally, a crisis, a catastrophe, and not just a very bad patch; that our society's manifest inability to face, let alone adequately respond to, the demands of ecological limitation threatens eventually to take us down; that this is the big one, the one we'll not be able to muddle through, the one that adaptation and denial will not avail.

Optimism is always possible, but consider what it means if the green apocalyptics are right. Consider what it means if local environmental crises are only the visible aspects of a global ecological crisis that will not yield to piecemeal reform or half measures; if, only two and a half decades after the first Earth Day, and just years after the West won its epochal battle against the "evil empire," we find ourselves a mere forty or fifty years from the abyss; if we are in fact facing a catastrophe that will present our children with conditions far worse than those we suffer today. Hard-core greens have imagined these possibilities in considerable detail. Is it any wonder that they see in calm deliberation and "political realism" only equivocation, complicity, and decadence?

Overwhelmed by our daily lives, we find global ecological decline a prospect difficult to take seriously. Worldwatch's forty-year warning was treated as hard news by the *New York Times*[8] (a fact notable in its own right), but of course it failed to penetrate the ruling optimism, or to displace what Worldwatch's Sandra Postel has called "denial in the decisive decade."[9] Despite vast libraries of terrifying fact and evidence, the consensus still judges warnings as urgent as Brown's to be misguided, almost banal attempts to rally the troops with millenarian ravings. Everywhere, innocents and skeptics echo the same arguments. Not only will we likely muddle through, but attempts to frighten people into action, to "organize on the basis of fear," will ultimately breed despair, cynicism (when prophecy inevitably fails), and passivity.

My experiences are, I think, typical of those who travel in both environmental and mainstream circles. I have been asked "what psychological needs" I thought lay behind "end-time thinking" in the environmental movement, and had to force a smile when a friend, a physician and medical researcher, told me he feared the existence of a fin de siècle virus. Another friend, a bright, sarcastic software engineer, found the nub of the green movement's public relations problem. He listened as I argued that "ecological crisis" is not too strong a term, then retorted that "environmental catastrophists" were like "gloom and doom economists, always predicting a crash," and "Marxist crisis theorists, always on the lookout for the final crisis of capitalism." All, he said, had "a professional relationship" to "their predictions of apocalypse."

This is a good point, but it is not decisive. Maurice Strong, secretary-general of 1992's Earth Summit, certainly did have a professional relationship to his prediction, delivered during the Summit's opening speeches, that "if we continue along this path of development and destruction, we will destroy our civilization," that if we do not act decisively and soon, "nature will, and in a much more brutal manner."[10] But who will altogether discount this as mere professional exhortation?

I should say that, with caveats and reservations, I am an apocalyptic. Watching the advance of the deterioration, I can only conclude that trouble lies on the horizon. I don't wish to wait for "proof," nor can I believe that minor institutional reforms and tech fixes will add up to "sustainability." Poverty and desperation are on the rise, and for a huge number of people (perhaps one-sixth of the world's population),[11] Brown's "downward spiral of social disintegration" has already arrived. I see the logic of crisis all around me, and though I want to be a realist, I wonder what that word can possibly mean.

Forty years or fifty, or a hundred, this is a technical matter. Any specific prediction is likely to be proven wrong. Even weak half measures have unpredictable effects. Randy Hayes, the director of the Rainforest Action Network, makes sense when he says, with his typical pragmatism, that "things drag," and "if Worldwatch says forty years we probably have seventy."[12] It's a reasonable hedge, one that expects the unexpected and respects the power of adaptation and denial. The difference between forty and a hundred years is, of course, no real difference at all.

Once and Future Catastrophes

It may be more difficult today to accept the full reality of the environmental crisis than it was around 1970, when books like *The Population Bomb, Blueprint for Survival, The Closing Circle,* and *The Limits to Growth* caught us unaware and undefended, and were able briefly to hold environmental crisis theory at the center of the media storm. Here we are several decades later, and aren't things still basically okay?

They are not. Despite advances in isolated technical areas, significant reductions (in the richer areas of the world) of the most visible air and water pollutants, a new vogue for Panglossian futurism, and a striking increase in the overall level of environmental consciousness, most — though not all — of the predictions of the early eco-doomsters have come, are coming, true, in outline if not always in detail. Take the grand old eco-apocalyptic Paul Ehrlich, who, in a series of late-1960s appearances on *The Tonight Show*, put "population explosion," and ecological apocalypse in general, onto the map.

It is almost a tradition to slam Ehrlich as a hysteric whose predictions have been disproven by time. But have they? In 1968, when *The Population Bomb* was first published, the human population was 3.5 billion. In 1995, it hit 5.7 billion. These are facts and are not in dispute. And what of Ehrlich's 1968 prediction that as population increased life would get nastier? About 1 billion of 1968's 3.5 billion people were "doing well," but of the more than 1.8 billion people born by 1990, only a few — perhaps 200 million — were. Today more people are starving, more are trapped in the terrible purgatory that development experts call "absolute poverty."

Numbers can be spun in many ways. To accept these, you need not accept the Malthusian view that "overpopulation" is the essential cause of the environmental crisis, and you certainly need not accept Ehrlich's early advocacy of both triage ("India . . . will be one of those we must allow to slip down the drain") and forced sterilization.[13] In fact, the population numbers must be separated from the old pseudo-debate between Malthusians and anti-Malthusians, for only then can we understand one of the most important, and most unexpected, dynamics on the planet — the rapid drop in population growth rates in much of the South. This drop, manifest even in countries as poor as Bangladesh,[14] is occurring without the improved conditions so long said to follow "development," and is far different from the "demographic transition" that, over the years, turned the affluent citizens of the North to smaller families. It is often called, in honor of that difference, a "reproductive revolution,"[15] and of it we will hear a great deal in the years ahead. For the moment, remember that while the reproductive revolution is good news, it has not falsified the old predictions. Trends still indicate a global population of 10 billion people in 2050, rising to a peak of about 11.6 billion people between 2150 and 2200.

The Limits to Growth, too, is holding up better than its many critics predicted. From the farmlands of Africa to the fisheries of the North Atlantic, the overall pattern anticipated by *Limits* seems far less speculative today than when it was written. Its once inflammatory statement that, barring profound changes in "growth trends in world population, industrialization, pollution, food production, and resource depletion, the limits to growth on this planet will be reached within the next 100 years,"[16] is now so strongly corroborated by empirical observation that it is well on its way to becoming the mainstream view.

Take "growth," that most vague and abstract of all economic processes. In 1990, with an annual output of $20 trillion, the global economy produced in seventeen days what it took an entire year to generate in 1900.[17] The economy is, more immediately, now four times as large as it was in 1950[18] and, by 2050, is projected to be five times as large again.[19] Will it happen? And what will be the consequences if it does? Sandra Postel sums up the situation with an image that almost defies denial — the economy as a cube growing within the ecosystem's larger sphere, a cube whose points have already risen high above the planet's crust.

Growth is a sloppy concept, and it is quite impossible to use highly aggregated statistics about growth (like those above) to absolutely prove that the existing economy cannot be reconciled to the limits of the physical world. Technological optimists seize upon this indeterminacy and argue that, increasingly, economic activity will come not as "growth" proper but as a "development" in which change and refinement yield ever more usable "goods," though the physical size and throughput of the economy do not actually expand. It's a nice thought, but let's be clear about the current situation, as suggested by one of the most frightening scientific papers of all time, published in 1986 in *Bioscience* under the dry title of "Human Appropriation of the Products of Photosynthesis."[20] In it, a team of scientists try, as far as the data will allow, to estimate the total human impact on the planetary ecosystem, and conclude that, while humans *directly* consume only 3 percent of the products of the land-based ecosystem, "nearly 40% of potential terrestrial net primary productivity [of the ecosystem] is used directly, co-opted, or foregone because of human activities."

If this figure is even approximately correct, we are in big trouble. Poverty, or rather the economic polarization between rich and poor, is now widely recognized as a wellspring of both political conflict and ecological destruction. Yet "realism" tells us in a thousand ways that justice, or even a more equitable distribution of wealth, is simply not in the cards, not anytime soon. Growth is the only way out, and it is to growth that practical men and women always appeal. The authors of the Brundtland report imagined the alleviation of poverty in the expansion of the economy "by a factor of five or ten,"[21] and in their footsteps thousands of others have followed. Too bad that biological science must intrude with a harsh realism of its own. Think again about the products of photosynthesis. What would the world be like if humans, instead of co-opting 40 percent, took 80 percent? 100 percent? Would it be like England — "no real wilderness, the landscape under human control, many wild species extinguished, not much room for expansion or mistakes, but a livable world"[22] — or would it be worse? Would it be much, much worse?

There are good reasons to worry, one of them being soil erosion. *The Limits to Growth* vastly underestimated this crucial index of ecosystemic health — the years since its publication have seen *six times* as much soil lost as it predicted.[23] Moreover, since the loss is greatest in the areas with the greatest population density, and since population density is generally highest where the soil is best, we are losing the earth's best soil.[24] Worldwatch, which tracks planetary trends with great care, looked back on the two decades after 1970's first Earth Day, and noted that in that time the "world lost nearly 200 million hectares of tree cover, an area roughly the size of the U.S. east of the Mississippi River. Deserts expanded by some 120 million hectares, claiming more land than is currently planted to crops in China. . . . The world's farmers lost an estimated 480 billion tons of topsoil, roughly equivalent to the amount on India's farmland."[25]

Things are going about as the early apocalyptics predicted. As Earth Day chairman Denis Hayes asked in 1990, "How could we have fought so hard, and won so many battles, only to find ourselves now on the verge of losing the war?"[26] It is not at all difficult to see why so many greens have become so desperate. Occasionally, as in 1989, when politicians as varied as Mikhail Gorbachev and Margaret Thatcher tried to outdo each other in declaiming green, or at 1992's thousands of Earth Summit press conferences, it has seemed that the political elite were just about to take the environmental situation seriously. But each time the illusion has passed, leaving always the same question: What must happen before we finally act?

This has been a pressing question for decades, though only in 1974 did it become unavoidable. That was when Sherwood Rowland and Mario Molina conjectured that chlorofluorocarbons (CFCs) and other chlorinated compounds were damaging the planet's ozone layer, and the scientific community, after reviewing their research, reached a near consensus that they were right. There was, unfortunately, a small wrinkle — the Du Pont chemical company did not agree. Instead, it launched a campaign of avoidance and stonewalling that included heavy lobbying, a groundbreaking greenwashing campaign, the concoction of twisted scientific studies that seemed to exonerate CFCs from any role in damaging the ozone layer, and even attempts to discredit individual scientists.[27] The news media, true to form, reacted to the flack by stressing the "uncertainty" of the ozone-depletion "theory."[28] The pattern was set, and Du Pont's managers were so sure it would hold that in 1981 they discontinued all research into CFC alternatives. The issue was revived only in 1985, when hesitant scientists finally announced their discovery that a hole was opening in the earth's ozone layer, and in so doing transformed a merely theoretical catastrophe into a terrifying physical reality.

It is fashionable to claim that much has changed since the unenlightened old days, and that environmental deterioration is now taken seriously. In a sense, this claim is justified, for in a weak way matters have improved. In 1972, when *The Limits to Growth* was first published, it was banned in the Soviet Union and earned at least one man a place on Richard Nixon's "enemies list."[29] (*Limits* was finally published in Russia in 1991.) In other ways, too, there has been progress. The level of environmental literacy is up, and even "unproven theories" — according to antienvironmentalists, global warming, the extinction crisis, overpopulation, and the ozone hole are all in this category — are generally taken, at least rhetorically, as clear and present dangers. Primitive antienvironmentalists rake in corporate donations, use their radio and TV pulpits to endlessly broadcast no-limits pseudo-science, and find remarkable electoral success, especially where local economies are depressed. But, still, they do not hold the mainstream. The Montreal Protocol on ozone depletion, for example, remains extremely popular, the attacks of talk-radio scientists like Rush Limbaugh notwithstanding.

In these matters, though, nothing is simple. There are, for example, excellent reasons to suspect the usual happy citation of the ozone treaty as a firm basis for optimism in the future of global environmental governance,[30] and this despite its virtues. The treaty's governing committee is relatively democratic (unlike most global organizations, it is not completely controlled by the North), and the ozone-protection protocols have, certainly, proven that, as Richard Benedick, U.S. ambassador to the ozone negotiations, put it, "the international community is capable of undertaking cooperative actions in the real world of ambiguity and imperfect knowledge."[31] But even with this most crucial of all environmental treaties, there is less than meets the eye. First, the CFC phaseout is based on a transition to the chemical industry's own carefully chosen alternatives, the so-called soft, or lite, CFCs, which can honestly be called "ozone safe" only in strange comparison to CFCs themselves. Some of these lite CFCs, the HCFCs, or hydrochlorofluorocarbons, still contain chlorine, and still damage the ozone layer by lifting it to the upper atmosphere. They cause less ozone damage than CFCs themselves, but a great deal more than the chemical industry originally admitted. The others, HFCs, or hydrofluorocarbons, contain no chlorine but are extremely powerful greenhouse gases.[32]

Further, and just as significant, the fund set up by the ozone treaty to help the South phase out CFCs is no real precedent for a workable greenhouse abatement fund. Estimated costs of the CFC transition in the South run as high as $5 billion,[33] but the fund was initially set at a mere $240 million for the three years, and even that tiny amount was slow coming in. Countries designated as donors because of their high per capita CFC usage often simply ignored their commitments under the treaty. In late 1993 the fund was renewed at the higher level of $455 million, again for three years, and the treaty's collection provisions were strengthened to deal with deadbeat states like France that did not pay their bills. It was progress, but not much. As Bill Walsh of the Greenpeace Atmosphere and Energy Campaign said, "The size of the fund is in no way tied to objective realities, to what it will cost to get the job done. It was just a question of how much you could squeeze out of the donors."[34]

Eventually, a CFC phaseout will have finally taken place. When it has, the newspapers will brim with upbeat stories about hard ground crossed and lessons learned. But other ecological crises, and global warming in particular, will not so easily yield to exhortation and half measures. Global warming has as its major cause carbon dioxide (CO_2), the inevitable product of all fossil-fuel combustion, while ozone-layer damage is traceable to a small family of deliberately manufactured chemicals whose primary uses — air-conditioning, for example — are confined to a small number of industries, and which, being controlled by a small number of large corporations, are subject to particular dynamics that will not apply to the major greenhouse gases. As *The Economist* wryly noted in its Earth Summit issue, "A world ban on CFCs was obviously an ideal way to lock up the largest possible market for substitutes."[35] The fossil fuels, in contrast, have long played a fundamental role in shaping industrial society. If greenhouse theory is correct, and the preponderance of the evidence indicates that it is, humanity must drastically reduce its use not only of methane and CFCs (both greenhouse gases), but of coal and oil as well, even though such a reduction means that the entire planetary economy must be restructured, and to a degree that implies a fundamental break with the energy economy that has underlain capitalism from its earliest days. This is not a matter of a few technical fixes, of isolated reforms to an economy that can remain essentially unaltered.[36]

Scientists have run all sorts of computerized simulations of the earth's future climate, and of possible energy transitions. It is sobering to take a look at the optimistic cases. In one of the best of these, Greenpeace's "Fossil Free Energy Scenario," prepared by the Boston Center of the Stockholm Environment Institute, an international crash program draws humanity's carbon dioxide emissions down to zero in the year 2100. This is done by increasing energy efficiency, developing a renewable-energy economy, stopping the destruction of the forests, beginning serious reforestation efforts, and so on. No implausible technological assumptions are made, though a certain political will is assumed that today is nowhere in evidence (this scenario, after all, involves ending the use of coal, oil, and gas). It is depressing, then, to see that even in this ultimate "good case," global temperature rises 2.7 degrees Fahrenheit over preindustrial levels before flattening out.[37]

It's even more depressing to turn from technical potentials to the actual progress — or lack thereof — of the post-Rio climate negotiations. Recent science has only underscored the 1990 conclusion of the UN's Intergovernmental Panel on Climate Change (IPCC) — even an "immediate reduction in global man-made carbon dioxide emissions by 60 to 80%" could leave us with a global temperature increase of 3 to 7 degrees Fahrenheit by 2075. Yet, despite these grim numbers, and a near consensus that most of the damage caused by greenhouse gases will come as a result of extreme events such as droughts, floods, storms, and heat waves,[38] the climate negotiations remain a long slog through greenwashing, procrastination, rhetoric, "madhouse economics,"[39] front-group lobbying, and self-deluded attempts by Northern politicians to displace the problem to the South. The story today is essentially the same as during the run-up to the Earth Summit, which saw the Bush administration internationally vilified for refusing to support a European push for carbon-reduction targets. The criticism was justified, but it obscured the crucial fact that the Europeans, despite their greener rhetoric and the often honest efforts of their environment ministries, were intent on business as usual. Today a truer picture has emerged of what *The Economist* called "the West's rather quaint efforts to restrain carbon emissions."[40]

First, the national plans. In the United States, carbon emissions are soaring, and the Clinton "Climate Action Plan" is widely seen as just a lot of hot air.[41] It does increase funding for renewables and efficiency, and for this it has won a measure of praise, but even if it survives the current budget-cutting frenzy it will barely begin to meet its own very modest goals. "Emissions," as the administration admitted long ago, "will continue to rise well beyond the turn of the millennium,"[42] and how could they not? The plan doesn't begin to cut the billions in subsidies (from tax breaks to highway funds) that the government grants to the fossil-fuel industry each year, and besides, its central provisions are entirely voluntary. In this, moreover, it is representative — *The Independent NGO Evaluations of National Plans for Climate Change Mitigation* show that virtually all are extremely deficient.[43] The European Community, for its part, considers one carbon tax proposal after another but, despite recurrent rumors that it is about to act, carries none of them to law. In late 1993 a mild, loophole-ridden Greek proposal designed to break the deadlock was referred to a "high-level group" for further study, and today it is a virtual certainty that Europe, like the United States, will fail to meet its once-loudly-touted year 2000 reduction targets.[44] In Japan the situation is the same or worse. Despite an economy widely admired for its energy efficiency, and despite the recession that has plagued it for years, Japan's carbon emissions are soaring. And its climate plan is like most of the others — lots of statistical gymnastics and little real greening.[45]

The situation is not much better in international climate negotiations. As one observer at the August 1993 session in Geneva quipped, the working groups gave nothing so much as the sense of a "strong, almost desperate desire" to avoid noticing "the elephant in the room."[46] That elephant is the need for a rapid, globally coordinated transition from fossil fuels to renewables, a transition that would have to include a global New Deal to have any notable chance of success. Obviously, such a New Deal is nowhere on the horizon.

The climate problem, like the world, splits into two. On one side are the rich Northern countries that are already falling far behind on their carbon-abatement promises. On the other is the South, and in particular the "big poor countries," Brazil, China, India, and Indonesia. The North has historically been the source of most carbon pollution, but it is the "big poor" group that has the experts terrified. Intent on development, and with a good deal of high-level encouragement, this group is following the North down the only visible path, that of fossil-fuel-powered industrialization.

India is a tough, representative case. It is beset by civil conflict and almost entirely deforested. Three-quarters of its water supply is polluted, and its population will soon overtake China's. It is already a huge emitter of carbon dioxide, and rather than help it take a soft-energy path, the World Bank is pushing its eager technocrats into a future in which more coal-fired power plants emit ever more. In the name of "structural reform" and "free trade," its economy is being rudely crowbarred open, thrusting even its poorest people into the full gale of globalization. Its government, meanwhile, is hanging by threads. In the quite hypothetical instance that this government were someday faced with reformed international institutions dedicated to a campaign of healing and reconstruction, would India even be able to carry it out?[47]

Not unless the reform is both practical and thoroughgoing, and gathers together the zeal and creativity of people everywhere. Watch, then, for cosmetic climate deals, and "joint implementation" arrangements by which Northern countries try to buy their way out of their carbon-reduction commitments by financing minor cleanups in the South. Watch, too, as history continues to prepare its revenge — carbon dioxide emissions in the South will soon exceed those in the North.[48]

We've seen this pattern before. Back in the early 1980s, the Law of the Seas treaty was seen, as the climate treaty is today, as a vehicle for a global New Deal. The seas, like the atmosphere, are a "common heritage of mankind." By 1994, when the United States finally agreed to sign, the treaty's royalty and technology-transfer provisions had been weakened to the point of near meaninglessness.[49]

There are lots of environmental treaties on the books which do not live up to the promises of their names. Often they are not even enforced. To be sure, some environmental treaties enjoy good compliance records, but in many cases — for example, the control of acid rain in Europe — compliance is not strictly defined in the first place. As one overview of the treaties put it, "Compliance with these agreements is fairly high. However, much of this may be an artifact of the standards."[50]

Nations, that is, generally comply with environmental treaties that are easy to comply with. How many environmental treaties really enjoy compliance, or if that compliance means anything, is difficult to say, because with very rare exceptions there is *no verification at all*. Instead, rules that, according to one expert on environmental treaties "are generally imprecise and not wide ranging" are "enforced" only by the examination of national compliance reports, which are usually all that a signatory state is required to agree to by way of verification. Environmental treaties are still not considered an aspect of "high politics," and "expectations concerning the compliance behavior of countries [do] not seem to be very prominent in the international environmental protection sector."[51]

This situation could change, but not without some realism about existing circumstances. The ozone and greenhouse crises are bad enough, but other problems bear mention as well — soil loss and extinction and deforestation, certainly, but also the genetic erosion of the major grain crops and the terrifying condition of the major oceanic fisheries. These have gotten far less attention than greenhouse warming, though they are almost as dangerous and far more immediately pressing.

With the advent of two-hundred-mile coastal zones, the oceans have essentially been privatized, but many countries, now the owners of exclusive rights over vast zones, lack both the will and resources to police them effectively. The size of the world fishing fleet is at an all-time high, but fish populations are at historic lows. According to the UN Food and Agriculture Organization, all seventeen of the major oceanic fisheries are already at their limits, with nine in serious decline and four more threatened.[52] Yet they are still routinely "mined" by highly mobile, hugely mechanized, heavily indebted, opportunistically flagged trawlers that lease (or simply invade) rich areas and "reduction-fish" them at rates far beyond sustainable levels. Often, according to Anne Dingwall, a former head of Ocean Ecology at Greenpeace International, ocean fisheries survive biological extinction only because the fleets move on when fish populations become so low that no more money can be made from them — when, that is, the fisheries reach commercial extinction. As for domestic regulation and international treaties, Dingwall is quite unambiguous — there is no Law of the Seas. "Any treaty that doesn't mandate implementation and enforcement measures is just a piece of paper, useless. As far as the oceans go, well, except for the direct dumping of toxic and radioactive waste, it's a free-for-all."[53]

All this has real consequences, especially for the poor. Overfishing means scarcity, and thus rising seafood prices. When combined with global markets (a staggering 38 percent of all fish caught is exported),[54] this puts seafood — traditionally an inexpensive source of protein — altogether out of the reach of the people who need it most.[55] The extreme example is bluefin tuna, the price of which had reached $135 a pound in Tokyo as of January 1994. The bluefin is in trouble, and at prices like this, it is almost certain to be hunted into extinction.[56]

There are countertendencies. Ever-rising seafood prices could ignite an aquacultural "blue revolution" that, like the green revolution before it, would sharply increase production. But it is not at all obvious that this would be good news. In the United States, the easy availability of salmon farmed in Norway and Chile obscures the collapse of the local salmon fisheries, at least to the average supermarket ecologist. A boom in export aquaculture, in addition to making new demands on already strained grain supplies (fish farms, like feedlots, burn huge amounts of grain)[57] and degrading natural aquatic ecosystems,[58] would further conceal the decline of the oceanic fisheries. Besides, large-scale aquaculture hardly implies affordable fish in local markets. In Bangladesh and India, industrial aquaculture has caused widespread mangrove destruction and water pollution, forced the displacement of numerous coastal communities, and, in general, brought misery to the poor and powerless,[59] even as it has helped ensure that affluent consumers can enjoy a continued supply of "cheap" prawns.

And there is the crisis stalking industrial agriculture. As the global fish catch per person has peaked,[60] so too the long rise in global per capita grain production (up 40 percent between 1950 and 1984) has apparently ended. Since its peak in 1984, it has dropped by 8 percent, and it appears to be dropping by about 1 percent a year. Even worse, the drop is concentrated in the poor countries, where it will do the most damage.[61] Not that "we" are running out of grain, by no means. Forty percent of all grain is fed to livestock, so the effective supply could be greatly increased simply by phasing out cows.[62] Phasing out cows, however, means phasing out the meat-centered diet, and in the real world meat consumption only continues to rise.[63]

In the past, technology radically increased food production, and it was easy to claim that this trend could go on indefinitely. It does not seem to be doing so. The population continues to grow, the meat-centered diet continues to spread at a breathtaking clip, and farmland per person continues to drop; yet "smart farming" experts scan the technological horizon in vain for a means by which they can again increase production as massively as they did by introducing the large-scale use of fertilizer between 1950 and 1984.[64] Surprises are always possible, and technological optimists revel in tales of ever-increasing agricultural yields, but just now their rhetoric is wearing badly. Even the most modern biotech-driven dreams of agricultural plenty depend on the underlying genetic diversity of the major food crops, and with the dominance of industrial agriculture, that diversity is fast eroding. Indian peasant farmers, for example, are thought to have grown about thirty thousand different varieties of rice during the last century. In fifteen years they are expected to be growing only fifty, with ten accounting for three-quarters of the planted acreage.[65] Many of the lost rices are, or will be, preserved in massive gene banks, but there they lie, static and vulnerable, and do not evolve. And so it is as well with corn, and wheat, and potatoes.

The agricultural engineers are not worried, but ecologists are, as are many political analysts, who do not always share the hubris of the powerful. Some of these analysts, including many who cannot bring themselves to fear a *global* ecological crisis, now believe that increasing scarcity is likely to lead, even in the near future, to increased numbers of local and regional wars.[66] In 1992 the U.S. National Academy of Sciences and the Royal Society of London offered a summary that bears repetition. "If current predictions of population growth prove accurate and patterns of human activity on the planet remain unchanged, science and technology may not be able to prevent either irreversible degradations of the environment or continued poverty for much of the world."[67]

There are, of course, still cards to be played. New and more productive grains will be bred and hybridized, and biotech vat food may be a possibility (it wouldn't be the first time science fiction anticipated reality). But the chemically sodden, globally integrated, free-traded system of factory farming that is modern agriculture — a system that helps divide the world's people into the dieters and the malnourished — is running hard into a blind alley.[68] Soon, if we are lucky, deteriorating conditions may force even the elites among us to recognize what UNICEF once called the "paradox of plenty" — increasing food productivity does not necessarily mean that more people are fed.[69]

There is so much to consider — not only the futility of seeking technological solutions to the social-ecological crisis, not only our absurd dependence on oil and coal, but also militarism and weapons proliferation, pollution on a magnificent scale, uncontrolled urbanization, human suffering without end, political paralysis. There is latitude for improvement, vast and qualitative improvement, but taking advantage of the alternatives, finding a path to sustainability, will require fundamental social changes. And if our society is not "sustainable," what then is it? To recall a term from the ancient days of the early 1980s, when NATO's deployment of intermediate-range cruise and Pershing missiles threatened nuclear annihilation throughout the "European theater of war," it may be "exterminist." Edward Thompson, a great British historian and the author of the term, had something precise in mind. "Exterminism," he wrote, described "those characteristics of a society — expressed, in differing degrees, within its economy, its polity and its ideology — which thrust it in a direction whose outcome must be the extermination of multitudes."[70]

Exterminism — a dramatic term, perhaps, but one that makes its point. Controversial even at the time, the term is easily discounted today, when the collapse of the enemy superpower makes it easy to imagine ourselves relieved of the burden of nuclear weapons. We are not, of course, so relieved. Some of the most destabilizing weapons are being eliminated from the superpower arsenals, but the cuts are hardly decisive. Besides, proliferation only continues, and takes on new forms. Weapons-grade plutonium is now available on the black market,[71] and the know-how and technology needed to manufacture nuclear and high-tech near-nuclear weapons, chemical and biological weapons, and ballistic missiles only becomes more available. The spread could be contained, but not while peace means only that war is elsewhere, on TV but not in town, not while the world's elites spend the better part of a trillion dollars a year on their armies.[72]

Despite the likelihood that sooner or later we will see nuclear weapons again used, nuclear exterminism is no longer the defining nightmare of the modern age. It no longer seems that the "fate of the earth" is sudden war and nuclear winter. Such war remains possible, but we have wakened as well to a more gradual despair. It must, then, be said that ecological exterminism is no fine improvement. In fact, being more diffuse, it is harder to imagine, and even more difficult to prevent.

Optimism as Backlash

It is amazing that the burdens of proof still fall on those who plead for radical changes and not on those who keep faith with dreams of business as usual.

William Safire, newspaper columnist and foundation stone of U.S. conservativism, gives it to us straight. In a 1991 farewell to Mikhail Gorbachev, he used his *New York Times* op-ed pulpit to rail against the "high priesthood of deep pessimism" that cannot see "this glorious moment in history," and instead spends its energies "wailing about hard times, nuclear instability and holes in the ozone layer."[73] The problem, according to Safire, is "declinism."[74]

It is as if this whole terrible denouement that is our time could be finessed by denial, as if the grind of ecological decline, coming inconveniently at a time when a rolling global recession and chaotic restructuring already make things complicated enough, could be jawboned out of existence, or at least down to manageable proportions.

There are two very different matters at issue here. The first, necessarily, is the ecosystem itself, and its fate. But the second, the political mood, and in particular the political mood of environmentalism, may be as fundamental. Though it will be politics that decides the future, it may be mood — desperation and despair, or a sense of better possibilities — that decides the fate of politics.

Having managed to sound the alarm about whaling, drift nets, and ozone, environmentalists are straining for ways to up the ante, to make the roots of the crisis visible, to act in basic ways. And yet now they meet denial and backlash. There are so few ways to engage the larger situation, and most of these are blocked. Little that seems significant is possible, and little that is possible seems to offer a global solution, a stable alternative.

Throughout the world, greens of all kinds have come to suspect that a sustainable society cannot be born within society as we know it. In general, facing such a thought, they choose one of two paths. Some, startled by the magnitude of the challenge and the brutality of the emerging world, embrace the need for expansive new agendas. Others, finding themselves in a tougher game than they had thought to play, demur, withdrawing to the safe boundaries of old-school environmental politics.

The good news is the emergence, in the last few decades, of a wildly diverse, internationally aware grassroots alternative to the environmentalist mainstream. Good news, yes, but few are naive enough to think that grassroots activists can win the war while the legalistic, legislative environmental mainstream continues to lose the battles. Is it any surprise that many people, unable to believe that mainstream strategy will make the difference, and seeing no real alternative, drift into the politics of fear? Is it any secret why so many greens, finding themselves at loose ends, retreat into rhetorical escalation — announcing dangers of cancer everywhere, epidemics of strange new distempers of all varieties, the need for social changes "beyond politics," the "crucial decade," the end of nature?

Helen Caldicott, the eco-feminist physician who is so often cited as the conscience of the movement, makes a telling, canonical example. She is, admittedly, an extreme case, as when, with typical enthusiasm, she claimed that nuclear energy was producing scores of anencephalic births along the U.S.-Mexico border. "Every time you turn on an electric light, you are making another brainless baby."[75] It's an odd claim (chemical poisons are the culprit here), but it does not appear that her fans see it, or its fellows, as such. Some even think hyperbole justified by the ruling paralysis.

We are not, though, all true believers. Appeals to fear (and, inevitably, to guilt) meet not only approval but also what Frank Kermode, in his classic analysis of apocalyptic culture, *The Sense of an Ending*, calls "clerky skepticism."[76] The problem is that skepticism about ecological crisis is usually only the abstract inversion of apocalyptic hyperbole. The skeptic sees the bitter sadness of green culture as evidence only of apocalyptic yearnings and does not interrogate it further. The skeptic takes it as an obvious truth, known by all sophisticates, that green Cassandras need not be taken seriously.

Thus, Lewis Lapham, editor of *Harper's* magazine, can be deeply confident of his virtue in the face of "conventional sermons of doom."[77] In a critique of an outstanding work of modern green apocalypticism, he commented: "*The End of Nature* plays to the superstitions of the environmental left. The author, a young man of sensibility named Bill McKibben, strives for a sanctimonious effect that is earnest, doom-ridden, precious, and tear-stained. In New York, a city not known for its farms or its morals, his essay was received as a work of rural piety."[78]

Lapham, though, is blinded by the flash of his own rapier. He dismisses McKibben's *cri de coeur* solely on the grounds of its mood, without once engaging or even noticing its factual core — the destruction and tragedy that would predictably follow from massive global warming. *The End of Nature* is earnest and doom-ridden, and McKibben wrote it as an apocalyptic; but an open-eyed response to attempts at ecological honesty, "tear-stained" or not, must go beyond elegantly written dismissal. It must, if nothing else, acknowledge that the sense of an ecological ending cannot simply be treated as a cultural phenomenon, as just another literary style.

The problem here is a basic one — apocalyptic fear has long dogged rationalist optimism, and this inevitably colors attempts to tell the whole grim ecological tale. Greens cannot hope to avoid the echoes of doomsday and biblical retribution that fill their visions, any more than sincere optimists can avoid confusion with the long tradition of skepticism-as-denial. And there are the burdens of this strange, frozen moment. Apocalypticism thrives in the soil of timidity and confusion, and is nurtured by fear and powerlessness. As long as the gridlock remains, as long as the sense of danger so overwhelms the few opportunities to effectively respond, catastrophe will seem all too plausible.

Moreover, since the chance confluence of the "crucial decade" with the big year 2000 will bring out low-rent prophets in record numbers, those wishing to deny the seriousness of the environmental crisis will have plenty of chances to ridicule it as a pseudoscientific belief, a variant of Christian Rapture or New Age millenarianism. Nineteen ninety-four's eco-apocalyptic Cult of the Solar Temple is just the beginning.

Return to Paul Ehrlich. His *Population Bomb* not only predicted a catastrophe. It also asserted a mood, and a theory about the causes of the catastrophe. More than an eco-apocalyptic text, it is a specifically Malthusian work in which Ehrlich embraces that infamous eighteenth-century British parson's all-excusing credo that "population, when unchecked, increases in a geometric ratio. Subsistence increases only in arithmetic ratio."[79] In *Bomb*, humans breed like animals, just like animals, and then, their vast numbers outstripping the "carrying capacity" of the land, fall victim to a mass "die-off." Ehrlich told that tale, moreover, with verve and breathless prose:

> I came to understand the population explosion emotionally one stinking hot night in Delhi. . . . The streets seemed alive with people. People eating, people washing, people sleeping. People visiting, arguing, and screaming. People thrusting their hand through the taxi window, begging. People defecating and urinating. People clinging to busses. People herding animals. People, people, people, people.[80]

Ehrlich predicted famine by the late 1970s or the mid-1980s at the latest, and on a stupendous scale. It did not come, though, not in the sharp, undeniable way he anticipated. There was famine, to be sure, but it was contained; a mere 200 million people, by his own figures, died from hunger and hunger-related diseases in the two decades that followed *Bomb*'s publication.[81] Life went on, and in the sheltered North famine remained an abstraction, an occasional TV image. The sense of ecological crisis, though, had been strongly, perhaps permanently, colored by Erhlich's loud cry of wolf, by his modernization of parson Malthus's venerable half-truths.

"Overpopulation" is a real threat, a multiplier of stress and tension, a variable in the equations of crisis, but it is as well a heavily warped political category. Malthusians see overpopulation as the *cause* of a biological crisis, not merely as one of its key biosocial factors. Barry Commoner pointed this out decades ago in *The Closing Circle*, and he did not lack evidence. *Bomb* is quite explicit, and brimming with lurid, self-damning quotes. Commoner chose this little chestnut: "The causal chain of the deterioration is easily followed to its source. Too many cars, too many factories, too much detergent, too much pesticide, multiplying contrails, inadequate sewage treatment plants, too little water, too much carbon dioxide — all can be traced to *too many people.*"[82]

Ehrlich, laboring under this insight, made predictions that have not come to pass. The core ecological problem is not too many people, and global environmental crisis will not come as a "bomb." For society, if not always for individuals, ecological tension comes not suddenly but by degrees — as rigidity, adaptation, denial, and, of course, deterioration. For just this reason, the limits to growth, with all their implied sudden finality, did not arrive, and, waiting within a culture of organized denial, it was easy — it *is* easy — to think they never will. The real ecological crisis, unfortunately, proceeds unabated.

Environmentalism, though, has been deeply marked as a Malthusian, apocalyptic science. It is a crippling slant, for it implies, above all, the willingness to blame victims and overlook injustice. The Malthusian hypothesis, it should be said, does not always come as vile nativism and self-regard — it can also be softened by the liberal virtues. Donella Meadows, coauthor of both *Limits to Growth* and *Beyond the Limits*, recently declared that "rich people have as hard a time learning to consume less, as people in poor countries have learning not to have so many babies."[83] She evidentally intended, with these words, to stress the significance of population and yet face the facts of Northern culpability, to avoid poor-bashing and apportion blame judiciously all around. Instead, she infuriated activists from Norway to India. And why not? Hundreds of millions of people lack access to birth control, let alone proper reproductive care, let alone health care in general, and yet this plague-on-both-their-houses ecumenicalism has them sharing some strange equivalence of responsibility with the rich.

It cannot too often be repeated that the population fetish debilitates the environmental movement. First, by hiding difficult political truths behind biologic pseudoexplanations, it affirms and promotes what longtime development analyst Gerard Piel, reporting back from preparatory negotiations for the 1994 UN Conference on Population and

Development, called "class condescension, eugenic anxiety, and morbid preoccupation with the procreative proclivities of the poor."[84] Second, by explaining the crisis in unconvincing reductionist terms, it exposes the green movement to cheap attacks by progrowth, sky's-the-limit "cornucopians."

Witness right-wing economist Julian Simon, not the first antienvironmentalist but one of the most persistent, and a longtime point man in cornucopian attacks on greens. Explicitly defining himself against Ehrlich, Simon argued in *The Ultimate Resource* that "natural resources are not finite. Yes, you read that correctly,"[85] and thereby positioned himself to exploit, in the service of his own mad optimism, the vulnerabilities of Ehrlich's reductionism. Simon argues that the more is literally the merrier, and this without limit. He also mimics Ehrlich in telling the tale of his own conversion: "I thought, have I gone crazy? What business do I have trying to help arrange it that fewer human beings will be born, each one of whom might be a Mozart or a Michelangelo or an Einstein — or simply a joy to his or her family and community, and a person who will enjoy life?"[86]

In *The Ultimate Resource*, Simon challenged "the Doomsayers to Put Their Money Where Their Mouths Are." With a style rare among economists of any stripe, he offered "to stake $10,000, in separate transactions of $1,000 or $100 each, on my belief that mineral resources will not rise in price." He further offered his opponents the chance to choose both the minerals and the payoff date. In 1980 Ehrlich, along with two other green professors (one of them being John Holdren, chair of the Energy and Resources Group at the University of California at Berkeley), took the bet. They specified a basket of five metals — chrome, copper, nickel, tin, and tungsten — and a lag time of ten years. In 1990 Simon won.

The whole story was told in December 1990 in the *New York Times Magazine*, in a snide cornucopian tone that demonstrated just how much environmentalism has been hurt by its reliance on apocalyptics. Simon gleefully offered to take the bet again, this time for as much as $20,000, so confident was he that we have yet to approach the limits of the planet's bounty. *Times* reporter John Tierney agreed, asserting (without evidence) that "among academics, Simon seems to be gaining in the debate," and then going on to attack Worldwatch's Lester Brown ("another widely quoted doomster") for his anxiety about the falling per capita production of grain. Ehrlich, for his part, tried to insist that the real issue was "the declining capacity of our planet to buffer itself against human impacts. Look at the new problems that have come up: the ozone hole, acid rain, global warming . . ." But Simon, who was after all the winner, had the last word. Saying that "Ehrlich has never been able to learn from past experience," he launched into the antienvironmental hard line on global warming, arguing that, in Tierney's words, "even in the unlikely event that the doomsayers are right about global warming, humanity will find a way to avert climate change or adapt, and everyone will emerge the better for it."

Ehrlich and Holdren are not stupid men, but in confidently taking Simon's bet, on Simon's terms, they were indulging the stupefying habit of trend-chasing. George Orwell described the process while railing against a justly forgotten futurist of the past, James Burnham, but his comments on simple extrapolation bear repeating today. Orwell considered it "not simply a bad habit, like inaccuracy or exaggeration, which one can correct by taking thought"; rather, he argued, with his usual lucid simplicity, trend-chasing is "a major mental disease" that leads "to the belief that things will happen more quickly, completely, and catastrophically than they ever do in practice." In consequence, "the slowness of historical change, the fact that any epoch always contains a great deal of the last epoch, is never sufficiently allowed for."[87]

Trend-chasing is basic to environmentalism today, as it was to futurism in days past. What is really notable, though, is the clumsiness with which it is often practiced. The price of metal is not a good indicator of eco-systemic health, as Ehrlich and Holdren certainly knew even as long ago as 1980. They clearly know it now. In 1995, after Simon insisted that "any trend pertaining to material human welfare will improve rather than get worse,"[88] Ehrlich finally responded and, with climatologist Stephen Schneider, took him up on his offer of a rematch. Simon backed down. Despite taunting rhetoric about being willing to bet on "any trend," he didn't like the ones Ehrlich and Schneider chose: they challenged him to take $1,000 on each of fifteen trends, including global warming, sulfur dioxide emissions, fertile cropland per person, rice and wheat production per capita, species diversity, per capita fisheries harvests, AIDS deaths, and sperm counts.[89]

It is not extrapolation as such, but the simpleminded extrapolation of poorly chosen indicators that is the real problem of environmentalist trend-chasing. Paul Ehrlich, again, is not innocent here, for the best example, and the most important, is the pseudodebate between Malthusian pessimists and anti-Malthusian optimists. *The Atlantic*, in a cover story on population, argued that we should grant both Cassandras and Pollyannas their due, but omitted even to consider the possibility that population might not be the key issue after all.[90] Liberal historian Paul Kennedy set up his widely read *Preparing for the Twenty-First Century* by recalling Malthus's challenge that "the power of population" must exceed "the power of the earth," and then going on to examine high-tech means of increasing food production in far greater detail, and far more seriously, than the possibility of more equitably distributing the planet's bounty. Even 1994's UN Conference on Population and Development, though a milestone in the history of population politics,[91] did not break the frame. The conference, held in Cairo, was the largest feminist meeting to date, and finally enshrined in an official UN Program of Action the obvious fact that women and men, if they are given sufficient information, free choice, and adequate means of birth control, will voluntarily limit their own fertility.[92] It was an advance, but it had its price. Only two years before, at the Earth Summit, the UN had given its stage to the open-ended task of redefining development. Cairo, in contrast, affirmed that "population," taken more or less alone and certainly as cause, is the core problem.

Step back and consider the population pseudodebate itself. Not long before Cairo, Betsy Hartmann, director of the Population and Development Program at Hampshire College, and a leader in the green feminist attack on Malthusianism, did just this. She concluded that "Ehrlich has probably done more than any other single scientist to legitimize and popularize the belief that overpopulation is the main cause of the environmental crisis. He has been aided immensely by the U.S. media, which persists in presenting New Right, cornucopian economist Julian Simon as his primary critic."[93]

The problem with Ehrlich's view, according to Hartmann, is that "he sees the human species through the same lens with which he views animal and plant populations that multiply beyond the carrying capacity of their environments," and in so doing, "ignores the historical variability of human demographic dynamics." Humans may breed like animals, but not when they have some reasonable degree of control over their conditions of life, not when they are fully human.

Ecology, a rising science, offers its own reductionist temptations. We inhabit physical and biological worlds in which denial is not indefinitely possible, but we also inhabit political and economic worlds in which physical limits are merely factors among others. In these social worlds, scarcity, population, and all the other keystone notions of the ecological perspective are less simple than they may appear. Erhlich and Holdren, for example, misjudged the direction of metal prices in the 1980s by taking price as an index of scarcity, which, as Donella Meadows told me, it is "exactly not." (The price of oil is, most strongly, a function of current pumping capacity — of the number of wells, not the amount of oil in the ground.)[94]

Natural scientists, in particular, overlook the seams of inequity that run deep though the foundations of society. Think of Holland, which has the highest population density in the world but is not generally considered to be overpopulated. Think of Japan, a country that has long been unable to feed itself.[95] Why, when we hear the word "overpopulation," do these countries not pop immediately to mind? Why do we think instead of India, China, and Bangladesh? Obviously because "population" is a code word that reveals certain matters but obscures others.

The population debate is a sterile one, for in it too much is unsaid. In it, typically, Malthusians, eco-apocalyptics, and worried scientists of all kinds are opposed to a corrupt cabal of (mostly) right-wing optimists who actually welcome population scares as chances to flog their favorite nostrums — "free markets" and the transcendence of social problems through advanced technology. Rarely are they faced instead with the stronger arguments of progressive greens and feminists, who point out, whenever they get half a chance, that "high birth rates" are often nothing so much as a "distress signal that people's survival is endangered."[96] Thus, the real question is rarely asked. That question, the one hidden within the rhetoric of population, the one Thomas Malthus was addressing in his *Essay on the Principle of Population*, is "Where do the poor come from?"[97]

To see this question in its modern form, one need only attend to Europe, where unemployment, already at historic highs, promises to rise still higher as companies shift jobs to low-wage countries,[98] and to the United States, where the sense, as one woman put it, that "our economy is in a bad state and we should take care of our own"[99] is once again overpowering the American tradition of hospitality to strangers. Poverty, and fear of poverty, and fear of the poor, are again the baselines of politics. It may surprise the many who imagine environmentalism to be always on the liberal side of the political spectrum, but within the context set by nativism and immigrant bashing, environmentalism has become a wellspring of xenophobic resentment. Its asocial and populationist habits of mind encourage those who would scapegoat the poor, and especially the foreign poor, for all social ills, who imagine endless waves of aliens stealing jobs, driving up healthcare costs, consuming welfare, and even causing smog.[100] The Sierra Club, the largest grassroots environmental organization in the United States, is deeply torn over immigration,[101] anti-immigrant groups take names like Californians for Population Stabilization, and right-wing organizations like FAIR, the Federation for American Immigration Reform, emphasize the "ecological" as well as the "cultural" dangers of immigration.[102] Not that the real issue is immigration; it is money, or, rather, those without it. German essayist Hans Magnus Enzensberger put it well: "Where the bank accounts look good, xenophobia disappears as if by magic. But strangers are all the stranger if they are poor."[103]

"Surplus population," the notion upon which Malthusianism pivots, is an economic concept masquerading as a biological one, a concept irreducibly bound to fear, social insecurity, loss of place, unemployment, and what linguist Noam Chomsky called the "unmentionable five-letter word" — class.[104] Even Ehrlich now occasionally points this out, in articles with titles like "Too Many Rich People."[105]

A Realist Interlude

Optimists make few distinctions among pessimists, preferring instead to lump the most balanced and scientific of green Jeremiahs together with the most emotional of doomsters, and to answer them all by appeal to the dynamism of the market. Here, they say, is the source of all creativity, the device that, unfettered, will solve all problems. It's a simple rhetorical strategy, and it does have its audience. Conservatives in particular prefer ridiculing greens to facing their strongest arguments (witness the success of "satirists" like P. J. O'Rourke),[106] and thus cornucopians — even Julian Simon, the thinking man's Rush Limbaugh — respond by treating optimism as a sport, as well as, of course, a career path.[107]

But technology will not enable us to indefinitely avoid ecological realities. In part this is because the old cliché is true — in the end, there are rarely "technical solutions to social problems." It is also because technological advance, as we know it, invariably pays its tithe to the merchants of denial. Birth control is offered as a tech-fix for poverty, and for ecological crisis in general.[108] Solar energy, an infinite resource, is cited as evidence that there are no real "limits to growth." Less familiar devices meet similar fates. One of the brightest of technological trends is that known as dematerialization, by which ever smaller quantities of material are made to yield the same final measures of utility. (The classic example is the computer, which shrank from sprawling ENIAC to the microchip in only decades.) Where dematerialization is cited, it is almost invariably said to promise, in and of itself, a new and sustainable industrialism, a new age of growth and consumerism all around.[109]

It will not be so. Our technologies are now so powerful and so adaptable that it is difficult to overstate the potential for their reform. But how can this potential be realized while technology is shaped to, and serves, merely private ends? "Democracy" is not a word often heard in reference to technological and industrial policy, but this only indicates the severity of our predicament.

Paul Ekins, a green economist at Birkbeck College in London, has run some relevant numbers, in an essay he called "A Sustainable Consumer Society: A Contradiction in Terms?" He begins with a back-of-the-envelope estimate that "sustainability" means cutting the overall ecological weight of human society in half, then goes on to remind us that best projections have the population leveling off in about fifty years at between ten billion and twelve billion people — a doubling from the current level. It follows quite simply that consumption patterns and technology must change enough so that each person fifty years from now makes only a quarter of the ecological impact he or she makes today. This is possible, Ekins notes, but it would not be enough. The poor of the world seek to improve their lot, and the only means they are offered to do so is "growth." The Brundtland Commission, the World Bank, and politicians everywhere therefore assume that a

3 percent annual rate of economic expansion, at the very least, will be needed to alleviate poverty.

But even a 3 percent growth rate would double the total size of "the economy" (in the most abstract, aggregate sense) every twenty-three years. The math (most of which I am skipping here) is inexorable: "If sustainability is to be achieved by technology alone, in 50 years time technology must have reduced the environmental impact of each unit of consumption to one sixteenth its present level . . . more than a 93 percent reduction." If population growth levels off in the mid-twenty-first century and that 3 percent rate of "green growth" continues to 2100, then "every unit of consumption would [have to] be making only 1.6 percent of its current environmental impact."[110]

This would be tough under any circumstances, and it is *not* the direction in which we are heading. Energy efficiency is increasing, but not nearly as fast as overall energy consumption, which only continues to rise.[111] Solar technology is, as usual, stalled on the margins of the economy. Dematerialization is a nice trend, but it is hardly dominant; the total mass of material passing through the economy keeps increasing.[112] Ekins thus suggests that if room is to be made for the world's poor, rich countries must be allowed "no growth in consumption per head." Like John Holdren, who has similarly sought a transition scenario that is both socially and physically realistic,[113] he notes that the South's economy could expand while ecological damage was held to current levels, but only along a path that promises security rather than affluence, and only if a lid were kept on the rich. Nor can Southern economies be allowed to explode — Ekins would hold the resource consumption of the poor down to less than one-fifth of per capita consumption current in rich countries. It wouldn't be the American Dream, but with the right technologies it could be a blessing for the poor — and since it demands only that the impact of the average unit of consumption be reduced to 21 percent of its present level (rather than 1.6 percent), it has at least the virtue of historical plausibility.

Ekins winds up his calculations by calling upon the "gung-ho technologists" to please get to work, and asking the rest of us to "help them by embracing green consumerism and green investment with all our hearts and wallets."[114] In so doing, he inadvertently demonstrates that politics and not technology is the real problem. We know what the techies should be doing, but how we will get past calls for "green consumerism and green investment" to even imagine a world in which "no growth in consumption per head" in the rich countries is a politically realistic goal is a mystery beyond us all.

Seeking realism, we find it far easier to imagine successful technical fixes than meaningful social change. There can be no better example than the conclusions now being drawn from declining Third World fertility rates — that the catchphrase of the 1974 World Population Conference, "development is the best contraceptive," is simply not true. The population debate has shifted since 1974, but not so much that the feminist agenda of education and independence for women, and health security for all, defines the new consensus. Rather, the "demographic revolution" is explained by the influence of the mass media, and especially in the easy availability of birth control. The new watchword is that "contraceptives are the best contraceptive."[115]

Unstated here is that contraceptives have had plenty of help. Fertility rates in poor countries like Bangladesh have been dropping not only because of television and condoms, but because "the sharp economic contraction of the late 1970s and early 1980s" made many Third World families realize that with more children "their standard of living fell." This isn't how it was supposed to be. The theory of "demographic transition" had it that development would bring security and even affluence, and thus smaller families. Instead, insecurity, urbanization, and the cosmopolitanism of a global society in which people increasingly have a sense of their bad prospects, have stepped in to do the job. *The Economist*, speaking fondly of domestic piecework, one of the most brutal forms of labor ever contrived by capitalist managers, notes that "women get the work only if they can produce a minimum amount of clothes. That is a strong incentive not to interrupt money-making with maternity."[116]

Is this too harsh? "Development" and family planning are more effective together than either alone, and no one is suggesting that development can be altogether dispensed with.[117] But then, people have become careful of what they say. The Vatican, in its bitter Cairo fight against reproductive rights, named its enemies as "contraceptive colonialism" and "cultural imperialism,"[118] while the conference's Program of Action rings with politically correct calls for health security and women's empowerment, and affirms that human needs rather than numerical targets should drive population policy. That's the rhetoric. Money tells a different story. Cairo's Program of Action budgets $10.2 billion for "family planning" between now and 2000, while reproductive health care will get $5 billion. As for health security in general, the *New York Times* put it well — the money is "supposed to come from other United Nations initiatives."[119]

Besides, the world's activists don't want "development," they want "justice," and have long argued that justice is needed to stabilize population.[120] Increasingly, they meet the answer that birth control technology is the real key. The pattern can be seen in the media coverage of falling Southern fertility rates. Where do we hear of the Latin American and Caribbean countries where high levels of poverty are found with low and decreasing birth rates?[121] And where, outside professional UN and NGO circles (and the pages of *The Economist*) do we learn that increasing rates of women's employment is a key factor in fertility declines? Why, in coverage of the "reproductive revolution," does birth control get the vast share of the attention? Isn't it because contraception is cheap and requires so little in the way of social renewal?

The irony is that the optimism engendered by declining Third World fertility is likely to be a rapidly wasting commodity, for the simple reason that population per se has never been the chief cause of the ecological crisis.[122] Moreover, tech fixes often worsen the inequities that *are* chief among its causes. To see this, turn from population to the other side of the Malthusian equation — food. Turn, in particular, to the devices that promise to increase food supply without requiring the inconvenient social upheaval that would follow from the redistribution of land or the empowerment of small farmers. Turn to "high-yield" industrial agriculture.

The road to technologically increased food production will be a cruel one. This would already be widely appreciated, were it not that the green revolution's partisans have managed to avoid any sustained public examination of their brave experiment in the industrial farming of genetically hybrid, chemically dependent, and, often, proprietary grains. Grassroots greens have worked hard to set the record straight. For example, Indian ecologist Vandana Shiva has taken a careful look at the Punjab region of her country, where the green revolutionaries concentrated much of their effort, and which has since the mid-1980s been torn by "communal violence." This violence is commonly interpreted as ethnic and religious conflict, but she finds it to be strongly linked to the "ecological and political demands" of the green revolution. According to Shiva, the green revolution itself, designed "as a techno-political strategy for peace, through the creation of abundance," has instead brought "diseased soils, pest-infested crops, waterlogged deserts, and indebted and discontented farmers." The green revolution, not alone but as a culmination of long-standing inequities, has "left Punjab ravaged by violence and ecological scarcity."[123]

In a world facing the possibility of massive food shortages, few stories can be as important as this one, in which the green revolution appears not as a milestone of hope and progress, but as a "techno-political" strategy that, supported by global corporations and development agencies and administered by opaque bureaucracies controlling policy, credit, standards, and technology, has destroyed the cultures and ecologies of innumerable regions. All this has been excused in the name of industrial "abundance," and it would be unforgivably naive to think it could not happen again.

As long as technological change displaces social change, pessimism must return. The world's most productive agricultural systems are traditional Asian rice-centered agro-ecosystems that rely on the sophistication of vernacular techniques and, crucially, on at least a "relatively equitable" distribution of land.[124] Traditional agro-ecosystems, though, are altogether irrelevant to agricultural engineers. In their lexicon, abundance is inseparable from "efficiency" and mass production. And yet efficiency and mass production, taken alone, have their limits.[125] Despite all its infamies, the green revolution at least increased grain production. Turn to the even more baroque forms of biotech farming now on the horizon and even this is too high a compliment — not only are they ecologically unsustainable, but by many accounts they don't even increase productivity.

Such details do not bother the right wing, for faith in technology is fundamental to its creed. George Reisman, the angry professorial voice of the ultracapitalist Ayn Rand Society's attacks on the ecology movement, argues that "the free citizens of industrial civilization" can and should manage the ecosystem to whatever ends they find the most profitable. Problems only betray a lack of vision. "Privately held, electronically fenced, ocean fish farms" are, for example, an ultimate solution to the food crisis.[126] The authors of *Free Market Environmentalism* agree, though in restrained and academic cadences. In their view, environmentalism, with its apocalyptic imagination, its weakness for bureaucratic regulation, and its penchant for "focusing on maximum sustained yield and ignoring economic factors," forces us to suffer "lower profits and economic waste." The lesson of overfishing is that it is past time for "establishing property rights on the ocean commons," past time for "homesteading the oceans." Even if "chicken little is right" and the sky is warming, this only indicates the pressing need for the "privatization of highways." After all, when combined with "strict liability rules," highway owners would have "an incentive to reduce emissions, so cars with better pollution control equipment could receive lower tolls and those with no equipment might be banned altogether." This wouldn't be a complete solution, but it would be a step in the right direction, a step toward "the evolution of property rights to the atmosphere."[127]

In the face of such schemes, one should recall Orwell, who after dismissing trend-chasing, made a further charge against extrapolation. It is a charge that casts cold light on green doomsters and even harsher light on right-wing cornucopians. In Orwell's view, the fallacy of "predicting a continuation of the thing that is happening" has its roots "partly in cowardice and partly in the worship of power, which is not fully separable from cowardice."[128]

This is certainly true of the cornucopians, who revel in an aggressive Panglossian view of the present, and see the future as only an indefinitely protracted version of an idealized, sanitized past. But while cornucopians have thus far proven justified in rejecting the green fixation on resource depletion, there are excellent reasons to suspect that the future will be less forgiving than the past. As Thomas Homer-Dixon argues in "On the Threshold: Environmental Changes as Causes of Acute Conflict," a 1991 essay that quickly emerged as the keystone text of the new field of "ecological security studies," humanity will soon "face multiple resource shortages that are interacting and unpredictable, that grow to crisis proportions rapidly, and that will be hard to address because of powerful commitments to certain consumption patterns." Nor will the free market help much. "It is a bad gauge of scarcity," and, crucially, "market-driven adaptation to resource scarcity is most likely to succeed in wealthy societies." Further, as conditions get worse, "social friction" will increase. "Future environmental problems, rather than inspiring the wave of ingenuity predicted by cornucopians, may instead reduce the supply of ingenuity available to society."[129]

The greens also suffer cowardice, though theirs is a more complex case, for they generally intend their jeremiads to dramatize the consequences of inaction, and to speak for changes they fear to openly advocate. In any event, Orwell was quite correct. It is cowardice to plot curves to catastrophe and yet refuse to name the forces shaping those curves. It is also cowardice to suggest paths to recovery without implying the political changes necessary to take those paths.

In *Earth in the Balance*, Al Gore cites the Indian state of Kerala as a model of Third World population control, noting that the enlightened policies of its "provincial leaders," including programs of literacy training, health care, nutritional support, and freely available birth control, have sharply reduced infant mortality and population growth.[130] But the rest of the story, told elsewhere, is that Kerala's "radical reforms" have emerged from a long history of struggle for land reform and "fair prices," and against the caste system.[131] Kerala has a rich left tradition, an unusually democratic one, and it is just because of this tradition that it has been so much more successful than other Indian states in caring for its people, and in controlling its population growth.

It's easy to understand why Gore, a professional politician, glossed over this rather inopportune material. The problem is that Kerala's left history is the *reason* it has made the transition to a low-fertility society while other areas of India are drifting deeper into a demographic crisis. Like all the thousands of Northern greens who made Chico Mendes the martyr of the Amazonian rain forest yet somehow forgot to mention, or even to learn, that he was a proponent of "socialist ecology,"[132] Gore offers us only a pale, inadequate education.

Apocalyptic Temptations

According to environmental historian William Cronon, we use prophecies to tell ourselves stories about what we both do and do not wish to become. If this is so, then how shall we understand the bias of so many greens toward prophecies of collapse, of crisis and impossibility? Is it a charm against softheadedness? A demand for fundamental change? A wish fulfillment? A desire, in the face of deeply felt impotence, to stop an evolution we fear even to imagine clearly?

Optimism, certainly, is a greater danger than apocalyptic fear. Consider the world of the right-wing cornucopians, of Ayn Rand, Julian Simon, and all their innumerable imitators. What if they are right? What if there are no limits, and we can indefinitely keep adding people, dams, chemicals, power plants, and all the rest? What if nuclear fusion can be made to work? What if it is even clean? What if the earth can be made to support a human population of even fifty billion?

Few people today would think this a pretty thought. It has been a long road from the 1950s, when science fiction told childish tales of high-tech happiness and PR flacks could hope to argue plausibly that "atomic" energy would be "too cheap to meter." These days, we have lost the deeper confidence that came so easily three or four decades back. Suspicion abounds, and technology is generally regarded with ambivalence. Even science is often seen as the instrument of an elite that has lost touch with the fundamental realities of life.

Today dystopia, not utopia, sets the tone.[133] Green radicals are hardly alone in imagining a sterile, brutal future. Foreboding is everywhere, and is everywhere justified. Inner-city desperation speaks it eloquently. So does the terror that comes to children when they learn that the animals in their books and toy worlds are being stalked by extinction.

Even the post-industrial boosterism of the "computer revolution" is only a shallow countercurrent in a broad river of pessimism. Where has that current taken us? To Internet fever not as emancipation (the "information revolution") but rather as stark social and economic necessity; to high-toned futurism like Alvin and Heidi Toffler's *Creating a New Civilization* (complete with a foreword by Newt Gingrich).[134] Techno-optimism is, increasingly, a product intended for mass consumption. In more sophisticated circles, progress is admitted to be a painful matter.

Optimism and pessimism are deeply political standpoints, and fear is anything but simple. Do chlorine compounds in general, and not just CFCs, destroy the ozone layer? Are the clouds changing in strange and mysterious ways?[135] Ultimately, only the scientists can say, but there are many among us who distrust the judgments of science, especially corporate science, and they often know quite a bit of science them-

selves. Does electromagnetic radiation from common household devices cause miscarriages and cancer? Is irradiated food safe to eat? Is
bioengineered food safe to grow? Is biotechnology eroding the "sanctity" of species by intermixing their genes?[136] Can even infinitesimal
amounts of chemicals damage the immune system? Do Alar-sprayed
apples harm children? Do nuclear reactors breed brainless babies? Are
dioxins as dangerous as the Environmental Protection Agency says?
Do we really have only ten years to "get it," and forty years to make
the turn, or can we honestly hope to muddle through?

Ecological fear is heavy with the decay products of impotence —
frustration, anger, and paranoia — and with the contingencies of class
and social position. Often, where we stand depends on where we sit. If
you happen to be an officer of a waste-management corporation and
community activists are preventing you from laying in a profitable
and, to your mind, entirely reasonable new dump, you can be expected
to have a certain sympathy for pundits who dismiss the activists' anxieties as "ecophobic" or "chemophobic."[137] Those anxieties may seem
less strange, and certainly less absurd, if you are a householder and
that dump is slated for your neighborhood.

Think of the pejoratively named and willfully misunderstood
NIMBY movement. The term NIMBY (for "not in my backyard") is the
slur of developers and professional optimists, the charge that what
some call "community self-defense" is only a matter of selfishness,
fear, and small-mindedness. This accusation is justified in some cases,
as when affluent homeowners in Los Angeles's San Fernando Valley
organize against everything from airport expansion to an arts park to
trailers for the homeless.[138] But it is a strange charge to level against
antitoxics activists, who note that dumps and incinerators seem always
to come to the poor and nonwhite (rather than places like the San Fernando Valley), and who see themselves as standing not only for their
personal interests but for "environmental justice" in general.

Even this honorable side of the so-called NIMBY movement is complex and contradictory, a fact that almost invites distortion by corporate spin doctors. In 1989 C. H. Grennert of Union Carbide's public
relations group distributed a memo among company management
that called the Citizen's Clearinghouse on Hazardous Waste, a major
antitoxics group, "one of the most radical coalitions operating under
the environmentalist banner." This it may be, though as he then ad-

mitted, the CCHW includes "all manner of folk."[139] Community self-defense movements can be expansive, communitarian, paranoid, or parochial — or all these together. What makes them comprehensible, and what concerns us here, it that they are often bellwether movements of otherwise ordinary people who feel forced to hyperbole and confrontation by, in the words of writer Charles Pillar, "a process of scientific and technological development that makes obstructionism the only antidote to impotence."[140]

What's the alternative? Rationalists often dream that cost-benefit analysis or some other analytic magic will someday put unwarranted fears to rest by concocting a scientific ranking of "risks," but this will never happen. The objectivity of cost-benefit analysis is largely illusionary, with politically loaded assumptions affecting outcomes by a hundred- or even a thousand-fold. Nor is this skew a neutral one — costs are easily inflated, while benefits are often impossible to quantify.[141] Cost-benefit models simply cannot capture the social reality in which community activists confront transnational corporations with huge research staffs and bottomless legal budgets. And even if an objective ranking of risks were possible, it wouldn't have much of a soothing effect, at least not on the many people who feel so strongly, and with such good evidence, that they face more than their fair share of the dangers.[142]

Science is not the issue here. Tobacco and fried foods both kill far more people than toxic waste but do not invoke a similar dread. Why not? Antienvironmentalists claim that ecophobia and (once lawyers get involved) "speculative fear" are the reasons, but this is not the whole story. What if people feel that since they *elect* to smoke and eat fried foods, the "risks" they thereby take are of a different order than those that come to them by way of the obscure workings of chemicals and machines? What if, like so much else in life, our view of risk turns on our power to choose?

Even *Fortune*, a magazine not particularly prone to ecological angst, will sway against the wind when the health of its executive-class readers is at stake. That, at least, is how it seemed when, investigating a possible link between cellular phones and cancer, *Fortune* granted that "maybe the Swedes are right" about the links between electromagnetic fields and childhood leukemia.[143]

The Environmental Protection Agency (EPA), as it happens, is coming gradually to confirm what antitoxics activists have long claimed — garbage incinerators emit dioxin, and dioxin causes cancer.[144] Nor is this the first time that ecophobia has proven justified. Traditional antibiotics are rapidly declining in efficacy, and it is now clear that their heavy use by industrial cattle ranchers and dairy farmers is a very bad idea. The ozone hole is real, and early green warnings about nuclear power only look better as the years go by. The paranoids, it happens, don't have a bad record at all.

Still, there are the temptations of hyperbole. Are sheep in southern Chile being blinded by cataracts induced by ultraviolet radiation streaming down through the Antarctic ozone hole? Even Greenpeace, a scientifically scrupulous outfit, repeated this often-rumored claim, though it issued a retraction when a San Francisco TV station took it to task for "sensationalizing" the evidence. The station produced its own medical expert, who, after an on-camera examination of a Chilean sheep's eyeball, concluded that the epidemic of blindness was caused not by ultraviolet radiation but by the diseases keratitis and conjunctivitis.[145]

The question here is how Greenpeace was led to such a lapse in the first place. Was it a product of overeager campaigning? Or was it part of a larger pattern in which greens reach beyond the all-important "precautionary principle" (which "recognizes the need for environmental regulation in the face of inevitable scientific uncertainty")[146] to abandon science and broadcast even poorly substantiated claims of impending catastrophe?

The answer may be found in desperation. Greenpeace is rare even among environmental groups in thinking the ozone crisis to be continuing, and in criticizing the ozone treaty, the Montreal Protocol. Even "ozone skeptics" like Patricia Poore and Bill O'Donnell, writing in *Garbage* magazine that both greens and antigreens are "engaging in hyperbole and lies of omission," call the treaty "the fastest, largest nonmilitary global response to a perceived threat in human history."[147] In the face of such a vast consensus, the ozone "debate" has almost completely narrowed to technical chatter about funding models and abatement schedules. Greenpeace, though, persists in charging that the treaty panders to chemical corporations, encourages unnecessary investment in the production of "soft CFCs," and, in general, takes a dangerously long and twisted road to a CFC phaseout.[148] Friends of the

Earth also gets in an occasional kick,[149] but Greenpeace is almost alone with what it views as frightening truths. It is a position that cannot but encourage apocalyptic shortcuts.

Extreme ecophobic fears often turn out to be justified. In the summer of 1993, when good data finally became available, they showed that surface-level ultraviolet radiation in Chile *is* dramatically increasing.[150] It may not cause cataracts, but it is certainly a threat to oceanic plankton — a crucial foundation of the planetary food chain. And there is the case of chlorine. Greens, feminists, and workplace safety activists have been campaigning for years to phase out *all* chlorinated hydrocarbons — not just PCBs (polychlorinated biphenyls), dioxins, and pesticides — as biotoxins.[151] Does this seem crazy? The chance to judge for yourself will arrive soon enough, for the evidence against the organochlorines is really starting to pour in,[152] and the once derided view that even infinitesimal doses can fatally disrupt biological processes by mimicking reproductive hormones is fast becoming the mainstream scientific opinion. It has been firmly established, for example, that specific organochlorines are linked to breast cancer. The *Journal of the National Cancer Institute* has published studies indicating that women with higher concentrations of DDT in their blood have up to four times the chance of developing breast cancer as those with lower levels.[153] Unfortunately, this knowledge, and all the rest cascading after it, has not led to meaningful DDT restrictions, except in the United States and Europe. In fact, DDT plants are still being built in the South, sometimes even with World Bank funding.[154]

Science is one thing, business is another. At least that's how it is in the textbooks. In reality, matters are just a bit more complicated, as the example of DDT shows. DDT is only one chemical, yet more than thirty years after *Silent Spring*, its phaseout has barely begun. No wonder that chemical company executives take particularly strong issue with the notion that organochlorines *as a class* pose monumental health and ecological problems. They may perhaps be forgiven their views, as they already have about eleven thousand chlorine-based products on the market and are forever concocting new ones.[155] As Francis Bacon put it centuries ago, "What a man had rather were true he more readily believes." In practical terms, it may seem absurd to even imagine phasing out an industry as gigantic as that erected on chlorine chemistry. But would it still seem absurd if the chlorines were in fact the force behind today's rapidly rising rates of breast and testicular cancer, if reports of plummeting sperm counts were borne out by further research,[156] if chlorines were implicated in a vast number of other reproductive and carcinogenic disorders across the animal kingdom? Would it still seem absurd if you, or your mother, or a dear, still-young friend were being consumed by breast cancer?

The Long Good-bye

In what was once the Soviet Union, the last few decades before the fall of communism, the Brezhnev years, are sometimes called "the period of stagnation." At least they have a name for it. Here in the West, we also suffer a profound stagnation, but the superficial dynamism of technology, trade, and fashion mask it beyond daily notice.

"Change" has become the political mantra of the American polity, though few can imagine real change. Or rather, few can imagine how real change might come about. There is a sense in the United States as in Europe that a self-interested, self-deluded "political class," a capitalist *nomenklatura*, has captured the government. Cynicism is the normal state of normal man, and gridlock the normal state of government.

Who really believes the world's executives will face the facts of ecological deterioration before events compel them to do so? Certainly not the planet's more experienced activists. The sense of overdetermination and inevitability, of economic tides too powerful to resist, of government's capture by private interests — these are the commonplaces of routine politics, and the grounds of environmental despair. There is so much that can be done; it is only that so little of it is.

Herman Daly, the dean of ecological economics, once said that our best chance may be an "optimal crisis: bad enough to shake us up, but not so bad as to impair our ability to react." [157] It's an odd notion — and a peculiarly honest one. Before the Wall fell, Norman Myers, a naturalist and environmentalist, seemed to suggest an answer, almost welcoming global warming as a "global wake-up call": "One day we may thank the greenhouse effect for sending a message that even the most optimistic politician could not ignore." [158]

Such is the hope of the apocalyptics. And who knows? It could even be rewarded. Climatologists and, notably, insurance industry planners have observed a pattern of intensifying frequency and severity of both tropical cyclones and midlatitude windstorms. With scant regard for the professional sophism of greenhouse skeptics, storms are tearing ever more destructively through the planet's vulnerable, overdeveloped coasts. Hurricane Andrew, in 1992, was the wake-up call — it caused almost $30 billion in damage in Florida and Louisiana, and was easily the most expensive natural disaster in U.S. history.

Global warming may still be an "unproven theory," but, says Jeremy Leggett, scientific director of Greenpeace's Climate Campaign, "whiffs of panic" are stirring among insurance executives, who pay the bills for catastrophic storms. Their attitudes, it seems reasonable to hope, will not forever dovetail with those of their comrades in the fossil-fuel business. "In high places in the industry," says Leggett, "there are real fears for the future of stable insurance markets should current climate models prove accurate, or even worse — underestimates."[159]

Leggett's dream is that the insurance industry, in a "strategic defense" of its future profitability, will lobby hard to strengthen the climate treaty (the Climate Change Convention), even to the point where it might conceivably make a difference. This would be a bruising fight, for it would mean going head-to-head against the oil and coal lobbies, which oppose all attempts to set enforceable targets or timetables for limiting the dumping of carbon dioxide into the atmosphere, and even reject weak regulatory devices (like carbon taxes) designed to improve energy efficiency or promote alternatives. According to Leggett, "It is time the insurance industry redressed this situation."[160]

It's a wild hope. Insurance executives are not likely to leap to sudden heroism. The well-informed among them have indeed come to see global warming as a threat, and a brave few have even begun to say so,[161] but the industry's major response has been on adaptation, not prevention. Far from heeding Greenpeace's urgings to champion a solar transition, the insurance industry's post-Andrew innovations have focused on "shorelining," an actuarial device by which construction codes are strengthened and coastal zones declared uninsurable,[162] and on the development of "Act of God" bonds and "catastrophe futures" that will actually allow investors to *speculate* on natural disasters.[163] According to George Lloyd-Roberts of Lloyds of London, such adaptations, in combination with government bailouts for insurers hit by "super cats" ("cat" is industry lingo for "catastrophe") "should be able to secure a stable insurance market even in the age of global warming."[164] Such opinions, of course, can change, and a major hurricane over Tokyo or Manhattan would, as Munich Re, the world's largest reinsurance company, pointed out in 1992, get people's attention.[165] Such a storm could, perhaps, be a small sort of "optimal crisis."

Does this seem a cruel hope? Remember where we are. It is a long time since the environmental movement shuffled onto the stage, but despite seas of rhetoric, and changes in the regulatory practices of the planet's rich areas — cleaner waters in the United States, more recycling in Germany — not a single major aspect of the *global* ecological crisis has been reversed. There is much to say about this failure, and its denial, and all the time that has been wasted, but finally the failure itself is the central fact.

Nor is humanity alone on this planet. If we were, we could wait out the paralysis and the lies, confident that despite our personal fates, despite the suffering of the poor and powerless, and barring only a major nuclear war, the future would be redeemed. Unfortunately there are the corals, the wetlands, the forests, and the reefs, and the hundreds of species that are perhaps being lost every day. It is only an estimate; the ecology of extinction is a young science. All we really know, according to Harvard biologist Edward O. Wilson, is that this "extinction episode" seems "destined to approach the great natural catastrophes at the end of the Paleozoic and Mesozoic eras." He adds that it is "the folly our descendants are least likely to forgive us."[166]

The details are terrifying. About 1,000 of the planet's 9,000 bird species are already in danger of extinction, and about 70 percent, fully 6,300 species, are in decline. The major cause of this downturn is habitat loss, though pesticides play their role as well. As bad is the extinction overtaking the world's amphibians, and here every manner of deterioration seems to combine into a single deadly synergy — habitat loss and pesticide pollution, increases in ultraviolet radiation, acid rain, the raiding of ecosystems by exotic outsider species, all seem to be at fault. The red-legged frog, probable protagonist in Mark Twain's "The Celebrated Jumping Frog of Calaveras County" is in serious trouble, and no one knows exactly why.[167]

We are adaptable and will no doubt survive, as will the various "weed species" — sparrows, starlings, roaches, thistles, carp, and rats. The same, however, cannot be said for a much larger number of less flexible plants and beasts. Barring only the most unlikely of surprises, many of them will disappear in the years soon ahead. This is clear, as it is clear that our society, as we find it, is "unsustainable."

We know this word — unsustainable — but we seldom consider its logic, its sadness, its bloody mechanisms. How can we? To know ecological crisis intimately, as extinction can compel you to know it, is to welcome anguish. And just now anguish makes demands we cannot meet. About 5,100 languages are spoken on earth. Within a generation or two, all but about a hundred may perish.[168] These are cultures dying, and communities, and forests and grasslands as well. In the face of such death, what can anguish suffice? What can any feeling suffice?

Where we cannot act, we can only deny and adapt. And so we will adapt. We will adapt even to Lester Brown's "downward spiral of social disintegration," as we have adapted to silent skies, endless suburbs, endangered predators as cartoon corporate mascots, falling standards of living. We will adapt, as we always do. Gary Evans, an environmental psychologist, showed as much in a suggestive and frightening series of experiments. To Los Angeles residents he showed slides of landscapes that ranged from clear to somewhat smoggy. The longer people had lived in the city, the less likely they were to acknowledge the presence of pollution. He is not sure why. "It may be a passive, helpless response, but they just seem to get used to it."[169]

The "social amnesia" that Russell Jacoby described long ago — "memory driven out of mind by the social and economic dynamic of this society" — is a powerful force in our lives.[170] What we cannot see, we cannot remember. What we cannot remember, we cannot mourn, or even miss. Ultimately, if we believe Evans, what we cannot change we do not even see. Memory, strained by powerlessness, fades into nostalgia, and our ability to adapt becomes our undoing. In The End of Nature McKibben argued that "even as it dawns on us what we have done, there will be plenty of opportunities to forget — at least for a while — that anything has changed."[171] It is a crucial point, especially when amended to include a simple reality of social class — distraction and forgetfulness come more easily, more elegantly, to those with cash.

Two hundred years ago, Tom Paine wrote, "It is the good fortune of many to live distant from the scene of sorrow." Little could be more true, or more frightening. In a world at the edge of global ecological crisis, the division between rich and poor is no longer a merely moral problem. The rich, those who "live distant from the scene of sorrow," have at once the greatest power to act, and the greatest ability to forget.

"Radical Environmentalism"

> *Two Legs Bad! Four Legs Good!*
> *Two Legs Bad! Four Legs Good!*
> *Two Legs Bad! Four Legs Good!*
>
> Rally chant, Redwood Summer,
> Fort Bragg, California, 1990. (And,
> of course, Orwell's *Animal Farm*.)
> Ironic intent unclear.

During the 1980s, with the environmental mainstream visibly stalled, a new "radical environmentalist" opposition turned away from legislative maneuvering to invent a new kind of *very* direct action — "monkeywrenching" bulldozers and "spiking" trees, camping high in ancient redwoods threatened with clear-cutting, and even shooting "slow elk" (cows) caught grazing in national parks. Earth First! stands out in the history of those times, for through its media-savvy irreverence it was able to put the corrupt management of the U.S. Forest Service, and the imperative of preserving biodiversity, into political play in a way that the environmental establishment had never dreamed to do. Like the early Greenpeace and Sea Shepherd before it, Earth First!, motivated by a rough-and-ready realism and a desire to value nature above all compromise, put a powerful new green activism into motion.

Unfortunately, Earth First! was in all ways a product of its times. Brave enough to face truths that most people shrank from, it was also — with its weakness for Malthusian horror stories and its knee-jerk rejection of the left tradition — squarely in the main line of eco-apocalypticism. Its turn toward deep ecology, and its desire (as Dr. Seuss put it in *The Lorax*) to "speak for the trees," came packaged with a frustration that deepened into green fundamentalism and flirted (and more) with self-hatred and misanthropy. Its fate, and the fate of the ideas it came to be associated with, thus make important cautionary tales.

Earth First!'s unraveling was announced to the world on May 1, 1987, when "Population and AIDS" — an article written by one Christopher Manes, right-wing deep ecologist extraordinaire, under the pseudonym "Miss Ann Thropy" — appeared in the *Earth First! Journal*. The article argued the classical Malthusian line that human population growth is the root cause of the ecological crisis, but this, obviously, was not news. That came when, with a stunning, self-satisfied consistency, Manes asserted that "if radical environmentalists were to invent a disease to bring human population back to ecological sanity, it would probably be something like AIDS." Seeing no other way to stop the "biological meltdown" than by sharply reducing the human population, Manes observed that AIDS was ideal for the job because "it only affects humans," and that, "[as] radical environmentalists, we can see AIDS not as a problem, but as a necessary solution."[172]

There was, not surprisingly, a storm of protest. But Manes soon returned to justify himself. On December 22, in the same journal, he wrote that a die-off in human population was inevitable, one way or another, and while it would inevitably cause terrible suffering, it was still to be welcomed because it "will mean the end to the industrial tyranny which controls every aspect of our lives, which determines how we work and where we live and even what we think."

This is a dark apocalypticism, as brutal and arrogant as Christian millenarianism. Nature stands in for God, but she is as hard as ever was old Jehovah. Her retribution is strong but just. The chosen few will be redeemed by their survival and, as Manes explains in *Green Rage: Radical Environmentalism and the Unmaking of Civilization*, live lives defined by "the simple ecological modesty of primal society." The way forward is back to the garden, "back to the Pleistocene."[173]

Most radical environmentalists objected to Manes's fond words for AIDS, but they were hobbled in their efforts to denounce him by their general sympathy with his posture, if not all his conclusions. Earth First! cofounder Dave Foreman was quick to disavow Manes's excesses, but has made some injudicious statements himself. He once told Bill Devall, coauthor of *Deep Ecology*, that "the worst thing we could do in Ethiopia is to give aid — the best thing would be to just let nature seek its own balance, to let the people there just starve."[174] On another occasion, Foreman explained the roots of his pessimism:

There is no way to take five billion people in the world today, with the worldview they have, and the economic and industrial imperatives they live under, and turn it into a sustainable Earth-harmonious culture. That's just not going to happen. What is going to happen is that the system is going to collapse of its own corruption. The next several decades are not going to be a very pleasant time to be alive.[175]

It must be stressed that these words express not malevolence but despair. In a 1990 open letter of resignation from the Earth First! movement, written with his partner Nancy Morton, Foreman made his beliefs and their pedigree clear:

Yes, we do believe that overpopulation is a fundamental problem. William Catton in *Overshoot* restates Malthus's dictum in ecological terms as "the biotic potential of any species exceeds the carrying capacity of its habitat." We believe that human overpopulation has led to overshooting the carrying capacity of the Earth and will result in a major ecological crash. We do not think that believing this means that one is racist, fascist, imperialist, sexist or misanthropic even if it is politically incorrect for cornucopians of the Left, Right or Middle.[176]

Radical environmentalists are in a fix. Unable to accept the solaces of either techno-optimism or political resistance, they are left with only the mock-heroic posture of the beautiful loser. Thus, while radical environmentalism played a crucial role in the 1980s, it is difficult to believe that it, or anything like it, will again make a decisive difference. There are many reasons for this, but chief among them is that Malthusian pessimism is so debilitating a hobble.

Thus, Earth Firsters, too, are adapting to the new world, either by embracing expansive new social agendas and thus ceasing to be "radical environmentalists" proper,[177] or by digging in their heels and embracing apocalyptics as politics by other means. This second road, by the way, is not without its political theory, though it is rarely articulated. The Australian John Young is an exception. He writes: "The hope is that when the crisis comes . . . there will be enough converts to the side of ecological sanity to take advantage of the situation. This apoca-

lyptic tradition has much in common with the earlier Doomsday tradition of the 1960s, based as it is on the fantasy of standing alone in the
smoking ruins, having been right all along."[178]

Malthusianism, the radicalism of those without hope, is always a
bad business. It is also, and this is true of other rigid, all-explaining
ideologies, an invitation to stupidity. We may not be able to imagine
the social reforms that will allow the establishment of a stable, ecological society, but before we define the problem as population and imagine that AIDS will solve it, we might do a bit of research. Worst-case
projections have another 100 million people being infected by AIDS by
the end of the millennium, but in that same time almost ten times as
many children will be born. Paul Kennedy is right to say that, in the
more likely future, "Africa's overall population would still be growing
rapidly, therefore, but in the midst of an appalling scene in which millions of people were dying of disease."[179]

In the face of such a world as this, we would like to ask Lenin's old
question: What is to be done? Unfortunately, it is difficult, these days,
to do so with hope of an answer that is both clear and convincing.
Philip Raikes explained why in his study of African famine, *Modernizing Hunger*. Impending tragedy demands practicality, but, "it becomes
increasingly difficult to say what are practical suggestions when one's
research tends to show that what is politically feasible is usually too
minor to make any difference, while changes significant enough to be
worthwhile are often unthinkable in practical political terms."[180]

Thus, despair. Instead of an impossible practicality we dream of de-
liverance by catastrophe. We reinvent old stories, with plots dominated by necessity and rough justice. William Ophuls, in his 1977 green
Hobbesian classic *Ecology and the Politics of Scarcity*, wrote that ecological crisis makes "the individualistic basis of society" — "inalienable
rights, the purely self-defined pursuit of happiness," and "liberty as
maximum freedom of action" — all "problematic," and concluded that
"democracy as we know it cannot conceivably survive." His solution
(of course he has one) depends on a class of "ecological guardians"
who would "possess the esoteric knowledge" needed to run a "complex steady-state society."[181] Christopher Manes, for his part, takes a
postsixties route and proposes to avoid altogether the need for hard
choices by denying complexity and returning to the Stone Age.

These two visions share a tradition of political despair. Their differences are cultural, generational, even aesthetic. Both are dreams,

not strategies, and both products of a school of thought that can properly be called Cold War environmentalism. Both tell us that adequate changes in the real historical world, the world of power and politics, are impossible. Both articulate an abstract model that we will all be forced to follow for the good of the ecosystem. In the end, both come to illustrate the wisdom of an old critique of apocalyptic radicalism — easily frustrated, it easily degenerates into a coercive utopianism that cares more for its own prejudices than for sober confrontation with reality.

There's no good reason to expect that we'll soon see a political opening encouraging enough to push pessimism from the stage. Radical environmentalism and its cousins — ecocentric philosophies that allow humanity no place in nature, reductionist technology-bashing, eco-primitivism of all varieties — will likely haunt the green movement for years to come. They are the shadows of its political failure.

Worse, volunteers have stepped forward to blame radical environmentalism for that failure and, by strategic caricature, to imply that in the worst excesses of green fundamentalism they have found the dark secret of the entire movement. Martin W. Lewis, the academic author of *Green Delusions: An Environmentalist Critique of Radical Environmentalism* (1992), was the pathbreaker, painting it as "an ill-conceived doctrine that has devastating implications for the global ecosystem," and making much of the claim that its "ideas are beginning to lead the environmental movement towards self-defeating political strategies, preventing society from making the reforms it so desperately needs."[182]

This is nonsense, if only because radical environmentalism is old news. The excesses and dangers of deep green culture are obvious. When Father Thomas Berry, in his widely praised *The Dream of the Earth*, tells us, "We are an affliction of the world, its demonic presence. We are a violation of the Earth's most sacred aspects,"[183] he hardly encourages clear thinking or bold new political departures. And Lewis's particular concern — revealing the much-idealized ecological "purity" of primal societies as a myth — is an ugly job that must be done. Chief Seattle did not speak those beautiful, endlessly quoted words that have it that "the beast, the tree, the man, they all share the same breath,"[184] and somebody, sooner or later, was going to rub it in. It might as well be Lewis.

Since *Green Delusions*, the literary marketplace has evolved. Richard Preston, searching for a rousing ending for his bestselling *The Hot Zone*, revived the spirit of Miss Ann Thropy by painting "AIDS, Ebola and any number of other rainforest agents" as evidence that "the earth is mounting an immune response against the human species."[185] Meanwhile, new titles — Paul R. Gross and Norman Levitt's *Higher Superstition* is a notable example, as is Gregg Easterbrook's momentously sloppy and Panglossian *A Moment on the Earth* — have stepped forward to attack both green "radicalism" and "pessimism" (which are typically treated as equivalents), and to tell us that realism lies in optimism, rationalism, moderation, science, and the unimpeded logic of the market.[186] Like Lewis, they have their points, but like him they both caricature radicalism and avoid the real problem of "pessimism" — it is more a symptom than a cause. Nicholas Wade, reviewing *Green Delusions* for the *New York Times,* got it just right. "Radical environmentalists are not a potent political movement, nor are they likely to become one as long as the establishment can show that it is responding, however grudgingly, to serious dangers like ozone layer depletion, the destruction of species and the possibility of global warming."[187]

"The establishment," unfortunately, has yet to make any such demonstration.

False Choices

Environmentalists live double lives. As activists and politicians, even as technicians and entrepreneurs, they must think their efforts worthwhile, they must believe that they will win. In these roles energy and initiative are essential, and it is optimism, not any depressive realism, that opens paths to profit and advantage. Yet greens are lost without their darker suspicions. Optimism tilts almost inevitably toward complacency, naïveté, and greenwash. Fortunately, and despite all the comforts of pragmatism, greens know this well. In private moments, even public optimists often profess themselves powerless, and dream of upheavals sudden and wrenching enough to open more adequate spaces.

It is a movement commonplace that political diversity is crucial, that radicals back up pragmatists, stiffening their spines, and that the two groups combine into a stronger force than either could muster alone. Despite all bitterness and friction, this is true. It may be, however, that it is not the whole truth. The rest, I think, is that environmentalism is trapped in a tense, sometimes panicked oscillation between liberal optimism and radical despair, a false choice that has hobbled the movement for decades if not from its beginnings.

The big picture was long easy to ignore. The world's political structures were frozen in place, and viewed from the North, life in the peripheries appeared exotic and inconsequential. Besides, in the early glory days of modern environmentalism, faith in pragmatism and liberal reformism was easy to justify. In the United States the 1960s ended with a spate of almost visionary legislation — the Clean Air Act, the Endangered Species Act, the Occupational Safety and Health Act, the National Environmental Policy Act — and with the first Earth Day. In Europe the green parties began their rise less than a decade later. The rest of the world existed, more or less, only in vague outline. It was easy to imagine a future in which rationality would prevail.

In the 1980s the Cold War reached its final denouement. In the United States, the antienvironmental backlash began in earnest with the election of President Reagan, and this was more than a backlash against the greens. By the late 1980s, a new round of economic globalization — embodied in burgeoning cross-border capital flows and trade deals like NAFTA and GATT — revealed economy, ecology, and human rights as a single inextricable tangle. The illusion of "the environment" as a politically distinct area, one that could be saved alone, passed away. The world was roiling, at once shrinking within a tightening electronic net and dividing into warring camps of rich and poor. By 1992 anxiety set the political tone. Despite "success stories" like South Korea and Taiwan, the South as a whole continued its decline. In the North the middle classes imagined themselves among the poor, and realized that their future held no certain comfort, security, or even opportunity. Ecology was part of the stew, but only part.

Today it is easy to believe that matters will worsen in both North and South. Then, Northern democracies will likely be besieged by anxiety, anger, and a terrifying turn to the strange and volatile mix of fear and nationalism that pundits call nativism. Add a long ecological decline, and it's easy to finally imagine what Murray Bookchin has long called ecofascism.[188] Here pessimism would rule, and ideology would teach that only monumental, centralized initiatives are worthy of support.

Ecofascism is no groundless fear. Despair is everywhere in the green movement, and despair has its own crazy logic. A few more decades of decline could themselves seem to justify a functionally (if not explicitly) ecofascist regime. The biologist Garrett Hardin argued as much years ago, in his famous essay "The Tragedy of the Commons": "Coercion is a dirty word to most liberals now, but it need not forever be so." He met a loud chorus of agreement from the apocalyptic greens of the time.[189] More recently, and anxiously, German green jurist Birgit Laubach has warned that the failure to control the ecological crisis within the "democratic constitutional state" may lead to a time when an "ecological emergency state" will appear as the only remaining alternative.[190]

In the end, we fall easily into the apocalyptic narrative because it is difficult to imagine social changes large and rapid enough to avert catastrophe. Things look particularly bad in the South, where the grounds for pessimism are all too manifest. Martin Khor, a tired and dignified Malay activist who emerged during the run-up to the Earth Summit as a spokesman for the South, drew his conclusions even before the Summit, when it was still possible to hope for major new initiatives to emerge from its tortured but still-unprecedented negotiations. Khor, though, expected nothing. "The fading of the Cold War has left the South much more vulnerable to the power of the North," he wrote, and it was "likely that the governments will keep on haggling for years to come, whilst the global environment continues to be degraded and destroyed." He concluded, with an honesty rare among politicians of any stripe, that "the problems of humanity appear too complex and deeply entrenched for Earth to be saved."[191]

Such pessimism is not lightly held. In researching this book I found that many of the best-informed green activists have decided not to have children, or have yielded to their desire for children only after protracted ambivalence. I also found that optimism was often, as the Italian Marxist theorist Antonio Gramsci remarked long ago, a matter not of intellect but of will. One person I spoke with comes particularly to mind, a thoughtful economist named Lyuba Zarsky who spent a long hour extolling the virtues of a strategy aimed at "greening" markets through a flexible, adaptive politics. Then, in reply to a question about her deepest feelings, she burst out:

> I'm afraid it's too late, that we won't be able to turn things around, that the world will be so ugly that we won't feel any joy in living in it, that the things I love most will be gone, that my daughter

will never know them. When I say an ugly world, I don't just mean a paved-over and polluted world. Even maintaining compassion will be difficult. Sometimes it seems that all our attempts to get a handle on the destruction will just not be enough.

But she soon recovered:

I feel that I have to cultivate a sense of optimism. We all have to. We have to search for and do what can be done even if we just don't know if it will be enough. . . . We're in for a bumpy ride the next fifty years. The next ten to twenty years is going to be crucial. If the greens can get it together not just to fight but to build, the twenty-first century could look pretty different.[192]

It is traditional when discussing matters such as these to call for hope. Christopher Lasch did so in The True and Only Heaven, his history of "progress and its critics," but with a twist. In this almost final book, Lasch spoke for a "more vigorous form of hope, which trusts life without denying its tragic character." This is not hope against dread and pessimism, but just the opposite, hope against cheap confidence. "We can fully appreciate this kind of hope only now that the other kind, better described as optimism, has fully revealed itself as a higher form of wishful thinking."

The apocalyptic mood is no guide to action, and it certainly fails as a "more vigorous form of hope," but at least it breaks with denial. As Lasch wrote: "It is the darker voices especially that speak to us now, not because they speak in tones of despair but because they help us to distinguish 'optimism' from hope and thus give us the courage to confront the mounting difficulties that threaten to overwhelm us."[193]

This comment is just, and well timed. Here we stand, at the end of an almost century-long war against communism, with nature groaning beneath our feet. Obviously, new paths must be pioneered, but who will take them? It is the old paths that still claim the most attention, the old paths that are thick with traffic. With energy and vast impatience, people around the planet seek to emulate our lifestyles, if not our fading democratic traditions. Given the vast power of consumer culture, and given its consequences, what surprise is there in the apocalyptic mood?

After the Cold War

*We are approaching you both in our own and your interest. We aren't
making sacrifices, nor are we unduly exploiting you. Of course, we are
approaching you on behalf of Western companies, whose interests lie in
increasing their markets and in using your cheap labor and raw materials.
Some people say that this is a form of neo-colonialism. Certainly, it may
look that way, but then it's for you to be strong, to create mechanisms to
protect that which you hold dear.*

— A. Frohmeyer,
European Commission[1]

*Sell the forests. Sell the minerals. Sell the gold, the diamonds. Let the
West take what they want. Let them come in and give us what we need to
start over.*

— "An old and ailing Siberian man"[2]

In December of 1991, in the surprisingly plush basement conference
room of the Paris Youth Hostel, an "East Meets West" activists' caucus
met to distill from their dilemmas a few common understandings. It
was an odd, exciting affair, held as part of a huge international conference of "environment and development NGOs" funded by the French
government to prepare for the Earth Summit (and, so said the cynics,
to shore up its eroding reputation as a friend of the poor). Roots of the
Future, or, simply, "the Paris conference," was a rare opportunity, no
typical United Nations jamboree. NGO representatives from more than
160 countries were present, and there were no diplomats around to
confuse matters. The networking was easy.

About thirty people showed up at East Meets West, from as far east as Siberia and as far west as San Francisco. Chaired by an amiable Andrej Kassenberg, a pioneer of Eastern European environmentalism, the meeting took form around a series of resolutions, each to be discussed, refined, finalized, and submitted to the conference secretariat for inclusion in the final "common action plan" that was the formal goal of the conference. The plan, *Agenda Ya Wananchi,* would just be words on paper, and we all knew it, but we still took it very seriously. It would do what the presidents and ministers in Rio would not — it would tell the truth.

Matters dragged, as resolution followed resolution in a spirit of surprisingly convivial democracy. One, by a Polish delegate, would survive to be incorporated into the final draft, for it summed up the East's predicament with a rare and simple clarity. The end of the Cold War had left the countries of the East burdened with problems, yet the solution to these problems "to a large extent lies in the hands of the West." Why? Because "severe debt problems, the lack of the capital resources and the gap in technologies reduce the autonomy of these countries in determining their own development pattern." This "period of transition is their biggest chance" to "develop in a more sustainable way," but instead of being helped to seize that chance, they are being pulled in "two opposite directions simultaneously, both unsustainable." On one hand, "there is a strong drive within these countries to uncritically adopt the development model of the overconsuming North." On the other, "it is also likely that they face a new kind of colonization and will follow the same track as the South."[3]

After about an hour, a young Czech, Josef, stood to read, in rough but serviceable English, his draft of a resolution calling for a *total ban* on advertising, because of its "fateful" role in "promoting unecological lifestyles." The crowd, much of it older than Josef's perhaps twenty years, was amused. There were giggles all around, and an attempt to drop the subject and move on. Few people seemed to think that advertising would be phased out anytime soon. Josef, however, was unyielding. Procedure dragged, and finally, amidst the tittering, a (Western) wit commented that his proposed ban was "socialist" because it attempted "to limit the rights and mobility of capital." At this, Josef, had he been older, would surely have had a stroke. He responded with an intemperate, hard-edged *"No one ever called me a socialist!"* and suddenly reality had intruded on our small cloister. With smiles fading, the mood turned pragmatic. I expected to see him altogether squelched, but curiously (at least to my eyes), the talk turned to "propaganda" in general and advertising as "capitalist propaganda." In the end, Josef's resolution, much modified, was adopted — as a call for the banning of racially or sexually discriminatory advertising, and of advertising that promoted antiecological industries like "Swedish monocultural tree farms and French nukes."

The next day, seeing Josef in the hall, I buttonholed him and tried to explain why, to my American eyes, his resolution seemed leftish in intent. After all, a ban on advertising? I was friendly, but he was not amused, nor was he interested in my absurd views. I knew nothing. This was an emergency. Capitalism must come, and he would have it now. If there was an incongruity to his call for banning advertising, he didn't see it. And if the restoration of capitalism would be hard and even brutal, that, too, was only necessary. No safety net should be contrived to ease the pain. He was emphatic on this last point, as he was about his appeals to nature. It would be best for "the weak to be weeded out." Josef had one thing right — he was no socialist. If that now almost meaningless word still denotes anything at all, it is that societies should protect at least their weakest members from at least the most hideous of life's possibilities. This notion he rejected, though with perverse misanthropic consistency, he welcomed the strictest of environmental protections. Josef, it seemed, was a hard right-wing East-bloc radical environmentalist. Atypical, he was nevertheless a product of his times, the child of a political and moral confusion that makes little enough sense to its own citizens, and even less to the citizens of the West. In lands littered by street hustlers turned *biznesmeni*, doctors turned street hustlers, Western shock therapists, and neo-Keynesian communist industrialists, a few young ecofascists will fit right in.

How shall we approach this confusion, and the choices being made under its influence? How, more generally, shall we understand the opportunities that have been, and are still being, squandered in the East, opportunities to do something better? What is the meaning of these peculiar, tragic years, and of what the *New York Times*, in a knowing comment about aid to Russia, called one of the "mantras of the 90s" — "structural reform"? This reform, it went on, speaking of the West quite as much as the East, means "preparing governments, industries, and workers geared to Cold War prosperity for the new austerity."[4]

We can approach "structural reform" in the East by way of questions of immediate relevance even to die-hard, single-issue Western environmentalists. For example, is there really no alternative to the breakneck redevelopment of the Soviet oil fields, and to the spills and "accidents" that are regularly and predictably resulting from it? The ecological consequences of the postcommunist oil rush are rarely considered, and this silence is of far more than academic interest. Is this only "the market" that is remaking Soviet society, and must it be so cruel? The question has analogs far outside the former Soviet bloc.

There are other questions, too. Western nuclear firms are rushing to flog their wares even in the Chernobyl region of Ukraine, and at some point we must decide if we will admire this as rough entrepreneurial vigor or condemn it as predatory and even cannibalistic. U.S. and South Korean transnational corporations are clear-cutting the old-growth forests of Siberia, and this too demands judgment. Should it be attacked, or regulated, or simply welcomed as a source of hard currency? Much follows from the choice. The North Koreans, and for that matter the Russians, are also logging Siberia with great energy, and with the additional competitive advantage of slave labor. (There are, according to the Russian Socio-Ecological Union, about 200,000 Russian prisoners living in "severe conditions" in "forestry prison camps" left over from the Gulag system.)[5] Is all this inevitable, necessary, even admirable? Is all this simply the "creative destruction" of the capitalist restoration?

The Restoration

This has been a cruel century, and its cruelty is unabated from the brutal days that spawned the original Russian Revolution. Today, in the backwash of that revolution's long, terrible failure, we should spare a moment to consider its original animus, to know that it was not simply a Bolshevik coup, but as well a popular uprising, fought for bread *and* freedom, and against, in the words of Victor Serge, one of its greatest chroniclers, an "autocratic Empire, with its hangmen, its pogroms, its finery, its famines, its Siberian jails and ancient inequity."[6]

When, nearly a century later, a rotten "communism" came finally apart, no one knew what was in store. At first, few people thought much about it. In 1989, when the Wall fell, as in 1917, when the czar fell, the hope was too great, the intoxication too thick and sweet, to trade for any realism. Among radical democrats, there were some who insisted that "the people of the East have won the Cold War," but even at the time there was something hollow in such words. The TVs overflowed with pundits pronouncing "The Victory Of The West," and obviously the pundits were the more correct.

The West had won. Much remained unsaid, and the price of victory remained unreckoned, but at least the Cold War was over — that was the single overwhelming fact. Change was possible, and optimism, in its excesses, could be very high. Christian Slater, a young East German pacifist, told me his comrades in Dresden had reacted with "such hope! In 1989 a Europe without armies seemed a real possibility."[7]

Today such crazy optimism is ancient history. Today, at least in the former Soviet Union, even the last broken shard of the old socialist vision — that people are entitled to adequate food, clothing, and shelter — is under siege. The ruling dream today is the dream of affluence. The small rich minority flaunt their wealth with grotesque abandon, while for the majority life is both hard and galling. There is food in the stores, but many lack the money to buy it. On the island of Kronshtadt, where in 1921 the officers and sailors of the Russian Baltic Fleet fought and died in a valiant battle *against* the Red Army and *for* the revolution, well-heeled Russian tourists can now take pleasant breaks from the stress of "transition."[8] Dale Carnegie's *How to Win Friends and Influence People* is a blockbuster bestseller.[9]

Today all serious thought of leapfrogging the West — in environmental policy or on any other terms — has been postponed into an indefinite and barely imaginable future. As Tim Jenkins, a policy analyst for Friends of the Earth International, wrote in 1992, "The opportunity to integrate environmental goals at the start of this new development process is being lost in favor of purely economic goals."[10] That's putting it mildly. In fact, "purely economic goals" are the only ones consistent with the logic of this restoration. All others — planning and cooperation, for instance — are discounted as residues of communism, or thrust aside in the mad scramble for riches. "The market," as former Civic Forum leader Jan Urban put it, "is becoming a kind of idol. Instead of the leading role of the party, now we have the leading role of the market."[11]

In the East, to quote Alexi Danchev, an unhappy Bulgarian economist, it is widely thought "that state interference in economic activity is a holdover of the old system, and should be limited" — even when it comes to "such matters as environmental protection."[12] His words date from 1992, another time long past. Today, with the utopia of "shock therapy" having fallen sharply out of fashion, with Washington, the IMF, Russian "reformers," and Harvard University having been caught without any Plan B up their sleeves, it is easy to imagine that "state interference" will soon again be deemed necessary and even desirable. Even so, an appreciation of regulation will not come easily. In the delirium of postcommunist marketmaking, it is not even considered irredeemably disreputable to trade in nuclear materials. Trade, after all, is business and thus inherently good, the source of wealth and progress. And if hatred of the state is a legacy of the "old system," it is also an elemental theme of the capitalist religion of "deregulation," one incessantly sung by Western politicians, investors, and consultants.

Recall the zeal of the West's early postcommunist punditry. Jeffrey Sachs, the conservative Harvard economist who emerged in the late 1980s as the high priest of privatization, even used to advise his Eastern clients against Employee Stock Ownership Plans, as if they were a kind of Bolshevik contagion.[13] That was in 1992, about the same time that John Redwood, Margaret Thatcher's guru of privatization, told a Hungarian audience that privatizing the British bus companies had led to "stunningly lower fares, more travelers, better quality services." He omitted, as political analyst Susan George later pointed out, "to inform them that these effects occurred only on a few well-traveled routes, whereas most of them — including socially necessary routes in more deprived neighborhoods — have suffered effects that are exactly the opposite."[14]

Today such zeal is not so innocently displayed. The downside of this rush to capitalism is too visible to completely ignore, and no one seeks the blame. The sense now is that the reformers have done badly, and that perhaps they had no choice. Necessity is always a fine defense, and as long as Russia remains stable enough to avoid conflagration and civil war, few people will insist that other paths were possible. And yet they were, and still are. What is needed, then, is clarity about the transition and especially about its lessons, for these go far beyond the immediate problems of the old Soviet bloc. Roger Manser, the British author of *Failed Transitions,* put the case quite precisely:

> The transition which the region is now undergoing constitutes a test of the flexibility of the capitalist system. For economic change to succeed in the eyes of the local population, it should bring real higher incomes; in contrast, for environmental success it would have both to clean up those areas which were polluted by the communists, and to stop the exploitation of the environment.[15]

This is not at all what is unfolding. Nor is there a widely shared confidence that, as the West's cheerleaders invariably announce, good times will soon replace the disappointments of the present day.[16] One afternoon in 1993, in the cramped, fantastically smoky offices of the Polish Ecology Club, I asked Tomasz Terlecki, a bright, sarcastic member of the national staff, what he saw in the East's future, Brazil or Sweden. His answer was crisp and immediate. "Brazil, this is totally clear." It is not totally clear, but it is a depressing thought — Brazil's society is the most economically polarized in the world.[17] If matters got this bad in the East, with its hangover of disoriented egalitarian expectations, bitterness and mass hatred would certainly bloom.

It is fortunate, at least for the citizens of the East, that such extreme and indefinite polarization is not likely. Life in the East will improve, if only because it doesn't take much to constitute improvement in places like Moscow, which between 1970 and 1992 experienced a deterioration in health care and environmental conditions so severe that there was a full ten-year decline in life expectancy, a sharp drop in the birth rate, and an unprecedented population *implosion.*[18] The question is what kind of improvement it will be, and whether, in the larger global context, it will be anything to be happy about. In any case, the likely future is not "Brazil." David Hunter of Washington's Center for International Environmental Law, a man who has seen a good deal of the new East, put it this way: "They are white, they have the bomb, they do have an industrial base, even if it is archaic, and they are, some of them, really part of Europe."[19]

The tenor of the times is displayed in the character of its opposition. There may be, as a few optimists believe, a "second wave of dissident movements" in formation, in which ecology — along with feminism and human rights — will be central concerns. The immediate prospects for such movements do not, however, seem very great.[20] The days when Solidarity, the Danube Circle, Charter 77, and other flowers of civil activism pushed tendrils through the cracked foundations of the communist state are today old episodes in a long, bitter history. Independent political life still exists, of course, and still takes environmental forms, though the grassroots resistance once aimed at state-owned firms now focuses as often on the East-West joint ventures that have so readily joined the state in polluting the towns and rivers of the East. But the hope that drives deeper opposition is rare, and it is easy to see why. Capitalism was anticipated so fondly, and for so long, but it made such a rude entrance, and few anticipated the bitterness of its inequities or the completeness of its hegemony. In Poland, where the East's implosion began, subsequent "economic reforms" have benefited the "old boss" far, far more than the rank and file that propelled the changes.[21] Adam Michnik, formerly a key member of Solidarity's "oppositionist elite," put the point quite without apology. "Where else were we to find banking and other sorts of administrative talent, in the great numbers needed, if not from the ranks of the former *nomenklatura*? Who else had the necessary experience?"[22]

The East is a region in which, as writer Andrew Soloman remarked, "all anyone wants is dollars and muscles." He was, to be sure, speaking of Russia (the extreme case), but his comment applies elsewhere as well. These are lands dominated by "the rhetoric of ideology, until finally ideology itself lost its meaning," lands in which the young, pretty, fast, and smart "seem to understand" that democracy "is a euphemism for capitalism, and capitalism they take to be a system in which everyone grabs for himself whatever will be most useful to him."[23]

This climate has consequences for environmental protection, as it does for every other aspect of life. Take laws. In Russia, there are fine environmental laws on the books, but they have long been unenforced, and there is absolutely no chance that they will be enforced soon. Take direct action. In Warsaw, the 1993 Earth Day protest against rising dominance of the car involved a paltry forty people briefly closing one road. Iza Kruszewska, a Greenpeace antitoxics campaigner who focuses her work in Poland, put it bluntly. "Action means signing a petition. Short-termism is everywhere."[24] Andre Laletin, the slight, serious cochair of the Krasnoyarsk Ecological Movement, a Siberian nature-protection group, reports the same mood, or one that is even worse. Whereas 1990 saw his group win a number of seats on the local council, in 1992 the rapid impoverishment that followed price decontrol saw almost everyone, even formerly eager green deputies, lose all interest in politics. Most have gone "into business," and he does not begrudge them their choice. "People have no money, even for food, so they have no time, even for meetings. They must have money. In many cases they can steal or starve."[25] Tomasz Terlecki, of the Polish Ecology Club, concurs: "No one had any idea how much it would cost you to live. Now, no one has any time. I call my friend and ask him to work on a campaign, and he says, 'Fuck off, I have to work for my money. You have a job!'"[26]

Tomasz talks about a "mass psychosis" in which "anyone who takes part in power, on any level, is considered to be absolutely corrupt. It makes it almost impossible to get anything done." The term wins instant recognition among activists throughout the East, for they must constantly swim against this "psychosis." Yet it is easy to see why cynicism is so widespread. Hustlers are everywhere, as I learned in 1993, when I met Zygmunt Fura — who in 1988 had helped to found the Polish Green Party — at his "office," the Blue Box Disco in the heart of Krakow's old-town tourist district. After telling me that "demonstrations are not attractive unless they are forbidden" (as they no longer are), he went to the bar to get the photo albums he needed to explain his new organizing strategy — the monthly "Miss Eco" contest. "Young people," Fura explained, "think with symbols." No doubt he is right about this, as he is about his claim that "we are not an orthodox green party."[27]

All this could be only a momentary daze. There are thousands of green groups in the East, and many of them are serious. The European green parties, far from being demoralized by the hustlers who have joined their ranks — ex-*nomenklatura*, police agents looking for a new home, career politicians, opportunists of all description, weirdos in general — have founded a Continental Federation, and look to the future with wary optimism. New laws are being passed, environmental laws among them, and someday they could be enforced. The "psychosis" could fade into the routine frustration and envy of modern life. "Nationalist populism" (read fascism) could remain a subculture among others.[28] "Liberal authoritarian" regimes like that emerging in Russia could yield to genuine democracy. The conversion of Eastern arms industries to peacetime uses — which collapsed in bitterness when the West not only failed to provide assistance but actually went after East Europe's arms markets[29] — could be resumed. The chaos lapping the edges of the Russian sphere could be indefinitely contained. The wave of anti-Western backlash could break before it swamps the region. Shock therapy, as a long stream of articles once assured us, could even work.

Shock therapy — draconian programs of fiscal austerity and neo-liberal structural adjustment — is key to these events. The most striking thing about shock therapy is that anyone could have believed it would work in the first place, in any unambiguously positive sense of the term. It's not as if austerity came as part of a package of reforms that included, say, adequate social programs and coherent industrial and trade alliances. Rather, "reform" came to the East, as it does to so much of the world, as a process in which the West's fiscal enforcers shoot first and ask questions later. In Poland, the testing ground for the reintegration of the East, few questions were ever asked. Most early reports indicated that despite a few rough patches, everything was going excellently. Warsaw began to boast its Gucci parlors, and they received their full measure of publicity. Nineteen ninety-three entered with a particularly heavy stream of bright prose.[30] As we learned from endless articles like "21 Months of 'Shock Therapy' Resuscitates Polish Economy," the East was "turning the corner."[31] The only question, according to an adulatory profile of Jeffrey Sachs run by the *New York Times Magazine* in June 1993, was whether "this uncompromising free market economist," so "instrumental in curing Bolivia and Poland," could "cure Russia" as well.[32] A mere three months later, Polish farmers and industrial workers, who despite the fastest-growing economy in Europe were being reduced to grinding poverty, dismayed the West by voting the shock therapists out of office.[33] Three months more and there was the Russian election in which the huge vote won by Vladimir Zhirinovsky, no protofascist but the real thing, put the backlash on the political map.

Despite increasing criticism, Western press reports remain upbeat and selective. In Kraków, a tourist-heavy pearl of the new East, Professor Maria Guminska, the widely respected former president of the Polish Ecology Club, told me that only a few hundred kilometers away, in the countryside of southeast Poland, there was "virtual starvation." I confess that I did not make it to Bieszczady, the village that she named, but I heard the same report from others.[34] Darek Sved, an activist with Krakow's anarcho-pragmatist Green Federation, put it this way: "The cities are okay, but in the countryside, the poverty is extreme. This is true of the whole Central European region. The Western journalists don't see it. They can always get a coffee or a beer in the cities, and talk to some interesting people, and maybe even get invited to a party. But in the countryside things are really terrible. There are many people starving, and not only in Poland."[35]

Actually, the cities are not all "okay." Old industrial centers like Lodz — Poland's second largest city and its textile capital — where production, and real wages, fell by a third between 1989 and 1992, do not seem "cured" to their inhabitants.[36] Nor for that matter do even the centers of Prague, Warsaw, and the other capital cities — at least not from an environmental point of view. In the capitals, unlike cities like Lodz, there is money — but there are also streets clotted with ever-increasing streams of traffic, a contrast between rich and poor that is jarring even to jaded American eyes, and, everywhere, the brightly packaged Western products that, soon to become bright garbage, are the most banal tokens of the new regime.

It almost seems absurd to mention garbage in the face of the infamies sweeping the East, but it is actually revealing, for in its onslaught, garbage itself and its significance are *visible* in a manner rare in the West. Dr. Adam Gula, an engineering professor and frustrated, would-be pioneer in the energy-efficient retrofitting of shoddy communist high-rises, vividly recalls the arrival of disposable packaging. "First came canned beer. Teenagers threw them away with gusto."[37] Nor is he alone in taking garbage as a serious issue — in Poland the amount of solid waste generated increased 40 percent between 1989 and 1992.[38] As Gyorgy Viszkei, secretary general of the Hungarian Packaging and Material Handling Association, put it, packaging is "a hallmark of consumer society, and is a focus for confrontation between different philosophies of life."[39]

The same could be said of ecology in general, which, in the East as in the world, plays the spoiler. The explosive impotence of proud people now suddenly impoverished is a matter of wide concern, but it is the greens who worry most about the character of the new wealth, its material foundations, and the "successes" as well as the failures of the restoration. Marie Haisova, a thoughtful woman I met in Prague, at the office of the Czech Republic's Green Circle, asked me which I thought more decisive, the active discouragement that the West was giving to any possibility of a "third way" in the East, or the fact that the people of the East did not seek such an alternative.[40] She wasn't sure. Neither am I.

The world being born in the East has little in common with that so triumphally predicted only a few years ago. Carbon emissions are down sharply, but this is due more to the terrible recession that struck the region in the early 1990s than to better laws or technologies. Valentin Vasilev, Bulgarian minister of environment, put the matter clearly in 1992, noting that the reason for the 30–40 percent drop in pollution in his country was "economic decline."[41] In that decline a great number of communist-class factories were shut down, and cleaner air was thereby purchased with privation and unemployment. Since then even greater ironies have visited the region. The air and water are often cleaner, but even this is not always so. The Vistula, Poland's principal river and chemical dump, is still deteriorating,[42] and in Russia the percentage of industrial wastewater that is treated is actually falling. In the new East, there is no shortage of desire for ecological reform, but the economic free-for-all that is wild capitalism makes it impossible to raise money for even the most pressing cleanups.[43]

The East picked a bad time to surrender to the West. Today only the most enlightened policy activists see real alternatives to shock treatment, kinder paths to structural reform. Perhaps there can be slightly better safety nets, more compassion for the millions who cannot afford the glitzy new shopping districts — this at least is the hope of the many people voting for the various parties of repackaged old communists. But pessimism rules. Hope for a humane turn to an equitable society has long faded, and talk of a "sustainable transition" would only be an embarrassment, a relic of naïveté and childhood. The dog-eat-dog realities of capitalist reconstruction are quite undeniable. Vast injustices are taken as routine, inevitable, and even salutary.

In 1990 a joke in Bucharest had it that "socialism is the longest road from feudalism to capitalism." Today, as their future has come upon them, the people of the East have become less sanguine. A more recent

Russian joke has it that "capitalism has accomplished in only a few years what communism failed to do in seventy — it has made communism look good."

Ecocide in the East: Act I

Is it still necessary to review the ecological catastrophe in the East? By early 1991 the story had already been extensively reported, in articles with titles like "Poland Left Choking on Its Own Wastes," "Word Is Out: East Europe Is a Disaster Area," and "The Polluted Lands."[44] More recently the focus of Eastern reportage has shifted from the legacy of the communist past to the turbulence of the capitalist present — though the ecological destruction and industrial decrepitude handed down from the past remain major themes, and will for some time. They are the fruits of idiocy on a heroic scale.

The photos in particular leave deep impressions. There are dead forests, mounds of leaching wastes, "Satanic mills," sooted children at play in grim, industrial landscapes. There are rusting boats and tractors, and dead or dying soils and waters. There is, especially, the nuclear terror, the terror of Chernobyl and Chelyabinsk, of shoddy nuclear technology and its incompetent, duplicitous managers, of invisible sickness and of fantastic, insane waste dumps. One of these, a lake named Karachay near the formerly secret city of Chelyabinsk — sometimes called the most polluted spot on earth — is so radioactive that were you to stand on its shore near a pipe that has dumped hundreds of millions of gallons of nuclear waste since 1951, you would absorb a lethal dose of radiation in a single hour.[45]

Even this is not the worst of it, for Chelyabinsk, as a key link in the Soviet Union's nuclear weapons complex, is the product of a military-industrial culture that we in the West, despite all protestations to the contrary, can well understand. Chelyabinsk has its U.S. equivalent in the Hanford Nuclear Reservation in eastern Washington State. At Hanford, as at Chelyabinsk, officials poured liquid nuclear wastes directly into the nearest river, in their case the Columbia. At Hanford, too, the powers that be routinely lied to area residents, and to themselves, about the risks of living in the area. At Hanford, too, we have a sprawling radioactive legacy that defies easy remediation. There are major differences, to be sure, and Russian nuclear managers have generally outdone their Western brothers in sheer idiocy, but still the differences are differences of degree. If we can understand the one we can understand the other.

The wastes generated in weapons production are among the most dangerous in the world, and thus the toxic legacy of the Cold War arms race — nuclear, chemical, and biological — constitutes a huge proportion of the overall toxic legacy.[46] It is tempting to explore the point in detail, to weigh cause and consequence East against West, and to make military wastes the symbol of the overall ecological legacy of the Cold War. It is tempting, and it yields its truths, but they only go so far. In the former Soviet bloc, as throughout the world, the larger patterns of ecological destruction cannot be explained by anything as simple as the pathologies of industrial militarism.

The Aral Sea, a freshwater sea once larger than Lake Huron, fell victim to one of the most insane irrigation schemes in human history. Its feeder rivers were diverted — sometimes by *nuclear explosives* — to support a massive cotton monoculture that, once in place, generated chemical runoff in such profusion that the region's mothers cannot safely breast-feed their children. What put the Aral on the map, though, was its revenge. It is a desert sea, and as its volume dropped it lost its moderating influence on the local microclimate, even as its waters receded to expose vast sterile, saline plains. The storms of chemically laden dust and salt were first noticed by cosmonauts in 1975, and by the 1980s were poisoning farmlands as far as 1,200 miles away.[47]

Chelyabinsk and the Aral Sea represent the whole poisonous legacy of communism — its nitrate-sodden fields, its heavy-handed industrialism, its bureaucratic gigantism, its vast ineptitude. Add dead forests and soot-laden villages for good measure — for the primitive coal-based energy system that spawned them was a large part of the problem. The details, though, are not the point here, for they are easily found elsewhere. Let us ask instead what the whole catastrophe signifies, and how it was reported in the West, and what we imagine as its lessons.

The great communist ecocide is almost alone among ecological disasters in being nowhere denied, in being taken, at least rhetorically, with the seriousness it merits. In sharp contrast to their typical treatment of ecological destruction in the West, Western pundits eagerly embrace systemic and historical explanations of the Eastern catastrophes. The whole polluted debacle of the East was a ready-made parable for the "failure of Marxism and Stalinism, of centralized planning and socialist economics." Its root cause was a "model of economic development that demanded rapid growth of heavy industry and made no provisions for environmental concerns." The "accumulated filth" was "an inevitable by-product of a centralized totalitarian system."[48]

But even this is not the whole truth. There was no single cause for communism's industrial ineptitude,[49] save perhaps the utter absence of democracy. Given this absence, *everything* made matters worse. Even the lure of Western lifestyles did so, for as worried Eastern elites increased production to try to pacify restive populations, they ignored both the quality of goods and the environment.[50] Communism was, as we've been incessantly told, a sick system. The only problem with that phrase is that it implies *the* sick system, as if there might not be more than one. As David Gergen, Washington's bipartisan chief of spin control, said in 1990 (without bothering to cite evidence), "The leaders of Pittsburgh didn't know they were killing people."[51]

This is a wildly implausible claim. The "leaders of Pittsburgh" (which in its 1950s form as a center of heavy-metal industrialism bore a remarkable resemblance to a 1980s Soviet manufacturing city) certainly did know, to the extent that they troubled themselves to know, that they were killing people. Anyone familiar with Dickens's novels knows that captains of industry have long professed ignorance about the social and environmental consequences of their enterprises, one that turns far more on willfulness than on lack of information. Yet we have lived so long and so intimately with such comforting summations as Gergen's that we scarcely notice them. Cold War culture taught us well. Our insensitivity itself is testimony to its lessons: always to compare ourselves to the East, and be glad of what we see, to accept the corruption, inequity, and violence of the West as somehow benign compared to the greater evils across the divide.

In the old days, such comparisons had a power they no longer hold, for Soviet communism was always presented as a deadly, well-functioning machine. The truth — that it has long been crumbling — would not have so well justified ever-expanding Western military budgets. There were plenty of Western dissidents who saw through the hype, but they were generally discounted as communist sympathizers.

There was Daniel Ellsberg, the Pentagon whistle-blower who earned the undying hatred of the national security establishment by documenting the cynical lies behind the Cold War's "missile gaps" and "bomber gaps."[52] There was Noam Chomsky, who with bitter realism explained the benefits each side won by exaggerating the strength of the other.[53] There was Edward Thompson, the British historian whose analysis of Cold War culture inspired a generation of antiwar activists during the 1970s and 1980s.[54] There was Andrew Cockburn, an independent investigative reporter who in 1983 managed, with hard work and clear thinking, to discover what had somehow eluded entire phalanxes of massively funded "intelligence" apparatuses — that the Soviet military, far from being a fine-tuned killing machine, was burdened with dilapidation and demoralization on a monumental scale.[55]

Eventually the truth came out.[56] The Soviets had built a high-tech industrial military machine, but at tremendous cost. Mao Zedong had been wrong yet again — the "paper tiger" had lived in the East, not the West. Today this is simply taken for granted. Today the mad pas de deux of the Cold War is over — and with it the endless mobilization against a known, single, worthy enemy; with it the long, vile series of anticommunist "proxy wars" and the policy realism that condemned us all to a Manichaean ideological flatland, and cast the United States, in particular, as the world's self-appointed gendarme.

What is *not* gone, however, is the gap between rhetoric and reality, and the deeply ingrained habit of justifying that gap with lesser-evilisms of all varieties. Environmental protection well illustrates the bent of such "negative comparison." The best way to make Western environmental regimes look good is to compare them to the old East; placed against today's deteriorating global situation, they don't seem nearly as appealing. It takes nothing from the West to note that, as Roger Manser put it, Western environmental experts coming to the East are the "half blind leading the blind."

How then should we understand the shortcomings of our own regimes? Should we weigh them against the task at hand — the creation of a new "sustainable" society — or may we bask just a bit longer in the knowledge that at least things are better here in the bastion of democracy? Today, I can quote a 1980s Polish censor's manual — "Information on direct threats to life or health caused by industry or chemical agents used in agriculture, or threats to the natural environment in

Poland, should be eliminated from works on environmental protection"[57] — and no one is the least surprised. This kind of censorship was always the best proof that the Eastern regimes, whatever they called themselves, were hateful and repressive. But what about the other side of the story? Do we in the West, amidst the floods of information that assail us daily, get a balanced view of the "direct threats to life or health caused by industry or chemical agents" used on *our* side of the old Iron Curtain? If ecological destruction in the East was caused, ultimately, by an economic model that "made no provisions for environmental concerns," does this imply that such concerns are, in contrast, adequately represented in our own economic model?

Not at all. In fact, the terms of the standard East-West comparisons are badly misleading. Poland and Slovakia are about as "developed" as Turkey or Iran, and the Czech Republic and Hungary compare more fairly to Greece or Mexico than to the United States or Britain.[58] This doesn't let the East off the hook for the damage its managers have done, but it does recast the issue: Greece, Turkey, and Mexico are no shining models of environmental management. And if "the West" is taken as a whole — to include its service areas in Latin America, Africa, and Southeast Asia — is it still so certain that its ecological record is superior in every way to that of the old East bloc?

Taiwan, perhaps the best example of the modern capitalist miracle, proves the double standard. One of the poorest countries in the world only forty years ago, it is now the thirteenth largest trading nation in the world. With South Korea, Singapore, and the other "Asian tigers," it is the basis of the myth of the "newly industrialized countries," and is often cited as evidence that newcomers can break into the ranks of the "developed" countries, providing only that they "work hard and work smart." In 1991 Taiwan's average per capita income was twenty times that on the Chinese mainland.

Less often noted are the ecological costs of the miracle. In some parts of the country, only 1 percent of wastewater and sewage is treated — as a result, the lower reaches of virtually all rivers are biologically dead. Three million metric tons of hazardous wastes are dumped each year. Emissions from twelve million cars and motorbikes choke the air of the cities. Cancer rates have doubled since 1960. A government report has warned that parts of the island could be uninhabitable by the year 2000.[59] All in all, the costs of Taiwanese development are comparable to those paid in the old communist world. Nor is this much of a surprise, for the two cases are more similar than is usually supposed. In both Taiwan and the former Soviet Union, industrialization proceeded by way of a technocratically encouraged crash program in which utter ecological insensitivity was assumed to be the price of growth.[60]

The question here is why these horrific conditions, in sharp contrast to those in the former Soviet bloc, are almost unknown in the West. Why, as Taiwan begins a weak and belated cleanup campaign, do its more viciously regulation-resistant firms move on to that latest last frontier of primitive capitalism, the People's Republic of China?[61]

China is a country to watch. A pioneer of "Market-Leninism," it is also "buying, building and consuming as if there were no tomorrow."[62] For all the fine talk of its smooth transition to capitalism, China's development curbs are quite as unenforced as were environmental laws in the former Soviet bloc. Its croplands are going fast — estimates of loss range from 50 million to 100 million acres since the 1950s, out of a total of 272 million to 346 million acres![63] Its roads are clotting with traffic.[64] Its air, land, and water are thick with pollution,[65] and it is entering what will certainly be a catastrophic national water shortage. Most of its energy is generated by burning dirty, high-sulfur coal. Millions of internal refugees, many of them "environmental refugees," are wandering the country in search of a chance, or at least a job. A green movement is desperately needed — and strongly discouraged. "The government," as the internationally known journalist and environmental activist Dai Qing put it, fears "an environmental organization will develop into a Green Party."[66]

Asia is booming, and its boom is an ecological catastrophe. In the former Soviet bloc, too, the ecological situation is in many ways worsening. Yet after years of triumphalist talk of communist ecological catastrophe, how can we be made to understand that these two trends express a single pattern? That capitalism has not come softly to the fields and streams of the old communist lands?

We need to register the fact that, as a group of Eastern greens put it in 1991, communism's environmental legacy is actually "ambiguous." There are vast polluted areas in the old Soviet lands, but at the same time there are many extensive and undamaged areas of high natural value."[67] This is indicated by the presence of three times as many wolves in Central and Eastern Europe as in West Europe, and more bears in Romania alone than in all of Western Europe.[68] Gary Cook, director of Earth Island Institute's Lake Baikal Watch, put the situation simply and truly: "Localized pollution hot spots are clearly *much worse* in the East, but there are huge areas that are in *much better* shape than they would be if they were in the West, because they haven't been 'developed.' "[69]

Meanwhile, in former Soviet lands like Turkmenistan, hunters with enough cash are welcome to hunt endangered species that once, under the communists, were protected. Environment Ministry employees have actually been instructed to assist them.[70]

Ecocide in the East: Act II

Today, of course, the East has joined the mainstream. And as the citizens of the East have found in their insecure new lives something quite different from what they had imagined, so the forces shaping the new East highlight realities that we, the citizens of the West, often prefer to avoid. The World Wildlife Fund's Richard Liroff clarified the issues. A man deeply involved in supporting environmental activists in the East, and fully aware of the many unpleasant aspects of Western policy and investment, he was nevertheless puzzled when I asked him about the role of the West in the continuing destruction of the Eastern environment. "Why blame the West?" was his immediate response,[71] and given the weight of history in the region, it has an air of immediate justice. Still, it is possible, and important, to answer him.

Nuclear Power

It is best to begin the answer with nuclear power, the defining technology of the Cold War. With more reactors in the West being shut down than started up each year, the East is one of the nuclear industry's last frontiers. The story of the industry's marketing offensive in the new East has everything:

• Expatriate Cold Warriors like Hungarian-born Edward Teller, the father of the American hydrogen bomb, who was reborn as a pronuclear salesman-diplomat, flogging Western reactors in his ancestral home.[72]

- Clever marketing savvy, in which the very shoddiness of Eastern reactors is magically transformed into advertising for Western nukes.[73]
- Helpful Western corporations — such as Siemens KWU, Electricité de France, Asea Brown Boveri, Westinghouse, General Atomics, Bechtel, and Atomic Energy of Canada — which have generously offered to build nuclear facilities of almost every description.[74]
- Friendly Western governments willing to offer easy financing. (Zoltan Illes, state secretary of the Hungarian Ministry of the Environment: "A French company would like to sell a very nice nuclear power plant to us. It is better than Chernobyl but not acceptable in the EC [European Community]. The French government will give the loan, then Hungary will buy the plant.")[75]
- Moves by the nuclear industry to outflank Western antinuclear forces by generating nuclear electricity in the East and importing it into Western Europe. The best-known such scheme turns on the Soviet-style VVER-1000 reactors near the Czech town of Temelin, which will export electricity to Italy and Switzerland, both countries with nuclear moratoriums. The Temelin scheme almost died after "the turn," but the Swiss utility NOK and Westinghouse lobbied hard to bring it back from the dead. They have made changes in its design, but these cannot remedy basic flaws, and Temelin could never be licensed in the West. Still, it will be a historic reactor, the first in the East to go online after Chernobyl.[76]
- Rank opportunism, in which nuclear lobbyists play to nationalist sentiments (not rare in the new East), pitching their wares to politicians and bureaucrats as means of gaining "energy independence."[77]
- A sense of pessimism and inevitability, in which the need to *do something* about energy, and the refusal by ruling institutions to seriously explore efficiency and renewables, make nuclear redevelopment appear inevitable.
- Disputes at the "highest levels." What, after all, is the problem, nukes themselves or only "unsafe" nukes? Should unsafe

reactors be shut down, or only "upgraded" by Western experts? The World Bank officially advocates a "low nuclear scenario," while the U.S. Export-Import Bank (Eximbank) and other such semiprivate export-promotion outfits have, with the strong encouragement of the nuclear industry, been funding nuclear development whenever they can get away with it.[78]

The pivot here is fear — fear of another Chernobyl, fear of energy shortages, fear of nuclear weapons proliferation and political instability. Or, if you are a nuclear executive, fear of losing what may be your last best chance to revive your dying industry.

"One of the lessons which the western industry is keen to impart to nuclear utilities in the east," according to Friends of the Earth, "is public relations."[79] And no wonder. Of the sixty-three operating reactors in the East, forty-three are based on designs unlicensable in the West. The industry's problem, then, is to convince Western governments that the "emergency" in the East should be managed by "upgrading" these plants rather than shutting them down. The happy result would be a huge surge in the river of public money that the industry has always relied upon for its profitability.

The industry is lobbying hard. Western funding for nuclear projects of all sorts has long been dribbling into the East — a few million here, a few million there — but until 1991 it didn't really amount to much. Then a major lobbying push by Westinghouse won a funding breakthrough in the form of an Eximbank "preliminary commitment" to provide a $136 million low-interest loan to the Czech Republic to upgrade and complete the reactors at Temelin. By 1994, when (with the support of "environmentalist" Al Gore)[80] the deal finally went though, the loan had risen to $317 million — a block of cash that, along with a good deal more in privately loaned funds, will pass through the books of CEZ, the Czech electric utility, and on to Westinghouse, which will add new instrumentation and control systems to make Temelin the first-ever East-West hybrid reactor.[81]

The East's "unsafe" reactors figure large in the industry's PR campaign, but Western taxpayers, through semipublic agencies like Eximbank, the European Bank for Reconstruction and Development, and the International Atomic Energy Agency, have spent more than twice as much money *expanding* nuclear power in the East as they have making existing reactors safer.[82] The Eastern ministries, for their part, are glad to take the money. For they hold what a confidential World Bank study on nuclear energy in the East, leaked to Greenpeace, called "different views about nuclear risks."[83] They also worry about balance of payments problems, and have been repeatedly advised by Western "experts" that nuclear power can help solve them — that it is the only realistic alternative to expensive imported oil and high-sulfur coal,[84] and that, moreover, there is a bright future in exporting electricity to West Europe and China. Given the shape of the local economies, these are seductive arguments. In Bulgaria the high price of imported coal, and the invisibility of energy alternatives, have helped keep the Kozloduy nuclear power station open, though it is one of the most dangerous in the region. Temelin, too, has long been defended with the claim that it would allow three coal plants to be shut down,[85] though the Czech Republic is already exporting power, and the World Bank itself notes that 30 percent of the republic's energy needs could be met with simple, inexpensive conservation measures.

The same, more or less, holds true in Ukraine, Bulgaria, Slovakia, Romania, and Russia itself. Western countries are gradually increasing the amount of "aid" targeted at improving the most dangerous of the Eastern reactors, rather than rapidly phasing them out.[86] This "go slow" approach is strongly supported by the Western nuclear industry, which argues that its technology and expertise can make the risk of operating most Eastern reactors "acceptable." There is no good reason to think this true. What this strategy will actually yield is a motley collection of nukes jury-rigged out of new control systems and badly designed, aging Eastern reactors that would be immediately shut down under Western regulations. Meanwhile, U.S. and European nuclear firms dream about billions of dollars in contract work and lobby for release from all legal liability for their new contraptions, just in case they fail.[87] Phalanxes of Western executives are chanting "safety," and the liability-relief deal enjoys the assistance of both European governments and the Clinton administration, so it just may go through. If it does, one thing at least is certain — the East, already staggering under archaic infrastructures and huge external debts, will become even more deeply bound in long-term entanglements that preclude more rational alternatives. "The West," as Lydia Popova of the Russian Socio-Ecological Union put it, "has been greeting the East with full hands, and those hands have been full not of energy efficiency technologies and renewables, but instead full of nuclear plants."[88]

Even the World Bank agrees. According to Bruce Rich, a veteran critic of the Bank and an expert on its history, for reasons that "are not clear, though definitely political,"[89] the Bank has long had "an unwritten policy" of not investing in nuclear power. "It deserves credit" for this policy, says Rich, and coming from him this is high praise indeed. Still, it would be nice to know the logic behind the Bank's nonnuclear policy, and getting a good answer is *not* easy. Peter Hayes, a senior analyst at the Nautilus Institute for Security and Sustainable Development, traces it to a "subliminal" desire to prevent nuclear proliferation, plus the judgment that, in any case, export-promotion agencies like Eximbank have the job of funding nuclear exports covered.[90] It seems a plausible interpretation and is consistent with the drift of events. Eximbank fought hard for the Temelin deal, while the Bank quietly and gently opposed it as economically unjustified.

There are factions within the Bank. Some go along with the "low nuclear scenario" that involves shutting down the East's most dangerous reactors, but still investing tens of billions of dollars on "safety upgrades" to the rest. Others do not support even this investment. Richard Ackermann of the Bank's Environment Department, an author of the *Environmental Action Programme for Central and Eastern Europe*, an international and interagency overview of environmental issues in the region,[91] spoke for this second faction when he told me, "Projections indicate that primary energy demand in the region, as well as electricity demand, will decline until at least 1995. This gives us a breather, an opportunity to do something else."[92]

The *Action Programme* is based on cost-benefit analysis, a controversial technique by which complex phenomena both social and ecological are mapped into quantitative economic models, and those models are then used to adjudicate pseudo-objective "trade-offs" and to maximize payoffs. Leaving aside the question of why the Bank — which, according to Bruce Rich, routinely "has its economists cook up appraisal methods that yield the numbers it wants,"[93] — would take cost-benefit analysis seriously in the case of nuclear power, it does seem to do so. Perhaps it really comes down to the belief that, as Ackermann described the core principle of the *Action Programme*, "money is scarce." With Western governments providing only tiny measures of overall assistance to the East and the cost of patching up just the worst East-bloc reactors estimated at $22 *billion*,[94] it's not hard to wonder at the size of the bill.

It may even be that, despite what Rich calls the Bank's "ceaseless struggle to keep the money flowing,"[95] Eastern realities have taught the Bank a bit of respect for unvarnished fiscal analysis. If so, it must be said that its new sensitivity has not spread through its bureaucracy. Despite fine rhetoric about least-cost planning and "demand-side management," the Bank continues to disregard energy efficiency and conservation in order to fund expensive new generating capacity — in 1994 only 1.4 percent of its current loans was allocated to renewables and 0.8 percent to end-use energy efficiency.[96] And of forty-six power-sector loans in the Bank's loan pipeline, loans totaling over $7 billion, only two were consistent with its own policy papers recommending energy efficiency.[97]

The Socio-Ecological Union, Russia's largest environmental organization, does a good deal better. In a 1992 statement entitled " 'Good' Western Nuclear Technology Is No Answer to 'Bad' Soviet Nuclear Plants," it argues that "given the economic and political instability of the region, only the replacement of nuclear power stations by non-nuclear energy sources can guarantee the ecological security of the continent." It then goes on to propose that if more energy is needed it can be gotten by using "modern gas-fired, co-generation plants to replace the aging and unreliable nuclear power stations." This option would cost *far* less and be far safer, could be based on available, domestically manufactured equipment and prolific Russian gas reserves, and, most crucially, would be a big step toward a renewable-energy economy.[98]

More energy is *not* needed. The Moscow Center for Energy Efficiency estimates that cheap, simple forms of energy efficiency, from compact fluorescent lights to building insulation, could easily reduce electricity consumption by 40 percent,[99] and other studies peg the figure as high as 55 percent. Friends of the Earth International has proposed a phased shutdown of Eastern nukes, in which the most dangerous (all fifteen Chernobyl types and eighteen others) are immediately decommissioned while the rest continue to operate until energy alternatives — gas cogeneration, small-scale hydroelectric projects, efficiency measures, and solar power — allow them to be shut down without causing any hardship. The total estimated cost of the FOE plan is $18 billion, far less than it would cost to "backfit" a fraction of the same reactors with Western safety features. (The "cost" of the Chernobyl disaster, by way of reference, is estimated at about $300 billion and forty thousand lives.)[100]

With nuclear power, there is blame enough to go around. Can we even judge the West completely innocent in the damage done by the Soviet nuclear program? To do so, we must judge it blameless for the nuclear arms race, and for the Cold War itself, which spawned that arms race. However historians eventually apportion overall responsibility for the Cold War, they must likewise apportion some measure of blame for the nuclear detritus it has left behind. This is true of the nuclear industry, born in the U.S. Atoms for Peace program of the 1950s, of the radioactive landscapes of Chelyabinsk and Rocky Flats, Colorado, and — unless sanity prevails — of RT-2, a "waste-reprocessing plant" (more likely to end up as a dump for high-level wastes from around the region) planned by ex-communist entrepreneurs for the banks of the Yenisei, a major river in remote central Siberia.[101] Likewise Chernobyl and the atomic warheads now spreading around the globe; where there is nuclear danger, there is a measure of blame for the West.

"Natural Resources"

The "extractive industries" may not have the catastrophic potential of nuclear technology, but when it comes to sheer brute damage, they can definitely hold their own. They sure do in the former Soviet bloc. The context here is the struggle for the far-flung properties of the old Soviet state. Natural resources, factories, buildings and military installations, technology — all are sources of potential power and profit. The story of their exploitation is largely the story of their "privatization," which Stephen F. Cohen, an expert on Russian culture and politics, once lamented was "corrupt even by Soviet standards."[102] It is, specifically, the story of how that privatization is being played out in the context of a global economy dominated by transnational corporations.

Here is a quick tour.

Of all the fronts in all the battles over drilling, logging, and mining in the old communist lands — and there are many — one of the most important, and most revealing, is the European Energy Charter.

Launched in 1991, the charter defines a framework for future energy-related ventures between the West and the East. Based on GATT, it fails to meet even the pallid environmental provisions of that much-criticized master trade agreement.[103] Dozens of countries have signed it, and the World Bank, the International Atomic Energy Agency, and the Organization for Economic Cooperation and Development (OECD) have observer status at its conclaves. Environmental advocates, however, are entirely excluded.

The charter sets terms in keeping with the desires of the Russian government, which has worked diligently and successfully to attract Western oil companies. At the end of 1991, thirty-six Western oil companies had Moscow offices and were dreaming of Russia's oil fields, which are even larger than Saudi Arabia's. Greenpeace's Jeremy Leggett has summed up the significance of the charter in simple, certain terms:

> The European Energy Charter seeks to open the Russian republic to a new bonanza in oil and gas production. It ignores the economic opportunities and environmental imperatives of energy efficiency, demand management and renewable energy supply. It opens the door to energy developments which run precisely counter to the existing agreement by governments, at the 1990 World Climate Conference, to stabilize concentrations of global warming gases in the atmosphere.[104]

The Energy Charter is the reality behind the rhetoric of a rapidly greening West Europe. It is proof, if proof is needed, that the integration of the East into the global energy economy will take place on terms that do not threaten the dominance of the fossil-fuels industries. It will probably be a stupendous mess as well. Given the very bad environmental record of the Soviet oil industry, the poor environmental performance of the American oil industry in Alaska, and the fragility of the Siberian environment, where almost all Russian oil and gas is found, there is little reason to be optimistic about the conditions that will prevail in the Russian oil fields of the future. If even more cause for anxiety were needed, it surfaced in early 1992, with the news that Russia's new petroleum laws were being written in conjunction with the University of Houston Law Center. The law center, heavily supported by the oil industry, was developing the new laws by a process that effectively excluded public-interest advocates, yet allowed oil companies to review draft legislation and even to help draft the very laws that will govern them in their future Siberian ventures.[105]

Another impending resource catastrophe lies in the taiga — a vast swath of boreal forests that carpets more than two million square miles of the Russian Far East and Siberia. Here, too, the "development" of the former communist lands threatens to take an all-too-familiar shape — in this case "slash for cash" logging of just the kind so exuberantly practiced in British Columbia. The taiga holds about 42 percent of the world's temperate forests and covers an area larger than the rain forests of Amazonia. Though not as magnificently biodiverse, it is a "carbon sink" similarly critical in the control of global warming.[106] Trees absorb carbon dioxide as they grow, and must be protected to stabilize the climate. Too bad, then, that the world market for lumber is vaster even than Siberia. The Japanese are exploring the situation, but two corporations — South Korea's Hyundai and the American-based Weyerhauser — quickly emerged as the taiga-logging pioneers.[107]

Weyerhauser's major venture is in the Botcha River basin, one of two remaining first-growth forests on the Far East Pacific coast. (Hyundai's, in the Svetlaya area, is in the other.) This venture is notable for the fact that the Botcha River basin was for a time protected as a temporary nature preserve, and had been slated to receive permanent protection. After Weyerhauser expressed interest in the area, the regional government withdrew its endorsement of the permanent protection plan, and the logging deal went through. All this is particularly telling, for the Soviet green movement fought some of its formative battles against the communists in defense of nature preserves. That was then; this is now. Hyundai began its logging in a joint venture that had received two negative ecological *ekspertizy* (the Russian version of an environmental impact assessment) and was quite illegal. In this it is all too typical of the Wild West capitalism now rife in the fragmented Soviet empire, where local authorities often seek advantage in ventures illegal under federal law. Hyundai made its deal with cash-strapped local officials nine time zones east of Moscow and pays about one-twentieth of the world market price for the timber it extracts.[108] Recently, in part because of an international letter-writing campaign, the Moscow-based Ministry of Ecology and Committee of Forestry has asserted itself and at least temporarily stopped the expansion of the logging into the Bikin River basin, home to the Siberian tiger and a dozen other endangered species.

The Bikin River basin is only one isolated area. As home to the Siberian tiger, a "charismatic megafauna"[109] if there ever was one, it is atypically easy to popularize and protect. In other forests, other oil fields, other mines, the dollar's rule is less easily modulated, as the St. Petersburg Green Party learned in the summer of 1991, when its antilogging activities led several of its members to severe beatings by a "forest mafia" specializing in illegal timber. One of those beaten, Vladimir Gushchin, was a cochair of the Russian Green Party, and thus it earned the very dubious honor of being the first official political party to be the victim of postcommunist economic terrorism.[110]

Things can get worse. Under the name of "environmental forest management," the World Bank is promoting heavy logging in cash-starved Slovakia.[111] And according to the Socio-Ecological Union, the new Russian forestry law, adopted in late 1993, is so riddled with "unresolved points of conflict between federal, regional and local forestry administrations" that it will invariably lead to "an increasing inability of central forest authorities to control federal forests," allow "local officials to expediently and independently carry out sales of forest resources in their own self-interest," and encourage "increasing involvement of organized crime in the Russian forest sector."[112] No doubt this judgment is correct — the perhaps 1 percent of the Russian population that makes up "the new rich" is formed largely of the "well-connected" people who have learned "to capitalize on their country's abundant natural resources."[113]

Finally, consider raw materials, which are notable for the destruction their extraction can cause — and did cause under the communists — and for the West's long, rarely remarked willingness to profit quietly from that destruction. The East has traditionally been a Western service area. Western Europe, for example, long imported Polish copper with no more thought to the belching smelters that produced it than to the labor conditions in the copper belts of Zaire and Zambia, from which it also benefits. Similarly, Albanian chrome, iron, and nickel, Czechoslovakian timber and steel, Bulgarian tobacco.[114]

What has changed? R. Dennis Hayes, an American journalist, has shown just how closely "democrats" will follow in the footsteps of the communists, if only doing so is profitable. His report from the Czech Republic, "Liquidating Libkovice," is the story of a Bohemian town as it is consumed by a spreading open-pit brown coal mine that had briefly been halted by the collapse of the old regime. State-run mining companies had, during the age of forced industrialization, destroyed more than one hundred such towns — but Libkovice's citizens had dared to hope theirs saved. That was before Hlubina, a state mining company directed by Zdenek Struzka — former dissident, cofounder of Civic Forum, professed environmentalist — began to court a Western partner. The coalfields beneath Libkovice fueled the deal. Where do liquidated villages go? Into gaping, open pits. Vaclav Havel, in earlier, more hopeful days, had spoken out against such liquidations, and promised change. "Where," Hayes asked, "do promises go when they are broken?"[115]

The Toxics Trade

Garbage — the most routine domestic effluvia and the most noxious toxic waste — reveals a great deal about the society that produces it. When that society seeks to forget it, to have it "go away," it reveals even more. Certainly this was the case with the *Khian Sea*, the infamous "ship of death" that left Philadelphia in August of 1986 loaded with fourteen thousand tons of toxic incinerator ash and — after trying to unload it on a Haitian beach (where its captain claimed to be dumping "fertilizer"), being driven way, and spending twenty-six months wandering the oceans — finally disposed of the waste somewhere in the Indian Ocean.

Toxic incinerator ash, like that the crew of the *Khian Sea* buried at sea, is among the least publicized of all the "goods" now in routine international trade. For decades, but now at an ever-increasing rate, these poisons have been shipped from rich countries to — quoting now from *Romania: The Toxic Assault*, a Greenpeace Germany report of surprising drama — countries "whose environmental movements are less influential, whose laws are less rigorous, whose administrators are less vigilant, and whose economies are less affluent than the ones 'at home.'"[116]

The toxics industry is nothing if not entrepreneurial. As waste-disposal regulations in the rich countries have firmed up, costs have increased as well. In the United States, they rose twelvefold between 1980 and 1992, and in so doing created a market that has not gone unserved. "Africa," according to Andreas Bernsdorff of Greenpeace Germany's waste-trade campaign, was the first "victim continent," but it did not long retain its unique status. In the late 1980s, despite their desperate need for hard cash, African countries made a strong effort to seal their borders to waste dealers who, undeterred, turned then to Latin America and, of course, Eastern Europe.

The West-to-East toxic trade was big business during the old regime. West Germany, by far the world's largest exporter of hazardous wastes, paid the East at least four billion DM for accepting its wastes *before* the Wall came down, and pacesetter Italian firms were already dumping toxics in Romania's Danube delta back in 1987.[117] The real "waste invasion," though, arrived around 1989, in Poland. Poland was hit hard, largely because of its proximity to Germany, its need for hard currency, and the difficulty it had, initially, enforcing even the toxic import prohibitions it had on the books. The opening of its borders saw Poland inundated with toxics. By late 1990 Greenpeace was easily able to show that twenty-two million tons of toxics had been offered to Poland, and that forty-six thousand tons had definitely crossed the border.[118]

The total size of the waste trade, in Europe and around the world, is rapidly increasing.[119] South Asia is emerging as the favorite target of the waste traders, as Africa, Latin America, and the Caribbean move to shut them out.[120] In Europe similar dynamics prevail, with the waste traders targeting the most indifferently regulated areas. By 1993 the Polish border was at least partially sealed and the preferred export targets became the Balkans, Russia, Ukraine, Georgia, Albania, and, in the lead, Romania. In 1994 Ukraine banned the import of hazardous waste, and again the trade moved elsewhere.

One especially sleazy aspect of the waste trade is that much of it (much, that is, of the unknown fraction of it that's legal) passes through the infinitely flexible conceptual loophole that is "recycling." Greenpeace studies of recorded waste-import schemes in Poland and the Caribbean in the early 1990s found that more than 62 percent of them declared there would be recycling or some other kind of further use.[121] There almost never was, but the cover story was extremely convenient.

Now the East is wide open and being treated to the same fate that has long befallen the South. All roads, it seems, lead to the same destination. The widely celebrated new German waste and recycling laws — Dual System Deutschland — may actually mean a vast increase in plastics "recycling" in Poland.[122] On another note, "waste mafias" (like "forest mafias") have begun smuggling toxic garbage throughout the East. In the former Soviet bloc, particularly, borders are in chaos, and it is often impossible to know what is crossing them.[123]

In 1994 waste-trade campaigners won a hard-fought battle. Germany, England, Australia, Japan, and Canada (all of which, along with the United States, had long opposed a total ban on the toxics trade) bowed to international pressure and voted, via amendments to the Basel Convention on the Transboundary Movement of Hazardous Wastes, to ban exports of toxic waste from OECD to non-OECD countries, including the countries of the East. It was a significant event, for two reasons. First, it was a rare victory for environmental justice — in the East, as in the South, as in poor communities in the North, powerlessness is often rewarded with inordinate numbers of toxic landfills, waste incinerators, dumps, and "recycling" facilities.[124]

Second, the 1994 Basel Amendments will, starting in 1998, begin to ban exports for foreign "recycling." The problem is that even countries that are parties to the convention must pass laws to enforce their Basel commitments, and this offers vast opportunities for legalism and evasion. The coming battles will be long — the United States still seeks to overturn Basel, as do Canada, Australia, and France[125] — and these battles will turn on the diplomatic details, on the official definition of "waste." This, after all, is a world in which pesticides can be banned and yet be exported as "humanitarian aid," so it is hardly a surprise that one man's "waste" is another's "raw material." But if waste is defined narrowly, as material that has fallen altogether out of the "chain of utility," then almost nothing will ever be "waste," at least not by the letter of the law. Most industrialists strongly prefer such a strict definition, which would make it nearly impossible to prohibit the toxics recycling scam, and would establish no precedents by which the transfer of dirty technology to the South might someday be resisted.

It is the West that must first do some leapfrogging — in this case to "clean production," which consumes "a minimum of raw materials and energy, uses sustainable resources wherever possible, and avoids or eliminates toxic waste and hazardous inputs and products."[126] If the West does not do so, it will continue to generate toxic wastes in great

profusion and, given the world's division into rich and poor, perpetu-
ate the vile economics that drive the waste trade. Joel Hirschhorn, a
clean-production expert formerly with the U.S. Congressional Office of
Technology Assessment, put the bottom line bluntly: "The greatest
misconception is that we have to produce toxic waste. That is simply
wrong."[127]

Traffic

"Everyone," said the Polish Ecology Club's Tomasz Terlecki, "is pissed
off about cars."[128] It's an exaggeration, of course — in the East, like
everywhere else, people want cars — but it's easy to see his point.
Throughout Eastern Europe's cities, traffic is much worse than in the
old days. There are cars everywhere. Tram systems are deteriorating.
Between the cities, the roads are thick with trucks. Air-quality improvements that came, at such heavy costs in unemployment, from
shutting down old communist-class industrial plants, are being eaten
away by increased auto emissions.[129]

Not only are many of its cars old, but the East has also become a
huge market for hand-me-down autos from richer Western countries.
More important is the total size of the fleet, which is increasing by
about 10 percent a year, the same rate as in Southeast Asia.[130] This is
the future celebrated in 1991 by the *Financial Times* as a "Potential New
Market of 420M."[131]

In Eastern Europe the largest Western investments have, from the
beginning, been in auto production, roads, gas stations, and the rest of
the auto-industrial complex.[132] The World Bank, for decades the major
source of highway construction funds in the South, has jumped in with
both feet. In fact — and this is quite peculiar for a "development bank"
chartered to invest in the *public* interest — the Bank has pumped hundreds of millions of dollars into *private* motor-vehicle manufacturing
in Eastern Europe.[133] And there is the flip side of all this investment,
the underfunding and shutdown of public transportation systems. The
Czechs abolished about ten thousand bus lines in 1992, leaving countless villages entirely cut off from the public transportation system,[134]
and in 1994 the European Bank for Reconstruction and Development
(EBRD) offered "restructuring loans" to the Bulgarian state railway
that required it to fire thousands of workers and close "inefficient"

local lines. Likewise for the World Bank and Hungary.[135] For those stranded, cars and trucks are the only option. In Poland, local bus fares have skyrocketed because of "cost-recovery" measures urged by the Bank. At the same time, there is money for a major expansion of the road network — the old regime left Poland with 225 kilometers of motorway; the new regime quickly negotiated a huge loan from EBRD to build 2,500 more.[136]

These are facts. What varies is their spin. Darek Sved, the Green Federation activist, told me that "there is tremendous pressure to shut down train lines and build new motorways. Gas is way too cheap. The cost of roads is not factored in, so the car is being subsidized, as usual. Private banks, and Mitsubishi, and, I think, Western car companies are behind the push for more motorways. All this, of course, is represented as 'aid.' "[137] Stanislaw Juchnowicz, a highly respected Polish town planner, went further and insisted that "it is capitalism itself, by way of traffic and 'redevelopment,' that is destroying the central cities of Eastern Europe, as it has already destroyed those in Western Europe. Just compare Krakow to Stuttgart!"[138] On another line altogether, the *Environmental Action Programme for Central and Eastern Europe* prefers the inevitability of the bureaucratic voice: "As living standards begin to recover, both the size and use of the automobile fleet are likely to grow rapidly which will lead to increased problems of photochemical smog and ozone exposure."[139]

There is much more at issue here than increases in "living standards" and the lust for cars. Also at stake is the overall direction of "development." Rail modernization is a fine example. Should the existing system as a whole be upgraded, or should only the "economical" lines be modernized while the rest are shut down? Should the rails be maintained as an alternative to the car for general intercity use, or devolved into a long-haul passenger and freight transportation system designed to integrate the East tightly into West European trade networks? Is such integration even desirable?

Is the East to be renovated in a rational fashion, with an eye to the future, or will it be shaped into a poor look-alike of the West? The second path has already been chosen. Amidst all the opportunities being squandered in the East, the opportunity to establish non-auto-based transportation will be among the most difficult to recover from. Once alternatives to cars have been destroyed, once suburbanization has taken hold, bringing in alternatives is almost impossible.

The myth of the East as an altogether devastated toxic pit is directly relevant here. Even EBRD admits that the environmental impacts of transportation systems are worse in the West than the East,[140] a point that bears emphasizing. There have been so many thousands of images of smog-enshrouded communist cities in the Western press that, recalling them, we almost automatically think that things are not really so bad here in the West. In fact, the best data indicate that, even in 1987, with East-bloc emissions at their peak, Western air pollution transported 520,000 tons more sulfur to the East than was returned. Central and Eastern European countries, writes Polish environmental economist Grzegorz Peszko, "severely pollute one another," but they also "have significant net pollution inflow from Western Europe (mainly from Germany, but also from Italy and the UK)."[141] It may only be an accident of the prevailing winds, but with sulfur dioxide as with toxics, it is more the West that pollutes the East than vice versa.

Lost Opportunities

Nuclear power, Arctic oil drilling, clear-cut logging, toxic dumping, automobile dependence — all are recognized environmental dangers. They are also the tip of a far larger iceberg. Most ecological destruction results not from the operation of mafias but via the routines of daily life, of daily business. Now the East will share those routines. Or, better to say, it will eventually share those routines. In the short run, the going will be even rougher. As one Western tobacco executive put it, "There is little awareness of health and environmental problems in Hungary. We have about ten years of an open playing field."[142]

Western commentators, observing the chaotic transition in the East, are quick to seek out local causes. They find plenty. There are delapidated factories, habits of passivity, ethnic hatred, arrogant commissars, frustrated consumerist longings, bitter and debilitating legacies of all kinds. But even these do not explain the single most glaring fact of the new East — that despite vast opportunity, there has been an almost complete lack of genuinely new departures, that the future has come not as internationally assisted hope and reconstruction, but as a mad scramble for profit and position. This is why greens, and all those who seek a better future, should attend to the East. These are lands embroiled in deep, sudden structural transformations. They are precious test cases, and their lessons are all too clear. The history of the East is unique, but its trajectory is into the same single world that will have us all.

The laws tell part of the tale. Throughout Eastern Europe, great efforts have gone into creating Western-style legal systems, including systems of environmental law. Helping to create these laws has been a strong focus of Western NGO assistance, especially in Poland, Hungary, and the Czech Republic. No one can say whether this effort will meet with success, but certainly there are no guarantees. Here as elsewhere, passing laws is only a beginning.

Are environmental laws being enforced? Ask first if *any* laws are being enforced. In Romania, or the new Russia, even to imply that they might be is to be quickly, and justly, branded the fool. In Bucharest in 1992 the traffic police had to start shooting out tires to reassert the red-light-means-stop rule, and in Russia driving as one may is now considered (by those with cars) to be a basic "human right."[143] In Siberia, a land fated to suffer vast destruction in the years ahead, there is no Environmental Protection Agency, or even a Bureau of Land Management, to erect a shield of regulations. Even in Eastern Europe, where proper laws are often on the books, enforcement is haphazard. In the Czech Republic, the *tax laws* are indifferently enforced, so one may be forgiven a bit of cynical realism about environmental law. As Erica Bassin, a Canadian legal researcher, put it, "Inspectors are not well trained and not motivated . . . and fines are low. There is little incentive to comply."[144]

It may be that this will change, but there are grounds for skepticism. The first is history. Greenpeace's Iza Kruszewska recalls the old regimes — which often had *better* environmental laws than West Europe. "It's a mistake to think that laws are the problem, or the answer to the problem. Poland and the USSR actually banned PVCs for meat wraps in the mid-1980s, while they are still legal in the West. Microwave standards were higher, too, and there are lots of other examples. These laws were all unenforced, of course. It was just communist greenwashing."[145]

The opening to Western investment has often made matters worse. In Poland under the 1988 Solidarity-brokered Roundtable Agreement, environmental grounds alone could justify refusing entry to foreign investors. But the 1991 Joint Venture law dropped this constraint,[146] and greens lost a powerful means of resisting the flood of detergents, plastics, and chemicals now inundating their country. This is the pattern throughout the region, and though time may see it broken by the passage and enforcement of new regulations, just now contract law is almost unique in the civil code for being taken seriously. This, too, could change, but even if it does the habits of the present will likely persist. Ignoring environmental laws is a tradition in the East, one that is now being reinforced, not broken.

And environmental laws are hardly the bottom line. Better to look at patterns of privatization, investment, and capital flow. These suggest a future in which Central and Eastern Europe, and the East in general, become to Western Europe what Mexico is to the United States — "a source of basic commodities, cheap labor, toxic disposal sites, and markets."[147] Is this too pessimistic, or simply realistic? The most obvious point is also the crucial one — the thrust of the East's restructuring has been on the elimination of "state controls,"[148] a process usually known in the West as "deregulation" and one enduringly popular with businesses around the world. Besides, how can any pessimism be less justified than the optimism of the "reformers," who pretend to believe that privatization and fiscal discipline will cohere, in Russia, as in Indonesia, Brazil, and everywhere else, into a rising tide that eventually lifts all boats?

The situation has changed since the early 1990s. At first there was little foreign investment of any kind, and it seemed that the East's markets and raw materials would be its sole entrées into the global economy.[149] Today it is clear that outside firms, aware of the rock-bottom wages in the East, and its lack of effective regulatory controls, are willing to transfer manufacturing there as well, if only social stability can be maintained. As one senior manager at Borsodken, a Hungarian chemical company, put it, "Foreigners come here because of cheap labor, because of lower environmental demands and the lower health and safety standards in the workplace."[150] The East is one "emerging market" among others.[151]

The organization of the global economy virtually ensures that such shifts of manufacturing make a zero-sum game — at least for the majority of people in the formerly secure but now "anxious" classes.[152] This is nowhere more obvious than in West Germany, where the long post–World War II economic boom and strong social democratic unions pushed wages far above the global mean. During the May 1992 public workers strike, the chairman of Daimler-Benz warned that his corporation could respond to strikes by transferring its Mercedes plants elsewhere, perhaps to Russia, with its ample supply of trained, healthy, and, it was hoped, docile workers.[153] A rough road, perhaps, but it will be taken. As U.S. firms look south to Latin America, so European firms look east. The differences are local and incidental, the fundamental truth clear. Capital can freely move; people are far more constrained.

It would be absurd to claim that the West can control events in the East. But it would be equally absurd to claim that the West has done its best to ease its vanquished enemies into a humane new world, or that the "creative destruction" now ravaging the East is a hopeful precedent for the larger future. The key distinction here is between the legacies of the East's own past — its delapidated industries and "old-style thinking" — and the eager advantage being taken of it by Western firms and governments.

Are the huge debts Central European nations inherited from the old regimes, debts now growing ever higher, simply legacies of communist mismanagement, or do the West and its banks hold a large measure of responsibility for them? What are we to make of the fact that unemployment and poverty in the former Soviet bloc have quite predictably skyrocketed, and that it took the beginnings of a neofascist backlash before Western "reformers" even remembered social safety nets? What does it mean that the Czech Republic, the country generally agreed to be the biggest success story in the new East, early in 1994 adopted new labor laws that both restrict unions and lower wages?[154] To know our predicament, we must see just how, and in favor of just what preoccupations, the vast opportunity in the East is being squandered.

Western debates about "reform" always seem to degenerate sooner or later into talk about "aid," as if loosening the strings normally attached to official "development assistance" would be a major step toward a better future. Aid, though, is an extremely warped lens, all the more so if it draws attention from the policies that structure the private economy. Note these words by Jacques Attali, spoken before he lost the presidency of the EBRD. He was speaking of the EC and its policies toward Eastern Europe, but his point is a general one.

The European Community has intentionally chosen to keep the Central and Eastern European countries that have most successfully wrestled [themselves] from communism at a distance from the western markets. Instead of being treated as new member states of Europe they are being considered as potential economic rivals for the rich Western Europe. Why else should the European Community have insisted in the Association Treaties with Poland, Hungary and Czechoslovakia on trade restrictions in areas like agriculture, textiles, coal and steel — exactly the areas that are most promising for the East to earn scarce currency.

One would like to avoid the remarkable conclusion that the Association Treaties of 1991 between the European Community and Poland, Czechoslovakia and Hungary are meant, in the first place, to help the European Community instead of the former communist countries, but it sometimes looks as if the European Community itself has more problems [adjusting] to a post communist Europe than Poland, Czechoslovakia and Hungary.[155]

This "remarkable conclusion" is hard to avoid. East European countries are allowed very limited agricultural exports to the EC (in 1991 these composed only 3 percent of the EC's total agricultural imports), and this limit is only being allowed to increase very slowly. The result is that the EC (now the European Union, or EU), a world center of industrial agriculture and a huge exporter of food in general, is a net exporter of food to the more rural Eastern Europe. This is crucial, for the EU also tightly limits textile, steel, and coal imports from East Europe, and thus locks it out of Western markets in most all its strongest areas.[156] The same is true of Russia, which finds Europe's markets far less welcoming than its rhetoric. Manufacturing, to be sure, is a complex case, and the East has historically manufactured little that is wanted in Western Europe. But this is changing, and as it does the advantage accrues not to the Eastern people, but to the Western firms and Eastern elites that control the vast bulk of the East's new ventures. The pattern is of Western-dominated joint partnerships that manufacture in the East, where labor and environmental costs are low, and hope soon to distribute not only locally, but to the West as well — a prospect that terrifies West European unions.[157]

The Soviet Union was once Eastern Europe's largest trading partner. Now both blocs are trading more with the West than with each other, and this trade is heavily skewed toward raw materials rather than finished goods — hardly a situation favorable to the balanced development of the East.[158] And who is to blame? Western protectionism and marketing are clearly among the culprits, but they do not stand alone. By the early 1990s, trade within Eastern Europe had plummeted to a fraction of its former level, as had trade between the former Soviet republics, and these sudden falls cannot be explained by Western policies, not in any simple sense. An almost mythic longing for Western goods, nationalist bickering, the every-country-for-itself character of the rush to the West — these factors, too, helped impel the East to offer itself dirt cheap as a junior partner in an already overcompetitive global economy.

Still, the West is the beneficiary of the East's desperation, a fact that makes Western pretenses about "trade" being always to the good ring deeply hollow. On the one hand, the East is being told to reform its economies, while on the other it is being denied credit, encouraged to dismantle its social security systems, and integrated into the world economy in a manner that has embittered the majority of its peoples.[159] Even the eagerly procapitalist president of Poland, Lech Walesa, felt the anger, and expressed it — as when, in early 1992, he told the Council of Europe, "It's you who have profited by the Polish revolution."[160]

The West's policies can be traced in the physical details of the reconstruction. Highway networks dominated by international truck traffic, as the East German Green League's Christian Koth argued in 1991, make "the East European countries a welcome market for Western Europe but hinder their sound economic development."[161] The same can be true of electrical-power networks. Sebastian Pflugbeil, a former East German politician turned member of the Berlin parliament, wants to see an innovative energy sector built in the East, one based on modern gas turbines and alternative energy. Instead, the Western power grid is being extended east. "The old structures are all being destroyed," said Pflugbeil, "and many people feel they are out on the street without a future."[162]

No wonder that people, according to the Polish Public Opinion Research Center, "prefer being poisoned slowly to losing their jobs."[163] No wonder there are so many opportunities to frighten people into thinking environmental improvements will cost them their jobs, to practice what Western greens have long called "job blackmail." No wonder the restoration is breeding such dark forces. In Russia, reports

Sergei Fomichov, copresident of the League of Green Parties, "the authorities are turning people against the Greens, claiming that it's environmentalists who are responsible for factories closing down."[164] Scared people want scapegoats, and greens are perfect, for they are weak.

Duncan Fisher, the director of the East-West Environment Programme at London's Ecological Studies Institute, captured the problem exactly.

> The working class . . . is highly conservative and antagonistic to change, including towards environmental issues if they are seen to be related to factory closures. A television documentary made in Romania by a small NGO, Friends of the Living Planet, showed a series of interviews with workers in the factory town of Zlatna. Awareness of and concern for appalling local environmental conditions were found to be high, but there was no suggestion that anything could be done about it.[165]

The key phrase is "there was no suggestion that anything could be done about it," and it implies the key question. Can anything be done, and if so, why is there "no suggestion" that this might be the case? It's been decades since groups like Environmentalists for Full Employment demonstrated that solar energy, rationally pursued, would create good jobs in vast profusion.[166] But even in the West, despite seemingly permanent levels of high unemployment and the urgent need for solar reconstruction, such ideas remain on the margins of political debate.[167]

Nor do state-of-the-art green technologies fit well into the postcommunist prospect. How could the East, a dazed region desperate for admission into the hypercompetitive capitalist world order that evolved while it was trapped inside its stiff, decomposing utopia, lead the way to a new economy? On this point, Andrej Kassenberg, now the head of Warsaw's rather optimistically named Institute for Sustainable Development, was clear. "Little shortcuts are all that we can hope for. All our time is spent trying to make privatization marginally less destructive."[168]

It is a poignant situation, particularly because so short a time has passed since the euphoria of 1989 and 1990. That euphoria was both powerful and beautiful, and its loss brought a bitter knowledge. Margaret Bowman and David Hunter, a married team of American environmental law experts, were caught up in the moment, along with thousands of others throughout the world. In 1990 they quit their Washington jobs and moved to Eastern Europe, where, said Bowman, "we thought there was a chance to do something really new." They found, instead, that "there was no third way." Returning to the States, they wrote that the region had moved from "high hopes to hard reality," specifically from the high hopes that

> the new governments could learn from forty years of mistakes (in both the East and the West) regarding environmental protection, and could leapfrog over the years of struggle that have taken the West from the uncontrolled industrial destruction of the 1940s and 1950s to where we are today (wherever that may be). The hard reality of today's Central Europe is that the emerging democracies in the region have taken a place in line behind all other industrial nations in what is at best a slow trudge towards sustainable development.[169]

Instead of leapfrogging the West, the East is becoming its pathetic grotesque. Public transit systems are decaying as the auto-industrial culture masses for a full attack. Reconstruction on the basis of green technology remains the rare exception. People are angry, afraid, and thrashing with frustration. Already in 1991 Romanian environmentalists were attacked as "antination." By 1992 Slovakian antidam activists who had recently been hailed as heroes of both ecology and democracy were suffering public attacks by protofascist politicians as "internal enemies." Three months after their "revolution," 90 percent of Slovaks said they considered environmental degradation to be a serious threat; by January of 1992 this figure had dropped to a mere 5 percent.[170] No wonder. By then the Slovaks had other problems, and they knew it.

"Structural Adjustment"

Why blame the West? Why blame anyone at all? Is it not the case, as Henryk Wujec, a veteran Polish dissident and now a deputy, told writer Laurence Weschler, that "first capital is always wild"? Why worry at all? "Large fortunes get generated through wild swindles, but then they serve as the foundation. In America, after all, you first killed all your Indians."[171]

Such massive and cynical optimism manages simultaneously to counsel complacence and leave everyone off the hook, for everything. Like the ideology of laissez-faire, this notion — that the brutality of the restoration is a natural fact — denies that policies are in place, that choices are actively being made every day. Obviously the East must change, but the names by which we know such change — deregulation, shock therapy, privatization, free trade, and so on — do not designate a just or sustainable future.

The operational euphemism here is "structural adjustment." What is structural adjustment? One point is key — "adjust" is an active verb. In sharp contrast to the assiduously cultivated view that the economy moves along lines designated by a sovereign market logic, "adjustment" implies an adjuster, a policy maker. And in fact, whether by design or default, the team formed by the World Bank and the International Monetary Fund does in many ways act as the architect of global economic policy.

Structural adjustment begins with loans, or, rather, with debt. It begins with the fact that most of the IMF's lending, and a large fraction of the Bank's, is not spent financing specific projects of any kind — good, bad, or debatable — but is rather aimed at changing, often by draconian means, the economic policies of recipient nations. These are "structural adjustment loans" (SALs), and in the East as in the South, they come with heavy strings attached. The strings are the "structural adjustment programs" (SAPs) — the policy.

SALs were introduced by the Bank in 1979, when rising Third World debt was widely taken as a crisis demanding official action. Their founding justification was that the ailing, debt-ridden economies of the South needed new loans to avoid defaulting on their old loans, but that these new loans had to be conditioned by fiscal discipline and tough debt-management strategies, and by the opening of inefficient local economies to the cleansing winds of the world market. Today, with most Southern countries having undergone adjustment, the focus of "reform" has turned to the former East bloc and to India. In the post–Cold War world, no nation can refuse the bean counters — without the seal of approval that only the IMF and Bank can bestow, countries are not deemed creditworthy and cannot qualify for loans of any kind.

Few matters are as contentious as structural adjustment. In the orthodox neoliberal mind, it is the best means of correcting the "severe imbalances" that distort "protected" economies. The East is easily cited to support this view — its economic imbalances are many and extreme. Greens and development activists prefer to stress that SAPs are radically unfair to the poor; they long ago labeled SAPs as "austerity programs" and made them notorious throughout the Third World. Despite all their talk of balance, the neoliberals promote a model of adjustment as distorted as the old Soviet economy. The typical SAP:

- Privatizes state corporations and severely downsizes public institutions. This exacerbates unemployment and undercuts public service ministries — health, education, transport, housing, environment, and so on — through drastic budget reductions.

- Promotes raw-materials exports and export-led industries to earn foreign exchange. This means import liberalization and the elimination of trade barriers or quotas.

- Eliminates or sharply reduces subsidies for agriculture, food staples, health care, education, and other necessities. Such austerity is justified as tough, necessary medicine. Notably, it does not often extend to the military.

- Restricts monetary policies, raises interest rates, and reduces real wages, all in order to control inflation. The reduction of wages, when mandated by a SAP, is generally called "demand management."[172]

This is not a menu calculated to encourage creative new departures, sustainable development, rational long-term planning, high levels of social welfare, or even economic growth. The typical end result of these "reforms," according to Rudiger Dornbusch, an economist at the Massachusetts Institute of Technology, is that the economy "falls into a hole."[173] In late 1994 the collapse of Mexico demonstrated just how deep such a hole can be.

The similarity between SAPs in general and "reform" in the East is a fundamental one. The essence of structural adjustment is getting the state out of the economy. Walden Bello, a Philippine activist intellectual and an authority on neoliberal economics, put it this way: "Structural adjustment was still experimental when it was being developed for the South. By the time it got to the East, it had become a dogma, the dogma of 'Shock therapy.' "[174]

Moreover, SAPs are often ecologically disastrous, as East bloc environmentalists are learning for themselves, and from their fellows in the South. Structural adjustment causes environmental destruction in at least three ways, all of which demonstrate that environmental and social protection cannot reasonably be separated.

• It increases economic insecurity and poverty, and thus forces people into ecologically destructive situations. In the South this often means forcing peasants onto marginal lands. In industrial contexts it means job blackmail and hostility toward environmentalism.

• It forces indebted countries to accelerate exports of natural resources in order to generate export earnings and balance their budgets. This leads to deforestation, soil erosion, desertification, and water pollution.

• It slashes environmental protection budgets, thus seriously and even fatally undermining the enforcement of environmental laws. Lax enforcement is also likely when "developing countries" are locked out of the global economic mainstream and then seek their "competitive advantage" in exploited labor and ecological rapine.

Structural adjustment became controversial in 1987, when a UNICEF report showed that women, children, and the poor "bore the brunt of economic contraction associated with adjustment programs"[175] — a delicate way of talking about immiserization and even starvation. More recently, a great deal of evidence has filled out the story of SAPs by spelling out their role in environmental destruction.

Examples of structural adjustment promoting environmental destruction are numerous and depressing. In Thailand, for instance, industrialization has followed the deregulatory neoliberal model, and come at the cost of severe environmental degradation, resource depletion (especially deforestation), urban pollution, and congestion.[176] Thailand is a country in which adjustment lending has played a role secondary to "development" in general, but that role has nevertheless been notable, and has helped define an economy in which, in 1989, hazardous waste–generating industries accounted for 58 percent of industrial GNP, up from 29 percent in 1979.[177] Thailand, still a beautiful country, is now positioned to be a full participant in the ecological holocaust now overtaking Southeast Asia.

In the Philippines, a country being overcome by ecological crisis, direct structural manipulation by the Bank and IMF has been a stronger force. The main direct environmental impacts of SAPs in the Philippines, according to a 1992 study by Washington's World Resources Institute, were results of policies designed to stabilize its external debt. The chain of causation is not difficult to trace — the trade regime, investment incentives, and credit policies all favored capital-intensive industries and larger farmers; this directly reduced income and employment opportunities for the rural poor; this set off mass migrations to forested upland regions, marginal land, and coastal areas; this in turn led to depletion of forests, mangroves, and fisheries, and greatly increased soil erosion.[178]

Ghana is a deeply troubled country which, not coincidentally, has enjoyed one of the longest-running IMF/World Bank "economic reform" programs in all of Africa. There, a fixation on expanding export income led to massive investments in logging and to a reduction of the country's forest cover to 25 percent of its original size. At the same time, in testimony to the logic of this strange "reform," Ghana's external debt increased from $1.4 billion to $4.2 billion in only nine years.[179]

SAPs lay the groundwork for new trade relations. As Ross Hammond, an analyst with Washington's Development Group for Alternative Policies (Development GAP), put it, "They reorient economies outward. That's the whole point. Basically, during adjustment, you provide incentives to invest in your country — low wages, loose regulations, easy access to raw materials, and so on."[180] SAPs, in other words, impose a "sound policy environment"[181] favorable to a model of global integration that leaves countries, and particularly weak countries, at the mercy of international capital flows. This is "free trade," though not trade freely chosen.

Smitu Kothari, an Indian activist, expressed a common Southern view when he told me he was "convinced that the Bank is playing a key role in the restructuring of the world economy, a role integral to the emerging nexus of GATT, the IMF, and so on." Why did he think so? The numbers. Ten years ago, about 5 percent of the Bank's lending was directly earmarked for the restructuring of Third World economies. By 1992 it had risen to 25 percent, where, much of the job done, it peaked.[182] This comes to plenty of adjustment, Kothari said, plenty of "the kind of economic development that relies on the intensive *extraction* of natural resources, their flow from the country to the cities, and from the cities to markets abroad," plenty of "marginalization and impoverishment, and, of course, environmental destruction."[183]

The history of structural adjustment flatters neither the World Bank nor the IMF. The Bank is nominally a development bank, founded after World War II to build a durable peace, not as an instrument of global deregulation and environmental destruction.[184] If it and its kin — the IMF, EBRD, the regional development banks in Africa, Latin America, and Asia — are widely thought to pursue goals other than honest development, then major changes will not only *be* on the international agenda, they will be *seen* to be on it as well. This is happening, in the East as in the South. For years, senior Russian officials have been denouncing IMF bureaucrats as "neo-Bolsheviks" who are "imposing alien rules of economic and political conduct and stifling economic freedom."[185] By 1992, with the dismemberment of Yugoslavia and instability in Russia, pressure for more "realistic" transition programs sharply increased, especially for Russia.[186] By late 1993, when Al Gore, as U.S. vice president, announced to the world that "the IMF board has been slow to recognize the hardship caused by some of what has been done in the past. . . . That may cause a diplomatic incident, but I don't care,"[187] it was clear that the development managers had a major public relations problem.

The Bank's trail through the East is equally fascinating, as is the impact it has had on the green debate about the Bank's future.[188] Briefly, as a report to the Charles Stewart Mott Foundation explained in 1992, the positions within the debate are drawn between "'reformists' that generally accept the reality of the continued existence of the international financial institutions, at least for the medium term; and 'abolitionists' that identify their goals as elimination of the multilaterals altogether."[189] Ideologically and tactically, the lines are not clearly drawn. In early 1993 Lauri Udall, now of Berkeley's International Rivers Network, called herself a "closet abolitionist."[190] In this she is not alone. Few people, however bitterly they hate the Bank, expect it to be abolished anytime soon.

One thing is certain: the East is a key test case. Alex Hittle of Friends of the Earth, in a tutorial on the Bank that he wrote for Eastern activists, summed up the challenge of the East. "It will be a difficult test for the Bank and the people of the region. . . . If the Bank does well, then it may learn lessons that can be applied in other developing countries. If the Bank does badly, it will strengthen the arguments of those who believe it must be shut down."[191]

There was a stir a few years back, when the European Bank for Reconstruction and Development was first organized, for its charter contains the promise that the bank will promote, "in the full range of its activities environmentally sound and sustainable development," as well as democracy and human rights.[192] The main product of that clause, though, has been cynicism. David Hunter, of the Center for International Environmental Law, told me that European activists, having been seduced into optimism once, would not fall so easily again. "The clause caused a lot of euphoria about greening the banks a while back," but "the trend is in just the opposite direction. EBRD's policies and procedures, as opposed to its charter, are worse than the World Bank's."[193]

John Hontelez, chair of Friends of the Earth International and coordinator of its Central and Eastern Europe program, agreed, and even expressed optimism. "It may be that the problems of the ex-socialist countries are more appropriately addressed by the kinds of large-scale industrial programs that the World Bank is capable of. In the South, where small, somewhat self-subsistent communities still form the basis of society, the Bank has been a bulldozer, but in the East you have massive industrial apparatuses that simply need to be modernized."[194]

Bob Wilkinson, founding dean of the graduate program in environmental science at the new Central European University in Budapest, is, for his part, "guardedly optimistic . . . because unlike the early 1980s, when the Bank had a flood of petrodollars, now they have to be sure that their investments are going to pay off." And with "the proper accounting, and the right people making decisions, the Bank will promote some reasonable development strategies, especially in the areas of water and energy." He added, though, that "the EBRD has been a real disappointment. It's picked up a lot of recycled Bank people, and is even more committed to being a true bank, with the majority of its loans going to the private sector. And it's even more secretive than is the World Bank itself, which isn't easy."[195]

Richard Ackermann, of the World Bank's Environment Department, is, of course, optimistic. Ackermann was involved in developing the *Environmental Action Programme for Central and Eastern Europe* and considers it to be "ahead of the curve, not only in Central and Eastern Europe, but in the West as well." "It's not a matter of greening the bank, but a matter of learning to produce good projects in the first place. There's no real difference between environment, poverty alleviation, or other aspects of development in this regard."[196]

Margaret Bowman, the former director of the Environmental Law Institute's Program for Central and Eastern Europe, rejects not only Ackermann's confidence, but even the idea that the *Action Programme* is a departure.

> It says so many things it says nothing. It's like the Bible. You can read through it and justify anything you want. In a way, it's destructive, because its clearest message is that the market will take care of everything. In its executive summary it says that "market reform — especially industrial restructuring — in combination with appropriate environmental measures will take care of a large part of the emissions causing health and economic damage in the regions." Well, in Eastern Europe, when people read that, they don't see the part about "in combination with appropriate environmental measures."[197]

In 1994 an EBRD team approached Bulgaria with an energy-efficiency plan that would reduce sulfurous brown-coal fumes and save energy by cutting industrial waste. Coming from EBRD, this was a major advance, but Bulgaria rejected the idea out of hand. The Ministry of Energy wanted to produce more energy, not less, and cited concern for the thousands of miners whose jobs would be lost in serious moves toward an energy-efficient economy. This, EBRD's staff complained, was "old thinking,"[198] and perhaps it was, but it nicely illustrates the limits of isolated technical reforms. "Better projects" alone will not cure nations locked in neoliberal economic trajectories. And if concern for unemployment and poverty is "old thinking," we have a real problem.

Energy-policy reform will not come easily at EBRD, which has as its principal goal the privatization of the East. Indeed, it has come to pursue this goal with such vigor that, *The Economist* wrote, "it may even become an example for other development banks."[199] Too bad, then, that privatization, glorified above all else, breeds insecurity and even hatred, and does not encourage "sustainable development." There are alternatives, but they are not on the EBRD's agenda, nor that of the World Bank itself. Certainly they are not on the IMF's! If there is hope, it is that the story of the East, like that of the South, makes the need for new policies obvious. As Sovietologist Stephen Cohen told me back in 1992, "Even the IMF knows that its prescriptions are not working, and even making the situation worse. Of course, they are going to have a hard time making changes. If they make an exception for Russia, then Mexico and Brazil and everyone else will want the same treatment."[200]

Turning South

In early 1993 Richard Nixon, reborn an elder statesman, wrote that "shortsighted Western governments and bankers have to face up to the fact that if the [Russian] debt is not rescheduled, they are likely to get nothing from any government which replaces Mr. Yeltsin's. We should demand that the bureaucrats running the International Monetary Fund not treat Russia like a third world country."[201]

To which the obvious reply is, Why not? Why should the IMF treat *any* country like a Third World country? We fear the rise of fascism in Russia, but certainly the danger is not confined to this one disappointed nation. Are Russians special because they have nuclear ICBMs? Because they are white? It may take an effort, but we must manage to remember that the people of the East have no monopoly on frustrated aspiration.

At the Earth Summit, Eastern countries pleaded that their special status "in transition" to capitalism justified special consideration. Southern politicians, not surprisingly, were both angered and frightened by this initiative, and by signs that it had not fallen on deaf ears.[202] During the Summit's final preparation conference, when the debate over "financing" began to quicken, the Northern countries had rushed past one another to plead poverty — yet somehow they found $6 billion to prop up the ruble. Then, at Rio, there were persistent rumors of an attempt, led by Germany, to assemble a large fund of cash to upgrade Soviet nuclear reactors before they blew. The *Earth Summit Times* commented:

Few would deny the importance of these expenditures. But the apparent ease with which these funds were assembled leads many in the G-77 [the "Group of 77," the UN's Southern bloc countries] to question the poverty of Northern treasuries. And Chancellor [Helmut] Kohl's remark yesterday that Germany wants recognition of its huge expenditures in Eastern Europe as it proceeds to [meet its foreign aid targets] must have set off alarm bells in many delegations.[203]

Just after Rio, I asked Andrej Kassenberg how he would describe relations between the East and the South. "Delicate" was the word he chose. But is the East receiving money that would previously have gone to the South? "Yes, but no one wants to put it on the table. It remains in the shadows."[204] Margaret Bowman was more forthcoming. "I suspect, but cannot prove, that money is being taken from other places" to go to the former East bloc. "It's obvious that Central Europe is getting all this attention because the people there are like us. Sometimes I'm embarrassed to be an expert on Central Europe."[205]

A year later, the fog had lifted. "Sub-Saharan Africa," the *New York Times* noted, "has been the biggest loser as the cold war has ended." The World Bank, as if to prove the point, had reduced loan commitments to sub-Saharan Africa by $1.2 billion in its 1993 fiscal year. In East Europe, meanwhile, these commitments rose from $1.7 billion to $3.8 billion.[206] The world's rich nations have forgotten the Rio speeches in which they pledged increasing aid to the South. Sweden, the EC, Canada, and even Holland have *cut* their development assistance budgets and, under the pressure of deficits and recession, "clarified" the rules by which they tie strings to their aid. Canada has not only reduced its aid budget, but has also diverted much of what remains from the South to Eastern Europe and moved to tie the aid it grants to "middle-income countries" more closely to Canadian corporate interests.[207]

We would all be better off if we understood the realities that hide under the term "aid." Accustomed to the assumption that "aid" is always to the good, I was unprepared when recently, in a bar in Berkeley, I found myself in semisurly confrontation with two gentlemen who wanted to know why "we should give more damn aid to Africa." Logic failed me, and so, I'm afraid, did facts. Between 1985 and 1992, Africa gave back $81.6 billion — a quarter of its export earnings — in debt repayments, and this despite its falling far behind on its obligations. This is the bill for the aid that was *loaned* to Africa in the past, aid that was once confidently touted as the catalyst that would bring Africa into the modern world. Instead, it financed the vanities of the powerful, buttressed Cold War alliances, erected the high dams and deep ports of a dubious industrialization, and eventually solidified into a crushing debt. "Aid" became just another burden, just another chapter in a long and brutal history. So much of Africa's debt is owed to the IMF that between 1983 and 1990 the Fund took $3 billion from that devastated continent — much of which African countries had to borrow from the World Bank. "In effect," noted one wit, "money just moves from the World Bank side of Nineteenth Street in Washington to the IMF side."[208]

Of all the conundrums that bedevil environmental politics, none is as difficult as "aid." Aid, my barroom friends were convinced, was "like welfare," a "handout" that, as right-wing Republican Jesse Helms later put it, just drains away down "foreign rat-holes."[209] When I told them that most aid came as loans, or as "tied" or "linked" aid that could only be used to purchase goods and services from donor-country firms, it simply did not register. And yet the details are amazing. For example, more than half the World Bank's 1992–93 "aid" to the poorest nations ended up in the world's ten richest countries, where it was spent on equipment and technical advice.[210] In fact, the U.S. Treasury Department defends the World Bank's procurements to an increasingly skeptical Congress by arguing that more of the Bank's aid expenditures are spent in the United States than in any other country, and that the U.S. share will only rise: "Improving U.S. performance in this area is a key item in [the Clinton] administration's agenda for change in the multilateral development banks."[211]

Throughout the West, moreover, most bilateral "aid" is given with an eye to domestic payback. Eighty percent of Canadian aid is tied to the purchase of Canadian exports, while as much as 98 percent of British aid is said never to leave Britain. In the United States, according to the Agency for International Development, a "Buy America" program holds that figure to 70 percent.[212] No wonder true humanitarian assistance programs like Child Survival or the distribution of polio vaccine make up only about 10 percent of U.S. foreign aid.

The Japanese grant more "aid" than any other nation, and are explicit about the strings they tie to it. In 1994 Japan virtually ordered four of its Caribbean aid-recipient nations to support its diplomatic assault on the global whaling ban.[213] More routinely, Japan uses "aid" to finance exports, to build large-scale facilities for exploiting and processing raw materials in countries like Brazil and Indonesia, to introduce Japanese banks and trading companies into developing countries, to move hazardous plants to offshore sites, to secure access to Pacific fishing waters, and even to ease the phaseout of industrial sectors that are no longer economical in Japan.[214]

Yet "aid," in the South as in the East, is almost always the answer, whatever the question. Richard Nixon, a sincere friend of the Russians, spent much of his last year lobbying the IMF to cut Russia large new loans, and ever since December 1993, when Vladimir Zhirinovsky won a huge percent of the popular vote, Nixon had had plenty of company. NGOs in the East and politicians in the South want Northern countries and the World Bank to greatly increase aid budgets, though they know that, with more aid, their countries will fall deeper into debt. NGOs around the world constantly stumble over the rhetoric of aid, though many of them should know better.

Aid, an old saw has it, is the transfer of money from poor people in rich countries to rich people in poor countries, and it does not seem that it should figure large in the NGO program. Yet it does. NGO activists, like liberal reformers and Richard Nixon, *want* aid to be good. For decades now, titles like *Aid as Obstacle, Odious Debts, Lent and Lost,* and *Lords of Poverty*[215] have bloomed on the sharper edges of the development literature. But how can the clarity of such volumes — clarity about what Kristin Dawkins, the research director at the Institute for Agriculture and Trade Policy, in Minneapolis, sums up as the "trade-debt-aid cycle"[216] — stand against the desire to *do something,* something that is possible *now?*

At the Earth Summit, Southern activists made no secret of their fear that the evolving world trade system would lead to their "recolonization."[217] But what about the East? As of 1992 about 15 percent of all Western aid to Poland, Czechoslovakia, and Hungary had come as grants, the rest as highly restricted loans. In early 1993 the papers were filled with ballyhoo about the West's $24 billion bailout for Russia, but with few exceptions, the bailout was criticized only for the glacial pace at which it was moving, not for the fact that it was composed largely of loans and tied aid.[218] By late 1993, with anxiety high, money began to flow a bit more freely, but still it came largely as loans. This may be the capitalist way, but let us at least admit that it is dangerous.

The East is not ours to lose, but that subtlety aside, it is likely that we will live to see the shortsightedness with which the West has met the collapse of its traditional enemies deeply and bitterly recriminated. No doubt, too, we will hear that there were no real choices, that nothing could have been done differently. It may clarify matters to recall the Marshall Plan, and to know that more than three-quarters of its funds were straight grants, many of them made to a West Germany that had lost only about 12 percent of its physical capital stock in the war. Compare that to the 40 percent or more that is estimated to be altogether worthless in the East today.[219]

It takes a world banker to remember the truth. When I asked Richard Ackermann what he thought about the transfer of development aid from the South to the East, his answer startled me with its unselfconsciousness. "Sweden giving money to Eastern Europe instead of to the South? Of course. That's only natural. They're neighbors, after all. Besides, most of the loans to the South just haven't been performing."[220]

Those Who Do Not Remember the Past . . .

The Cold Warriors left us a depressing world, and a tough question — what comes next? In days long gone, it was the dream of socialism that shaped hopes for a better world, especially among the poor and powerless. Only later, and perhaps in response, was there the dream of "development," a dream crazy with images of wealth, blue jeans, and big automobiles. Today those who reject development reach for hope in "sustainable development," but just now, after the much-advertised death of socialism, amidst a brutal globalization, they may be forgiven if they suspect it a vague and colorless notion.

We know that major social changes are needed, but we have no good idea of how they might come about or what might be possible if they did. The "revolution" in the East, certainly, offers no useful model of renewal. The collapse of communism is less an inspiration than a warning, more a tale of exhaustion than one of rebirth and historical opportunity.

In 1989 a little-known U.S. State Department official named Francis

Fukuyama won instant international fame with his essay claiming that the "triumph of Western liberal democracy" was the "end of history," and would usher in a long period of stability and even boredom.[221] It was a timely prediction (made before the fall of the Berlin Wall), but today it is best remembered for the eagerness with which it was received, and for the fantastic speed with which its moment passed. Capitalism has triumphed, but capitalism is many things, and it is difficult, in the face of ecological decay and a booming arms trade, to believe that its liberal-democratic variant has won the day, that the future will be painted in colors of stability and prosperity.

We cannot know what would be possible if "sustainable development" were taken seriously, if real efforts were made to phase out fossil fuels for a renewable-energy economy, to strike a global New Deal, to invent the egalitarian modernization that is the real hope of the poor and the weak. Instead we see the rapid globalization of Latin American–style capitalism, and try as we may, we cannot avoid an increasingly obvious conclusion — that the new order will not be pretty, nor will it deal gently with the hopeful.

In the early days of industrial capitalism, the "worldly philosophers" — Adam Smith, David Ricardo, Thomas Malthus, Karl Marx — spent much of their time wondering about the fault lines they saw running through the substrates of the new economy. Now, in the age of ecology, those fault lines have risen into easy view. With the whole world seeking its fortunes in exports, who will import? What will happen to the several billion people who find no welcome in the new economy, and the tens of millions more who will join them yearly? Consolation comes only in necessity. Our planet is small at last, and we will not forever be able to seek prosperity in the impoverishment of others and the destruction of first nature. Ecology compels us, finally, to ask if there is a decent future for any if there is not a decent future for all. Frieder Wolf, a veteran activist of the German Green Party, offered me a cogent summary:

> The easy way of posing ecological problems is past, because it is no longer possible to go the way of tech fixes and mandatory controls. The restructuring is taking place in such a negative way that, unless the ecological problem is raised in the context of that restructuring, it is no longer possible to be taken seriously. It is nec-

essary to tell people, for example, that ecological transformation will create jobs, will create a new future and a new kind of social security, or else there is no possibility of being taken seriously.[222]

Long ago George Santayana told us that "those who do not remember the past are condemned to repeat it." If this is true, then we are in for a rough time. Already there is a vogue for "green-baiting," in which environmentalists are attacked as "reds" by those who know well the power of anticommunist fearmongering. In early 1991 George Sessions, coauthor of *Deep Ecology*, warned me against "tomatoes, who start off green and turn red."[223] At the time I thought it only the bitter remark of a man whose creed was being overtaken by history. I soon learned that the joke was everywhere, even in Russia. Its twisted essence was well voiced by George Reisman, a poisonous Ayn Randite professor, who in 1991 told an audience of Berkeley students that "the support of most intellectuals for the environmental movement comes from guilt feelings about humanity rooted in their support for socialism. . . . They have blood on their hands."[224]

George Reisman's students will not likely remember the past. How could they? Which of our historians tells them, today, that even the Russian Revolution was born of a longing for justice and emancipation, and that it sank into its authoritarian passion during a terrible civil war in which, not incidentally, the czarists were armed and funded by the West? Who tells them that the Cold War, according to no less an authority than George Kennan, the U.S. State Department "wise man" whose policy of "containment" virtually defined the Cold War, was a product of "the extreme militarization" of American discussion and policy, which "consistently strengthened the comparable hard-liners in the Soviet Union." Who tells them that, again according to Kennan, "the general effect of Cold War extremism was to delay rather than hasten the great change that overtook the Soviet Union at the end of the 1980s."[225]

It is odd to live though a historical moment, one we must remember if we would avoid eternal repetition. It would be best if we remembered the truth — that after its victory the West was paralyzed by ideology and cheap preoccupation, that it offered the East only the IMF, the trade-aid-debt cycle, and a second-class ticket on the slow trip into a devastated and desolate future.

New World Orders?

Free trade and a level playing field are illusions. If I told you the details of social and environmental policies in Brazil I would make you weep. Suffice it to say that they consist mainly of bullets, bulldozers and boxes of matches. Farmers in the UK can never hope to compete with that and I don't advise them to try.

— "An international farmer
from Kent and Brazil"[1]

Goods produced under conditions which do not meet a rudimentary standard of decency should be regarded as contraband and ought not be allowed to pollute the channels of interstate trade.

— Franklin D. Roosevelt[2]

The 1846 European harvest was a failure. The wheat crop was thin, oats and barley "deficient," rye and potatoes total losses. Everywhere food supplies dropped, prices rose, and a "general famine" ensued. In Ireland special conditions led to a special catastrophe — the potato famine that was the largest single "starvation event" of the nineteenth century.

Few of those special conditions are adequately stressed in the routine histories of the potato famine. I have, for example, a British encyclopedia that says only that the famine was caused by a "parasitic fungus."[3] This is true, but hardly adequate. In fact the blight, *Phytophthora infestans,* was able to flourish as it did, wiping out almost the entire Irish potato crop, because that crop had become a monoculture — and monocultures will always be vulnerable to sudden and fatal pesti-

lence.⁴ Add the feudal conditions and grim poverty of the Irish countryside, a poverty that encouraged early marriage and high population
growth, and even in good times reduced the peasant's diet to an un-
healthy, potato-heavy monotony, and you have the well-known part of
the story.

The rest? Different writers tell different tales. Al Gore, in one of the
most interesting chapters of *Earth in the Balance* — "Climate and Civilization: A Short History" — chooses a green revisionism that empha-
sizes the potato famine's position at the end of the "little ice age," the
long cold spell that lasted from about 1550 to 1850. The potato blight,
it seems, reproduces well only under very specific conditions, and
these were provided in 1846, when long and heavy rains arrived to
moisten fields already stressed by one of the hottest summers in memory. The blight had probably arrived in Europe decades earlier, but
only in that strange summer did it thrive.⁵

For the deeper story of the potato famine, go to *The Great Hunger*, by
Cecil Woodham-Smith, where you will learn that "throughout the famine years the 'native produce' of Ireland was leaving her shores in a
'torrent of food.'" In fact, "'during all the famine years,' wrote John
Mitchel, an Irish revolutionary, 'Ireland was actually producing sufficient food, wool and flax, to feed and clothe not nine but eighteen millions of people'; yet, he asserted, a ship sailing into an Irish port during
the famine years with a cargo of grain was 'sure to meet six ships sailing out with a similar cargo.'" Mitchel's remarks were supported by
those of others far more loyal to the British crown.⁶

What was on those "six ships"? Export grains in the form of wheat,
oats, and barley, or, as we would say today, cash crops. The peasants
grew far more than potatoes, but they "dared not" eat the rest, to the
point that "the Irish people did not regard wheat, oats and barley as
food — they were grown to pay the rent and to pay the rent was the
first necessity of life." In time, a movement to oppose food exports
grew, and spread, and won support from the more humane among
the landed gentry. It did not, unfortunately, impress Britain's Lord
Trevelyan, who largely controlled the Irish relief effort. An avid supporter of laissez-faire capitalism, he cautioned others "not [to] encourage the idea of prohibiting exports," and explained that "perfect Free
Trade is the right course." The less ideological Sir Randolph Routh of
the Relief Commission estimated that sixty thousand tons of oats alone,

apart from much other produce, had left Ireland by the end of the 1846 harvest, and argued that these exports, amid rising famine, were a "serious evil." Trevelyan, however, was unmoved. According to free-trade doctrine, such exports would serve the "greater good," as the export of high-priced grains would provide Irish merchants with the money to purchase and import low-priced foods to replace the potato.[7] When reality did not conform to doctrine, starvation came.

Thus it was during the nineteenth century, as the industrial revolution allowed Britain — with its military power and its monopoly on the techniques of mass-production — to force open the borders not only of Ireland but of India and China as well. India was the leading textile producer in the eighteenth century, and had a stable agricultural system. Both were wiped out in the nineteenth century. In China, too, modern history began the hard way, as the doctrine of free trade found good use, along with the guns of the British navy, in opening Chinese borders to the free flow of opium.

Thus it is today — with crucial variations. The naive colonialism of the past, when Rudyard Kipling could unabashedly write about the "white man's burden," has faded into the larger and still almost uncomprehended movement called globalization. This time, *all* the borders — from Ireland to China to India to Mexico — are being opened, and less by guns than by the "inevitable" expansion of industry and world trade. This time it is not only Irish peasants who eat by virtue of fragile and exotic monocultures. And this time, too, ecological destabilization is destined to play a large role in shaping history, and not only because the climate is warming — though it is, and not by so natural a cause as the end of a little ice age.

The Second Coming of "Free Trade"

During the 1980s the world's elite politicians set out on a program of trade liberalization that was unprecedented in its ambition. Negotiations over the European Common Market, the North American Free Trade Agreement (NAFTA), and the Asia Pacific Economic Cooperation Forum (APEC) defined three vast regional trade blocs, overarched by the General Agreement on Tariffs and Trade (GATT), the mother of all trade treaties. By the end of 1994, when GATT and its new World

Trade Organization (WTO) became an institutional fact, nations everywhere had been wired into a single hair-trigger planetary economy.

Recall the 1980s. In the United States, Ronald Reagan was president and the economy seemed to be booming along. Corporate lobbyists, especially U.S. agricultural lobbyists,[8] set out an ambitious trade agenda based on economic dogma and the short-term self-interests of largely stateless transnational corporations. "Free trade" became the defining political orthodoxy, taking over the role that anticommunism had played during the 1950s. Few people foresaw the debate that lay ahead. The idea that "trade" had something basic to do with "environment" would have sent the average economic bureaucrat into a state of irritated incomprehension. Trade negotiations were still the private pursuits of cloistered corporate and diplomatic specialists who all spoke the same, narrow, technical language. The enemy of "free trade" was "protectionism," pure and simple. "Fair trade" was a term that hadn't been heard much for the better part of a century.[9]

Those days are over. Hardly a decade into what U.S. economic historian Doug Dowd calls "the second coming of free trade," NAFTA, GATT's WTO, the Common Market, APEC, and the ever-threatening trade war between the United States and Japan are constant front-page news. Everywhere trade is the focus of incessant heated conversation, and it's not hard to see why. Unemployment and economic insecurity are high and rising, and trade, a fundamental mechanism of global economic integration, is always implicated. Together with automation, and global financial markets, and all the other devices of the new globalization, "trade" comes to the losers in garments far more somber than those it wears to greet the rich and even the comfortable.

Life in the North is cheap, but life in the South is cheaper still. In Mexico, the Third World country that most Americans know best, the "economic openness" of the 1980s set off a dramatic increase in malnutrition and in economic desperation of all kinds. It brought, too, a sharp increase in the number of millionaires and even billionaires,[10] even as between 1982 and 1990, real Mexican wages dropped by over half.[11] In the wake of 1995's financial collapse and Mexico's reborn commitment to "economic discipline," they do not promise to rebound. Meanwhile, once-lovely border rivers, now the unregarded sewers of unregulated export-processing zones, have grown so profoundly toxic that in some cases their waters cannot even be safely approached, let alone entered or drunk.[12]

Trade pacts come and go, but the larger pattern of events does not often change. There are striking, damning similarities between the 1840s world of free trade and potato famine and our 1990s world of stateless capital, breakneck technological revolution, anxious but self-satisfied elites, globally integrated production and marketing, and ecological deterioration. The parallel was borne out by the 1984–85 Ethiopian famine, which killed a million people, but did not interrupt the export of green beans to England,[13] as well as by the civil war and famine in Somalia in 1992–93. Somalia is a clear marker of the new times. The first famine broadcast live on satellite TV, it was as well a tale of trade — the arms trade, the oil trade (four oil companies have leased drilling rights to two-thirds of Somali territory),[14] and the seafood trade. Even at the height of the UN-U.S. joint pacification and relief operation, Operation Restore Hope, fleets of fishing trawlers (Taiwanese, Korean, Spanish, Greek, and Italian) were working the undefended Somali fishing grounds, removing far more protein than was entering the country in "aid."[15]

After the potato famine, a great wave of Irish headed to America to start new lives. Today no country would accept so many refugees, for today immigration is not so free. Today it is goods and investment capital that can ignore national boundaries. There is no longer a New World, and the old is enclosed by GATT, the master free-trade deal that governs over 120 countries and more than 90 percent of all international trade.[16]

GATT is an institution far too few of us understand in any detail. Aside from a few brief moments — first the early 1990s, when the ratification or death of GATT's "Uruguay Round" negotiations was imminent and the related maneuvering took on the air of a high-stakes horserace, and then again in late 1994, when the U.S. Republican establishment pretended to oppose GATT's final passage though Congress[17] — newspapers rarely discuss it, and then only in the business pages. Most people find it only another incomprehensible acronym, another boring detail of a winner-take-all economy no one expects them to understand. And yet GATT is anything but boring. The World Trade Organization, GATT's newly created implementing body, could easily evolve to be the most powerful institution since the World Bank and the IMF, and certainly it will have a profound effect on the shape of global environmental treaties. Maurice Strong, secretary-general of the Earth Summit, repeatedly warned negotiators that their final treaties would have to be "GATT legal." It is a phrase (often softened to "GATT consistent") well known to politicians, executives, and, recently, green activists.

Strong's meaning was clear. The Earth Summit treaties would not be allowed to contradict the doctrine of free trade as codified in secretly negotiated trade agreements (many key GATT documents were, and still are, classified) interpreted by an unelected cabal of unknown, Geneva-based bureaucrats. GATT was not even nominally a democratic institution,[18] whereas the Summit was organized under the auspices of the United Nations and was being hyped around the world as a new beginning for both mankind and nature. But none of this mattered much. It was GATT, not the Summit, that embodied the emerging future.

Until recently, environmentalists seldom gave much thought to geopolitics, and those few who did were almost always of the World Resources Institute school of "global environmental governance." In this elite circle, it has long been taken as an unchallenged truth that we all, whether officers of planetary corporations or residents of impoverished Brazilian favelas, have the same ultimate interests in enlightened planning and rational global management. Today this is no longer a near-universal illusion, and the trade debate is one of the reasons why — it has made it impossible to deny that this is a world of winners and losers.

The character of the late 1980s should be recalled. The Bush years, following upon the Reagan "boom," saw the bill come due. The United States had become the world's largest debtor nation, and the Bush administration, ideologically zealous in a fashion Lord Trevelyan would have easily understood, took the opportunity to prescribe for the country a mild dose of the bitter medicine so well known in the South as structural adjustment. Bush's men fell to the job with gusto, setting out anew on the path that Reagan had cleared — to cripple regulatory agencies like the Environmental Protection Agency and the Occupational Safety and Health Administration; to privatize national forests, mines, and oil fields; to promote "free market reforms" in agriculture, education, and low-income housing; to cut social programs from health care to alternative energy development; and, of course, to pursue aggressively both the GATT and NAFTA agreements.

The trade deals that crystallized in the 1980s were of a piece with a larger agenda, and to understand that agenda is to understand the challenge of ecology. As Mark Ritchie, director of the Institute of Agriculture and Trade Policy and, according to no less a source than the *Wall Street Journal*, the man who jump-started the anti-GATT campaign in the United States,[19] put it, "Since many of the citizens active in the trade debate started out as committed environmentalists, this debate has generated a pool of people with a serious understanding of the links between ecology and economy — the fundamental knowledge needed to prosper in the next century. Thank you, Ron and George."[20]

As GATT and its cousins — from NAFTA to APEC — have become better known, "trade" has lost its aura of unchallenged promise and prosperity. *The Economist*, for over a century the ideological flagship of free trade, notes that "if liberal capitalism is to continue advancing it must overcome the entrenched skepticism of the people that it benefits."[21] This is surely true — which is just why that skepticism must be understood. *The Economist*'s editors cannot print "fair trade" without adding "whatever that means,"[22] and have written of the "sinister alliance of environmentalists and economic isolationists"[23] that threatens their chosen creed. But this is only smoke and self-delusion. The actual cause of the skepticism is an economy now mutating in strange and frightening ways. "Free trade," long an incantation designed to conjure images of affluence and "growth," has come for many to denote instead an "upturn" for the few, and for themselves only pain. "Fair trade," for its part, names the almost unnamable, unbearably difficult project of reforming the economy.

Harmonic Convergence

Since its establishment after World War II, GATT has evolved through a series of negotiating sessions called rounds. Initially, its business was the elimination of tariffs, and by the mid-1970s this goal had been largely achieved. GATT's Uruguay Round (1986–93) did not focus on tariffs, subsidies, quotas, or any of the usual fronts in the ongoing low-intensity conflict that is international trade. Instead, the Uruguay negotiations broadened GATT's agenda to include investments, services, and intellectual property rights, and drew attention to the at first obscure goal of eliminating "technical" or "nontariff" barriers to trade.

These bland and abstract terms name the real trade controversy, or would, if only more people understood that in the minds of free-trade true believers, ecological protection and human rights are just such barriers.

GATT looms large on the trade and environment landscape, but it is hardly the whole of it. We come to it with lessons learned elsewhere, lessons that, in North America, were first taught by the 1988 U.S.-Canadian Free Trade Agreement (FTA). It was the FTA that first awakened U.S. and Canadian environmentalists, health and safety advocates, and labor activists to the fact that their most crucial laws and regulations, precious fruits of decades of hard-fought campaigns, were actually "import restrictions" and other forms of "protectionism." In 1989 Quebec, on behalf of its huge asbestos industry, invoked the FTA to attack a U.S. ban on the import, production, and use of asbestos. At about the same time, urged on by its pulp and paper industry, Canada challenged U.S. laws requiring that a portion of the fiber used in the manufacture of newsprint be recycled; weak though they are, these laws remain, according to a Canadian industrial group, "disguised non-tariff barriers to trade because Canada does not have the supply needed of recycled fiber to maintain market share in the U.S."[24] In the United States, too, industrial interests sprang into action, invoking the FTA to attack Canadian acid-rain reduction programs, energy export rules, reforestation and fish conservation policies, pesticide laws, and even automobile fuel-efficiency standards as "nontariff trade barriers."

The pesticide episode illustrated with particular clarity the deregulatory dangers hidden in the free-trade agenda. It is not simply that corporations sought to open Canada's markets for their products by attacking its pesticide laws. It is that they made this attack by challenging the legal foundation of these laws. Unlike U.S. rulings, which require only that the benefits of use be "shown" to outweigh the risks, Canada's laws went so far as to require that a pesticide be *shown to be safe* before it could be approved. Six out of seven pesticide products legal in the United States could not be used in Canada,[25] a situation viewed by transnational agrochemical corporations as an unfair and even irrational restraint on trade. In the end, Canada defused the dispute by agreeing to work toward "equivalence" with U.S. laws. The larger matter, however, remains. It is "harmonization," trade jargon that means nothing less than the global leveling of divergent national rules about exactly what can be traded, and under what social and environmental conditions.

"Harmonization," pursued intelligently, could be a boon to both humanity and the earth. The question, to use the jargon, is whether we will get "harmonization up" or "harmonization down" — that is, whether trade agreements will treat international standards as "floors" that nations are free to build upon as their people wish, or "ceilings" that define maximum standards that no country will be free to exceed. It's a simple question to pose, but in a free-trade world that pits every nation and community against every other, a world in which ecological rapine and human slavery are both means of lowering prices on merciless global markets, it is anything but simple to answer.

We cannot know where the trade debate will take us, though we can easily understand what is at stake. Harmonization, as brought to us by Uruguay GATT and NAFTA, is, in the words of Lori Wallach of Public Citizen, a key U.S.-based fair-trade organization, "a one-way ratchet down."[26] The weight of the evidence argues that she is right. GATT demands that American food safety laws be watered down to conform to rules set by a highly secretive, industry-dominated, Rome-based organization named Codex Alimentarius (literally, "the law of food"), which consistently sets standards far laxer than those in force in the United States and Europe. Under Codex, peaches sold in the United States would be allowed to contain fifty times as much DDT as they do today.[27] NAFTA says that the United States will not have to lower its food safety standards *if it can be proven that those laws are necessary in the first place,* a test that precious few laws would pass.

This is just the beginning of the threat. There is a fundamental conflict between the logic of social and environmental protection and the demands of deregulated international trade. The roster of U.S. laws that face challenges as restraints on trade includes the Marine Mammals Protection Act, the Endangered Species Act, the Resource Conversion and Recovery Act, the Pelly Amendment (a key enforcement tool for whaling and other treaties), various food safety laws, Corporate Average Fuel Economy (CAFE) standards, and even (according to a European Commission study) the Nuclear Non-Proliferation Act.[28] All these laws are easily interpreted, under GATT rules, as nontariff trade barriers. Internationally, matters are even worse. At least seventeen environmental treaties involve limitations on trade and are highly vulnerable to challenge under GATT.[29] They include not only the Convention on International Trade in Endangered Species and the Basel Convention on hazardous waste export, which have as their explicit *purpose* the restriction of trade, but also the London Dumping Convention, the Migratory Bird Treaty, the Montreal Protocol on Substances That Deplete the Ozone Layer, the International Convention on the Regulation of Whaling, the International Agreement for the Conservation of Fishes, and a variety of UN environmental protocols.[30]

The inclusion of the ozone treaty on this list should make the issues crystal clear. The Montreal Protocol is constantly cited as the strongest basis for reasoned optimism about the future of global environmental governance. And although the Montreal Protocol is flawed, it is a model of serious intent in comparison with most other environmental treaties, for it explicitly allows nations to block imports from countries that violate its terms. Judged by GATT rules, it would be illegal, though it is unlikely to be challenged. The Protocol is too popular, and such a step would loudly advertise both GATT's antienvironmental bias and the public secret of most other environmental treaties — that they are not only indifferently enforced but also largely unenforceable. Steven Shrybman, a counsel to the Canadian Environmental Law Association and a leading fair-trade theorist, put the point succinctly: "When countries are serious about enforcing environmental measures, they include trade sanctions among the enforcement measures."[31] The question is, why is the Montreal Protocol almost alone among environmental treaties in containing such sanctions?

There are myriad issues here, but the most difficult of them is "national sovereignty." GATT, as an instrument of economic globalization, ultimately implies a deregulation of trade so complete that it would circumscribe the ability of even *strong* governments to control health and environmental standards within their own borders. The pattern was visible as early as 1981, when a landmark Danish law mandating the use of returnable bottles was overturned as a barrier to the European Common Market. By the early 1990s, GATT had already been used to challenge European rules against hormone-tainted beef, to force Austria to abandon plans to introduce a 70 percent tax on tropical timber, and to overturn Thai smoking restrictions in the interests of U.S. tobacco companies. In this last and particularly notorious case,

GATT ruled that no country could use trade restrictions to enforce public health laws *unless it could demonstrate that they were the least trade-restrictive means to that end.*[32]

Conflicts over sovereignty are crucial to the politics of the new world, which is just why *The Economist* derides concern for sovereignty as "economic isolationism." The real issue, however, is not isolationism but democracy, not nationalism but a globalization that is swamping nation-states and putting nothing in their place but global corporations and unregulated international markets. Fair traders, to be sure, have often been less than coherent on these points, but the debates they provoked in battles against NAFTA and GATT at least made the stakes clear. In 1993, for example, Public Citizen, joined by the Sierra Club and Friends of the Earth, filed suit to protest NAFTA's summary enactment in terms that stressed not vague nationalism but the specific matter of national legislative sovereignty. Their argument was simple — since NAFTA would affect the U.S. environment, it was properly subject to the terms of the National Environmental Policy Act, and required a U.S. environmental impact statement before it could legally go into effect.

The lawsuit failed, but it marked the frontiers of a new territory. Environmentalists worry about the efficacy of their hard-won laws, as food safety advocates worry about theirs, as just about everyone worries about security and jobs. We are all, today, subject to the logic of almost unregulated global economic processes that are far more powerful than the laws of individual nations. It is a sign of the times that concern about national sovereignty, long a hot button in the South, has become an issue in the United States as well. The North no longer stands above the global fray, and judging by the strength of 1993's anti-NAFTA coalition, a lot of people know it.

Environmental standards, and the fight to maintain and even raise them, is only one aspect of a larger argument over the terms of globalization. These standards, along with health standards and labor rights, are part of the living history of the United States and Europe, a history that, from a hard-line free trader's point of view, has an inconveniently democratic character. GATT review panels seek to iron out the resulting frictions, usually by lowering our "unreasonably high" standards to the levels enjoyed throughout most of the world.

Free trade inevitably pits the relatively strong health, environmental, welfare, and labor rules of the North against the far laxer standards that can always be found somewhere else — in Asia, the former East bloc, Latin America, or Africa.[33] Moreover, it *must* do so, and precisely because it proposes to throw the poor together with the rich, the weak together with the strong, in one fantastic, chaotic, unregulated, planetary marketplace.

The sultans of globalization argue that a harmonized "level playing field" will be fair by definition. "Free trade," in the textbook-perfect world of economics, is said to improve life for all, even the lowliest, by removing economic "inefficiencies" and freeing the economy to approach its optimum performance. These, though, are illusions possible only to those who can ignore the population's increasingly sharp division into rich and poor, into a well-equipped and adaptable minority habituated to consumption and affluence and a hard-pressed majority still reeling from the destruction of their traditional cultures.

The richest can harmonize up, if they must. The rest lack both the ability and the means to raise social and environmental standards, and could not in any case do so without risking the small "comparative advantage" that world markets allow them, an advantage that turns on low wages and ecological looting. In a world thus partitioned, "free trade" can only be a hoax, as David Ricardo, the nineteenth-century economist who invented the idea of comparative advantage, would almost certainly have admitted. Ricardo believed that

> the fancied or real insecurity of capital, when not under the immediate control of its owner, together with the natural disinclination which every man has to quit the country of his birth and connections, and intrust himself, with all his habits fixed, to a strange government and new laws, check the emigration of capital. These feelings, which I should be sorry to see weakened, induce most men of property to be satisfied with a low rate of profits in their own country, rather than seek a more advantageous employment for their wealth in foreign nations.[34]

Adam Smith himself, when discussing his famous "invisible hand," assumed it to be in the interest of capitalists to invest at home:

> By preferring the support of domestic to that of foreign industry, he intends only to his own security; and by directing that industry

in such a manner as its produce may be of greatest value, he intends only his own gain, and he is in this, as in many other cases, led by an invisible hand to promote an end which was no part of his intention.[35]

Today's world, Ricardo and Smith would find, is one in which such homey nationalism is visibly absurd; it is a world in which capital is free to roam the planet in search of investment opportunities, in which goods are free to travel in search of better markets and higher prices, in which only labor is enjoined, by law and fortified frontier, against easy mobility. Chinese manufacturers may dump cheap clothes and shoddy artifacts on the U.S. markets, but this does not mean the Chinese people are free to follow. Not unless they can shell out $30,000 to risk their lives crossing the Pacific on a tramp steamer.

Social Environments

Dave Phillips is a well-spoken, almost dapper man, and sometimes he seems a bit out of place in the hippie world of the dolphin wars. He is not. Phillips, as the director of the San Francisco–based Earth Island Institute's International Marine Mammal Project, was responsible for setting off a chain of events that not only made "dolphin safe" a household term, but also inadvertently put the previously obscure central issue of the trade-environment battle into play. That issue, more fundamental than even national sovereignty, is usually named "process standards," and if ever there was a crucial matter hidden in an abstract bureaucratic term, this is it.

Earth Island's initial concern was simple enough. Dolphins often swim above schools of yellowfin tuna. Why they do so is an ecological mystery, though the result is all too easily understood — archaic purse seine tuna nets scoop up dolphins as well as tuna, and kill them (slowly, by drowning) by the tens of thousands. The Marine Mammals Protection Act (MMPA), passed in the United States in 1972, forbade the use of purse seine nets in the American tuna fleet, which at the time was the largest in the world and was killing about 400,000 dolphins a year. By the late 1980s, intense pressure by U.S. greens had won the domestic enforcement of the MMPA, and the number of dolphins killed by the U.S. fleet dropped to about 1,000 a year. It might have been cause for celebration, save that during those same years the tuna industry had gone global, and the United States, with its MMPA rules, was now far out of harmony with the rest of a decidedly less-punctilious world. U.S. tuna boats began to reflag under the banners of other nations, and hundreds of tons of dolphin-unsafe tuna were pouring into the United States.

In response, in 1988 Earth Island decided to pursue a legal strategy aimed at forcing the U.S. government to *completely* enforce the MMPA. It was able to do so because the MMPA, almost alone with the Montreal Protocol, includes provisions that forbid the import of tuna caught using fishing techniques ("processes") that violate U.S. law. Under pressure, the federal government began to enforce those provisions, and *that,* finally, was when push came to shove. Mexico, a major exporter of dolphin-unsafe tuna to the United States, appealed to GATT, and in August 1991 a GATT dispute-resolution panel, staffed by unelected trade officials from three landlocked countries, ruled that MMPA's import provisions were in reality "green protectionism" and therefore illegal barriers to trade.

GATT's secretariat explained in simple terms befitting a self-evident truth. "A country may not restrict imports of a product solely because it originates in a country whose environmental policies are different from its own."[36] Dave Phillips, older and wiser, says, "Though looking back it makes perfect sense, at the time we were amazed that the dolphin issue was being inserted into the international geopolitics of trade."[37] Today people are still amazed by the implications of the tuna-dolphin decision, for it *does* make perfect sense — from a free trader's point of view. GATT is the high church of free trade, and it has its cardinal tenets. One of the most sacred is that national laws may not distinguish between "like products." If a country allows a domestic commodity (such as tuna) to be sold on its markets, then it must allow imported "like" commodities to be sold as well. The fine point is that products are "like" even if produced by completely different processes. There is no GATT-allowable distinction between tuna caught by means that kill dolphins and tuna that is dolphin-safe. In the end, says GATT, tuna is simply tuna.

The fishing industry is global. It can be reached by national laws only if they "proscribe imports" of products judged to have unacceptable conditions of production, and such laws are GATT-illegal. The consequence, Steven Shrybman argues, is that "the GATT decision removes the only compliance mechanism — economic sanctions — that is available to a nation seeking to enforce international environmental norms."[38] Moreover, the same logic applies to labor rights, health and safety rules, and consumer-protection standards. Nor is this an accident. As Carla Hills, President Bush's chief trade negotiator, put the matter, in a rare moment of candor, "We want to abolish the right of nations to impose health and safety standards more stringent than a minimal uniform world standard."[39]

As it happened, GATT's ruling did not stand. A federal judge soon decreed that American law remains in place, and Mexico, alarmed by the attention being drawn to its abysmal environmental record and anxious about rising environmental opposition to NAFTA, chose not to press its anti-MMPA case before a GATT tribunal. Then in mid-1994, after NAFTA's adoption, came "Tuna-Dolphin II." GATT, supporting European complaints, ruled that the United States could not ban the import of dolphin-unsafe tuna that was imported into Europe, canned, and reexported into the United States, for the now familiar reason that it could not ban the import of any product based solely on judgments about its conditions of production. There will be more episodes in this tale, many more, but the point has been made. Nations have their limits, and in the free-trade regime they quickly meet them: If they attempt to ban the social and ecological "dumping" into their markets of products that do not meet their standards, they are charged with the sin of protectionism.

Such is free-trade orthodoxy, and if there is to be hope of greening the world economy, it must fall. And it may. Rod Leonard of the Washington, D.C.–based Community Nutrition Institute, an NGO expert who has watched for years as process standards slowly made their way onto the diplomatic agenda, thinks their time is finally coming. A green trade system, Leonard says, must distinguish between products on the basis of criteria that are not "physically embodied" in them when they are traded. Never mind, for the moment, what it *is* — ask how it was caught, cut, mined, manufactured, farmed, transported. These are the real questions, the questions that imply that "the whole conceptual framework of the trade system be changed."[40]

The tough case is not exemplified by, for example, imported pesticide-laden food, for in this case there is something physical about the food that can be named, measured, and banned. Broccoli tainted with DDT and Aldrin is not "like" organic broccoli, and the toxicological difference can be measured with scientific precision. Mexican tuna caught with purse seine nets bears no such identifiable traces. Neither does Brazilian steel produced by low-cost methods that, using charcoal as a fuel, cause large-scale deforestation. Neither do electronic components made in the toxic sweatshops of Taiwan or Indonesia, or the electricity generated in nukes and large dams and distributed over "the grid." In all these cases and millions more, a product leaves the pain of its origins behind and enters vast international markets, later to be consumed anonymously, and with carefully guarded innocence.

The very size and complexity of the global markets, and the variety of the societies being thrown together within them, means that regulation as we have known it will fail. Free traders oppose efforts to use national laws to protect the environment, and for just this reason environmentalists tend to support those laws — to consider them crucial and, sometimes, adequate. It's a natural enough conclusion, but in the face of globalization, it is both wrong and dangerous. Here, for example, a 1993 Greenpeace report explains how the tuna industry evades even the strictest (and probably GATT-illegal) clauses of the U.S. MMPA:

> Literally hundreds, if not thousands, of fishing ships operate without any monitoring or control at all. They use flags of convenience to avoid regulations, or change their names to avoid inspection. . . . The vessels are able to move from ocean to ocean very quickly when necessary, mixing tuna caught in different regions and using different methods. For instance, a boat can fill most of its hold with tuna caught in areas where there are no observers and control, and then "launder" its catch by a brief trip to the Eastern Pacific, where there are inspectors and controls. . . . Once the tuna arrives in port, it is further mixed with tuna from other ships, coming from other areas. By this point, buyers have an enormous choice of tuna, caught in different areas by different ships, and reliably identifying where and how the tuna was caught is almost impossible.[41]

Inspections in the eastern Pacific, and all the MMPA's other legal and procedural controls, have sharply reduced the number of dolphins killed by the fishing fleets serving the U.S. market. But this too has had its downside, and regardless of the fate of the MMPA, it is a downside that must be understood. In the absence of a uniform set of international rules, countries that unilaterally raise their standards can hope only to mark off their territory, and this is not an act without consequences. Mexico has charged that the MMPA is "eco-protectionist" and is quite correct.

"Eco-protectionism" names a treacherous shore. The issue, to put it with only a bit of exaggerated simplicity, is that poor nations often lack the means to do better. Rich nations that seek to uphold high environmental standards by proscribing the exports of the poor are treading on dangerous ground. This is why "technology transfer" was such a big issue at the Earth Summit, and during GATT's Uruguay Round negotiations. Kristin Dawkins, the research director of the U.S.-based Institute for Agriculture and Trade Policy, summarized the issues as follows:

> If the tuna-dolphin case is a precedent, it means that in any number of areas it would become illegal to restrict the import of products that were made with ecologically unsound production methods. Now if you're a poor, Third World country, you might want to invest in environmental technologies, but you can't afford to. This was one of the big issues at the Earth Summit: whether or not technology transfer would be made possible through international policy. The United States' position was, *absolutely not*: technology will be made available at strictly commercial rates.[42]

A year later, in early 1993, GATT took the same position. In fact, Uruguay's intellectual property rights provisions tighten and restrict the availability of environmentally sound technology and its innovation by granting the current patent holders — usually transnational corporations — virtual monopoly rights.

What's at stake? The logic of today's trade regime — of inviolate corporate property rights and export dependence for all — traps reformers in a Catch-22 in which only unilateral national regulations like the MMPA are possible, even as unilateralism is officially forbidden and widely denigrated as "environmental imperialism" and "a fast track to trade chaos and conflict."[43] More fundamentally, we must look beneath the exterior of traded goods to the conditions by which they are created, and by which they exist. Not only are many "goods" — clear-cut logs or prison-made blue jeans — actually "bads." But also, as Karl Marx noted long ago, "commodities," though appearing "trivial" and "easily understood," are actually "very queer" and abound with "metaphysical subtleties and theological niceties."[44] We could today use a similar exacting attention to the subtleties of traded commodities, for as "process standards" imply, the deepest truth of a harvested or manufactured object may not be visible or even testable, but hidden in its origins, its history, its conditions of existence.

Marx was less concerned with nature than with labor, and greens must turn, if only for a time, in the same direction. The tuna industry illustrates why, for it is as global as the ocean currents, and not only in the ranging of its fleets and the marketing of its wares, but also in its endless, restless search for cheaper workers, a search that it shares with most all global industries, from mining to sneaker manufacture. Dave Phillips:

> In the old days, California had the largest tuna canning industry in the world, but today — these are approximate figures — the wages in California are about $17 an hour. So the industry moved, first to Puerto Rico, where wages are about $7 an hour, and then, when they decided that was too much, to American Samoa, where wages are about $3.50 an hour. From there it moved to Ecuador, where workers are paid about $1 an hour, and then on to Thailand, where a great deal of the industry is today, and wages are about $4 a *day!* And now, amazingly enough, there is some movement to Indonesia, where wages are as low as a couple of dollars a *day.*[45]

A couple of dollars a day. Amidst the abysmal working conditions and trade union repression of some export-processing-zone slums, workers are lucky to get a couple of dollars a day. By September 1991 more than two thousand U.S. firms were operating *maquiladoras* (export-zone factories) on the unregulated southern side of the U.S.-Mexico border, employing half a million workers in the manufacture of goods slated for Northern markets. And, partially as a consequence, U.S. wages had dropped to their lowest point since 1964.[46]

In the fight over NAFTA, besieged fair traders took aid where aid was offered. When Ross Perot asserted, during the 1992 U.S. presidential debates, that NAFTA's passage would yield a "loud sucking sound" as U.S. jobs flowed south, anti-NAFTA activists were delighted. Exhausted by a tide of media coverage that uncritically accepted absurdly exaggerated and explicitly partisan estimates of the benefits of deregulated trade, even as it dismissed the fears of greens and working people,[47] fair traders thought they had finally found a champion. Only later, when the press and then the political establishment canonized Perot as leader of the anti-NAFTA campaign, did many of them become anxious about his unabashedly nationalist leanings. Then, on August 26, 1993, it became hard for even the most doggedly pragmatic fair traders to ignore the strains in their alliance, for that was when far-right politician Pat Buchanan came out against NAFTA. The labor and environmental "side agreements" that Bill Clinton had added to George Bush's NAFTA, and which greens and other fair traders were busily denouncing as cynical window dressing, were to Buchanan only infringements of American sovereignty and hidden "aid" to the Mexican government. "Why," he asked, "should the American people be responsible for cleaning up the pigpen that the Mexicans have made on their side of our common border?"[48]

Since 1993 the muddle has only worsened. Fair traders, having lost the anti-NAFTA battle and straining against GATT, were hurled into unwanted coalition not only with Pat Buchanan, but with Jesse Helms, godfather of the Neanderthal American right, and Senate Republican leader Bob Dole as well. Helms, in particular, was an embarrassment, for while fair traders tried, with some desperation, to defend the sovereignty of national democratic traditions without sinking to nationalism, Helms launched into eager and reductionist attack on GATT/WTO as a "world government." In such company, fair traders — who generally support "global governance" — have no choice but to clarify their stand. Do they aspire to bring ecological and social rights into one grand agenda, to build a new and visionary internationalism, or will they ride the coattails of economic nationalism? Perot, Buchanan, Helms, and Dole — these men make peculiar populists, for all are friends of "big business," and of the unrestricted global mobility of capital.

Why do Northern industries flee for the South? Sometimes, as with the scores of furniture manufacturers that have moved from Southern California into Mexico, where pollution laws are generally unenforced,[49] the move is primarily to avoid environmental laws. But such avoidance actually is the unusual case. In a study of plant relocations, Jeff Leonard, president of the Global Environment Fund, a leading green investment group, found that "there has been no wholesale exodus of industry to developing countries in response to stricter environmental legislation at home," though there are the special cases of "some very hazardous industries, including asbestos, benzidine dyes, a few pesticides, and some mineral-processing companies."[50] He also found that a few countries — including Ireland, Mexico, Romania, and Spain — deliberately kept environmental laws weak to attract foreign investment. In the majority of cases, though, access to cheap, unprotected (and often skilled)[51] labor was the crucial factor in the decision to relocate, a point that U.S. citizens may want to consider, along with the fact that many of the jobs that have left Canada since the North American free-trade deals began have gone not to Mexico, but to the right-to-work states of the American Deep South.[52] ("Right to work," as Noam Chomsky has noted, is a cute bit of Orwellian language that means that union organizing is effectively illegal.) Still, labor and environment are two sides of one coin — when firms do move in search of cheap labor, or for access to local markets, they are rarely unwilling to take advantage of lax environmental regulations to cut costs even further.

It is not quite fair to say that GATT allows no consideration of conditions under which goods are produced. There is one significant case in which these conditions can be taken into account — GATT explicitly allows countries to restrict imports of goods produced by prison labor. It is an odd provision, brief and isolated, but it does not exist by caprice, and its effect is anything but trivial. By outlawing one egregious form of "social dumping," it gives fair traders a platform from which to argue that labor and human-rights linkages to trade policy are, like environmental linkages, altogether just and proper, and not, as Democratic Senator Bill Bradley put it during 1994's debate over China's trade status, "cold war old-think."[53] With prison labor officially proscribed, the point has been granted, and it remains only to determine where and how to draw the line. Herman Daly and Robert Goodland, at the time both mavericks in the World Bank's Environment Department, pressed this opening when they argued that child labor, debt peonage, uninsured risky labor, and subsistence-wage labor all represent a greater degradation of social standards than requiring justly-convicted, reasonably-fed criminals to earn their keep. Of course, if people are thrown in forced-labor "gulags" for political reasons, then GATT's exception is understandable, but the case for extending it to child labor, etc., remains strong. The prison labor exception is an acknowledgement by GATT that standards-lowering competition can be carried too far. That is the thin edge of a big wedge.[54]

Economics has moral and ecological limits. Labor, human, and environmental rights are all "external" domains outside the core concerns of business, which aim, as any novice executive knows, at the pursuit of ever-greater profits. If we accept the logic of the free traders, our wages are too high, our environmental and workplace safety rules too strict, our entitlement programs too generous. How can Western firms, thus encumbered, hope to win the economic wars of the future? How can they hope to face down rising competitors able to exploit freely the vast unregulated expanses of the world's peripheries?

With communism in ruins and markets exalted on every side, we rarely hear the simple truth that markets, by their very nature, produce "externalities." If you and I compete, and if I suffer costs that you evade, you will, all other things being equal, drive me from business. The problem is that all other things — and labor costs in particular — are *not* equal, and thus we get what historian Jeremy Brecher calls a "race to the bottom." Daly and Goodland summarize:

> If by wise policy or blind luck a country has managed to control its population growth, provide social insurance, high wages, reasonable working hours, and other benefits to its working class (i.e., most of its citizens), should it allow these benefits to be competed down to the world average by unregulated trade? Through unregulated trade, Northern capitalists share the wages of Northern laborers with Southern laborers — although the Southern elites may also gain. This leveling of wages will be overwhelmingly downward due to the vast number and rapid growth rate of underemployed populations in the Third World. Northern laborers will get poorer, while Southern laborers will stay much the same.[55]

Northern environmentalists, who have kept themselves aloof from the worker's world, must eventually acknowledge the importance of the cost of labor. This was, in fact, the chief lesson of the infamous "Summers Memo," written in late 1991 by Lawrence Summers — then chief economist of the World Bank and subsequently assistant secretary for international affairs in the Clinton Treasury Department — while he led the effort to draft the Bank's 1992 *World Development Report*. It was the year of the Earth Summit, and thus the Bank's most prestigious annual publication took "Development and the Environment" as its theme. The *Development Report*, however, was entirely upstaged by the memo, which after being leaked to *The Economist*, reprinted, and cursed around the world, became a truly world-historic indiscretion. As José Lutzenberger, then Brazil's secretary of environment said, it was "perfectly logical but totally insane."[56]

"Just between you and me," Summers asked his colleagues, "shouldn't the World Bank be encouraging *more* migrations of the dirty industries to the LDCs [less developed countries]?" Doing so is entirely reasonable on economic grounds, he explained, because, for example, a carcinogen will have a larger effect "in a country where people survive to get prostate cancer than in a country where under-five mortality is 200 per thousand." Poor countries, then, are "under-polluted," and the economically rational course is to encourage "dirty industries" to move to them. While there is great disparity between wages in rich and poor countries, "the economic logic behind dumping a load of toxic waste in the lowest wage country is impeccable and we should face up to that." There are, to be sure, "arguments against all of these proposals" for exporting pollution to the South: "intrinsic rights to certain goods, moral reasons, social concerns, lack of adequate markets, etc." but the problem is that these arguments "could be turned around and used more or less effectively against every Bank proposal for liberalization."[57]

The tone of the memo, *The Economist* complained, was "grating" and "a curious one for a World Bank official to promote," but it added that "the issues raised in the memo are central: how far ought countries to pursue different environmental standards?"[58] Summers's real offense was that he stated a public secret too crassly. He pleaded that he had only "intended to provoke debate," and in this he certainly succeeded. The problem was that he provoked *real* debate about a significant issue. The "costs" of pollution can only be relative to the "value" of life, and if we put aside "moral reasons" and "social concerns," how can we avoid concluding that Northern lives are "worth" hundreds of times more than Southern lives? This is simply the result we get if we apply the test of the market and value lives by what they can be sold for; if we value people, that is, by what they can demand in wages.

The global inequality of wages reflects, as Summers pointed out, an inequality in the "value" of human life, as it is currently reckoned. This inequality is perhaps *the* essential problem to be resolved if we hope to save the earth. To see this, follow the global climate negotiations. In mid-1994, economists from the Organization for Economic Cooperation and Development who were active in the treaty's working group on "Economic and Other Cross-Cutting Issues" were arguing that the "damage cost" of a life lost in the South must be less than one in the North, because Southern people make less money, and have less money to spend on insurance.[59] As one green economist told me, off the record, "I really think the environmental stuff is a piece of cake compared to the labor stuff. The real problem, in a nutshell, is that a lot of people don't get paid shit."

False Promises

In early 1992, with the Earth Summit looming on the horizon, the GATT secretariat issued a public report, *Trade and the Environment*, that added an arresting variation to the hoariest of economic myths — that economic growth is the solution to poverty, that, in fact, economic growth *in the North* is the solution to poverty *in the South*. This is the "traditional view," which Daly and Goodland sum up as the claim that "Northern high-consumption societies should continue to consume yet more in order to help the South by providing larger markets."[60]

Trade and the Environment defended this claim, though not in such bald terms, and then added another:

Increases in per capita income — which are boosted by increased market access and expanding trade — provide more resources to contain environmental damage, helping to finance pollution control and remedial clean-up. . . . If the average citizen is convinced of the need to devote more material and human resources to achieve a better environment as his or her income rises, the growth of per-capita income ultimately will lead to increased expenditure on the environment.[61]

Accept these premises and there's no need for any anxiety about the impacts of "free trade" on the environment. The world according to GATT is a fine, tidy place where increased trade yields increased wealth, which in turn yields more resources for environmental protection and increased trade. Even child labor is unfortunately to the good, for it gives the poor a chance to survive, and even to succeed.[62] Round and round and round it goes, in a perpetual virtuous loop — trade increases economic activity increases wealth increases greening increases trade, and all is well.

But every link in this loop carries with it assumptions that, closely examined, dissolve. Global trade has increased elevenfold in the past fifty years, yet poverty and unemployment are not even close to being eliminated. Will more trade somehow change this? Will the wealth it generates trickle down to the poor? Will the poor become more affluent and more interested in environmental protection? Are the poor even the environmental problem in the first place? The free traders make all these claims, but none is as compelling as it may at first appear.

The most fundamental of these claims — that traditional, trade- and growth-driven economic development will make people richer and thus move them to protect their environments — is based upon the assiduously cultivated myth that it is the poor who are destroying the earth. But by far the majority of environmental damage is done by the planet's rich — the North, and among the elites of the South. Even in countries like Indonesia, Brazil, Honduras, and Zaire — all famous for environmental destruction — small groups of families control the great majority of economic and political power, and use it first of all to enrich themselves. In Brazil a good number of the miners and farmers who are pioneering the rain forest have been themselves pushed off farms by powerful agrobusinessmen intent on expanding their production of soy and other profitable export crops.[63] These fabulously rich free-trade farmers are the real force behind the destruction and murder in the rain forest. In a society that was until recently almost entirely rural, they control the bulk of the agricultural land.

Is it true, as orthodox economists never tire of asserting, as *Trade and the Environment* intones with perfect certainty, that "the growth of per-capita income ultimately will lead to increased expenditure on the environment"? Indeed it is. But what about the larger claim, the one so many people presume when reading reassuring words about increasing "expenditures"? Does environmental quality itself increase, or only the money spent on cleanup? Presuming that the Chinese people as a whole, including the poor, are destined for riches (a very dubious assumption) and that riches bring increased spending on environmental protection, does this mean that China's forests, rivers, and coastlines will someday in the future be restored to something like the state they were in when the big boom began about ten years ago? Isn't it far more likely that, after a few more decades of "growth," there will be irremediable horrors all around, and a great deal that has been tragically, permanently lost?[64]

A key question is, What kind of growth? It is a question the apostles of "free markets" and "free trade," with their constant counsel to leave the market to its own unregulated devices, never answer. GATT tells us that "countries near the top of the development ladder are likely to have different priorities from countries further down," but this remarkable insight is intended neither as a critique of inequity nor as a call for the redefinition of development. What follows instead is a call for trade, growth, and development as usual, a call crafted to appeal to Southern exporters. "The existence of less strict environmental standards in a lower income country, therefore, is not a sufficient basis for claiming that the environmental standards are 'too low,' that the country is manipulating its environmental standards in order to improve the competitiveness of its products."[65]

Trade and the Environment is a brief for unregulated international trade as the golden road to global prosperity, and by miraculous synchronicity, as the best method of prodding the world's impoverished masses to raise their environmental standards. It is as close to an official defense of free trade as a road to environmental protection as we will find. For all this, its arguments are only elaborations of the dominant economic creed. They can be found in one variation or another wherever the economic priesthood feels threatened by environmental heresies. Here is another variation — *The Economist*, defending the "distinctly economic premise" that "environmental policy involves trade-offs, and should seek a balance between costs and benefits":

If clean growth means slower growth, as it sometimes will, its human cost will be lives blighted by a poverty that would otherwise have been mitigated. . . . When a trade-off between cleaner air and less poverty has to be faced, most poor countries will rightly want to tolerate more pollution than rich countries do, in return for more growth.[66]

These arguments will be around for some time. Even now, after what economic policy analyst Robert Kuttner has called "the end of laissez-faire," they are far too convenient to fade away. We can expect to encounter them in ever newer and greener variants, for the same reason that "growth," "development," "progress," and all the other schools of official optimism still survive — they calm us, and counsel us that the existing social conditions are just and proper, and tell us that the poor are best served, in the long term, by policies that, in the short term, benefit the rich.

The danger lies in thinking that the times have changed, that GATT's arguments are artifacts of an unenlightened past. In fact, it is only our insulation from the daily realities of the very poor that allows us to imagine that this is so. Matters look different in the South. Here, for example, is the Indian activist Smitu Kothari:

Increased trade might bring an increase in per capita income, but this doesn't tell you anything about injustice, about how many people have fallen below the poverty line, about class. There is no reason to assume that an increase in wealth by a small portion of society will lead to the overall enhancement of the ecosystem, or to the increased control of more people over their productive natural resources, which is what must happen if there is to be true ecological sustainability.[67]

Observe how much Smitu's frame of reference differs from that of even the most fair-minded free traders. In their world the dangers lie in inadequate regulations, in unfair subsidies, in the threat of protectionism and the return of chaotic economic conditions. For Smitu, and for the movement he represents, social justice and political power are the pivots around which the future will turn.

There can be no better justification for this view than the effect that

NAFTA will quite predictably have on Mexican peasant agriculture, and on the *ejido* system, which protects it from utter destruction. This system, by which Mexican smallholders grow corn on communal lands they won formal title to during the 1910 revolution, is vastly "inefficient" by the standards of U.S. factory farming. As a result, in late 1993 U.S. corn at the border cost about $110 per ton, while in Mexico corn cost about $240 per ton. By June of 1994, with NAFTA in effect, U.S. corn exports to Mexico had increased 525 percent over their level a year earlier.[68] Conventional economic theory has it that "Mexico" will benefit from this trade as food prices drop, but this takes no account of the *ejido* system. And as it is destroyed, the results are not particularly hard to anticipate, for they are the continuation of well-established, well-documented trends.

Between 1960 and 1993, about nine million peasants abandoned farming and migrated to Mexico's cities and north to the United States.[69] Estimates vary, but NAFTA, if fully implemented, will likely drive millions of additional peasants from their lands, sending them in desperate poverty into choked Mexican cities and, of course, into the United States. Such vast homelessness is, of course, only an intensification of long-standing patterns, as NAFTA is only the institutionalization of a development path that the North American elites have long pursued. And though it is a path profitable to all those who manufacture for export, it is hard to see who else benefits from it. Certainly not the Mexican poor,[70] nor the U.S. workers who are forced to compete with them.[71] Nor does this "development" seem to be in the American "national interest."[72] Yet it will destroy an ancient farming culture that maintains an astounding variety of distinct genetic variants of corn in active cultivation.

Mexico's peasant farmers grow about five thousand varieties of corn, making their central and southern Mexican farmlands the earth's largest and most biodiverse reservoir of that crucial grain. In the United States, a mere six varieties account for almost half the acreage planted to corn, and only a few hundred are commercially available. The International Maize and Wheat Improvement Center has already cached thousands of varieties in a large Mexican gene bank (not that this is the same as keeping them in cultivation), but its directors fear they will not be able to keep up with the "rate of abandonment" under NAFTA.[73]

Abandonment is not a side effect but an integral part of the free-trade package. At issue here is what ecologists sometimes call scale. The corn monocultures of the American plains are closely adapted to the sprawling factory farms on which they are grown. The corporations that operate these farms, the fragile, overbred grains on them, the chemicals these grains need to survive, the shipping companies that dispatch them by hundreds of tons around the world, the free-trade agenda — all compose a single, immense enterprise, all are of a single piece.

Moreover, free trade greatly increases the prospect of a true ecological "crash" — a classical overshoot (in which a basic ecosystem limit is exceeded) followed by a collapse on a planetary scale. Free trade does so because, by globalizing markets, it ensures that localized ecological strains, and even collapses, are hidden from view. When the Maine cod fisheries went into serious decline, the region's fishermen knew it but most consumers didn't, because they could still buy cod — Russian cod. This is just the kind of "adaptation" that mainstream economists celebrate,[74] for though they do not often put it this way, it allows the planet's rich to escape the ecological carrying capacities of their local regions. The result, according to Donella Meadows, coauthor of *The Limits to Growth*, is that the world is getting more and more like the crashing computer simulations of that classic eco-doomster text. "The worst problem with our model is its global aggregation, and with GATT and NAFTA, they are making it true. The drive to globalize, from a systems perspective, is the drive to deny overshoot by making the economy global."[75]

Social-ecological matters will be the pivots of the future. They were not, however, much visible during 1993's NAFTA battle, and even less so in 1994's fight over GATT's ratification. These were defining moments of the new trade politics, but though they revealed widespread public anxiety about the terms of economic globalization, the battle lines were almost always drawn along lines of economic and political incantation as usual. The free traders spoke endlessly of "growth" and "jobs," of "economic imperatives" and, in a modern vein, "environmental protection," this last being typically defined in cramped and misleading terms, as a problem of the "pollution" of "dirty" Mexican industry. Pollution is a deadly problem, but it is not the only paradigm of trade-related ecological damage — recall Mexico's vanishing varieties of corn, and the vanishing of the peasant cultures that culti-vate them.

The U.S. environmental mainstream, in a spasm of legalistic op-portunism, declared NAFTA to be the greenest trade treaty of all time. Perhaps it is, but this is faint praise, and hardly explains the servile alacrity with which the environmental majors rushed to praise Clinton's environmental and labor "side agreements" to Bush's NAFTA. The executives of the World Wildlife Fund, National Wildlife Federa-tion, National Audubon Society, Natural Resources Defense Council, Environmental Defense Fund, Defenders of Wildlife, and Nature Conservancy all supported NAFTA, and many even campaigned for it. These groups were sometimes called the Shameful Seven by angry fair traders, and it's not hard to see why. Some of them had already agreed not to oppose NAFTA during the Bush years — before the treaty even wore its environmental figleaf.[76] Many were recipients of large cash donations from the very corporations that led the pro-NAFTA campaign.[77]

How will "green trade" be defined? If NAFTA is the answer, there is no reason for optimism. Its environmental side agreement explicitly does not tie trading rights to advances in environmental protection, but rather sketches the outlines of a byzantine appeals procedure by which failures of environmental enforcement can, perhaps, after tor-tuous bureaucratic maneuvering, lead to fines and trade sanctions. So far, little or nothing has improved, and the future does not look good. (The cost of cleanup in the border region alone is estimated at $8 bil-lion, but the North American Development Bank was kicked off with a mere $112 million. More is due, of course, but as the Mexican economy collapsed soon after NAFTA's ratification, it is not obvious that it will be forthcoming.)[78] Even worse, NAFTA's environmental rules do not even apply to natural resource exploitation. Strip mining, the clear-cutting of old-growth forests, the destruction of coastal fisheries, large interbasin water transfers, and export-oriented mega-energy develop-ments — like the huge James Bay dams built on Cree Indian land in Quebec — cannot be challenged under NAFTA's side agreement.[79] Yet NAFTA, by institutionalizing continental integration, will have major long-term effects on patterns of resource exploitation.

To call such a deal progress toward "green trade" is to stretch the bounds of even bureaucratic doublespeak — which is why the green movement's split over NAFTA marked a political watershed. Even in the Washington offices of the Seven, support for the pact was less than unanimous, and staff anger at the executives who backed it was often sharp. Among green activists, who repeatedly faced reports that "groups representing 80 percent of American environmentalists" supported NAFTA[80] and then watched as NAFTA's victory paved the way for GATT's easy ratification, bitterness at the Seven will not be soon forgotten.[81]

If you called their offices as a reporter, you got a different story, one reminiscent of President Clinton's post-NAFTA calls for "healing" and "reconciliation." Al Meyerhof is an attorney at the Natural Resources Defense Council, which supported NAFTA. When, just after the congressional showdown, I asked him if NRDC had been permanently marked by its support for the pact, he replied that, on the contrary, the debate was "a coming of age," a sign that the green movement was mature enough to contain "major disagreements on questions of policy."[82] True, in a sense. But also an argument that can justify all sins.

What is crucial is that environmental protection and labor rights almost entirely fell out of the official trade debate. When it came to congressional votes, nothing mattered but money, power, and position. The defining moment came in 1993, when Bill Clinton, in what the *New York Times* called "one of the most courageous acts of his young Presidency,"[83] won NAFTA's passage by allying himself with the Republican bloc, preaching progress and open markets, branding his opponents as representing the "politics of fear," and striking a hecatomb of sleazy cash-for-votes deals with cagey and otherwise reluctant House members. The price of the pork is estimated to be as high as $50 billion.[84]

Great Transformations

This is a moment of creation. As in that brief time after World War II, when the World Bank, IMF, and UN were founded and the world system we know today was established, the political-economic macrostructure is shifting. The need for new institutions has become a constant theme of policy wonks, diplomats, futurists, and assorted visionaries. Unfortunately, little seems to come of the talk but more talk, and still more. Greens hope that a new biopolitics will soon flower to fill the void — but this, too, does not happen.

The proof of this is in the official silences of the Earth Summit. Long before Rio, all efforts to force the issues fundamental to the modern world — international debt, the transnational corporations, poverty, militarism, trade — onto the Summit's official agenda were rejected, most visibly by the United States but by all the governments of the North, often with the support of Southern elites.

Yet these are the central matters, and it is only in their dynamics that the larger patterns of international power become visible. Debt, the corporations, the rich/poor split, militarism, trade — together they are delivering us into the embrace of a globalization so strange that huge areas of the planet are losing all hope for even the most basic kind of self-sufficiency, the ability to feed themselves.

Can ecological crisis provide the motivation and focus for an enlightened new managerial internationalism? Can new political institutions be contrived, and made equal to the challenges of the emerging world? Ask first how, when most all political institutions are being overwhelmed by power and cynicism, politics of any kind can become a source of hope. Ask first about the existing world. Certainly there is a chance for a strengthened and democratized United Nations, for radically reformed financial and trading systems, for an effective new species of ecological treaties. All this and more is possible — theoretically. But how to get from here to there?

Just now, too much utopianism is not wanted. To be realists, we should cut directly to the dominant institutions of the age, the transnational corporations (TNCs), which despite their power are rarely mentioned in the same sentence as ecology, or even in most discussions of international politics. For all the ubiquity of their logos, ads, and products, the TNCs are strangely overlooked by many who imagine they know the ways of the world. There are, according to the best estimates, now 37,000 transnational firms, controlling some 170,000 foreign affiliates,[85] yet the majority of texts on green diplomacy and global environmental governance (though they may mention specific corporations) fail to discuss TNCs in any but the most Pollyannaish manner, let alone to raise the crucial subject — the necessity of their regulation.[86]

The TNCs are the first institutions in history with the money, power, and technology to plan on a truly global scale. It is because of their global reach that "free trade" is a misleading term. TNC activities involve a third of the world's private-sector assets, 70 percent of the products in world trade, the bulk of international financial transactions, and the major share of advanced technology.[87] How can world trade be "free" when almost all manufacturing is globally integrated by TNCs? When — to focus on the largest of the large — 70 percent of *all* international trade is controlled by a mere 500 corporations?[88]

The role of TNCs in global environmental destruction is just as staggering. TNC activities account for half of all oil, gas, and coal extraction, refining, and marketing. TNCs are responsible for over half the greenhouse gases emitted by industry.[89] They produce almost all ozone-destroying compounds[90] and dominate key minerals industries. For example, aluminum, a dramatically overused and energy-intensive material, has 63 percent of its mines and two-thirds of its refining controlled by only six companies.[91] TNCs control 80 percent of the land that, globally, is given over to export agriculture, land often taken from local food production. Twenty TNCs account for over 90 percent of all pesticide sales and, in a terrifying development, given that they are chemical companies, have come to control a huge fraction of the world's seed stocks.[92]

Moreover, the TNCs control the bulk of global investments, decisive in shaping the future. For example, incalculably more money has been spent in the last forty years on nuclear rather than on solar power, not because of democratic decisions by communities or electorates, or because of rational decisions by well-informed managers, but simply because powerful firms have found in nuclear power a more profitable "energy alternative." Automobiles, electronics, chemicals, and agriculture all tell the same tale. Products and product lines are designed for global markets, and in the process, technologies and societies are shaped to the convenience of corporations.[93]

Nations as we know them are being overcome by international economic flows and recomposed into transnational economic blocs knit together by those flows. It's an old story, but its latest chapters are the most impressive. In 1986, $290 billion passed though the world's foreign-exchange markets each day. By 1990, the figure had topped $700 billion; by 1994, it may have reached $1.3 trillion.[94] Daily.

Since 1993 foreign direct investment has grown more than four times as fast as total world output,[95] and in the patterns of this investment we can see the shape of economic globalization. The American, European, and Asian economic zones are often designated as "super-blocs," but it is perhaps more useful to speak of them as together forming a single entity, "the Triad."[96] Composed of perhaps twenty-five countries, the Triad is the area of the world where the TNCs make most of their investments, the area where an increasing portion of all economic activity takes place. Triad economies now account for two-thirds of the global economic product, and this percentage grows every year. Being in the Triad does not guarantee a nation prosperity, but being left out is worse.

Further, the "newly industrialized countries" — the Asian Dragons like Taiwan and Korea, and even Latin Dragons like Mexico and Brazil — are largely creatures of multinationalization, because many of "their" exports are produced by subsidiaries of the TNCs. According to a 1992 World Bank report,

> by the early 1980s, intrafirm trade within the largest 350 transnational corporations (TNCs) contributed about 40 percent to total trade. More than a third of US trade is between foreign affiliates and their US-based parents. Similarly, East Asian affiliates of Japanese firms ship a quarter of their exports to parent companies in Japan and buy from them more than a third of their imports. In 1982, 47 percent of Singapore's exports were by US-owned firms. Fifty-two percent of Malaysia's exports to the United States were from US affiliates; and [Taiwan's] five leading electronics exporters are US firms. Similarly, exports of electrical goods by Japanese producers in Korea had much to do with the rise of Korea in world electronics.[97]

This economic transnationalism is hollowing out the state, leaving governments increasingly powerless; the process is most advanced in the South, though the United States and the nations of Europe have also lost a great deal of their former autonomy. Jan Knippers Black, a professor of international policy studies at the Monterey Institute of International Studies, writes,

> Whatever the inclination of its leaders, the state is no longer able to carry out what was seen a few decades ago as its primary func-

tion — serving as job or welfare provider of last resort. . . . The state cannot protect its citizens from the vagaries of a global marketplace or give them a voice in the externally rendered decisions that seal their fate. Nor can the state preserve for its citizens' use the essential life-sustaining resources of the national territory. Like the colonialists of centuries past, today's multinationals deplete, despoil and depart. The only reliable guardians of any ecosystem are those who do not have the option of leaving.[98]

The TNCs are both the architects and the building blocks of the global economy, though this situation is obscured by the existence of a press that incessantly reports on the activities of governments but relegates discussion of corporations to the business pages, where individual firms and economic sectors are minutely scrutinized but the overall economy treated in only the most discreetly abstract terms.

In the new global economy, the TNCs dictate the overall terms. The wild capitalism of the East is certainly more brutal, and the "crony capitalism" of the Marcos dictatorship was more devastating, but in these and all other cases the TNCs, with their routine and rationalized imperatives, set the stage. While the planet slides toward the cliffs, the TNCs are simply doing business. They are, as Alfred Sloan, president of General Motors, put it in 1935, "continuously exploring and capitalizing the secrets of nature, making it possible to create new luxuries to be turned into new necessities."[99]

What is crucial about the TNCs is that they pursue this imperative with organizations, tools, and methods that far surpass the power of either community resistance or governmental regulation. They are regional and global actors in a world broken into nations and tribes. They play country against country, ecosystem against ecosystem, simply because it is good business to do so. Low wages and safety standards, environmental pillage, ever-expanding desires — all are symptoms of economic forces that, embodied in TNCs, are so powerful they threaten to overcome all constraint by the society they nominally serve.

Mitsubishi, the model of the modern decentralized corporation, pursues "efficiency" and profit with a single-mindedness that would be almost admirable, were it not that its goals — the maximization of profit and the avoidance of accountability — are so much at odds with the demands of justice and ecological protection. With annual sales of over $150 billion, it is one of the world's largest single corporations, and the Mitsubishi "family" of corporations may be the largest on the planet. That family is deeply involved in deforestation and the tropical timber trade, but it cultivates a complex internal structure that allows it to deny involvement in the ecological crimes being committed in its direct interests. In 1992, when the U.S.-based Rainforest Action Network protested Mitsubishi's logging operations at an auto trade show, it was met by the staff of Mitsubishi Motor Sales of America with startled incomprehension. The car-company flacks denied involvement in the timber trade, and they probably believed in their innocence. Mitsubishi Motor Sales of America is linked only indirectly, by way of its parent Mitsubishi Motors, and then again via the Mitsubishi Corporation itself, to the Meiwa Trading Company, which actually imports timber from the endangered Malaysian Sarawak rain forest into Japan. Within such a structure, usually justified solely on the basis of efficiency, very few people need to have the big picture.[100]

Mitsubishi embodies to an extreme degree the fundamental process that sets the modern world off from its predecessors. Our time, to use words the economic historian Karl Polanyi wrote fifty years ago, lies after the "Great Transformation," in which "the notion of gain" so overcame the social framework within which it was once embedded, and by which it was restrained, that "human society" was turned into "an accessory of the economic system." We live, as Polanyi put it, within the "stark utopia" of the "self-regulating market," and finding ourselves within a long movement of social and ecological decay, it is not difficult for us to appreciate his 1944 warning against economic forces so unrestrained that "the laws of commerce" come to seem "the laws of nature and consequently the laws of God." As for Polanyi's conclusion, that "a self-regulating market" cannot exist "for any length of time without annihilating the human and natural substance of society," what is it if not an early statement of a now almost public secret?[101]

The political-economic question of our time is if anything can be done to force the market into channels less corrosive to life. Can a high-technology planetary economy be democratized and "greened?" How can such greening be possible while each year nations are weaker and government less admired, when economics is taken by so many as the sole source of sound judgment and virtue? These are not questions we will live to see finally answered. In the short term, though — and the starkness of our circumstances compels attention to the short term — they have a simple and almost manageable form. Can we, either by institution building or some other still unaccounted means, hope to meaningfully regulate the global economy, and if so, how?

A Coup at the United Nations?

In January 1992 the U.S. favorite for the post of United Nations secretary-general, Boutros Boutros-Ghali of Egypt, took office. Promptly, and without consulting the General Assembly, he began a "restructuring of the house" that included consolidating a number of the UN's freestanding economic and social groups into a centralized new Department of Economic and Social Development. A month later, the UN Centre on Transnational Corporations (UNCTC), founded in the early 1970s by the G-77, the UN's Southern bloc, was restructured, renamed the Transnational Corporations Management Division, and merged (minus its former autonomy) into the new department.

In 1992, still during the Bush administration, the right-wing Republican Richard Thornburgh was appointed to the post of UN administrative undersecretary-general. Thornburgh arrived on the job with a handpicked team that included at least two insiders from the Heritage Foundation, an ultraconservative outfit with a long, vehement commitment to UN-bashing, and bent to the task of deepening Boutros-Ghali's restructuring. Just before Boutros-Ghali's selection, the Heritage Foundation had called for a new secretary-general willing and able to "take the dead hand of statist socialism off the rudder of the UN."[102] With Boutros-Ghali and Thornburgh on the scene, Heritage was more than gratified. Burton Yale Pines of its UN Assessment Project was quite open about the reason: "The Heritage Foundation hasn't changed its position on the UN. Absolutely not. There's been a change in the UN." The change had evidently gone so far that the UN was no longer "a forum for world Bolshevism and anti-Americanism."[103]

This was the context within which the UNCTC was reorganized. The official reason for the move was "efficiency," but people familiar with the story find that less than candid. Political gambits are often disguised as bureaucratic restructurings, and if anything is clear about this particular "efficiency" move, it's that greens and development activists were its losers. A year later, *The Economist* noted the tranfiguration of the UNCTC in a more revealing manner. The UN, "which spent decades tut-tutting about these firms and drawing up codes of conduct to control them, now spends much of its time advising countries on how best to seduce them."[104]

The "UN Coup," as it was called during the Earth Summit's fourth and final preparation conference (PrepCom4) by an excited and anxiously anonymous UN staffer, did not inspire confidence in the approaching convocation, but it did offer a clear look at the realities of global power. The UNCTC had long been hated by the corporate elites for its critical research into the workings of the TNCs, and for its attempts to promulgate a corporate code of conduct. As *The Economist* said, the code would "control" the TNCs. In its original form, it went so far as to prohibit bribing public officials, to require that the dangers of products and production processes be disclosed, and to ban the export of goods or technologies that are prohibited as unsafe in their country of origin.[105] The code's current draft, after twenty years of relentless lobbying from the TNCs, is so eviscerated that even were it someday to find legal force it would be essentially useless.[106]

The UNCTC's final, fatal transgression was its report *Transnational Corporations and Sustainable Development: Recommendations of the Executive Director,* written for the Earth Summit.[107] Referred to as the *Recommendations,* the report was seen by the United States, Japan, and the TNCs themselves, which were intimately involved in the Summit negotiations, as "an attempt at international regulation." According to Harris Gleckman, a principal author, the report spells out "what would have to be done to have sustainably managed multinationals."[108] This seems a large statement, but it certainly is true that had the *Recommendations* found their way into the Rio accords, they would have been a step toward official standards of corporate conduct. It is a measure of the TNCs' influence that the *Recommendations,* as well as other proposals for regulating the TNCs, were shelved in favor of a "voluntary code of conduct" drawn up by the International Chamber of Commerce and supported by the dozens of corporate groups that were participants in the Summit negotiations.[109] In the end, the UNCTC's proposals were not even circulated to conference delegates,[110] and Agenda 21, the master treaty, contained only the vaguest of references to the TNCs.

Peter Hansen, the former executive director of the UNCTC, was clear about what had happened.

The *Recommendations* were focused on Environment and Development. . . . The U.S. and Japan both opposed them, as they had opposed the Centre on Transnationals. The U.S. and Japan had also made it quite clear that they were not going to tolerate any rules or norms on the behavior of the TNCs, and that any attempts to win such rules would have real political costs in other areas of the negotiations.[111]

Chakravarthi Raghavan, the editor of *Third World Economics* and a longtime UN watcher, saw no mystery in any of this. In New York during PrepCom4, he told an audience of NGO activists that the UNCTC's dismantling was "a move to strengthen the hand of GATT, the IMF, and the World Bank. Power is being shifted from areas where there is some transparency, however limited, to areas in which the peoples of the world have no way of participating."[112]

The reform of the UN is rarely considered within a fair and realistic appraisal of global power. Rather, it is usually confined to a sanitized center-right frame of reference in which "reform" is taken to imply nothing more than bureaucratic streamlining and cost cutting. Only rarely does reform mean more than the better management of a crushing "peacekeeping" agenda and, perhaps, an expansion in the membership of the Security Council (that least democratic and most military of the UN's bodies). Peacekeeping is essential, of course, but if ever there was a time in which peace could not be made solely by the generals, it is now.

The restructuring of the United Nations is a slow and disappointing story. But after the Earth Summit, we at least know how to keep abreast of it. The key is the UN's Economic and Social Council (ECOSOC) and, specifically, its new Commission on Sustainable Development (CSD). The CSD, founded in Rio to monitor compliance with Agenda 21 and the other Summit treaties, is arguably significant. Its establishment was not easy, and according to Bill Pace of the Center for the Development of International Law, can only be seen as a victory of "NGOs and progressive governments" against a large and powerful cabal that included not only the United States, but also "India, China, the United Kingdom, Argentina, Japan, representing most of the North, Brazil, Austria, and Sweden, all of which opposed the creation of the CSD." Most of them "just wanted to get UNCED [the Summit] behind them" and "send in reports for a few years."[113]

The CSD's founding, though, was only a fleeting victory in what promises to be an interminable uphill battle. It has scant financing, and rather than having its own secretariat, is embedded in the UN's ECOSOC bureaucracy. These are not the features of an organization seriously intended to help save the world, and it is easy to be cynical about its fate. Just after its founding Peter Hansen told me that "being placed into ECOSOC has led to other worthwhile initiatives suffering death by bureaucratic suffocation."[114] Since then the political landscape has shifted and shifted again, and we have seen at least glimmers of change. When Al Gore, speaking in 1993 to the CSD's first full meeting, declared that "a child born in the United States will have, in his or her lifetime, 30 times more impact on the earth's environment than a child born in India," and that "the affluent of the world have a responsibility to deal with their disproportionate impact,"[115] even Martin Khor, director of the Third World Network and a man not given to optimism about the goodwill of Northern politicians, reported a change in the air.[116] How long it will be before that change blows steadily, or indeed if it ever will, we do not know.

In the years to come, there will be a great deal of talk about the modernization and reform of global institutions, from GATT and the World Trade Organization to the World Bank and the IMF to the United Nations. There will be victories, and even optimism, and certainly we need them badly enough. But it would be wise to cultivate a certain skepticism. The globalization of power is hardly cheering news, and in all but the most extraordinary moments, even the finest and most well-meaning politicians can accomplish little. International institutions are democratic only in the vaguest sense, and the UN, the most democratic of the lot, is *not* in ascendance. During the Cold War, it lost much of its prestige and position to the Bank, even in its core areas of social and economic development, and although the friends of the UN system are making an increasingly focused and even desperate effort to regain position, it is not clear that they will succeed.[117]

The future should not blind us to the past, as the dramas of peacekeeping should not blind us to the more prosaic and more essential drama of inventing a workable international democracy. At the Earth Summit, when it might have mattered, the TNCs were able to control the political agenda. In the end, the UNCTC's mandate for tracking the TNCs, and the largest part of its staff, was transferred to the UN Conference on Trade and Development (UNCTAD) in Geneva. Little of its funding went with it.[118]

Earth Summit Blues

No adequate response to the social-ecological crisis was ever on the agenda in Rio. This bears restatement even now, for during the Earth Summit, U.S. president George Bush was singled out as "Earth enemy number one." As the *New York Times* commented, the Summit ended up "reviving anti-American sentiment rarely seen at international forums since the Vietnam war."[119]

The Bush administration did lead the battle to contain the green agenda. It lobbied hard to strip the new climate treaty of emissions-reduction targets and target dates, opposed many of the strongest clauses in Agenda 21, and, notoriously, fought against, weakened, and refused to sign the biodiversity treaty. Under Bush, the United States won the "Worst of Rio" contest sponsored by a group of large U.S. environmental groups. As the contest judges noted, it was under Bush that "unprecedented and almost brutal" pressure was applied to force weaker countries to follow U.S. dictates.[120]

Bush was singled out for criticism in Rio because, choosing to play to his domestic antienvironmental constituency, he spoiled the mood. And yet, contrary to the easy Bush-bashing that many environmental groups chose as their main Rio message, nearly every major nation played its part in the dark comedy that was the Earth Summit.[121] As Mark Valentine, then issues director of the U.S. Citizen's Network on UNCED, remarked just after PrepCom4, "The U.S. was rarely alone in obstructing progress on Agenda 21 and the Rio Declaration, and often was not even the principal malefactor."[122]

Here, as a baseline by which to measure the future, is a description of a diplomatic minuet that occurred in the late stages of the discussion of the Agenda 21 chapter on atmosphere. It is taken from the *Earth Summit Times*.

> The stickiest issue remaining is whether or not certain key phrases should be used repeatedly in the text. Saudi Arabia has objected to repeated references to "new and renewable" energy sources. On the other hand, the Saudis are insisting on multiple references to "environmentally safe and sound" technology. Some European countries with heavy investments in nuclear energy object to the words "safe and," suggesting that they approve of what is "sound" but not what is "safe and sound."[123]

Thus was the future adjudicated in Rio. The United States was the leader of the antienvironmental hordes, but it was never alone. The British led a long (and continuing) campaign to head off any serious European push for carbon taxes, an effort that was later joined by poorer members of the European Community and by the Organization of Petroleum Exporting Countries (OPEC). The EC as a whole played a more complex role — it proclaimed itself the world leader on the climate issue, and enjoyed countless favorable comparisons to the Bush administration, but somehow its emissions only continue to rise. The Summit had barely faded from the press when European and British "transportation planners" began a major push to expand their highway systems — not quite the thing for capping off carbon dioxide emissions.[124]

At Rio words were quite enough. The Germans in particular came off as environmental good guys. Chancellor Kohl, the first Western head of state to agree to go to Rio, pledged a 25–30 percent reduction in Germany's carbon emissions by 2005, and for this he was celebrated around the world. Today it is clear that Germany will not meet this pledge, or even approach it, and this despite the carbon-abatement windfall it enjoyed with the collapse of the archaic factories of the former East Germany. Carbon emissions in western Germany are rising, with traffic posing a particular problem. By late 1993 traffic-related emissions (which Germany has promised to reduce by 10 percent by 2005) had actually increased by 17 percent over their levels in 1987.[125]

The Japanese came off even better, and were widely reported in the press as "the first environmental superpower," a status Japan — a virtual environmental criminal state, especially with regard to tropical logging, mechanized fishing, and its role in the international plutonium trade — worked hard to win. According to the *Financial Times*, "Japan approached Rio with a carefully planned diplomatic offensive backed by the largest offer of new environmental aid made at the Summit" — some $500 million a year. "They're the owners of all the new issues, and they're getting it all so cheap," said a senior Brazilian official with mixed regret and admiration.[126] Walden Bello, then director of the U.S.-based Institute for Food and Development Policy, summed the situation well: "Japan and Europe didn't even have to do anything to look good. They just had to have the good sense to shut up."[127]

The South's story, too, is complex, and sordid in its own fashion. The Malaysian government, though a leader in the South's opposition to the North's most hypocritical initiatives, is a major force in the destruction of the remaining Southeast Asian forests. China, which insisted on the deletion from Agenda 21 of language detailing the ecological damage done by large dam construction and water channelization, was meanwhile pushing ahead with its almost incomprehensibly destructive Three Gorges dam. (If built, the dam will displace about 1.3 million people. There have been massive protests, and the Chinese public security forces are planning for many more).[128] And in the climate negotiations — at Rio and since — G-77 politicians have joined with their Northern brethren to oppose even a vague commitment to "study ways their policies subsidize unnecessary waste and pollution."[129]

In 1995 in Berlin, at the climate treaty's first major Conference of Parties, the drift seemed so familiar — with the United States leading an obstructionist bloc, and thus providing cover to every manner of diplomatic bad faith — that jokes quickly emerged about a "Rio re-run." There were real differences between Rio and Berlin, the most important being that in Berlin it was China, and the South in general, that won the chief benefit of looking good in comparison with the "carbon club." But despite this shift, Berlin's halls echoed with the old music. This, like Rio, was a festival of posed virtue.

The United States still led the carbon club, which had additional keystone members in Canada, Australia, Japan, and New Zealand, and of course the eager encouragement of the oil-exporting countries, fossil-fuel industries, and their assorted front groups. On the other side, the South crystallized around the Alliance of Small Island Countries ("front line" countries facing potential innundation by rising seas) and then the Philippines, Malaysia, and Bangladesh, and finally the "Southern superpowers" of India, Brazil, Egypt, and China. The Europeans played the role they so enjoyed at Rio — pressed by a public that wants action, they speak bravely, then in the relative privacy of the negotiating room slip back toward the studied equivocations of routine diplomacy.[130]

The details of the negotiations were, of course, byzantine. The ultimate question, though, is simple enough — was Berlin, and the process it capped, a failure or a success? (With environmental governance, this is almost always a crucial, undecided question.) Christopher Flavin of the Worldwatch Institute, like most mainstream greens, is upbeat. "The final agreement constituted a new global commitment to move forward on the climate issue. As a result, the 'Kyoto Protocol,' to be signed . . . in Japan in 1997, may one day stand alongside the Montreal protocol on ozone-depleting substances in its historic importance for protecting humanity from atmospheric damage."[131]

We shall see. Berlin marked the emergence of new global alliances, and witnessed the Business Council for a Sustainable Energy Future rise to challenge the oil lobby's claim to speak for all industry, everywhere. And it saw a rhetorical commitment to carbon reductions, one that could in fact be elaborated in years ahead. But it won no legally binding commitment to the all-important "targets and timetables" without which even "commitments" remain cruel tricks.[132] And Berlin, crucially, saw a fading of the "Spirit of Rio," which at least in its rhetoric emphasized the role of poverty eradication in environmental renewal, and suggested a road based on equity and a new seriousness.

It is often difficult to know what is important. In the United States, where official politics is trapped in a seemingly perpetual orbit around the Republican hard line, it is easy to hope, and then to imagine, that Democratic Party centrism is a viable alternative. The Clinton administration's role in 1995's climate talks, little different from the Bush administration's role in 1992's, does not support such a hope. But what of Clinton's eager earlier signature to the biodiversity treaty? Isn't it evidence that, for a while, he was able to break from the ingrained anti-environmentalism of U.S. foreign policy? In some ways, perhaps, but these may be less decisive than they seem.

The Biodiversity Convention, despite its name, is hardly a glorious milestone in the history of international environmental law. Peter Padbury of the Canadian Council for International Cooperation — a coalition of 130 Canadian NGOs — described it as "very complicated, very weak."[133] And the *Financial Times* echoed the most left-green of the Earth Summit's critics when it noted that the treaty "was originally proposed as a measure to preserve plant and animal life. But the real issue quickly became the exact opposite: how living organisms could be commercially exploited, and who should have the patent rights. The treaty that was finally agreed was more about commerce than about conservation."[134]

"Biodiversity" means different things to different people. Environmentalists use the word in its technical sense, to denote the ecological complexity that underlies the resiliance and beauty of nature, but governmental and especially corporate negotiators have another concern as well. Hearing "biodiversity," they think not only of life, but also of intellectual property rights, or, in the jargon of international treaty-making, IPRs. Once called "the most boring subject known to man,"[135] IPRs are key to the fair-trade debate, and to the politics of life in general, and they pose unprecedented questions — when can life-forms be patented, and by whom? Under just what circumstances should life be treated as property?

These are not abstract questions, not in the age of biotechnology, not in a time when TNCs are taking advantage of an international chaos in patent law to claim the ownership of entire species. The first such "species" patent — granted on *all forms* of transgenic (genetically engineered) cotton — was issued in the United States in October 1992, to Agracetus, a subsidiary of W. R. Grace. In March 1994 Agracetus won a second species patent — this time in Europe, on all forms of transgenic soybeans — and it is applying for others on rice, beans, and peanuts. Activists are appealing these patents, and there is a widespread sense among both scientists and patent experts that they overstep any legitimate claim. Still, as this is written, Grace seeks exclusive monopoly over any method of genetically transforming any variety of cotton or soy.[136]

The Human Genome Diversity Project (HGDP) was formed by U.S. and European scientists to collect blood, tissue scrapings, and hair samples from "endangered" indigenous communities. The very idea is grotesque to most greens, and not just because it takes the extinction of ancient human communities as inevitable. For the moment, though, think only of intellectual property. Under the IPR rules of the biodiversity treaty, the human genes collected and cloned by the HGDP will be patentable. Human-rights activists charge that biotechnology firms will thus profit from the extinction of indigenous communities, a point the HGDP's supporters can dispute in only the weakest terms. Henry Greely, a Stanford law professor and the chairman of the project's North American ethics committee, says that it "does not have development of commercial products as an interest or as a goal." He also says that such benefits, in any case, would flow back to "sampled populations."[137] On this last point he is almost certainly wrong.

The problem is that the IPR regime established by GATT's Uruguay

Round, a regime the biodiversity treaty's drafters sought to respect and strengthen, is directly at odds with the interests of "sampled populations" and sampled ecosystems. Property rights have little to do with ethics or the protection of biodiversity, and everything to do with manufacturing and royalty payments. As Indian ecologist Vandana Shiva said,

> Pepsi's tomato cultivation in Punjab and Cargill's sunflower cultivation in Karnataka are examples of biodiversity destruction, not biodiversity protection. Large scale commercial interests in agriculture, forestry, and fisheries are the biggest threat to biodiversity. IPR protection to these commercial interests will accelerate biodiversity erosion because the monopolies that are created though IPRs destroy the capacity of countries and small producers to protect biodiversity.[138]

There are, of course, non-IPR aspects to the biodiversity treaty, and they, too, are important. Its "biosafety" provision, for example, specifies that bioengineered organisms must sometimes be treated as "novel" rather than "natural," and thus are to be subject to a set of still-evolving, and potentially meaningful, restrictions on use and testing. And the treaty's all-important conservation provisions require ecosystem audits, the protection of endangered species, the conservation and even restoration of threatened ecosystems. But these other provisions are embedded in a treaty carefully solicitous of IPRs, a treaty that defines those IPRs to the benefit of planetary agricultural and pharmaceutical corporations, and that marks the formal globalization of economic models of life. However laudable the treaty's conservation provisions may be, it is hardly clear that they, or any formal conservation measures, will be as decisive as the ruling economic relationships.

Much was at issue in President Bush's refusal to sign the biodiversity treaty, but the politics of property was the basic matter. It requires a strange and willful imagination to believe, as do so many on the far right, that "environment protection has replaced communism as the great threat to capitalism,"[139] but it certainly *is* true that such protection has major implications for both the meaning and the regulation of "property." A memo leaked from Vice President Dan Quayle's office during the Summit argues against the biodiversity treaty because it "would require enactment of broadened environmental legislation," and particularly the expansion of both "the Endangered Species Act and the National Environmental Policy Act."[140] This might even be true, if the treaty was strongly interpreted, if a serious effort were made to stop genetic erosion.

In the increasingly influential view of the American right, environmental laws imply unacceptable violations of property rights. Some antienvironmentalists even nurture dreams of a radical form of deregulation based on a novel interpretation of the Fifth Amendment, which prohibits the government from depriving citizens of "life, liberty, or property, without due process of law," and from taking property "without just compensation." The amendment has traditionally been interpreted to deny the government the right to seize private property, but now, they demand, it must be extended to prohibit the "regulatory taking" that occurs when governments restrict "development" on "private property."[141]

This is the ideological context within which the Bush people opposed the biodiversity treaty, a context that reflects a larger antienvironmental assault and that will not soon dissipate. To speak of "property rights" is to invoke ancient and venerable prejudices. Nineteenth-century slave owners invoked their property rights as a defense against demands that they free their slaves. In the 1930s, industrialists argued that minimum-wage and workplace safety laws were a taking of their property.[142] Now the issue is the environment.

More specifically, the issue is genes. The debate over the biodiversity treaty begins with the gene banks in which, over the last decades, vast collections of economically significant plant tissue have been stockpiled. These gene banks are essentially huge refrigerators in which collections of seeds and shoots and, in particular, exhaustive collections of fundamental food-crop families — wheats, corns, beans, rices, potatoes — are stored against the anticipated loss of the ecosystems where they evolved, most of them in the gene-rich South. This, it is said, is necessary, for as industrial agriculture, free trade, and the green revolution have swept away traditional forms of farming, the majority of these varieties — many of them developed by selective breeding over the last fifteen thousand years — have been, according to Henk Hobbelink, an activist researcher with Genetic Resources Action International in Spain, "massively replaced by modern 'high yielding' variants, causing genetic erosion of unprecedented proportions." And though it is not often realized, high-tech hybrid crops require continual "injections" of genes from their parent ecosystems. These genes are banked by organizations like CGIAR, the Consultative Group on International Agricultural Research, which was long controlled by the World Bank and is still effectively controlled by the North.[143]

"Banked" is just the right word, for what is most at issue here is royalty payments. At least half of all the crop seeds ever collected in the South are now backed up in Northern gene banks, and these genes are treated by the biodiversity treaty as the property not of the South, where they originated, but of the countries that currently hold them. This is where the treaty goes beyond even GATT, for it eliminates the rights of countries to withhold germ plasm, and dictates that countries that had "donated" germ plasm lost all rights to it. Pat Mooney, the director of the Rural Advancement Foundation International and a leading biodiversity activist, put it clearly: "On December 29, 1993, when the biodiversity treaty went into effect, all biological resources became the property of those who had stolen them."[144]

Today 68 percent of the total world food germ plasm is held in Northern gene banks. Hobbelink estimates the value of the annual genetic infusion from these gene banks, in rice, wheat, and beans alone, into U.S. agriculture alone, as $680 million. At stake is perhaps $100 billion a year for all products based on the accumulated knowledge of indigenous peoples. Ethnobotanist Darrell Posey estimates that, for drugs alone, the figure has already reached $54 billion per year, though less than 0.001 percent of that has ever gone to the indigenous peoples who, in so many cases, led Northern researchers to their botanical "discoveries."[145]

Lost royalty income is just the beginning. A mere twenty crops account for 95 percent of all human nutrition, and although these crops originated almost entirely in the South, we have already reached the point where even Southern agriculture is dependent on the use of hybrid seeds that must be continually refreshed with genes banked in the North. Under the new biodiversity regime, Southern producers — even peasant farmers — must repeatedly pay royalties to transnational companies to use these seeds.[146] Moreover, because of CGIAR rule changes made simultaneously with the biodiversity negotiations, genetic creations based upon CGIAR gene banks, despite the fact that these gene banks are nominally being held "in trust" for humanity, can now be patented.

Why, then, did President Bush still refuse to sign the biodiversity treaty? Because of biotechnology, and property rights. The treaty exempts genes already in Northern banks from royalty payments, but it does grant that the South should, or might, share in the IPRs for in situ genetic materials, those that remain in field and forest. The Bush people would not accept even this, preferring to stand for the corporate right to "prospect" for new strains in the fields and forests of the South, and to win entirely unrestricted IPRs to those strains and all their progeny. In this hard-line view, neither the countries in which new strains are found nor the indigenous peoples who in many cases bred them and in many others pointed them out to corporate biologists have legitimate claim to any royalties at all. Moreover, the treaty contains language that, in Bush's day, was taken to imply that American agricultural companies would be "compelled" to share their genetic creations with the South.

The Europeans and Japanese, confident that the situation was manageable (the treaty is vague and obscure, so there is plenty of room to maneuver), and seeing a PR disaster in a refusal to support "biodiversity," decided to sign. Bush, under pressure from his right wing, and from biotech executives hypnotized by right-wing rhetoric, took the hard line, and plenty of heat. He looked so bad that few greens moved beyond their schadenfreude at U.S. clumsiness to wonder at the content of the treaty itself. In Mark Valentine's words, Bush provided "perfect air cover for everyone else to get away with anything they wanted. We were so good at being the ugly farting monster that no one else had any trouble looking great. Even Castro looked good. I mean, he gave a good speech, but jeez."[147]

Bill Clinton looked good as well. Reversing his predecessor's opposition to the biodiversity treaty was an easy path to an environmentally correct image. But, in fact, Clinton's support for the treaty was conditioned by an "interpretive statement" that calmed the U.S. biotech industry, and gave the United States what *Biotechnology* magazine called a "figleaf behind which to reverse its previously misguided opposition to the treaty."[148] Three U.S. biotech companies (Merck, Shaman, and Genentech) were involved in writing the statement, as were three of the more conservative U.S. environmental groups (the World Resources Institute, the World Wildlife Fund, and the Environmental and Energy Study Institute.) [149]

What does the statement say? First, that "technologies," even if built upon Southern genes, will be transferred to the South only on "fair and favorable terms," which the United States will interpret as terms "voluntarily agreed to by all parties in the transaction." [150] This put an immediate end to Southern hopes for a radically increased royalty stream. Second, the United States will "strongly resist any actions taken by Parties to the Convention that lead to inadequate levels of protection of intellectual property rights, and will continue to pursue a vigorous policy with respect to the adequate and effective protection of intellectual property rights in negotiations on bilateral and multilateral trade agreements," [151] meaning that the United States will see to it that the treaty is not interpreted in any way that would be GATT-illegal. Under Clinton, though, the U.S. hard line on property rights and royalties no longer appears as clumsy Republican rejectionism. "The Clinton position," according to Beth Burrows, an IPR expert with the Washington Biotechnology Action Council, "is worse than the Bush position, because it is the same." [152]

A World of Difference

Many Northern environmentalists left the Earth Summit with a new and not altogether comfortable sympathy for the view, common in the South, that saving the earth is less a matter of correcting isolated wrongs than of finding a route to fundamental social change. Southern activists, for their part, tended to both arrive and leave in a deeply skeptical mood, and it is not at all hard to understand why. During the PrepComs, even the mildest attempts of extravagantly polite Southern politicians to put global political and economic reform on the agenda had been coarsely rebuked. There were still some optimists around at Rio, but the hopes of the early PrepComs had long since faded — few informed activists imagined that Rio would mark a new beginning, a new realism, a new accommodation between rich and poor.

Such an accommodation is possible, and necessary, but it will not come easily As Martin Khor, the director of the Third World Network — a Malaysia-based group of activist intellectuals that was deeply and productively involved in defining the movement critique of the official Summit — wrote in early 1992:

> It is clear that [the disintegration of the Soviet bloc] has weakened the position of the South. . . . Since there is no longer an East-West contest for the hearts and minds of the South, the North is now also much less willing to accommodate Southern demands in economic negotiations. . . . The fading of the Cold War has left the South much more vulnerable to the power of the North.[153]

Rather than despair, Khor sought hope in the environmental crisis, arguing that it has reached a point where "solutions cannot be attained through technological means alone, but will principally involve fundamental changes in economy, development models, lifestyles, distribution of resources and income, and international political relations." The environmental crisis is an "opportunity to renew international cooperation," and to "focus the minds and wills of political and economic leaders as well as people and their organizations on broad cooperation strategies and mechanisms that will be mutually beneficial and ensure Earth's survival."[154]

Other observers see the collapse of the Cold War system in a more optimistic light. Xabier Gorostiaga, rector of the Central American University in Managua, told a 1992 conference of European development activists that though the end of the Cold War would bring "short-term" problems — "an imbalance of power favoring the North, a loss of support for needed changes in the South and submission to direct military control, exerted in particular by the United States" — and though the collapse of "real socialism" has sown confusion and demoralization among activists in the South, the longer term would reveal that this collapse had released the South "from an ideological dependency which hindered dangerously its capacity to construct its own alternatives."[155]

As for the Southern governments, they chose at the Summit to forget the egalitarian demands of past decades and, in Walden Bello's words, "to go the easy route, and make financing the centerpiece of their definitions of success and failure."[156] Their focus on money was justified as realism, as an effort to get beyond cheap rhetoric and seize the meat of the development debate, the meat, in other words, of the North-South conflict. In the end, though, they achieved just the opposite.

Cost estimates for programs of planetary ecological recovery are not often objective — they make assumptions and, inevitably, they imply blame. The estimate for fully funding Agenda 21 is $600 billion a year, of which the North was asked to supply $125 billion. This kind of money was never in the cards, not even as loans, and the Environmental Defense Fund's Bruce Rich was altogether justified in branding the whole Earth Summit funding debate a "uniquely cynical charade, even by UN standards,"[157] and this despite the fact that $125 billion is not a lot of money. It's only a small fraction of the world's annual military budget,[158] and (the numbers here are softer) far less than the *trillion dollars* that, according to a 1994 UN study, the world's governments waste each year on "environmentally damaging subsidies."[159]

But the Agenda 21 budget was framed, in the media coverage of the Rio negotiations, as "a demand for aid," or, as the World Bank's Richard Ackermann told me, a "bill for a hundred and twenty-five billion." So defined, it reinforces the illusion that ecological protection is essentially a matter of money (rather than will and political power) and that substantial changes would cost impractical amounts of money. Ackerman caught the spirit perfectly, telling me that "Agenda 21 lays out a program which is desirable but not necessarily feasible. Taken seriously, it would involve enormous expenditures, so it contains quite a bit of wishful thinking."[160]

Sheltered by such phony realism, in which meaningful changes are impossible by definition, Northern politicians fell back upon rhetoric. One hundred twenty-five billion dollars comes to 0.7 percent of the combined domestic products of the Northern economies, a figure that happens to equal the UN's decades-old, decades-ignored goal for development aid commitments from the North. Absent commitments of real cash, Rio heard talk of finally meeting that goal, "by the year 2000, or as soon as possible."[161] France agreed, but it was alone. Japan, Britain, Germany, and several other large donors agreed to the target but not the deadline. The United States, which has never accepted the 0.7 percent aid target, and allocates about 0.21 percent of its GNP to foreign aid, essentially ignored the whole discussion.[162]

The debate was confusing in the extreme. Even if the North did pay its 0.7 percent (and since Rio, international development aid has dropped, not increased)[163] this wouldn't have changed the overall patterns of North-South economics. "Aid" is not the real issue, for it generally comes as loans, is usually tied to the purchase of goods and services in the donor country, and always remains a part of the trade-debt-aid cycle — "aid" returns to the South only a fraction of what it loses in the routine course of daily economic affairs. Between 1982 and 1990, in debt service alone, the South sent the North $418 billion more than it received in all forms of Northern aid. That's about $50 billion a year (about six Marshall Plans, in inflation-adjusted dollars) paid by the poor to the rich.[164] And since Rio this pattern has only continued — in 1993, the world's forty poorest countries paid $19 billion more in debt and interest than they received in aid. Thirty of these countries are in sub-Saharan Africa.[165]

Even this is just the start of the grim tale of the international economic system, in which "trade" pits undiversified, postcolonial, export-dependent economies all over the world against each other in an economic free-for-all that depresses the prices of primary commodities far below sustainable levels. For the majority of Southern countries, which remain dependent on raw materials for export earnings, the numbers speak in cruel and undeniable cadences. At the end of the 1980s, West Africa earned 84 percent of its income from primary commodities, Latin America earned 67 percent, developing Oceania 76 percent, sub-Saharan Africa a full 92 percent.[166] Commodity prices vary, but the trend has long been down — the average prices of nonfuel commodities dropped a full 50 percent in real terms between 1980 and 1990,[167] and though there have been rebounds since then, they have been far more limited. The nuances of this decline can be traced, by specialists, in endless arcane detail, but as Ross Hammond of the Development GAP told me, "It doesn't take a rocket scientist to figure out that if everyone in the world is exporting, prices will go down."[168]

A great deal of money has flowed from South to North, and despite all rhetoric, it continues to do so. It flows as neverending debt service (Third World debt is still rising),[169] as low commodity prices, as royalties and fees, as foreign-exchange losses, as wealth bled off by a thousand obscure mechanisms. It is a very old story, and in the face of its interminable repetition, we should feign no surprise if money and not, say, democracy or sustainable development continues to define the North-South political agenda.[170]

Who is to blame for the condition of the South? The obvious answer is the North, to which so many of these sentences inevitably refer, the North that, in much of the rhetoric of Southern politicians, sits astride the planet like a cruel, fevered landlord. But this answer will not do.

"North" and "South" are unavoidable shorthand, but they will not serve to map the emerging world.

The Earth Summit proved this at painful length. In the endless hothouse of its PrepComs and plenaries, Northern greens were thrust into sudden contact with Southern NGOs and politicians, and more than a few Northerners became intoxicated by Southern rhetoric. What was there to choose between charismatic Southern activist intellectuals, speaking basic if sometimes oversimplified truths, and Northern politicians whose rhetoric, in constant contrast, was in the service of rapine? Even Greenpeace, which should have known better, told its members that at Rio the South had had "little choice but to abandon any nobler planetary visions and demand a larger piece of the disintegrating global pie."[171]

Such words excuse too much. In lumping Southern elites together with ordinary people, the rhetoric of "North" and "South" obscures the large roles those elites play in destroying their own forests, their own fisheries, their own people. The elites of Malaysia, for example, were ideological leaders of the South at Rio, though they've made a mission out of justifying both political repression and environmental destruction as the costs of "development." Malaysia is home to rapacious logging companies that have gone beyond clear-cutting their national lands to compete with the Japanese and Thais for rights to help destroy Papua New Guinea and Cambodia as well.[172] And Malaysia is by far the world's largest supplier of tropical logs, a title it evidently intends to keep until its forests are gone, which, at current rates, will be about the turn of the century.[173] Yet it was Malaysia that insisted that any forestry treaty would violate its "national sovereignty," and that "development" requires the destruction of the rain forest home of the indigenous Penan, who, according to Prime Minister Datuk Seri Mahathir, will have to decide if they want education and development or to "go to the jungle and live on monkeys."

Mahathir asserted that the North wants "a say in the management of our forests while we have no say on their carbon dioxide emissions. The day the North starts planting forests, and the day we have an Industrial Convention, we can have a Forest Convention."[174] Not an altogether unreasonable position, and one that illustrates a crucial problem — Southern politicians can easily adopt heroic poses, for it's easy to look good compared to the North. Before Rio and since, Mahathir has played his part in the ongoing tragicomedy of global forestry negotiations, but he has hardly acted alone. Northern politicians likewise prefer public relations to progress toward a meaningful treaty, and like Mahathir, they have their reasons. The Europeans seek easy access to the forests of the former East bloc,[175] and for the record, today's most extensive clear-cutting is in neither Malaysia nor Cambodia, but in Canada, the "Brazil of the North."[176]

There are far more substantial common interests between Southern elites and their Northern cousins than between Southern elites and the Southern poor. These elite commonalities, though, are continually being obscured. They are hidden by the abstraction of "the South," and by the development game, in which "aid" to "the South" takes the place of the democracy and empowerment that could make a real difference to poor communities and ecosystems of the Third World. As one movement wit told me, "Southern elites say 'equity,' but mean 'money.' "

Martin Khor, speaking before Rio to a group of Northern activists, sought to stress the environmental consequences of the "unfair terms of trade" that Southern exporters suffer in the world market. By these terms, Southern commodity prices fall far below their ecological value, and Khor's intention was to show that, while they remain so low, the destruction of the South can only continue. Unfortunately, he made another point as well. It is a measure of the confusion that surrounds North-South relations that Khor, a man who actively campaigns to save the Penan and their Sarawak rain forest home, seemed to pass imperceptibly, in the course of an altogether reasonable argument against low commodity prices and high external debt, into a defense of the clear-cutting of the Malaysian rain forest. "If Malaysia drops its lumber exports by eighty percent," he asked, "who will bear the burden? If it drops lumber exports by eighty percent, it must get four times as much per log."[177]

But if Malaysia (actually, a few well-connected Malaysian logging companies) must get better prices for its logs before it will stop the current rates of exploitation, then catastrophe is inevitable. In the short term at least, better prices are just not in the cards. Nor would they stop the logging.

In an unregulated cash economy, those with nothing to sell are doomed, and those who seek a new internationalism confront mind-numbing contradictions. According to a well-known U.S. development activist (who declined to speak of these matters on the record),

"Southern NGOs, at an impasse, have formed some pretty unfortunate alliances with Southern governments. They emphasize access to Northern markets, but deemphasize the ways in which such access distorts their economies. They emphasize aid, but deemphasize the quality of aid. It's still friendly at this point, but definitely dangerous."

It will get more dangerous as the market continues its expansion. Angela Gennino, a veteran environmental activist and the coeditor of a valuable guide to deforestation in Southeast Asia, told me,

> Logging is a metaphor for everything that is happening in Southeast Asia. The South is eating itself, turning on itself. Thailand is eating Burma. The Philippines, which has destroyed its own forests and is now being overcome by floods, is going after wood from other countries. While we're sitting here talking about the North and the South, the countries that have already used up their forests are attacking weaker countries, and the countries that are just opening up are sitting ducks. And soon, China is coming down from the North. And *nothing* can stop China. The Southeast Asian forests are *gone*. There is no country in Southeast Asia that can realistically stop logging. It is over.[178]

There are limits to economic growth, and it does not seem too bold to claim that, as we approach them, civility itself could easily become a scarce and precious commodity. Pragmatism is clearly in order, but simpleminded pragmatism can make matters worse. It tends to support the charge — commonly hurled by Southern elites intent on protecting their perquisites — that environmentalism is in reality an "eco-imperialist" plot against the South. Sometimes these charges are almost justified. In the early 1990s the U.S.-based Natural Resources Defense Council (NRDC) tried to broker a deal by which the oil transnational Conoco would trade $15 million — to go to a "foundation" that would, it was said, spend it to further the interests of local Indians — in exchange for access to a major oil field in the heart of the Ecuadorian rain forest. The local Indians, unfortunately, were never consulted, and neither were the local environmentalists, all of whom rejected the deal as arrogant green colonialism. Conoco, seeing its chance for cheap greenwash slip away, pulled out, another oil company, Maxus, moved in, and NRDC was left with nothing but scorn and a damaged reputation.[179]

NRDC will not make quite the same mistake again, and the whole Washington environmentalist corps may in the future be marginally less naive. The larger problem of environmental protection in a world riven into rich and poor will be harder to come to terms with. "Eco-protectionism" and "eco-imperialism" are names by which we know this dilemma, and they will be sources of pain and confusion for decades to come.

In the face of the claim — often made by Southern elites educated in the U.S. and Europe — that the "development" of their nations demands that Northern markets be opened to their exports, no matter if these were produced by virtual slave labor or at the price of vast ecological damage, we have no choice but to demur. There is no future down this road, not a future that we would wish to claim.[180]

What is needed is a new internationalism, and it will not likely be grown within the sterile frames of "North" and "South." In fact, "the South," as a cabal of political elites able to recognize and represent its own collective interests, has become an increasingly misleading term. The UN's G-77 bloc of "developing countries" has, according to no less an authority than Fernando Jaramillo, its outgoing chair, "accepted to be submerged in a scene of linguistic negotiations, procedural discussions, grandiloquent discourses, and in the elaboration of an immense volume of resolutions, many of them having little if any practical effect."[181] Where once there was cooperation, now, under the pressure of a relentless globalization, every country is for itself.

As one highly excited Latin American delegate put it at the pre-Rio Roots of the Future NGO conference — held in December 1991 amidst the high-tech extravagance of Paris's huge science and technology museum — it is past time "to stop talking about the 'North and the South' and the 'South and the North' and the 'North within the South' and the 'South within the North' and start talking about" (in rough translation) "the fuckers and the fuckees."

A Closing Circle

John Maynard Keynes, a humanist of a kind rare in the economics profession today, wrote in 1933 that he sympathized "with those who would minimize, rather than those who would maximize, economic entanglements among nations." His explication of this heresy is even more shocking to the modern ear: "Ideas, knowledge, science, hospitality, travel — these are things that of their nature should be international. But let goods be homespun wherever it is reasonable and conveniently possible and, above all, let finance be primarily national."[182]

This famous quote, taken from an essay entitled "National Self-Sufficiency," is interesting today for the degree to which, to quote an economist friend, it seems "utopian" and even "quaint." Economic globalization has, she says, "gone too far" for us to put faith in dreams of national self-sufficiency. I know this, yet like many fair traders, I read Keynes's words with sympathy, not so much as a claim about nations but as a statement about communities, as an early form of an impossibly difficult realization — we must find ways to delimit the global economy.

Keynes strained to be practical. After stating his sympathy with those who would "disembarrass a country of its entanglements," he added that "they should be very slow and wary. It should not be a matter of tearing up roots but of slowly training a plant to grow in a different direction." Today's greens, facing more desperate circumstances, likewise strain to be practical, and to understand the emerging world. As they do, their traditional calls for bioregional autonomy and "decentralization" are often joined by new calls that echo Keynes's attention to nations. Nations still have borders and can at least hope to stand against the storm of the new globalization.

In this spirit, Tim Lang, a longtime British food safety activist, and Colin Hines, coordinator of Greenpeace International's economics unit, have called for a "New Protectionism" that "aims to protect the environment by reducing international trade and by reorienting and diversifying entire economies towards producing the most that they can locally or nationally, then looking to the region that surrounds them, and only as a last option to global international trade."[183]

A new protectionist call for reducing international trade is, of course, utopian in the sense that it runs hard against the current of immediate history. Like Keynes's plea for national self-sufficiency and Herman Daly's claim that "the default position should favor domestic production for domestic markets,"[184] it makes great sense when read with an eye to ecological limits and the future. But turn back to the present and the picture shifts. The inability of politicians to link trade sanctions even to Chinese slave labor prisons, police beating of union-minded workers in Sony's post-NAFTA *maquiladoras*,[185] child labor, or any of a thousand other stories makes the point — it is unregulated economic integration, not any protectionism new or old, that sets the terms of globalization.

Today economic position is everything. Early in his administration, President Clinton talked bravely of tying China's trading rights to improvements in human rights. In 1994 he ate crow and embraced what Human Rights Watch called "commercial diplomacy,"[186] allowing China, that land of Market-Leninism, of capitalism without democracy, to retain its most-favored-nation trading status with the United States. The *New York Times* approved, writing that "the game of nations is now geo-Monopoly, and it is first of all about profits, not principles."[187]

Such statements don't seem servile and defeatist to those who make them. Capitalism unbound is simply the game, and effective regulation of the global economy is so far over the horizon that it need not even be discussed. The lack of democratic rights, and the environmental destruction that accompanies it, are admitted into polite conversation, but only as problems that markets will in time solve. Freedom will come with wealth and Levi's — this is called realism. There is only one small problem; globalization-as-usual is destroying human and natural communities around the world, and at rates that cannot safely be ignored.

What is the alternative? We must first ask where we are already heading. If it is utopian to speak of an economic regime of "upward harmonization," one in which minimal environmental and labor rights standards apply to all, or at least to all that seek access to global markets, then realism demands attention to at least one prior question: If we continue on a path of maximal global economic integration, where will we arrive?

In the vast cacophony of contending futurisms, a theme has formed. Today's future is marked by brutal globalism and disoriented localism, by high technology and dismal village poverty, by planetary TV, computerized back-office sweatshops, and frustrated, furious youth. It is a transnational future of nationalist backlash, in which twentieth-century institutions and twenty-first-century technology combine to yield an almost nineteenth-century capitalism.[188] Walter Russell Mead, during the anti-NAFTA campaign, described it thus: "The First and

Third worlds will not so much disappear as mingle. There will be more people in Mexico and India who live like Americans of the upper-middle class; on the other hand, there will be more — many more — people in the United States who live like the slum dwellers of Mexico City and Calcutta." [189]

Many of these people will be trapped in worn or devastated ecosystems, which is where ecology comes back in. The planet is starkly divided between rich and poor, but this is nothing new. What *is* new is that it has been girdled by amazing transportation and communications networks, and that its fields and forests are under siege. The logic of the situation is unclear, but clearly inauspicious. Not, if you please, that this is a prediction. We can see only the future in which current trends continue, which, of course, they will not. Change will come; the question is what kind of change it will be.

As we saw at the Earth Summit, it is not likely to be a coordinated and visionary change. The Summit was a failure not because its treaties are so mild (green treaties often start off timidly, establishing vague regulatory regimes that can later be strengthened), but because it did nothing to raise the key issue — restructuring of the global economic order. We know that order, concretely, as a trading system that, with its financial and institutional understructures, denies all meaningful decentralization, that makes even African peasants dependent on commodity prices set in the electronic bazaars of distant, foreign lands.

Free trade, as Walter Mead put it, has "crossed the threshold." It abets the evolution of a brutally competitive global regime in which democracy is swamped by a reductionist economics. It undermines communities everywhere, and erodes the political forces that could someday compel the "internalizing of costs" in "fair prices." It weakens nations, humiliates any politician who dares oppose the sovereign power of international markets, and allows large corporations to whipsaw nations against each other, beating each down toward the lowest worldwide environmental and labor-rights standards. Yet even free trade is only a symptom of globalization, not a cause, and after GATT's ratification, it is as well a fait accompli. During 1993, with battle raging over the future of GATT, Mead summed up the situation as follows:

Many participants and observers [at the GATT negotiations] reacted with horror to environmentalists' increasingly forceful objections to the talks: another set of demands, another set of issues that divided North from South added to an already impossible burden. But the environmental objections to GATT were part of a broader critique, and the ultimate effect of addressing these issues will be to enhance the scope for free-trade agreements and to disarm protectionism. . . . The liberalization of world trade increasingly and inevitably involves the establishment of a global system of economic regulation.[190]

Of course, it wouldn't be "free trade" as we know it today. Josh Karliner, an American writer and green activist, is more explicit about the shape of such a new regime.

Upwards harmonization implies creating and enforcing environmental standards within trade agreements as a way of controlling TNC behavior. While this concept has not been clearly defined, the idea behind it is that in a world of increasing globalization where power continues to accumulate in the hands of transnational corporations, the rules of the game are enshrined in these international agreements. . . . If we can turn the power of these agreements to our advantage by making them more transparent, democratic and accessible, this may be one of our best hopes to create a space for controlling global corporations, and limiting the negative impacts of free trade without resorting to protectionism.[191]

This is "upward harmonization" or, at the extreme, a "new protectionism" — a global economy in which social and ecological matters are fundamental even to prices. This could be called by more circumspect names like "managed open trade." It could be won by "greening the GATT" or by establishing a new global environmental organization with power over GATT's trade bureaucrats. The key thing is that the greening of international trade is necessary. It must come. That this seems utopian is only because, as Steven Shrybman told me, "all the articles of faith about the proper workings of the economy" must be overthrown before green trade becomes thinkable.[192]

It is important to realize how fast the trade debate is changing. In 1987 the UN-sponsored Brundtland Commission, in its famous report

Our Common Future, could only call in vague terms for GATT to find "more effective instruments to integrate environment and development concerns into international trading arrangements."[193] That today's greens are getting down to details can be seen in documents like *Making Trade Fair: A Social and Environmental Charter for North America*, prepared by U.S., Canadian, and Mexican fair-trade activists.[194] Imagine its "Suggested Minimum Continental Labor and Environmental Standards" as international law. One alone — "Prohibit the export of products extracted, manufactured, harvested, or grown under environmental conditions or workplace health and safety standards that undermine counterpart standards in the importing country" — would set off a virtual green revolution if it were enforced on a global level.

Such ideas are far from the policy mainstream,[195] but on the other hand the religion of unregulated trade is under attack as never before. What is unclear is where that attack will lead. It may even be that a classic isolationism is poised to return. Under Ronald Reagan, Republicans were the party of capitalist internationalism, but no more.[196] Today right-wing politicians everywhere are flirting with nativism of all sorts, and protectionism — old-style protectionism — makes a solid plank for their soapboxes. Fortunately, there is as well another alternative to "free trade," one that looks forward to the greening of the global economy instead of back to models of national and local autarchy that can no longer exist. Support for the greening of trade can be found in the UN, the EU, the OECD, in APEC, even on the fringes of the Democratic Party. The genie is out of the bottle, much to the concern of old-line trade negotiators, who, according to Rod Leonard of the Community Nutrition Institute, an NGO observer in the OECD trade and environment talks, "just can't accept that the environment now has equal status with trade. They're sitting on the tracks and see the train coming, but all they're doing is hoping it will stop."[197]

Their anxiety is understandable, for the improvement of global environmental and social standards is indeed an open-ended proposition. If unsustainably logged lumber is to be subject to reprisal, why not the products of child labor as well? Both, after all, are cheap because they are, as Franklin D. Roosevelt said, "produced under conditions which do not meet a rudimentary standard of decency." Should not both be "regarded as contraband," as FDR recommended, and kept from polluting "the channels of interstate trade"? And if child labor is to be proscribed, why not adult labor, if it takes place under unsafe or unacceptable conditions? And if unsustainably logged lumber is to be penalized, why not unsustainably grown rice, corn, and cotton? Why not cheap fossil fuels? Why not meat?

This is a changing game. Green trade is on the agenda, and the question is whether it will come in a form that makes a difference. In early 1993, Walter Mead, speaking of GATT's future, said that the real danger was a "quick green round" that would pacify mainstream environmentalists but offer little to the rest of the fair-trade coalition. The majors would cave in but declare victory, and this, Mead argued, would be a disaster — for "the coalition is the most important thing in all this," and "without the environmentalists, the human-rights and labor people look like grubby special interests."[198]

Today, as GATT's implementation passes into the hands of the new World Trade Organization and NAFTA spreads south into a larger American free-trade zone, such superficial greening is a clear danger. NAFTA's environmental side agreement was predictably ineffective, but this did not keep the environmental majors from endorsing it. Besides, the current batch of trade agreements — from NAFTA to the European Common Market to GATT — is so bad that almost anything can be claimed as progress. Forget NAFTA's environmental commission, which embarrasses even some of the very environmental legalists who once sang its praises.[199] Think instead of GATT. What will "trade and the environment" mean to the WTO? Not much, not soon. Its Trade and Environment Committee is an obscure, low-status backwater within GATT's larger apparatus, and its environmental "workplan," according to fair-trade activists, is designed not to reduce the impacts of trade on the environment, but to ensure that environmental issues don't get in the way of ever-increasing trade.[200]

Traditional environmentalists, who seek only to protect "nature" in limited but meaningful degrees, require social justice for their success. Wages in Mexico will increase, or wages in America will drop. In the end, one trend will predominate. There will be strong international norms of environmental protection, and social justice to animate those norms; or the condition of our planet, and the health of our democracies, will continue to deteriorate. Finally, and despite all complexity, it is that simple.

To win, greens, workers movements, and human-rights activists must go global, just as the corporations have done. To a small extent, this process has begun. The NAFTA battle moved some U.S. unions — including traditionally protectionist textile unions — into joint strategy talks with their counterparts from Latin America and the Caribbean, and into common commitments to defend the rights of workers throughout the hemisphere. At Rio greens and development activists from around the planet sat together for days to compose an Alternative Treaty on Trade and Development that expressed widely shared understandings of what was at stake. Among other things, it calls for a global trade organization that is "designed with a participatory and democratic structure ensuring transparent, accountable and equitable decision making in accordance with the public interest instead of corporate interest." (GATT's WTO, undemocratic by any measure, definitely does not fit the bill!) This is a small beginning, but at least it indicates a direction, at least it speaks for an alternative model of globalization.

Green trade is inching onto the diplomatic agenda. This is good news, and should be clearly stated. At the same time, it is unlikely that we will soon see any really meaningful form of ecologically and socially conditioned trade. The fundamental and inexorable problem is that a true green trading system would *reduce* long-distance commerce, which for basic ecological reasons tends to have higher environmental costs than decentralized systems of production. Such a change, obviously, is not in the cards, not in the immediate future.

Mike Rubin, a friend unencumbered by a formal education in economics, after browsing some of my "trade alternatives" files, pointed out that the various proposals for green trade systems have, despite their many differences, a great deal in common. All are "utopian." They make no clear connection between the new regime they advocate and daily events in the existing world, wherein every nation, every region, is straining to find its future in exports to all the others.

And even if strict new trade-related environmental laws were put on the books, how would they be enforced? Angela Gennino, the rain forest activist: "Who's going to go into Cambodia and make sure that the Khmer Rouge is doing sustainable logging? Who's going to tell Pol Pot, 'You didn't selectively cut this area, so you can't export the logs'? Give me a break."[201]

Return, finally, to the promises. Free trade and global economic integration are everywhere being sold with magnificent scenarios of export-led affluence. And what if GATT and NAFTA — despite the contributions they will certainly make to swelling the ranks of the Northern poor — do redound to the benefit of the U.S. economy? What if GATT is in fact a tonic for the economies of the North? These are at least plausible scenarios. But turn to the other side of the equation, and to the benefits that ever-expanding global trade will supposedly bring to the poor people of the South. Shall we believe that all the world's poor will soon live in export-driven "dragon" economies? That all the world's poor will someday be winners? Already, it's clear that sub-Saharan Africa and the Caribbean, two of our poorest areas, will grow poorer still under GATT/WTO rules.[202] But when will it be as clear, even to policymakers, that such inconvenient realities really matter? At what point will the plausibility of the free-trade fantasy finally snap?

The Age of Greenwashing

Crimestop means the faculty of stopping short, as though by instinct, at the threshold of any dangerous thought. It includes the power of not grasping analogies, of failing to perceive logical errors, of misunderstanding the simplest arguments . . . and of being bored and repelled by any train of thought which is capable of leading in a heretical direction. Crimestop, in short, means protective stupidity.

— George Orwell, 1984 [1]

If the truth of an idea is defined by its advertising campaign, who but a mug can seriously believe in one set of ideas or another? If perception is reality, what is the point of any difference at all — between Republicans and Democrats, between journalists and Government officials, between ideologues and copywriters, between the chatterers of television and the thinkers of the academy, between Washington and Hollywood?

— Michael Kelly [2]

In 1969, having faced years of bitter protest, Pacific Gas and Electric finally won the permits needed to break ground for the construction of a nuclear power plant in the pristine near wilderness of California's Diablo Canyon. Tension was high, and people were asking why the plant, if it was necessary at all, had to be built in an area so stunning and uniquely situated that it was being considered as a national park. PG&E had its nuke, but it also had a real public relations problem. [3]

As construction proceeded, it became obvious that serious damage was being done to the canyon. Worse from PG&E's embattled perspective, it was highly visible damage, including as it did the complete denuding of a large oceanfront hillside being leveled to make room for the plant's switching yard and transformers. The wounded slope gaped, visible for miles around. PG&E had a problem, but it also had, so it thought, a solution — spraying the exposed slope with a rich green paint.

It was a tacky move, and it did not buy PG&E much sympathy. It does offer a neat reference point, a marker by which to date the age in which ecological crisis met public relations, the age of corporate "greenwashing," the age we inhabit today.

Deep Lobbying

Green PR people are advised to ride the Republican fueled anti-environmental backlash as far as possible. But they should not be greedy because overreaching may come back to haunt them once the sun sets on the pro-business Republicans and greenies are again on the rise.

— O'Dwyer's PR Services [4]

Public relations, not physics — or even ecology — is the paradigm science of the modern age. Its roots trace back to the World War I years, in which life first took on the hard commercial glint we still associate with modernity, to the development of advertising as we know it today, and the emergence of professionally organized systems of appearance management.

By 1934, when Du Pont formed its PR department — in tardy response to a Senate investigation of the gunpowder industry that painted the company as "a merchant of death" — the pattern was already set. [5] By 1979, when Metropolitan Edison, in response to the near meltdown at its Three Mile Island nuclear reactor, quickly moved to expand its PR staff, it was following, if inexpertly, a well-marked path. By the late 1980s, terms like "spin control" were in common usage, and the ground was prepared for a specialized "green" PR industry.

In 1989, when the Exxon *Valdez* spewed heavy crude oil across the shores of Alaska's Prince William Sound, PR insiders almost rejoiced. Exxon managed the crisis with the arrogance of a dull giant, and as John Paluszek, president of Ketchum Public Affairs, put it, "brought to the attention of all CEOs the importance of good public communications."[6] By 1990, the Public Relations Society of America could focus an entire annual conference on the mechanics of corporate environmental positioning, complete with seminars like "Understanding Activist Publics: Making Allies Out of Enemies," and "Building Public Support by Resolving Disputes Through Consensus."[7] By 1992, only the most ideological and self-destructive of politicians would publicly trivialize the ecological crisis. President Bush's Earth Summit image disaster drove the point home to his comrades around the world. He called himself the "environmental president," but his act was just not up to modern standards. Today those standards are easy for politicians and executives to learn. Antienvironmental and "green" PR are a billion-dollar-a-year industry,[8] and the largest PR firms in the world are self-consciously involved in the fabrication of what they sometimes call a "new environmentalism," one that, as *Fortune* magazine put it, will be "more cooperative than confrontational — and with business at the center."[9]

"Everything about the rhetoric," says a sometimes bitter friend, "has changed, but nothing about the reality." If this is true, and in an important sense it *is*, then questions come immediately to mind. How, first of all, can we tell the difference between rhetoric and reality? And why has this strange change taken place? And by what peculiar dynamic?

Political journalist William Greider has called the subject "deep lobbying,"[10] an enterprise that goes far beyond filling TV screens with images of responsible corporations and trustworthy, informed politicians. Such images are the flagship products of an appearance-management industry, but focusing too much attention on them obscures the degree to which this industry has outgrown advertising and public relations to become a central element of the political system, and a standard part of the corporate tool kit. Harold Burson, founder and chair of Burson-Marsteller, the world's largest independent PR firm, is clear. "Our business is still considered by some as a facade, the practice of form over substance," he complains. "Our discipline is deprecatingly referred to as 'PR,' a now-pejorative term I've never cared for. But our contributions are, in fact, substantial, or can be. I believe they are mainly unrecognized."[11]

It is time to recognize them, and to know that the basis of the greenwashing industry is the slippage between reality and images of reality. A polluting firm is not "industry" in general, but it may still have a large PR budget, and it will certainly have motives to deny that environmental regulation both promotes economic activity and creates jobs.[12] Today the expertise needed to package such a denial is easily available. Image management is a mature industry. It has its case studies, its trade associations, its metrics, routines, and innovations. Politics will never be the same, and green politics least of all.

To understand greenwashing, start with its simplest form — ad campaigns. Examples are everywhere, but the baldest seem always to emanate from the energy companies. There is, for example, Chevron's infamous "Do people?" campaign. ("Do people keep an eye on little things so we don't lose sight of the big picture? People do!")[13] And, as evidence that nothing is impossible, there is the U.S. Council for Energy Awareness's closely targeted nuclear-power-for-postfeminist-women ads — "I want my kids to grow up in a healthy environment. . . . When I was in college, I was against nuclear energy. But I've reached a different conclusion."[14]

The key to greenwashing is manufactured optimism, which comes in many forms — as images, articles and books, technologies, and even institutions. Anything will do, as long as it can be made to carry the message that, though the world may seem to be going to hell, everything is in good hands. Examples are everywhere. Thin "beauty strips" of trees left along roadsides to hide clear-cut hillsides, paint sprayed over Diablo Canyon's wounds, NAFTA's "environmental side agreement" — all, to one degree or another, are greenwashing. So too are recycling, "inherently safe" nukes, bioengineered grains, double-hulled tankers, and plenty of other technologies designed to be framed as green alternatives, though they are at best palliatives. So too are whole ideologies. "Progress," that old warhorse, is the classic but now unrepresentative example. This is the age of green PR, and in it odes to "sustainable development," optimism about ecological economics, and even environmental treaties are suspect. All can be, and are, used to assure us that we are already turning the corner.

Corporate Environmentalism?

Today Pacific Gas and Electric, builder of the Diablo Canyon nuke, has become one of the greenest corporations in the United States, and promotes energy efficiency as eagerly as it once promoted atomic power. David Brower himself — the legendary archdruid of the American ecology movement, the man who in 1969, with a small group of allies, threw the genteel, corporate-friendly Sierra Club into chaos by demanding that it oppose PG&E's nuclear ambitions — has praised it as a corporate inspiration. Obviously, something in the eco-political landscape has changed.

Stories of corporate greening are endlessly cited as tokens of realistic hope. Too bad they are so routinely exaggerated, so routinely stripped of their proper context. PG&E, for example, is a regulated monopoly, and its turn from oil and nuclear energy to efficiency and conservation is a direct result of a decision by California regulators to grant it, in exchange, a high rate of guaranteed profits. PG&E has changed not because of any market-driven bottom line, but as a result of "shareholder incentives" that started off at 15 percent. Not bad for a guaranteed return.

Such devices cannot reform Du Pont, Chevron, or Monsanto, global corporations that, far from being regulated monopolies, are generally able to evade governmental controls of all kinds. Nor do easy regulatory fixes always work on utilities. They are, after all, corporations like any others, in business to make money, not energy. The executives of Southern California Edison — internationally known as a green utility — chose on at least one occasion to lobby *against* a bill that would have tightened energy-efficient construction standards. The problem was that such standards would have required better-insulated buildings, thus depriving them of some of "their" energy-saving opportunities.[15]

Welcome to the new world, where everything is changing, and changing not at all. Are corporations coming to see in ecology an unprecedented opportunity to reorder priorities and prepare for a new cycle of green growth? Or is corporate environmentalism better read as an ominous development in which well-advised executives, keen to hold off citizen activists and governmental regulation, pay ever closer attention to the orchestration of appearances? Can we even tell the difference between images and reality?

These are tough questions. To answer them, it may help to attend to the advice the executives are receiving from their green counselors. Nazli Choucri, a professor of political science at the Massachusetts Institute of Technology and a corporate environmental strategist, put the key issue with cool pragmatism: "Managing an inquisitive and possibly hostile public must be part of maintaining a positive image, but public relations without environmental action will surely backfire."[16]

There must be change, for images must have some substance to support them. But which is in command, the logic of change or the logic of images? When a scandal-ridden company called Nuclear Engineering Inc. changes its name to U.S. Ecology, wins the contract to build a hotly contested radioactive waste dump, and distributes slick brochures explaining the dump's displacement of a threatened desert tortoise as "A New Home for Endangered Friends," it is obviously the logic of appearances that sets the terms.[17] Is this the general case? If it is, then all the corporate greening in the world comes sooner or later back to public relations.

And yet reform movements do exist in the corporate world, and some of them are substantive. "Pollution-prevention engineering" is a promising discipline in which products and processes are redesigned to eliminate wastes at the "front end," by not manufacturing them in the first place.[18] But historian Robert Gottlieb argues that such engineering reforms are often responses to pressures generated by activist groups like the National Toxics Campaign,[19] and to some extent this is certainly true. This is the paradox of corporate greening. If activist and regulatory pressure brings corporate reforms, who deserves credit for those reforms? And if the PR department goes on to tout them as badges of corporate virtue, who, in the end, is their beneficiary?

Corporate greens will not appreciate the skepticism here, but neither will grassroots activists appreciate the willingness to take corporate greening seriously. Imagine that you have been an ozone campaigner for a solid decade, and that in the early 1990s you had to endure Du Pont's widely televised image remake, anchored by a TV spot in which seals, otters, dolphins, and penguins applaud the company's new green departures to the triumphal strains of Beethoven's "Ode to Joy." You could be forgiven your cynicism, especially since Du Pont is the largest single corporate polluter (by the pound) in the United States, and was, even as its "applause" ads blanketed the airwaves, conducting a high-pressure, misleading, and ultimately successful lobbying campaign against international restrictions on its new "lite" chlorofluorocarbons, the HCFCs and HFCs that, according to Du Pont's PR staff, are "environmentally enlightened" chemicals.[20]

It is also easy to see why the executives and environmental consultants of major corporations bemoan the distrust and resistance they get from green activists. Corporate greens see themselves as the good guys. Peter Schwartz, author of *The Art of the Long View* and head of the Global Business Network, spoke for many green executives when in 1991, at ECO/TECH, a green technology conference, he declared that "corporate environmentalism can be a successful partnership between private initiative and social good," and that it "provides multiple payoffs," because "efficient and high-quality products reduce both cost and environmental impact." Schwartz even called for regulation, because "environmental regulation forces companies to take the long view" and makes them leaner, more creative, and more competitive.[21]

The Global Business Network is a visionary among consulting firms (Stewart Brand, founder of the *Whole Earth Catalog,* is listed on its roster as a principal consultant), but it does not share the philosophy of activist greens. Peter Schwartz believes that "outside" environmental activists make the jobs of green insiders more difficult, for activists' fixations on "blocking" corporations and pushing their "knee-jerk views" create a climate of confrontation, and result in the "delegitimating of environmental regulation over time." In the face of such a dubious claim — in which greens are blamed for weakening green regulations — and especially in the face of the assertion endlessly repeated by corporate greens, that *they* are the true environmentalists, it is easy to relax into cynicism.

The classic statement of this view — that corporations are the hope of the environment — came from Du Pont's CEO Ed Woolard, who, in a 1989 speech to the American Chamber of Commerce in London, shortly after the Exxon *Valdez* spill, seems to have been the first to use the term "corporate environmentalism." In that speech, Woolard called for "an attitude and a performance commitment that place corporate environmental stewardship fully in line with public desires and expectations," and claimed that "the environmental groups cannot solve any of these problems. Governments can't do it. Corporations have to do it."[22] John Elkington, a leading European green business strategist and the coauthor of *The Green Business Guide: How to Take Up — and Profit from — the Environmental Challenge,* goes even further, claiming that "the main impetus for sustainable development in the future will probably come from business," an outrageous claim that he supports as best he can — with a pop-psych "generational transition" theory of institutional change. "The previous generation of industrialists saw environmentalists as the enemy. . . . They used the watermelon analogy, with the environmental movement seen as green on the outside and red on the inside. That's changed very substantially as the 60s generation and the people around it have grown up. Now there are people with green sympathies in board rooms." [23]

Though it is not often obvious from the rhetoric of its official representatives, corporate environmentalism may be as real a "social movement" as feminism or civil-rights activism. Social movement theorists stress that movements (unlike theories) are messy, and corporate environmentalism, like any green movement, is a fine example. It is naive, contradictory, compromised, and sometimes even sincere. It is tough to evaluate, and routinely manipulated, yet it is more than greenwashing. Talk to the rank and file, the liberal professionals who know corporations as fish know water. They complain that the real decision makers aren't sincerely interested in environmental protection, but they nevertheless want to change the corporations they work for. They are pragmatic and more than a bit worried. As one female middle manager told me, quite without Ed Woolard's overarching confidence, "The corporations have the talent, the resources, the R&D, and the ability to make a difference. If they can't be brought on board, there's no hope of reversing the environmental crisis in time."

Will the corporations, as green optimists believe, climb on board of their own accord? Is corporate environmentalism a movement destined to spread throughout the business world, or is it a creature at the margins, localized in a few sectors (like high-tech manufacturing) while other sectors (like the oil and mining industries) use it, if they even bother, as PR cover for ecocidal business as usual?

A small number of small companies are cited ad nauseam whenever it comes time to argue that business is becoming socially responsible: Ben and Jerry's ice cream, Smith and Hawken (a purveyor of high-quality tools and cotton clothing), Patagonia, The Body Shop. And in 1994 The Body Shop fell off this already short list, when an exposé in

Business Ethics revealed the half-truths behind its "hippie mythmaking." The company, for example, has long made its "Trade Not Aid" program a centerpiece of its marketing strategy, though "fair trade" accounts for less than 1 percent of The Body Shop's ingredients and, contrary to publicity, the company does not pay "first-world wages for third-world products."[24] Reading the article, many people in the "ethical investing" movement were scandalized. But even if The Body Shop (and, for that matter, the rest of these companies) were run to heroic standards, what difference would it make? A painfully long series of articles have leaned on this same group of small companies for hope, and this repetition itself reveals the weakness of the case. A 1992 book named *Companies with a Conscience* profiled a number of the most exemplary of such firms. Together, they employed 4,191 people. At about the same time, Du Pont employed 132,600.[25]

And Du Pont? According to corporate-environmentalist theory, it too will gradually become greener, even if it never becomes as green as Ben and Jerry's. Why? Because, says Hardin Tibbs, a charming and knowledgeable man on the staff of the Global Business Network, while "the company of yesterday restricted itself to the minimum effort necessary to ensure compliance and end-of-pipeline costs," the emerging "green corporation" willingly "accepts the environmental imperative" and "adopts a truly 'proactive' strategic posture, favoring voluntary product and process redesign, as well as the avoidance of pollution and waste." Why? For the most unimpeachable of capitalist reasons — because it has realized that "the speed with which a corporation understands and addresses these changing norms and values will define a large part of its competitive edge in the future."[26]

Du Pont, like PG&E, will become a green company because it can make money by doing so. The central claim of the corporate environmentalists is that in the end efficiency and "greenness" come to the same thing, that "well run" companies like 3M, Dow, and Polaroid have found that, with clear vision and hard work, they can redesign their production processes so as to eliminate toxic wastes and increase profits at the same time. The claim is that "leading companies" have cleaned up their acts, and that only bad management and obsolete ideas prevent others from following along.

The classic example of such a "leading company" is 3M, a diversified, U.S.-based high-technology manufacturing corporation that in 1991 was capitalized at over $24 billion and operated eighty-nine plants in thirty-eight different countries. 3M is perhaps *the* pioneer in corporate pollution prevention; its "Pollution Prevention Pays" (3P) program was founded in 1975, to encourage employees to develop manufacturing processes that eliminate or reduce toxic waste.[27] By all reports, 3M takes its 3P program seriously. Even Barry Commoner, a longtime radical known for his arguments that only a deep democratization of society can ensure a transition to greener technologies,[28] grants that "they understand that the way to reduce pollution is to eliminate the production of toxic materials."[29]

3M is seldom accused of overt, crass, PR-driven greenwashing. Unlike Dow Chemical, a company torn by conflicting tendencies, sometimes a budding corporate environmentalist and sometimes an antagonistic opponent of social activists ("This is the Dow that bitterly fought Oregon housewives and Vietnam veterans over herbicide sprays, and still denies the links between those sprays and cancer"),[30] 3M is not at war with itself. Its 3P program is consistent with its larger "corporate culture," which aims to generate ever greater efficiency and to encourage innovation. 3M's managers are acutely aware that new products are expected to account for at least 25 percent of every division's revenue every five years.

But greenwashing comes in many shades, and one of the oldest is the manipulation of statistics. 3M claims in its promotional materials that 3P prevented seventy-two million pounds of pollutants from being released every year between 1975 and 1989. It does not say that because of dramatic increases in production its total output of pollutants actually increased during that period. As Joel Hirschhorn, co-author of *Prosperity Without Pollution: The Prevention Strategy for Industry and Consumers*, told me in reply to a question about the 3P program, "To some extent it's bullshit." He went on to explain:

> The problem has to do with the lack of a frame of reference around their data. They say they have reduced waste by 80 percent. Okay. Are other wastes being generated? Sometimes they take credit for regulations that were rammed down their throats. Or claim waste-reduction gains when the reduction came from closing production facilities. 3M had the first serious pollution-reduction program, but they still have a lot of incineration prob-

lems in Minnesota. 3M is one of the top polluters in the nation, and in particular one of the largest producers of reproductive hazards. They do not present their data properly so that you can tell what is going on.[31]

Or, as Brian Lipsett of the Citizen's Clearinghouse on Hazardous Waste put it, while 3M is one of the few companies that has made "well-substantiated claims" of reducing waste at its source, it remains one of the nation's worst polluters. According to Lipsett, "Talk is cheap,"[32] and one might add that it is often edited. 3M got a lot of great press in 1989 for cutting emissions from two factories in Hutchinson, Minnesota. It did not tell reporters that it did so only after a community right-to-know law revealed that the plants had emitted twenty-five million pounds of toxic waste in 1989 alone.[33]

"Most of these corporations," according to Hirschhorn, "are green the way an apple is green, on the outside where you can see it."[34] To understand corporate environmentalism, you must understand this, and also understand that powerful economic forces are compelling changes in manufacturing technology that can contribute in real ways to a green transition. One promising trend is "industrial ecology," an engineering discipline that goes beyond pollution prevention to design "industrial infrastructures as if they were a series of interlocking man-made ecosystems interfacing with the natural global ecosystem."[35]

Industrial ecosystems, according to their eager spokesman Hardin Tibbs, are "a logical extension of life-cycle thinking" that involve the closing of loops by "recycling, making maximum use of recycled materials in new production, optimizing use of materials and embedded energy, minimizing waste generation, and reevaluating 'wastes' as raw materials for other processes."[36] It is an elegant idea that excites the technical imagination. The Dutch are funding research into zero-discharge manufacturing as part of their national environmental plan, international conferences are taking place, the Japanese are interested, and in the United States there is talk among the President's Council on Sustainable Development of funding a large-scale demonstration industrial ecosystem.[37] Nor is it all theory. In Denmark, west of Copenhagen, an industrial ecosystem has evolved that includes an electric generating plant, a pharmaceutical plant, an oil refinery, a wallboard producer, a sulfuric acid plant, cement producers, a fish farm, a large greenhouse farm, and a district heating system. Power plant steam is sold to the pharmaceutical plant, sulfur is removed from gas and used to make acid, fish-farm sludge is used as fertilizer by local farmers, and so on.[38]

All these activities can also be profitable, and thus the dream of the corporate greens — that an engineering revolution, along with managerial improvements, can obviate all need for jarring social changes and, as green cultural critic Marcy Darnovsky put it, "wean public sympathy for environmental action away from anti-business green activists, rallying it instead behind business leaders and mainstream greens."[39]

In some industries, some of the time, there is money to be made selling green products and greening industrial processes. In others the slope is toward greenwashing, pure and simple. Barry Commoner cites "oil, petrochemicals, and utilities" as industries where "pollution prevention will really cost them,"[40] and it is hardly serendipity that drove these same sectors to pioneer green public relations. Today green PR is ubiquitous, and corporations as a whole reap the goodwill that properly belongs only to the green sector. Corporations *in general* benefit from the sense that an ecological transition can be made within the unregulated global economy we suffer today, and from the official optimism that tells us that corporate greening is fated to overcome its many countertendencies to define the economic enterprises of the future. Corporations *in general* benefit from the sense that the green sector of the economy is already large, when actually the vast majority of stocks sold by "environmentally screened" mutual funds represent, as green-investment expert Mike Kieschnick of the Muir Fund once snidely noted, "trash companies that do everything to garbage but reduce it."[41]

And, always, greenwashing has as its primary purpose confusing the boundaries between the "green sector" and the much larger corporate world. The oil, coal, and auto industries have the Global Climate Coalition, organized and well funded to resist all moves to restrict carbon emissions.[42] The U.S. Council for Energy Awareness tells us that nuclear energy is essential to reduce dependency on imported oil.[43] The American Council on Science and Health, a food industry cabal that includes Seagram, General Motors, and Union Carbide, works to "prove" that pesticide residues pose only a negligible risk to human health.[44] The National Wetlands Coalition labors on behalf of mining, utility, and real estate interests to oppose wetlands protection. Besieged chemical companies circle their wagons behind the banner of "Responsible Care."[45]

The Earth Summit, that perfect creature of the age of public relations, demonstrated just how popular such intercorporate PR consortia have become. The green-and-white tents of its Global Forum included booths by corporate NGOs like the American Nuclear Society, Asbestos Institute of Canada, Australian Coal Association, Confederation of Brazilian Industry, International Council on Metals and the Environment, Edison Electric Institute, Japan Fisheries Association, and lots of other similar organizations. In response, Friends of the Earth International immediately distributed a list of suspect corporate attendees, and plastered their booths with skull and crossbones stickers announcing, "Warning: Toxic Information."

It was the Business Council for Sustainable Development (BCSD) that led the corporate assault on the Earth Summit, via *Changing Course: A Global Business Perspective on Development and the Environment,* the executive summary of which was everywhere at the Summit. In it, Stephan Schmidheiny, the Swiss billionaire who founded the BCSD at the request of UNCED secretary-general Maurice Strong, takes the high ground. "The title *Changing Course* was chosen with some care. While the basic goal of business must remain economic growth, as long as world population continues to grow rapidly and mass poverty remains widespread, we are recommending a different course toward that goal."[46]

This is a book that requires close scrutiny. Schmidheiny, its principal author, appears sincere in his fear of environmental crisis, and *Changing Course* even advocates "full-cost pricing," a device few corporations would willingly embrace.[47] Full-cost pricing means fully incorporating ecological and social costs into all economic transactions, and this in turn means strong and broadly conceived environmental laws and regulations, effectively enforced. Just getting started on this path demands an end to subsidies for environmentally damaging activities and the transition to a system of ecological taxes. These are not ideas often associated with the Du Pont, Alcoa Aluminum, Shell Oil, and Nippon Steel corporados who populate the BCSD's ranks. Something funny is going on here, and while you will not find it spelled out in the pages of *Changing Course,* there are clues:

> The fall of communism does not represent the total victory of capitalism. It is merely the end of a system that, as practiced in Eastern Europe and in the Soviet Union, reflected neither economic nor environmental truths. This should encourage those of us who believe in the efficacy of the marketplace to eliminate its failures and weaknesses and to build on its strengths. Market economies must now rise to the challenge and prove that they can adequately reflect environmental truth and incorporate the goals of sustainable development.[48]

This may be a bit self-serving, but it does not appear to be a call for business as usual. Still, Greenpeace, which at Rio made a mission of attacking the BCSD, sees it as greenwash through and through. Its *Greenpeace Book of Greenwash,* issued in anticipation of the BCSD's public relations assault in Rio, says,

> A leader in ozone destruction takes credit for being a leader in ozone protection. A giant oil company professes to take a "precautionary approach" to global warming. A major agrochemical manufacturer trades in a pesticide so hazardous it has been banned in many countries, while implying the company is helping to feed the hungry. A petrochemical firm uses the waste from one polluting process as raw material for another, and boasts that this is an important recycling initiative. A company cuts timber from natural rainforest, and replaces it with plantations of a single exotic species, and calls the project "sustainable forest development." . . . While they proclaim that "corporate environmentalism" is here, the TNCs are working to help create a new world order where international agreements and practices will give them unregulated, unparalleled power around the globe.[49]

This is the nub. Were corporate environmentalists proposing to transfer their best technologies to the lands of the poor, to democratize world markets, and support strict, uniform, and global environmental regulations, then, clearly, they would have broken in a substantial way from their more unenlightened colleagues. Questions would remain, dozens of them, but it would be clear that something large was afoot.

What is actually happening, though, is different. A small group of upper executives, many of them heads of major corporations with criminal environmental and social records, have signed on to a public relations manifesto that is notable only for its recognition of the need for reformed business practices more sensitive to the demands of efficiency and waste reduction. Schmidheiny himself sits on the boards of both Asea Brown Boveri, which builds and markets nuclear reactors, and Nestlé, which has long been notorious for its aggressive marketing of unaffordable infant formula as a breast milk substitute in the developing world.[50]

Changing Course speaks effusively of full-cost pricing, but BCSD's corporate members do not seem to have read it. During the runup to the Earth Summit, the International Chamber of Commerce (in which BCSD's membership is highly influential) pressed hard to purge all calls for regulating the TNCs from the Summit documents. That campaign included a trip to Stockholm, where the ICC lobbied Sweden to withdraw a proposal calling for TNCs to internalize environmental costs — a major aspect of full-cost pricing — and replace it with the meaningless "inviting [the TNCs] to participate in examining the implications for internalizing environmental costs."[51]

Corporate environmentalism is, in the end, notable for the threads of both sincerity and cynicism that wind though its tangled patterns. Compared to corporate antienvironmental activism, it is a token of rationality and hope. Yet corporate environmentalism also offers a misleading win-win fantasy of environmental protection in which tough choices will not be necessary. Environmentalists have long promoted the idea that companies can easily increase profits by reducing pollution, but many corporations believe, with evidence, that their relatively easy environmental problems have already been solved. As Noah Walley and Bradley Whitehead, consultants with McKinsey & Company, wrote in the *Harvard Business Review*,

> While tough environmental standards may yield significant positive results for the economy as a whole, individual companies will actually be battling increasingly complex environmental problems at a much higher cost than ever before. . . . Companies are

already beginning to question their public commitment to the environment, especially since such costly obligations often come at a time when many companies are undergoing dramatic expense restructurings and layoffs.[52]

Thus win-win rhetoric, Walley and Whitehead argue, is "not just misleading; it is dangerous." It is, moreover, at least as dangerous to the managers of the environmental mainstream as it is to corporate management. Corporations fall back on greenwashing when it suits them, but it was the green mainstream, with its fervent desire to believe that environmental protection entails no uncomfortable reckoning with power, that originated win-win rhetoric, and that holds the most faith in its exaggerations.

Technology is a special problem here, for it is an axiom of corporate environmentalism that social-ecological problems can be redefined, and resolved, in technical terms. Environmental technologies are the foundation upon which win-win rhetoric rises, yet that rhetoric obscures the larger situation, and even the role technology could play in a green transition. The ecological crisis does not grow from any lack of technological options, and to imagine that it does is to acquiesce in a deep greenwash. As Josh Mailman, a well-known U.S. green philanthropist, put it, "The goal becomes not to pollute, like *that's* going to be the gift of the corporations to the world, not to destroy it."[53]

Technology as Denial: Examples

The fascination with technology is an old one, as is the dream of what historian of technology David Noble calls the "technological transcendence" of social problems. What is new is the number, size, and complexity of the problems technology is expected to solve, and the widespread skepticism that proposals for technical fixes to social and ecological problems now routinely meet. That skepticism is entirely justified.

Today, largely because of green culture, technologies are seen not as dry or "neutral" bundles of science and artifice, but, in the words of technology critic Langdon Winner, as "forms of life" whose social consequences are far more than "side effects."[54] Fuel cells, fission reactors, bioplastics, and biotechnology — all can be seen as socially "neutral" artifacts and practices that do not affect the social ends in whose service they are constructed, but this, visibly, is a merely official truth. The choice to use industrial agriculture and biotechnology rather than organic farms to grow food has large and predictable consequences, and everyone knows it.

A technological revolution is an essential part of any humane ecological transition, and this we must grant while at the same time rejecting the chorus of voices that insist that technology alone will do the job. Technological choices are themselves social choices; technology is politics by other means. One classic example is in the comparison of solar and nuclear power. Both, we are told, are ideal in the age of global warming, for both generate electricity without also spewing out greenhouse gases. But one need only imagine the potential for semiautonomous solar villages, set against the weapons proliferation that is the inevitable consequence of *any* nuclear economy, to see how different are the worlds sketched in this "technical" choice.

Technological choices are usually made with, at best, a studied nonchalance about their larger consequences. And yet to build upon one technology rather than another is to choose a mode of life. This is now well known, for over the last few decades, greens have developed a peculiar politics based upon "alternative technologies." Whole industries rise and fall on the promise of these often elegant, sometimes state-of-the-art, generally convivial alternatives to technology as usual.[55] Now, as ideas long marginal — high-yield organic farming, permaculture, life-cycle design, solar architecture, small-scale aquaculture, biological pest control, and a thousand others — become known, respected, and even profitable,[56] it is time to ask if "alternative" technologies are finally poised to enter the mainstream.

Reagan took Carter's solar panels off the White House roof, but Clinton installed new and better ones.[57] Does this mean that a solar revolution is finally imminent? Despite major improvements in solar technology, this conclusion could be almost as misleading today as in the 1970s. Because machines are always embedded in life, significant technical changes require social changes before they can enter the mainstream. The mainstream itself must shift. Solar electricity is dropping in price, and we may soon see it used in boutique enclaves and centralized power stations,[58] but that is all. A true solar transition would require passion, planning, and commitment, as any generalized transition to green technologies must presuppose massive social change. Even industrial ecology, that brightest child of corporate greening, is making slow headway. In late 1993 I asked Hardin Tibbs for an update. His response was simply that there was "a lot of talk, but I don't know that I can tell you that a whole lot has happened."[59]

We inhabit a time when systems of machines — "technics," as cultural and social critic Lewis Mumford called them — constitute a technosphere that overlays the natural ecosphere. This technosphere is malleable as never before. There are thousands of paths, and each has different social implications. This must be understood, for only some paths will be taken, while the others will be called impractical, or said never to have existed at all.

Technology, then, has everything to do with politics, and with deniability. Here are three examples.

Recycling: Public Relations Cover for the Garbage Society

I encountered greenwashing early, in 1971, when luck and affinity combined to bring me to Berkeley Ecology Action, then operating one of America's first community recycling centers. It wasn't much, just a parking lot crowded with overeducated white kids smashing glass, baling newspaper, and handing out leaflets with titles like "Return, Recycle and Use Less," and "Water Conservation Fact Sheet." Earth Day 1970 had just passed, and Vietnam was still the name of the war. Barry Commoner had just written, in *The Closing Circle*, that "everything is connected to everything else," and this endless river of garbage, which I seemed to see for the first time, was a fine place to begin unraveling the long skein of industrial culture. Just where did all this stuff come from? Why was it all being made, and discarded, and made again? The tin in the cans — how much of it hailed from mines in Vietnam? These were the sort of questions that twenty-five years ago (and today) could set off a series of disorienting realizations, and more questions. Why, for example, were Owens Illinois Glass and Continental Can paying us so much for our few poor bins of redeemed garbage, when we could never hope to divert more than a tiny fraction of the "solid waste stream?" And what did it mean that so much of the money came from their public relations budgets?

Today the answers to such questions are more easily found. Recycling is everywhere (even the Mafia has gotten into the act),[60] and it is easy to suspect that recycling, as we know it, may be more compatible with the garbage society than with any serious green transition — and this despite the fact that TV's cartoon eco-hero, Captain Planet, tells his young fans that "the best way to deal with waste is to recycle it. Don't forget, Planeteers, the power is yours!"[61] *The Ecologist,* first among political ecology magazines, made the point with the bluntness it deserves — recycling is heavily promoted because "industry is keen to suppress the idea of reuse." Why? Because reusables "are best suited for a local distribution system," while recyclables are more compatible with large-scale production and centralized distribution. Mandating reuse would therefore be an indirect way of regulating the distance that a commodity could travel, and therefore "an interference with free trade that could not, in the modern scheme of things, be countenanced."[62]

There's more at stake here than soda bottles, or postconsumer waste, but soda bottles are a clear window on the world. Most of them these days are plastic, and according to a 1989 letter from the Society of the Plastics Industry, "The image of plastics among consumers is deteriorating at an alarmingly fast pace. Opinion research experts tell us we are approaching a 'point of no return.'"[63] The plastics industry, in response to this threat, has followed in the footsteps of the glass and aluminum industries, and concocted elaborate, heavily publicized recycling campaigns. Hundreds of millions of dollars have been spent to build a new image for a material once effusively celebrated as "disposable." Today plastic is a raw material. Today Patagonia and other "green companies" make their wares from EcoSpun, a high-tech fabric made from recycled soda bottles. Today polyester has become environmentally correct.[64]

Reality lags far behind rhetoric. In practice, plastics recycling often means that mixed plastic waste is shipped to Third World countries like Indonesia, Hong Kong, the Philippines, and China; that after being hand sorted in filthy conditions by child labor, much of it is abandoned in vile, unregulated dumps; that only a fraction of it is ever "recycled" (no one knows exactly how much), and that much of that winds up in degraded, dead-end products like plastic boards for park benches and EcoSpun sweaters, rather than as new bottles that are again recycled.[65] Moreover, plastic is only one part of a much larger hustle in which "recycling" is used to ease toxic waste exports. Car batteries, which contain lead and are thus extremely toxic, are "recycled" in the same countries as plastic.[66] Mercury-laden liquid wastes have generally been "recycled" in South Africa.[67]

"Recycling," moreover, can be a public relations scam even when it actually occurs, because it *seems* to be a step toward a green economy, and thus it displaces questions, and initiatives, that might cut deeper to the root. Why, after all, do we the citizens of the North generate so much garbage to begin with? Why are so many fundamental decisions — about product design and packaging, transport and energy — quietly resolved to the benefit of large companies? Why does the average U.S. "food item" travel almost two thousand miles between production and consumption?[68] Why, whenever we notice the downside of the modern cornucopia, do we always hear that "we" are the problem, that "we" can save the earth if only "we" consume more responsibly?

"Biodegradable," incidentally, is almost as slippery a term as "recyclable." "Bioplastics" are still experimental, but as they contain no chlorine and decompose easily into simple carbohydrates, bioplastics will almost certainly play a major role in the elaboration of a future green economy.[69] Too bad the image engineers sold them before the chemical engineers invented them. Mobil Chemical long ago marketed Hefty garbage bags that, it claimed, would biodegrade when stuffed into landfills. These were, unfortunately, only standard bags with starch added, and often did not decompose at all. A spokesman confessed that "degradability is just a marketing tool. We're talking out of both sides of our mouth because we want to sell our bags."[70]

Nuclear Power: Not Reading
the Handwriting

Some technical problems are difficult; generating cheap, safe energy is not one of them. It would only be necessary to remove the huge and quite unjustifiable subsidies that oil and nuclear power *still* enjoy, and the economic advantages of a renewable solar-hydrogen economy[71] would soon be altogether obvious.

Yet it does not happen. Consider Luz International, a southern California company that until its bankruptcy in November 1991 generated 95 percent of the world's solar electricity. Luz's strategy was prosaic —

to use proven technology in large desert collector farms, and to sell its electricity by feeding it into the existing power grid. No radical decentralism here. Luz's executives, like their comrades everywhere, wanted nothing but to grow and make money. It looked good until July 1991, when Luz canceled a major expansion, concluding that it could not compete with cheap oil[72] and thus proving a point made just after the Gulf War by Albert T. Sommers, a U.S. Conference Board economist and something of an unconscious wag. The U.S. victory, Sommers observed, had ensured that the price of oil would not soon be high enough to "impair consumption."[73]

Energy is fundamental. As long as the "soft energy" option can be plausibly denied, the very spirit of emergency that greens assert is a weapon to be used against them. If there is a climatic crisis, we must act immediately, and if renewables are not ready, then nuclear power, especially when redesigned to be "inherently" or "passively" safe — to shut down rather than melt down if there is serious trouble — seems newly attractive, a fact that has not been lost on the beleaguered nuclear industry.[74] "Advanced reactor" designs have charmed even environmentalists like Stephen Schneider, who advocated their use in his *Global Warming*, a book published in 1989 by the Sierra Club![75] He did so grudgingly, in the spirit of emergency, but he did so nonetheless, and in a manner startling for its lack of reflection.

Time magazine announced the campaign to revive nuclear power in 1991 in flat, hard tones. No 1950s-style techno-optimism, no blather about nuclear electricity being "too cheap to meter." Instead, *Time* offered a threatening cover photo of floodlit cooling towers and a brutally blunt question: "Nuclear Power: Do We Have a Choice?"[76] It's a question we should ask ourselves more often. Solar- and wind-generated power are cheaper than ever before, energy efficiency measures are far more cost-effective than new power plants, and nuclear proliferation is manifestly and inevitably the by-product of the fission economy. Given all this, the choice is clear, as is the cost of the nuclear industry's campaign to maintain its hold on the public purse.[77]

Nuclear power never has met the Promethean pretensions of its boosters, and now — with the important exception of Asia — it is clearly dying.[78] It's been decades since a nuclear plant was ordered in the United States, and even in France, a longtime industry stronghold, the true costs of atomic power are now widely known.[79] No wonder the nuclear lobby sees the need for drastic measures, no wonder its old school is being elbowed aside by young turks willing to argue for their "advanced" designs by agreeing with some (though hardly all) of the standard antinuclear arguments. Though the U.S. Council for Energy Awareness has ceded not an inch to the greens — as late as 1993, it was still running ads pushing nuclear (old and new) as "clean, safe, power"[80] — the pragmatists are willing to face the facts. Their new designs are intended to be standardized, and thus to be cheaper than the old models. Just as important, they are designed with public relations in mind.

Nuclear power is dying, but its agonies will be long. The industry is pressing hard to export into the former Soviet bloc and Asia.[81] In Japan, Korea, Taiwan, and Thailand, nuclear boosters have become eager advocates of new-generation reactors,[82] and in India, Indonesia, and China as well, construction proceeds. In the United States, the Clinton administration, though hardly as pronuclear as its immediate predecessors, stands for a high-tech centrism that is not altogether unfriendly to the nuclear industry. Al Gore, like Hazel O'Leary, head of the Clinton Department of Energy, is a booster of passively safe reactors[83] and will probably remain one as long as the industry retains its political power. When it comes to the longer term, Gore has only good words for fusion power, that ultimate love-child of cost-plus government financing and the science-fiction imagination.[84] Fusion is filthy with radioactivity, and still gets far larger federal subsidies than solar.

The easy conviviality between public relations, tech fixes, and business as usual can be seen in Japan. New Earth 21, launched in 1990 by MITI (the Ministry of International Trade and Industry), offers itself as a *one-hundred year plan* that, according to Shinji Fukukawa, executive vice president of Kobe Steel, "aims, over the next hundred years, at restoring the earth's functions to its state prior to the industrial revolution."[85] These words are not to be taken too literally, despite the fact that the plan is backed by the Keidanren, an influential council of major Japanese corporations. Japan's ministries are in the habit of issuing "visions" and "projections" that, taken together, indicate a willingness to take advantage of *any* new trend, if only it offers a chance of profits and economic expansion. Ecology is no exception, and besides, Japan is desperately in need of green PR cover. It does not seem a coincidence that New Earth 21 materialized during the runup to the Earth Summit.

Still, New Earth 21 is not merely a rhetorical initiative. Al Gore contrasted the minimal U.S. presence at a green technology trade show ("a handful of small businesses") to "the enormous, highly sophisticated Japanese effort consisting of hundreds of exhibits by businesses representing every sector of the Japanese economy, all working together within the framework of an ambitious '100 Year Plan' to save the global environment."[86] In choosing such a spin, Gore was emphasizing the competitive threat Japan's corporate greening poses to supine U.S. corporations. Thus, he took Japanese environmental rhetoric at face value. But the details of New Earth 21 tell a tale quite at odds with the rhetoric of "an ambitious '100 Year Plan' to save the global environment."

New Earth 21 divides the next century into two fifty-year periods. In the first, green technologies are to be developed and introduced, while in the second, according to one eager spin doctor, "future generations will be able to reap the benefits of the first half century to recreate a green planet."[87] The first fifty years is further divided into decades, each with a sharp focus. First, and not surprisingly, given the overall efficiency of the Japanese economy, comes the "Conservation" decade, while the second, "Clean Energy," decade is dedicated to nuclear power (passively safe, of course) and other "renewable energy systems." Next comes the "Technology" decade, in which harmless CFC substitutes are to be developed (this does seem a bit late), as well as large-scale means of recycling carbon dioxide! The fourth decade, "Sinks," focuses on increasing carbon sinks, not just through planting forests and reclaiming deserts, but also by "enhancing ocean sinks." Finally, the "Future Energy Technology" decade will go beyond both fossil fuels and conventional nuclear power with fusion reactors, orbiting solar platforms, magma power, and other ultra-high-tech energy sources.

New Earth 21 is a corporate engineer's fantasy. More than simple public relations, it seems a sort of Magna Carta of the corporate tech-fix mentality. Some of it, like "enhancing" oceanic carbon sinks, is probably impossible, and some, like its call for clean fusion and orbiting solar, is only a sad compendium of old high-tech fantasies. Still, it is worth noting how soothing a frame high-tech green dreams make for Japan's nuclear power program. It is standard practice in Japan to greenwash nuclear expansion, and there is no sign that this will change. In 1993 almost 60 percent of Japan's global environmental budget was ultimately absorbed by its nuclear industry, and it is working in the climate negotiations to define the export of nuclear power plants to Southern countries as an antigreenhouse strategy.[88]

New Earth 21 is perfect. It provides cover for nuclear business as usual, fits cleanly into Japan's push to become an environmental superpower, and, by defining ecological crisis as a technical crisis, suggests no changes whatsoever to the economic regime or the consumption economy. The message of this extreme technological optimism, in fact, is just the opposite — that no limit need interrupt the dream of consumption. Beef makes a fine, if absurd, example, for in addition to all their other unsavory qualities, beef cattle emit vast clouds of methane, an extremely powerful greenhouse gas. In response, at least one Japanese government agency is looking into applying biotechnology to stop cows from farting methane.

Agricultural Biotechnology:
The Specter of Ecology

Biotechnology is crucial to the tale of technics as denial. It has taken over the aura of mythic science from computers, which have become commonplace and boring. And in an age of ecological limits, biotech comes to us not only as a medical technology, but as a new way of farming — as "ag biotech," a means of manufacturing herbicide-resistant grains, or "more efficient cows" able to produce more protein per measure of fodder.

Biotechnology is a mythic science, but its myths are not always to the liking of its managers. There is a widespread public sense that "the engineering of life" is both overweening and transgressive, that it goes too far, and thus the industry repeatedly confronts what one panelist at a 1993 biotechnology conference called "ethics and other irrational considerations."[89] Agricultural biotechnology, in particular, needs deep PR cover, and it is notable that it finds that cover in "overpopulation," a slippery notion that can easily make biotech seem necessary. The ag biotechnicians have an active stake in the Malthusian nightmare, for once it has chilled the air they can rise to pronounce that with their emerging knowledge, the "power of the earth" can grow without limit, and overcome "the power of population." In their literature, conferences, and research programs, and especially in the air of smug, farsighted social responsibility that is the deep lobbying of agroindustrial corporations, there lurks the specter of hunger. In this time of rising population and famine, they say, productivity is the only important fact of agricultural life. The world needs more food, and biotech is necessary to provide it. Ask British multinational ICI Seeds, which published *Feeding the World* to argue that biotech "will be the most reliable and environmentally acceptable way to secure the world's food supplies." Or ask Eli Lilly, a transnational drug company diversifying into biotech: "We will need dramatic progress in the productivity of agriculture to limit starvation and the social chaos which overpopulation will bring."[90]

Biotechnology is no longer, as in the early 1970s, framed in steal-God's-thunder, engineering-of-life terms. Now it is just a practical science of genetic "modification," not so very different from brewing or bread making. As one essayist patiently explained, "Biotechnology is around us every day, just as it was for our ancestors."[91] If today's high-tech techniques, from gene splicing to industrial tissue culture, are more precise and more powerful, that is only an evolutionary difference, and one we should welcome.

Ag biotech has its critics, but according to the industry's spin they are generally naive greens and comfortable urban dwellers too coddled even to know they are speaking for starvation. According to the agricultural industry's new image, biotechnology is the true environmental alternative, a key plank in the second green revolution that will again massively increase the productivity of agriculture, feeding all the world's people and, as a bonus, solving the biodiversity crisis by allowing huge agricultural areas to be returned to nature.[92] As two eager Monsanto scientists put it, "Sustainable agriculture is possible only with biotechnology and imaginative chemistry."[93] In fact, biotech will allow ruinous chemical pesticides and herbicides (the chemicals that so concerned Rachel Carson) to be dropped in favor of a new generation of "safe" biopesticides, while still increasing yields. The industry is even lobbying the U.S. Department of Agriculture to get genetically engineered foods accepted onto the list of "certifiably organic" materials.[94]

Then there is reality, which is, according to Jane Rissler, a plant pathologist, and Margaret Mellon, a molecular virologist, both based at the Union of Concerned Scientists, that

if the agricultural biotechnology industry fulfills the hopes of its promoters, it could be producing hundreds of kinds of transgenic vegetables, grains, fruits, trees, fiber crops, and ornamentals by the end of the century. These plants will be grown on huge acreage in the United States and around the world. Most of these crops will contain combinations of genes and traits not possible in nature. Moreover, in many cases, the novel genes will be transferred via pollen from the crops to populations of wild relatives.[95]

Almost no research has been done to test the likely effects on the larger ecosystem of the widespread use of transgenic crops. Rissler and Mellon have a number of fears — that transgenics will become weeds, that they will transmit new genes into wild plants, which will then become weeds; that plants engineered to contain virus particles will facilitate the creation of new plant viruses; that all these effects and more will take place while transgenics, farmed on an industrial scale, become a new threat to the world's already besieged centers of crop diversity.[96]

Industry scientists dismiss such fears out of hand, and insist that there are environmentalists who favor ag biotech. There are, though not nearly as many as Calgene and Monsanto would have us believe. Agricultural biotechnologies do have positive potentials. The problem is that these potentials are easily advertised as being far greater than the risks, though we simply do not know, for the research has not been done. Moreover, biotech has potentialities that can be widely trumpeted but then allowed to quietly languish. Its boosters talk of altering grains to produce their own pesticides, and of thus being able to reduce the use of traditional agrochemicals by taking a biotechnological "soft path." But even if such a path exists, is there really any reason to think it will be taken soon?[97]

The main focus of ag biotech research is the development of herbicide-resistant crops. This does not inspire confidence in any soft path, for the herbicides in question here are the standard hard-path poisons of corporate factory farming. BXN cotton was shaped by Calgene wizards to resist bromoxynil, a highly dangerous old-style pesticide, and thus to support cotton monocultures in which bromoxynil is heavily used. It is, moreover, the representative case, one echoed again and again in the research programs of the biotech firms. Behind the rhetoric, ag biotech is being shaped along lines that will further entrench the existing agrochemical economy.[98]

None of this means that ag biotech will be rejected. Walter Truett Anderson, author of *To Govern Evolution: Further Adventures of the Political Animal*,[99] stated the truth when, in his keynote speech to 1991's National Agricultural Biotechnology Conference, he claimed that "environmentalists tend to be very suspicious of technological fixes, but the general public has no such reservations. Technological fixes will do just fine. They'll not only be tolerated, they'll be demanded."[100] It is a point that radical greens in particular must be reminded of.

The biotechnicians suffer their own comforting illusions, and Anderson sought to puncture these as well. There are "excellent scientific reasons for being concerned about adverse ecological impacts from genetically modified plants, animals, or microorganisms," and these cannot be avoided simply by yelling, "Get out of the way and let us save the world." Provocative words, these, though Anderson, a man with ambitions in mainstream futurism, immediately softened them by attacking greens who make "a religion out of being frightened." Future historians, he predicted, will be as hard on the "anti-biotechnology crusaders" as on the "alleged mad scientists," for the crusaders deny the responsibilities of modern life — and the fact that nature now falls explicitly within the ambit of politics, that evolution must be "managed," whether we like it or not.

To choose sides in the biotech debate, it helps to have some details about just what such management would likely mean. If food shortages are the problem, there are vastly different strategies available for improving yield, and we the ecosystem's "managers" must choose between them. It also helps to have some historical context, to know that when ag biotechnicians talk about developing "more efficient cows," they make an especially twisted homage to ecology. The common knowledge that cattle are wildly inefficient producers of usable protein, and that there would be much more food available if only the planet's consumers ate less meat, traces back to Frances Moore Lappe's *Diet for a Small Planet*, first published in 1971 by Friends of the Earth. The fact is, cows consume eight grams of usable grain protein for every gram of meat protein they yield, which is why still-spreading popularity of the meat-centered diet is becoming an *extremely* serious problem. As Bill Liebhardt, director of the University of California's Sustainable Agriculture Research and Education Program, told me (after first noting, "Hell, I like a steak as much as anyone else"), the reasons people are hungry have very little to do with a shortage of food. "Let's face it, you could free up tremendous amounts of food by changing social and economic conditions, and by using existing technologies to improve yields."[101]

Consider "using existing technologies to improve yields." Examples offer themselves by the dozen, and they are not all based on advanced technology. Liebhardt's favorite is "rotational grazing," a simple method of managing pastureland that, by giving it periodic chances to recover, increases total "productivity" as much as injecting dairy cows with bioengineered bovine growth hormone (BGH). Why then is BGH so much preferred by the "dairy science community"? Liebhardt says, "BGH is very popular" since it is seen as more "scientific," but this is only the start of the story. There is also money — and land, which in farming is about the same thing. Rotational grazing, being labor intensive, fits more easily into a small-farm economy, while BGH increases costs and, in so doing, promotes larger herds and the concentration of ownership.[102] Moreover, rotational grazing "produces few products that can be sold, and therefore does not attract large industrial research grants,"[103] while BGH is estimated to have a sales potential of $2.5 billion a year. Well over $250 million has been spent on its development, and much of this money has found its way to financially strapped university agriculture departments.[104] Thus is the research agenda set.

Margaret Mellon put it simply: biotechnology is being shaped neither by the joy of fundamental science nor by the hardheaded practicalities of a world on the edge of starvation, but by "the nature of its being a product."[105] Ag biotech is being shaped to fit the existing system of industrial agriculture, the world of chemical monoculture, cash crops, factory farming, and dying rural towns. Sustainability is only a gloss, as becomes obvious when you contrast industry claims that ag biotech will lead to new kinds of sustainable agriculture with the effects biotech research is actually having on farm science. By "siphoning off scientific talent into genetics rather than ecology," Mellon tells us, "it's actually going to make it harder for us to get to where we ought to go." Ag biotech is a booming field, while only the traditional pittance, or less, is going to agro-ecological research.[106] Jack Kloppenberg, a rural sociologist at the University of Wisconsin familiar with the clash between biotech and ecological agriculture, explains that "we're

at a pivotal point in which sustainability is being defined bureaucratically, so that scientists of all kinds will know how to write their proposals to get ahold of green money."[107]

True "sustainability" is a more difficult matter. At the least, that
much-abused word means nothing unless it applies to the rural South,
where the poor, forced aside by expanding plantations, must regularly
choose between brutal megacity slums and hard lives as forest or upland pioneers. In the industrial imagination, increased food production is simply the key to eliminating hunger. In the actual world, riven
by social and class divides, and saddled with a corporate economy that
seeks its own very private goals, things will not work out that way.
Already it is obvious that ag biotech will have a cruel impact on Third
World peasant agriculture, and thus on the local economies that actually feed so many of the Third World poor. As Edward Goldsmith,
publisher of *The Ecologist*, pointed out, "Increased yields actually produce starvation."[108]

Already, ag biotech is accelerating the shift from small farms to large
plantations by promoting techniques that smallholders simply cannot
afford, such as the mechanized harvesting based on bioengineered
vegetables that all ripen in machinelike unison. But imagine a future in
which matters have gone much further, in which the research now
aimed at developing bioengineered substitutes for such traditional
high-value Third World export crops as coffee, chocolate, sugar, va-
nilla, and coconut oil succeeds.

Paul Kennedy, the American historian whose 1993 book *Preparing
for the Twenty-First Century* attempted to bring the social-ecological
crisis into the mainstream of liberal anxiety, is sure that such in vitro
crop substitutions will happen soon, and on a vast scale. The prediction is difficult to judge, but he is on firm ground when he writes
that "it is bad enough for a developing country to be dependent
upon a monocultural export like cocoa or sugar, the prices of which
fluctuate sharply, but it will be far worse if such produce is no longer
needed by foreign consumers who can obtain it from domestic labo-
ratories."[109]

In such a future, what would be left for the South? Only the production of low-value feedstocks, the carbohydrates and sugars from which
more exotic substances would then be synthesized. For a portent, look
to the Dutch beef economy, which makes heavy use of industrial tech-

nologies to complete a highly profitable (and highly polluting) production cycle that is utterly, but quietly, dependent on cheap imported fodders, principally soya and tapioca from Brazil and Thailand. Holland is the world's single largest importer of livestock feed, much of it purchased at prices far too low to support anything like a decent standard of living for its producers. As the Brazilian cultural anthropologist Mercio Gomes drily noted, after realizing that the 60 percent of the Dutch land area given over to farms is still only a small fraction of that needed to generate Holland's prodigious output of meats and cheeses, "It seems Holland is using other people's land as the first step in their agribusiness."[110]

It is not technology that enslaves us, for technology is only an expression of paths taken, choices made. It is those choices that must change.

Plausible Deniability

Despite all the political disputes that swirl about it, ecology is first of all *natural* ecology. As much as greens interpret and even mystify it, as much as antigreens deny their claims, ecology remains a science. As much as philosophers dispute proof, fact, and objectivity, physical nature remains.[111] The earth is either warming or it's not. A species either survives or it doesn't. You are either eating or you're not.

The environmental claim is that social change — global change of a degree that ultimately must be quite profound — is not a matter of any moral or political longing, but of natural necessity. In the long run, biophysical realities will not be denied. For the moment, though, environmental limits are disputed, and crucial political questions (Must we really phase out the fossil fuels?) appear as scientific disputes about physical uncertainties (Is the earth really warming at all?).

The songs of the skeptics are all too familiar. Ecological degradation is sometimes real, but there is no "crisis." Environmentalists barrage us with statistics, but we all know that statistics are only pseudoscientific lies. Radical greens are hysterics, or frauds who use environmentalism as a stalking-horse for their real political agendas. There must be "proof" before any "expensive" action can be justified. If there are problems, they can be "managed" with technological change alone.

The pivot in all this is "uncertainty," as can easily be demonstrated with a look back to the Bush administration's heroic denial of global warming, a denial maintained in the teeth of rising scientific consensus, frightening weather, and acute international anxiety. In September 1989, just after a wilting heat wave and just before George Bush was to deliver his speech to the UN's Intergovernmental Panel on Climate Change (IPCC) — a speech that would insist that greenhouse policy "be consistent with economic growth and free-market principles" [112] — Richard Lindzen of the Massachusetts Institute of Technology and Jerome Namais of the Scripps Institute of Oceanography had written to the White House, arguing that global warming forecasts were "so inaccurate and fraught with uncertainty as to be useless to policy makers." The administration "welcomed the input," and it is easy to see why.[113] Lindzen and Namais are both noted meteorologists and members of the U.S. National Academy of Sciences. Lindzen has made major contributions to atmospheric theory. Their views carried weight, and even today, with the scientific community having finally acknowledged that the warming is both real and dangerous, they continue to do so.[114]

Yet Lindzen, a leader among antigreenhouse scientists, once described his views as of a "theological or philosophical" nature, relying on a faith in the existence of undiscovered atmospheric dynamics of sufficient magnitude to counter the known effects of greenhouse gases.[115] Time has passed since this admission, but it remains striking for the frankness with which it was made, and for the clarity with which it reveals the cultural and political currents running below the surface of supposedly "objective" science.

All scientists admit uncertainties in the atmospheric models, as they do in the animal models used to measure chemical and biological hazards. The real debate turns not on the existence of those uncertainties, but on their meaning — their interpretation and uses. At the extreme, these uses are both self-serving and cynical, as was demonstrated by a Bush White House memo, issued to the 1990 U.S. delegation to the IPCC. The leaked memo listed "debates to avoid," including whether "there is or is not" global warming and how much warming could be expected. "In the eyes of the public," it went on, "we will lose this debate. A better approach is to raise the many uncertainties that need to be understood on this issue."[116]

In the long run, science resists manipulation. Greenhouse theory is controversial in detail and mechanism, but the scientific community accepts it because it dovetails with routine laboratory physics. Carbon dioxide, methane, and CFCs trap heat — that's why they're called greenhouse gases. And complex though climatic dynamics may be — forests, oceans, ice sheets, jet streams, clouds, and even pollutants interact in highly variable ways that still resist definitive computer simulation — the rising concentrations of these gases are not in dispute, nor is the geological record, which shows that atmospheric temperatures correlate strongly with CO_2 concentrations. There has never been any good scientific reason to doubt that, with vast clouds of greenhouse gases being spewed into the air, the planet's skies will warm and its winds rise.

For a while it looked as if the seriousness of the greenhouse effect had finally been incontrovertibly established. In late 1992 several major and widely publicized studies of climatic history,[117] including ice-core explorations that went back hundreds of thousands of years, emerged to back up the worrying conclusions of the computer modelers. If present trends continue, the planet's carbon dioxide load will reach twice its preindustrial level sometime in the next century. When it does, the average global temperature will probably have increased by about 4.5 degrees Fahrenheit, and as the IPCC put it back in 1990, "the rate of [climatic] change is likely to be greater than that which has occurred on earth any time since the end of the last ice age."[118]

Then in 1993 the backlash began anew. Richard Lindzen and his fellows were reenforced by dozens of inexpert antigreenhouse newcomers. The procorporate Cato Institute called the chance of harm occurring as a result of global warming "ludicrously small."[119] The neoconservative *Commentary* magazine, after warning that substantially reducing greenhouse gas emissions "would require a fundamental restructuring of the global economy," asserted that there is "no solid scientific evidence to support the theory that the earth is warming because of man-made greenhouse gases."[120] A spate of right-wing books with titles like *Apocalypse Not*,[121] *Environmental Overkill*,[122] and *Trashing the Planet*[123] claimed to "debunk" global warming theory, and they were joined by the *Wall Street Journal* and the *Washington Times*. *New York Times* staff writer William K. Stevens reported the trend, and added the key to understanding it. Citing a 1991 National Research Council report, which concluded that "despite the great uncertainties, greenhouse warming is a potential threat great enough to justify action," he commented that "how much action, what kind and how soon" was now the issue. For this reason, Stevens concluded, "proponents of the greenhouse theory need not be surprised at the intense fire now being rained down on their ideas."[124] Nor need they be surprised if — though even the conservative mainstream of the scientific community has announced that the judgment is in — the media continue to broadcast partisan analyses that stress uncertainty and indecision.

The history of the ozone crisis, too, is one of scientific theory long ignored, environmentalists unable to contrive absolute "proof," corporate-sponsored chants of "uncertainty,"[125] eventual grudging recognition of ecological reality, and an astoundingly successful campaign to fabricate, virtually from whole cloth, the belief that the "ozone scare" is only the child of a fevered, apocalyptic imagination.[126] Everywhere, antigreen "skeptics" charge that greens are twisting the facts to support a "junk science"[127] that serves their political agenda. Are low doses of ionizing radiation[128] or electromagnetic fields[129] dangers to human health? What about dioxin and other xenobiotic (alien to life) chemicals?[130] In these and many other cases, nonspecialists soon find themselves with little choice but to decide which experts to believe.

There are few matters as difficult as "proof," for there are few areas where science and politics more closely intertwine. Still, debates about "uncertainty" cannot be dismissed as "academic," for they convert the honest question "What is to be done?" into "Should anything be done at all?" With the tobacco industry still profitably denying there is "proof" that smoking causes cancer, it is obvious that "proof," like "uncertainty," is no innocent scientific notion.

Julian Simon, free-market economist and champion of antienvironmental optimism, asserts that he has "documented the complete absence of evidence for the claim that the extinction of species is going up rapidly — or even going up at all,"[131] and the most notable aspect of his claim is how easily he maintains his determination to believe it. Simon is an economist, not a biologist, yet he finds himself more than equal to the task of sorting out detailed debates in island biogeography (a branch of ecology useful in estimating extinction rates) and pronouncing the "extinction crisis" to be a simple bio-dogma. His attitude toward the biological literature — which each month swells with monographs demonstrating the decline of one species after another —

seems to be that it is an ideological literature of green doomsters and can safely be ignored.[132]

In some cases the facts are clear — there were thirty-six birds listed as endangered in the United States in 1967, while today there are ninety — but on the whole the dynamics of mass extinction are not so unambiguously stated.[133] We know by direct observation that the tigers, sharks, and elephants are becoming rare, but rain forest flowers die unobserved. We know their loss, if we know it at all, only indirectly, by inference, over time, statistically. And where there is uncertainty and approximation there is, for Simon and his many "skeptical" and "optimistic" fellows, an opening for denial. For the rest of us there is the demonstration of a cruel fact — those who wish enough for blindness will have their wish granted.

Ironically, natural ecology itself will offer the skeptics the materials with which to modernize their claims of uncertainty. Like other sciences, ecology has, in the last few decades, abandoned the "machine models" that so long encouraged its practitioners to imagine in nature order and simple predictability. In ecology this turn to nonlinearity and (in the current cliché) "chaos" has caused the old notion of a simple balance of nature to be abandoned in favor of a new emphasis on the complexity of natural systems. As Daniel B. Botkin, an American ecologist and a spokesman for the "new ecology," put it, "Wherever we seek to find constancy" in nature, "we discover change." Today it is generally assumed that ecosystems are too complex to allow causal lines to be easily traced, or even to allow us always to be sure of "obvious" phenomena.[134]

Unfortunately, extinction is one of those phenomena. In the old days, when population dynamics were seen primarily in terms of balance and stability dictated by, say, prey-predator relationships, scientists did not know that perfectly healthy animal communities could exhibit wild population swings. Today such swings are taken for granted, as is the "chaotic" behavior of ecosystems in general. This would all be to the good, a simple advance of human knowledge, were it not that even the new ecology has become grist for the deniability machine.[135] Healthy animal communities sometimes undergo unpredictable population oscillations over short periods of time, and thus any population crash can be said to be healthy. It may be that other factors — a general degradation of habitat, or a pattern of population decline that spans species and extends over a large region — raise questions about whether a population crash is "normal," but these are not proof. Proof is rare. Biologists are concerned, and even panicked, by a global crash of amphibian populations,[136] but there are those who see this, too, as only a "natural fluctuation." The glorious orange swarms of the Costa Rican toad *Bufo periglenes* haven't been seen in years, but is this a true extinction? Certainty requires time, and time is one thing the toads do not seem to have.

What's It Worth to You?

Practical men, who believe themselves to be quite exempt from any intellectual influences, are usually the slaves of some defunct economist.

— John Maynard Keynes [137]

Imagine that you've just dragged yourself out of a cheap motel bed to the third day of ECO/TECH, a green business conference, and find yourself watching a distressingly self-confident Michael Rothschild, author of *Bionomics: The Inevitability of Capitalism,* display a profit-and-loss sheet for a beehive.

The "currency" of the beehive, as with most of nature, is, you see, energy. During the winter, the hive burns more energy than its workers bring in, but that's okay, since during the summer there's usually a surplus. There are those occasional bad summers, though, and there is the overhead — disposing of dead workers, feeding the queen, investing in new hives. Sometimes (too bad for the hive) the books just don't balance. You get the idea.

The capitalist economy, you see, is more like a rain forest than a machine. "Nobody runs it. It evolves." We need only to let nature (represented here by the "free market") take its course, through the "decentralized feedback loops" of the price system, and everything will turn out fine. Socialism is in the trash can of history, and it's time to get past "brain-dead, left-right politics" and realize that "resurgent capitalism and rising environmentalism" can reach an easy reconciliation if they both only realize that economies are like ecosystems, with technological innovation playing the role of mutation and economic competition that of natural selection. "This thing we call capitalism isn't an 'ism' at all, but a natural phenomenon." [138]

This extremely dubious proposition, it should be said, has roots not in biology but in conservative ideology. If any conviction is central to modern conservatism, it is that "the economy" functions best when unfettered by governmental regulation. Rothschild is notable for the naive eagerness with which he seeks in "nature" the proof of his political-economic preferences, but in this search itself he is no pioneer. Economics invites such projection, for in the desiccated categories of the "dismal science," abstraction reigns.[139] Here one may assert that capitalism functions like a rain forest and hope to be taken at one's word. In economics' formalisms all the flesh and marrow of life vanish away. What will be produced, and how much? By what designs, and by whom? Where, and from what materials? In the economic world, such questions are said to be the merely private concerns of "business." Democracy, hollowed, wastes away, for in the economic world, it is to "the market" that the last appeal is made.

It is "the market" that is incessantly exalted as the source of all good and creativity. Traditional environmentalism, with its faith in science and good government, is caught in a fatal squeeze. Having bequeathed us the pollution laws that ensure that Cleveland's Cuyahoga River no longer periodically bursts into flames, it is now routinely derided by conservatives who admit no need for any constraint on "the free market" *and* by a rising school of "third wave" market environmentalists who insist that economic logic can best save the world.

On the one side there is the *Wall Street Journal*, which in 1990 indicted the South Coast Air Quality Management District — the unfortunate bureaucracy charged with cleaning Los Angeles's air — for "massive social engineering."[140] On the other is Keith Schneider, who in 1993, as a *New York Times* journalist, emerged as one of the third wave's most visible spokesmen, arguing that only in the market was there salvation — "In the last 15 years environmental policy has too often evolved largely in reaction to popular panics, not in response to sound scientific analyses of which environmental hazards present the greatest risks." Cost-benefit analysis was the carrot, self-hatred was the stick. Those who try to adhere to the old ways are "in danger of becoming the green equivalent of the military lobby, more interested in sowing fear and protecting wasteful programs than in devising a new course."[141]

We are easy prey to the charms of "market-based solutions." Witness the third wavers. Always upbeat, and selective in their use of the historical record,[142] they see the question as simply determining what kinds of "market-based regulation" will best facilitate a shift to a greener capitalism. As the World Bank said in its 1992 *Development Report*, the "primary cause of environmental problems" is "the failure of markets and governments to price the environment appropriately."[143] If this is true, then what is needed is a green pricing system that reflects the full costs of all goods and services. Moreover, such a pricing system should be relatively easy to cobble together. Gus Speth — founding president of Washington's World Resources Institute and now head of the UN Development Program — is characteristic of third wavers when he says that "doing the right thing environmentally should be cheaper, not more expensive."[144]

The third wavers have a dream — an environmental revolution in which careful regulation leads the market to properly "internalize ecological costs." Paul Hawken, a U.S. green entrepreneur and a thoughtful third-wave writer, has summarized this notion, and its optimism about a postideological green detente:

In order for a sustainable society to exist, every purchase must reflect or at least approximate its actual cost, not only the direct cost of production but also the costs to the air, water, and soil; the cost to future generations; the cost to worker health; the cost of waste, pollution, and toxicity. Simply stated, the marketplace gives us the wrong information. It tells us that flying across the country on a discount airline ticket is cheap when it is not. It tells us that our food is inexpensive when its method of production destroys aquifers and soil, the viability of ecosystems, and workers' lives. . . . The prices in the marketplace . . . are lulling us into cutting down old-growth forests on the Olympic Peninsula for apple crates, into patterns of production and consumption that are not just unsustainable but profoundly short-sighted and destructive. It is surprising that "conservative" economists do not support or understand this idea, because it is they who insist that we pay as we go, have no debts, and take care of business. Let's do it.[145]

Let us construct a rational world, one where "least cost" economics combines with green taxes and technologies to compose a new environmental regime, while the old (command and control) model of regulation is, as the World Resources Institute put it, "held in reserve for scofflaws and laggards."[146] The same themes are heard again and again. Throughout the left academy, and in books published by the Harvard Business School,[147] the question is how and under what conditions capitalism can best be turned from its ecocidal excesses. Even Margaret Thatcher, during her green period, brought herself to support state intervention to save the earth. (She did so by analogy, noting that similar intervention is needed to manage currency markets.)[148] Moreover, the third-wave insight that markets can act as regulatory devices and thus be part of the solution, as today they are part of the problem, is both valid and important. But third wavers, eager to use markets as mechanisms, are quite insensitive to their role in promoting, and modernizing, the myth of the market as an ideal adjudicator of human affairs. They seek realism but practice what Pope John Paul II once called "the idolatry of the market."

Our society, all rhetoric to the contrary, is hardly one in which prices are set by "free markets." To be sure, prices in the West are not as much the products of bureaucratic decree as they were in the old East, where "production and not profit" set the pace. But, ironically, the subsidies buried in Western economies may be of the same order as those that destroyed so much of the Eastern landscape. The World Bank once estimated that energy subsidies in the late 1980s cost the USSR and Central Europe some $180 billion a year, and that more than half the region's air pollution was "attributable to these distortions."[149]

Compare the United States, starting with the auto-industrial economy. In 1993 there were 680 million motor vehicles on the planet, and this figure was increasing by about one a second — one car for every two babies born.[150] This rate would certainly be far lower without the sprawling network of visible and hidden subsidies, from government-subsidized roads to militarily supported oil prices, that keep the price of driving down. Estimates of the annual subsidy to the auto industry in the United States vary a great deal, but $400 billion is a good guesstimate. Justifiable numbers, based on reasonable assumptions, go much higher.[151]

Or look at livestock. Beef, the core of the traditional American diet, is held at its current rock-bottom price only by vastly underpricing water and grazing rights.[152] And think of the irrigation culture of the American West, as corrupt and self-deluding as it is unsustainable.[153] *New York Times* correspondent Peter Passell, a hard-line market booster, once quipped that "California's water system might have been invented by a Soviet bureaucrat on an LSD trip."[154] He has a point.

Finally, think of energy production. Apalling examples come easily, from subsidized coal mining[155] to gigantic, money-losing dams. Nuclear power, though, still deserves pride of place. According to one *conservative* study, the U.S. nuclear industry received $97 billion in direct federal subsidies between 1950 and 1990, and this figure *excludes* the costs of potential accidents, waste disposal, and weapons proliferation.[156] This $97 billion is nothing compared to the subsidies that have gone to fossil fuels and industrial agriculture in that period, but it is more than enough to have long ago established a large and viable solar industry. It is notable that NAFTA explicitly exempts oil and gas exploration and development subsidies from challenge as unfair. It does not do the same for wind, solar, or hydrogen.[157]

Gus Speth once commented that "the planned economies failed because prices did not reflect *economic* realities. It might also be said that the market economies will fail unless prices reflect *ecological* realities."[158] This explains why full-cost economics, despite the win-win pose cultivated by third wavers, is a deadly serious business. A green economy will come, if it comes at all, only after long and bitter confrontation.

The economics establishment still pretends to believe that prices as we find them today are somehow natural. Economists do admit that subsidies "distort" the functioning of "the market," but this is only a small nod to a looming problem. Within the profession's mainstream, few allow their qualms about subsidies to affect their positions in the all-important debate over greenhouse economics.

One must know a bit of jargon. Strategies aimed at reducing greenhouse gas emissions (i.e., carbon taxes designed to reduce the use of fossil fuels) are often called "prevention," whereas muddling along in the face of climate changes (i.e., building dikes against rising seas) is known as "adaptation." Greens, third wavers among them, are usually friends of prevention, while old-school economists prefer to concoct mathematical models that prove beyond all doubt that business as usual is the only business that is reasonable, and profitable, and, ultimately, possible at all.

Some adaptation is inevitable, but environmentalists fear to admit it. Adaptation is a weapon in the arsenal of denial, and granting its utility helps conservatives to force prevention from the agenda. It is far easier to breed drought-resistant crops (the Israelis are doing so), or to ensure against worsening oceanic storms by raising the height of off-shore drilling platforms (Shell Oil is doing so), than it is to turn society as a whole, with all its complexity, onto a postgreenhouse path. Moreover, economists, at least economists of the old school, see nothing at all worrisome in the bias against prevention. They are well represented by Yale University's William D. Nordhaus, an internationally recognized economist and a man whose views weighed heavily in the 1991 report of the Adaptation Panel of the National Academy of Sciences. Nordhaus believes that warming would most affect "those sectors [of the economy] that interact with unmanaged ecosystems." The rest of the economy, especially activities that take place in "a carefully controlled environment" — like enclosed shopping malls and, presumably, the hallowed halls of Yale — will hardly be affected at all.[159] "The main factor to recognize," he asserts, "is that the climate has little economic impact upon advanced industrial economies."[160]

This is a remarkable claim. A economist of the old school, Nordhaus is doggedly impervious to all the factors — mass extinction, drought and storm and flood, political instability — that fall outside his tidy econometric models. His "best guess" is that the economic impact of the doubling of atmospheric CO_2 is likely to be small ("around one-fourth of one percent of national income") while the costs of reducing CO_2 emissions by half come in at about $180 billion a year. Faced with such numbers, Nordhaus thinks that "societies may choose to adapt."[161] In late 1994 Nordhaus and his associates went even further. In a new study, they argued that since preventing global warming would be so expensive, and since U.S. agribusiness — with its access to capital, information, and technology — will be able to adapt to and even prosper in a warming climate, it will be difficult to raise the political incentive to wage the fight against it.[162] Prevention will be expensive, but adaptation will be profitable.

As always, it comes down to money. Third wavers argue that switching over to an efficient green economy would save money,[163] while old-school economics says it will cost a fortune. Who is right? This depends, first of all, on who is paying the bills, and as ecological deterioration continues, no amount of econometric abstraction will quite obscure this point. Today, though, the views so dominant after the 1988 greenhouse scare remain in place. The *New York Times* summarized them in 1989, in a front-page story, "Cure for Greenhouse Effect: The Costs Will Be Staggering." The drift of official expert opinion, briefly, was that for at least the next fifty years it will be cheaper to adapt to global warming than it will be to attack its causes. Harvard's Thomas Schelling was particularly firm, arguing that with the warming, increasing irrigation and flood control costs will raise the price of food by only 20 percent, that the quality of life a hundred years in the future will depend as much on technology and capital as on the temperature of the air, that "if money to contain carbon dioxide emissions comes out of other investment, future civilizations could be the losers."[164]

Fortunately, the choices are not as sterile as economic traditionalists believe. Prevention and adaptation can go together, as Stephen Schneider, the climatologist, pointed out by proposing a path of "anticipatory adaptation." Here, preventive measures are used to slow the warming, and a postgreenhouse infrastructure is phased in as the existing one wears out.[165] On this path, change would come slowly, one step at a time. And in true "no regrets," third-wave fashion, Schneider argues that it would be profitable as well, since prevention measures like energy efficiency are economical in and of themselves.

"Green cars" illustrate both the realism and the downside of such ecologically responsible adaptation. One need not admire the auto-industrial landscape to understand that *extremely* efficient automobiles would be a vast improvement over cars as we suffer them today. Three hundred miles per gallon is possible with gasoline-electric "hybrid" designs, and even totally nonpolluting hydrogen fuel can be made to power safe and comfortable cars that get far over one hundred miles per gallon.[166] Alternative technology guru Amory Lovins, a big fan of green "supercars," has it just right. "The only problem with green cars is that they would be better cars."[167] Technically they are quite different from today's cars. Socially they are about the same. The oil industry would not welcome them, but they threaten neither the car culture nor the auto industry. They might even aggravate the innumerable diffuse ecological problems of auto-based transportation systems — the eco-systemic destruction caused by roads and the suburban sprawl enabled by the car[168] — but they would vastly improve the energy efficiency of the economy. They are adaptation at its best, and thus they illustrate its nature, and its limits.

In all these debates, Lovins, the unacknowledged father of the third wave, delights in taking positions so at odds with the economic mainstream that they seem to describe a different world. While most economists still argue about how expensive a transition to a postgreenhouse economy would be, Lovins insists that it would be far cheaper to cut greenhouse gas emissions by taking the "soft energy path" than to continue business as usual. "Far from being costly, abating global warming should, on the whole, be immensely profitable. Improving energy productivity can save the world upwards of a trillion dollars per year — as much as the global military budget." [169]

Amory Lovins is not crazy. He may be, as energy expert John Holdren told me, "sociologically naive," and "underestimating the difficulty of actually achieving those improvements in the real world of imperfect human beings," [170] or he may simply be making a point about what is technically feasible. Lovins begins with the physical realities of heat and energy rather than the abstract economic world, and concludes that rational frugality can save the earth. In a classic 1981 study, Lovins led a team that calculated that a world populated by eight billion people could be industrialized to the West German level, and at the same time global energy use could be cut to a third. His point was not that such a level of global industrialization would be desirable, only that it would be possible, and without "acid rain, global warming, urban smog, nuclear proliferation and deforestation." [171]

Lovins's view that the market makes a good vehicle for such discipline is interesting in two respects. First, by showing just how far today's economy diverges from one based on "least cost" principles, Lovins gives the lie to analyses that treat today's corporate-controlled, subsidy-laden economy as the product of "efficient" market forces. Second, his faith in the market prompts a key question. Why is our society so monumentally inefficient? Is it, as he believes, because powerful forces prevent the market from pricing energy rationally, and in general from imposing economic discipline? Or, as green radicals have long claimed, are today's perverse prices better seen as the *successes* of a market that has been captured by the few?

Who can tell when so many costs are never priced, when so many costs are, in green terms, "externalized" to the benefit of powerful economic actors. Logging companies denude hillsides and clog distant streams with silt, factories spew out wastes (and products) and promptly forget them, businessmen around the world avert their eyes in a million different ways. Social costs are even more routinely externalized. Shall the lives broken by Union Carbide's 1984 accident in Bhopal, India, be counted against the modern world? What about the industrial serfdom the people of Bhopal endured before 1984 and endure still? How much does it all add up to?

What percentage of "full" prices are reflected in today's actual prices? Herman Daly, a leading light of green economics, could only tell me that "it's difficult to know, because we don't know the total." [172] "Costing the earth," as *The Economist's* Frances Cairncross calls it, is no established activity with tried and tested procedures. With green economics in ascendance, it is easy to imagine such procedures coming with time, but for the moment all is chaos. Andrew Stirling, a former director of Greenpeace International's antinuclear campaigns and now an energy economist, has reviewed a number of attempts to assign monetary values to environmental effects, and noted results that differ by a factor of fifty thousand. "Rather than making spurious claims to objectivity," he argues, "policy-makers should acknowledge that calculation is subordinate to judgment." [173]

One morning in 1993, the front page of the *New York Times* bravely announced that "Polls May Help Government Decide the Worth of Nature." Since there's no market for wild otters or wild nature, surveys ("calculation") must do instead. Charles J. DiBona of the American Petroleum Institute, seeing such techniques for "valuing" the "passive use" of unsullied nature as a threat, complains that in them "junk science will gain a companion — junk economics." [174] Does Mr. DiBona mean to say that the main currents of economics, so easily used, even in a warming world, to justify the expanded use of petroleum, are not also junk?

The difficulty is not markets themselves, but the utopia of the "self-regulating market." Green radicals as various as Murray Bookchin and Wendell Berry speak for living communities able to encapsulate and socialize the economy, but they are only tolerated as marginal figures, as philosophers and poets. The economy reigns, and pragmatists accept the need for "valuing" nature — by using markets to allocate "rights" to pollute, or even by contriving entirely abstract "markets" based on polling. They do so not simply because it strikes them as proper, but because they are trying to be practical, because, in accepting the hegemony of economic devices, they feel themselves to be facing inescapable realities.

There are numerous circumstances in which markets as regulatory devices have real advantages over bureaucratic decrees, but these are not so absolute and unambiguous as many people imagine. In the ongoing and vituperative debate about saving the African elephant from ivory poachers, proponents of "command and control" — the supporters of hunting bans — are under attack by third wavers who believe, as *The Economist* wrote, that conservationists would be wiser to "set up a toughly controlled trading system to market a limited quantity of sustainably harvested ivory" than they would be to attempt to prohibit its use altogether.[175] The third wavers have a point. There's no obviously greater morality in a ban than in market-based regulation — not if effectiveness rather than purity of stance is to be the measure of rectitude. The ivory ban campaign does not even begin to address the social conditions that engender elephant poaching in the first place. As conducted by apolitical groups like the African Wildlife Foundation, the campaign has favored gruesome images of mutilated elephants and simple-minded fund-raising campaigns that make not the tiniest effort to explain the political-economic roots of extinction. If there is moral high ground here, the supporters of hunting bans do not hold it.[176]

But does this mean, as *The Economist* claims, that "the elephant's main chance of survival will lie, counter-intuitively, in the value of its tusks"? In fact, the story of the African elephant's destruction is both tragic and complex, and no simple moral can be drawn.[177] The 1989 ivory-trading ban, though inadequate, did arrest the elephant's overall population crash. Desperate action is often necessary and can have real if temporary benefits. The long term is a different matter. Garth Owen-Smith, a Namibian who co-won a 1993 Goldman Environmental Prize for helping to persuade unarmed African herdsmen to guard black rhinos and desert elephants against poachers, explains. "During the colonial era, subsistence hunting became poaching. Now, rural Africans have been alienated from their cultures and resources, and the challenge is to link wildlife conservation and economic development." This, according to Owen-Smith, implies a "pragmatic approach" to conservation that will involve markets, but much else besides.[178]

A pragmatic approach to conservation may make use of markets, but if it is truly pragmatic, if it is intended to succeed, it will not fetishize them. The Endangered Species Act, a keystone of U.S. environmental law, is virtually defined by its attempt to hold to entirely scientific, *noneconomic* criteria for listing species as endangered. Economic impacts can be considered, but only late in the ESA process, when trading off mitigation, protection, and development. Attacks on the ESA focus on just this point. Its enemies long ago decided that their best strategy lies in getting economic factors considered *before* species are listed, and they often succeed.[179] Each time they do, habitat is lost, and usually forever. How many jobs is the spotted owl "worth?" Should private lands be exempted from the ESA, to allow logging near spotted owl sites? Do healthier salmon fisheries justify higher electricity rates? How much higher? What about an undistinguished bird like the gnatcatcher? What is it worth? Does its "value" drop if developers lust after its habitat?

Third-wave environmentalism is in ascendance, and with it the notion that markets can save the world. Even *The Economist* agrees, though in all its briefs for market-based environmental management, there is no special attachment to nature. *The Economist*'s true faith lies in markets themselves, as the solutions to all problems, everywhere, as it has been since 1843, when the magazine was founded as a public relations instrument for laissez-faire capitalism and the first wave of "free trade."[180] The editors of *The Ecologist*, founded in 1970, sing a different song. They grant that third-wave devices like "toughly-controlled trading systems" and "correct" prices can make useful tools, but they ask their readers to think first of life, community, and politics, and only then, if at all, of economics. "Under what circumstances is the hope these prices offer for a livable community sufficient to suggest that activists should concentrate their efforts on enclosing the environmental debate within economics instead of working to roll back the dominance of the market economy?"[181]

This question asks us to see economics as a political tool, much like lobbying or direct action, and restates the goal of green politics — a livable community. Markets, for all their power and popularity, have an ambiguous relation to that goal — they can only "see" that which is priced, and subtleties like ecological diversity and justice (both necessary to livable communities) escape them altogether. An economy of "full" or "correct" prices might help to remedy this blindness, but it also implies a world where everything and everybody — otters and whales, forests and fields, men, women, and children — has its price. This is the utopia of market environmentalism, and we should not imagine that it will finally make good on the false promise of economic objectivity. There are no "correct" prices, ecological or otherwise. Prices reflect the ways and means of power, and will always do so.

How can we price the rights of future generations to hear songbirds, or set the moral limits needed if market-based measures of value are not to overwhelm all others? And what about the many cases — car travel or beef — in which current prices reflect only a small percentage of "real" costs? In these cases, significant price changes could only follow major political and social changes, and to imagine otherwise is to fatally confuse cause and consequence.[182] Besides, people resist too deep an intrusion of economics into their lives, and it is hardly clear that they are wrong to do so. There is, for example, the revulsion that so many ordinary people hold for cost-benefit analysis, and for its assumption that everything has its proper price. Economists almost invariably see this revulsion as naive emotionalism, but Mark Sagoff, a green philosopher who has studied the public *experience* of economics, has concluded exactly the opposite, that people often "reject cost-benefit balancing as an inappropriate and illegal framework for making social policy" and believe that "it is only in this way — by lodging a protest — that [they] can begin to make their values known."[183]

The market may be a useful device, but it can never be the means by which livable communities shape their lives and cultures. The invention of "marketable pollution rights" (which "tactful economists"[184] call by less loaded terms like "emission reduction credits") forces this recognition upon us. The idea, according to its partisans, is "efficiency,"[185] and in fact regulatory systems that feature tradable credits are often more efficient than those that do not, at least on paper, because they grant pollution allowances the sanctity of tradable goods. Say you are an industrialist with plants that emit sulfur dioxide. In the old "command and control" days, your emissions were either above a legal limit or below it, you either violated the law or you didn't. In either case you had no "incentive" to do better than the law demanded. In the new world, the amount you are allowed to pollute is set by law and commodified. If you install new scrubbers, you may sell the unused portion of your pollution allotment to someone who would otherwise exceed his legal limit. It may be strange, but it is the capitalist logic. The 1990 Clean Air Act launched emissions trading into the regulatory mainstream, and if you can comply more cheaply by buying pollution indulgences at the Chicago Board of Trade or one of the many other pollution markets springing up around the country[186] than by installing new scrubbers, you will do so, right?

The idea is spreading fast, in all sorts of circles. The EPA is studying trading-based schemes as part of future clean-water statutes, Canadian environmental managers have gotten the bug, and in Los Angeles air pollution control authorities may soon allow emissions-permit trades for volatile, highly toxic, organic compounds. Massachusetts already does so.[187] The chemical industry wants to trade toxic air and water pollutants both between and within facilities.[188] In the climate negotiations, the realists place their hopes in "joint implementation," an emerging device by which Northern countries partner with poorer Southern (or Eastern) cousins, and get "credit" for carbon-emissions reductions they can purchase more cheaply in their partner countries than at home. Joint implementation isn't often pitched as such, but it is essentially a global pollution-trading device.[189] Meanwhile, in the United States, where markets are more evolved, a few visionary commodities brokers are even playing with the idea of "interpollutant trading." And indeed, as pollution trading becomes standard practice, and information systems are put in place to support it, there may be no limit at all to the kinds of "goods" that can be traded. The Chicago Board of Trade's Richard Sandor imagines abstract markets for "macroeconomic and microeconomic indices," which would not only allow pollution trading of various kinds, but also hedging against price hikes in natural resources, insurance contracts, and even wages.[190]

Political journalist James Ridgeway once remarked that "cancer bonds" are on the horizon, and green radicals have long attacked pollution trading for its vulgar commodification of life — an important moral point, but one that does not capture the full dilemma. Society is market society, and nature's "value" must be "internalized" in market relations if it is not to be destroyed, if it is even to be visible to the grinding mechanisms of the economy. To this extent the market environmentalists are certainly right. The problem is that "internalization" is no guarantee of either grace or protection. Conceived as pollution markets, it can be ugly indeed.

What will pollution trading mean in practice? Will it even work? In many cases, it will not. Alex Farrell, a researcher at the University of Pennsylvania Center for Energy and the Environment, has made a careful study of pollution markets.[191] He is a supporter of the 1990 Clean Air Act but is careful to defend only "properly designed market-based environmental control programs," and he asserts that "proper design" is a complex matter. This is an all-important qualifier. It means, first of all, that pollution trading be allowed only within limits set by scientific, not economic, criteria.

The 1990 Clean Air Act caps overall sulfur dioxide emissions in the year 2000 at about one-half the 1980 level, a level set in conformance with the "best science."[192] Not all pollution markets meet such criteria. In many cases, a "proper design" that protects human and ecological health will involve so many restrictions that markets become more expensive than old-school command-and-control regulatory systems.[193] And according to Farrell, it is almost always a "bad idea" to regulate toxics (even smog) with pollution markets, for they can be redistributed and concentrated in a manner neither safe nor equitable. Yet within today's markets-uber-alles culture, the prestige that pollution trading wins from a few "properly designed" markets will translate into a perverse momentum that engenders plenty of improperly designed ones as well.

U.S. antitoxics groups have been far less friendly toward pollution trading than the lawyers who invented it. They have rebelled against the notion — implicit in such trading — that industries have a preordained right to pollute their neighborhoods. This rebellion, according to friends of the 1990 Clean Air Act, has been irrational, for sulfur dioxide is not thought to have adverse effects on human health. The short history of pollution trading casts a different light. "Green markets," like their traditional brethren, shift burdens from affluent to less affluent areas. The very first pollution trade made under the 1990 Clean Air Act allows plants belonging to the Tennessee Valley Authority and Pittsburgh's Duquesne Light to increase their sulfur dioxide emissions. These allowances were bought from Wisconsin Power & Light, which can afford to operate without them. Is it any surprise that in the counties surrounding the TVA plants the minority population is proportionately seven times larger than in Wisconsin? That the percentage of people living in poverty is nearly twice as high?[194] Environmental justice advocates have gathered a great mass of evidence indicating that nonwhite people are far more likely to be the recipients of society's toxic effluvia than their richer white cousins. In this particular trade, the pollutant (sulfur dioxide) typically has no adverse human health effects, but can those who are constantly dumped upon be expected to take comfort in such fine distinctions? Given the rapid proliferation of pollution markets, is it even "rational" for them to do so?

There are no simple ways to locate the point at which a pollution market can fairly be said to be "properly designed." The Clean Air Act had hardly come into effect when Long Island Lighting sold pollution rights to AMAX Energy of Indianapolis. AMAX passes them along to utilities as incentives to use its high-sulfur coal. The utilities, burning that coal, will send acidic plumes that drift over the Adirondack Mountains, an area the Clean Air Act was specifically intended to protect. It is a problem that would seem to have an easy fix. New laws could simply prohibit such "upwind" trades. Wouldn't the Clean Air Act's authors welcome such laws as a sort of regulatory debugging? It does not seem so. Joe Goffman of the Environmental Defense Fund, the third-wave think tank behind the act's trading scheme, complains that in New York's move to protect its mountain park by banning upwind trades, "the Midwest is taking it in the neck to save the Adirondacks."[195]

Markets cannot be separated from the society in which they function, and in a society as wracked with division as ours they are guaranteed to work their magic at the expense of the weak. Would an international market in carbon-emissions rights be a "fair" market? Why should it be? Why should rich countries reduce their emissions beyond the pain point if they can cheaply purchase emissions rights from the cash-starved South? On another line, Herman Daly, the green economist, and John Cobb, a theologian, have suggested creation of a "transferable birth quota plan." Such a market in childbearing rights would grant more children to couples who "can afford the responsibility of nurturing a new human being." But Daly and Cobb argue that this is acceptable, since it will lead to children being born to parents able to take care of them properly.[196] This may be true, but somehow it does not seem the last word.

Market environmentalism is far more likely to succeed in wealthy societies, where large reserves of capital and knowledge open doors to technological change and social adaptation,[197] than in the lands of the South. It is no more for the poor than are efficient green cars and organic vegetables, and in fact it can even sharpen the class divide. In Alaska a tradable permits system has been introduced to protect strained haddock fisheries. It is, however, rapidly forcing small fishers out of business and turning others into "sharecroppers." That some of these are Indians whose people have been fishing haddock in the region for thousands of years matters not at all, nor does the fact that permits are being bought up and monopolized by large companies.[198] The bottom line? Simply this: the efficacy of market environmentalism is limited by the same division of humanity into rich and poor that has destroyed so many other dreams.

The Netherlands may "adapt" to rising seas by reworking its diked borders. In Bangladesh, if the oceans rise, floods are destiny. So will it be, year by year, on a thousand fronts. Despite the staccato of spills, accidents, and resource conflicts that is the background of environmental crisis, that crisis remains distant from daily life. It comes to each of us as a chaotic stream of bad news, but it does not come so brutally to the rich as to the poor.

Can our society, marked by inequity and denial, be turned to "sustainability" with only minor alterations? Green economics is part of the answer, for as a reform movement it seeks to substitute subtle measures for coarse ones, and to establish an economy less deluded about the true costs of business. It even seeks justice, to the extent that justice is convenient, and conceivable, in economic terms. All of this is to the good, but it is not decisive. The problem is simply that for the last few hundred years the market has been the principal device by which humanity has been divided into rich and poor.

I am aware of how excessive this claim seems. Yet this impression, too, is a sign of the times. When capitalism hit its stride, it was a matter of common understanding that its free operation generated poverty along with wealth. Adam Smith, certainly a friend of capitalism, stressed the point, writing in *The Wealth of Nations* that "wherever there is great property, there is great inequality. . . . The affluence of the rich supposes the indigence of the many." John Ruskin made the same point almost a century later:

Men of business rarely know the meaning of the word "rich." At least, if they know, they do not in their reasonings allow for the fact that it is a relative word, implying its opposite "poor" as positively as the word "north" implies the word "south." . . . Riches are a power like that of electricity, acting only through the inequalities or negations of itself. The force of the guinea in your pocket depends wholly on the default of a guinea in your neighbour's pocket. If he did not want it, it would be of no use to you.[199]

Our world is shaped by buying and selling, by the calculus of exchange, and yet markets are seen as neutral mechanisms, rather than as what they actually are — rationing systems based not on age, citizenship, health, merit, or geography, but simply on wealth. This denial is more than remarkable, it is dangerous. In capitalism's early days, its partisans were not so confident of their triumph, so foolish as to lie to themselves about matters as fundamental as the twin nature of poverty and wealth.

The Temple of Greenwash

Some will differ strongly with my characterization of change within the Bank. They would argue that the proliferation of environmental policies and staff, and of new kinds of projects has been substantial over the past several years, while conceding that more needs to be done. In fact, I agree with them, and add that by the norms of international bureaucracies, the changes are major. Indeed, this is precisely the issue, and the problem.

— Bruce Rich[200]

A few days into the Earth Summit, the staffers of the World Bank's Global Forum booth (the Bank, too, is an NGO) were startled by two hundred or so young activists, of no particular nationality, who approached and surrounded them, shaking rock-filled Cola-Cola cans in a Brazilian beat and loudly chanting, "No World Bank." The staffers had been busily distributing slick literature promoting the Bank's green initiatives, but now suddenly they were being assaulted by a rowdy crowd that, with hyena shouts, tore down their fine "World Bank" sign (substituting a rough "People's Bank" banner), then heaped their literature into a giant wheelbarrow and set it alight. A few hours later, the booth reopened, but the Bank's officials declined to reenter it. The flacks were left to carry on alone.

It was a fine moment, but in the end it mattered little. The Bank was one of the Summit's big winners, leaving Rio with its Global Environment Facility (GEF) — a new green grant-making arm — endorsed as the "interim" fiscal agent for both the climate and biodiversity treaties, and positioned to channel any funds the rich countries might eventually grant to realize Agenda 21. Some years later, despite a crescendo of damaging criticism, it is clear that the Bank's positioning will hold. The details will change, and change again, but the Bank has placed a strong hand on the financial tiller of green "development" and will not release it voluntarily. Mohamed El-Ashry, the director of the Bank's Environment Department, put the Bank's new line flatly: "In the past, the Bank used to be part of the problem. I think now it is becoming part of the solution."[201]

Thus the World Bank, one of the world's most undemocratic, opaque, powerful, and destructive institutions, one that, with its historic love of capital-intensive gigantism — deepwater export ports, forest-destroying dams, river-poisoning mines — has annihilated whole cultures, emerges as the planet's lead environmental funder. The Bank's official spin on its past has become, as Bruce Rich, the director of the Environmental Defense Fund's International Project, summarized it, "That was then, this is now."[202] But is it? The Bank has a long, sorry history, and its future will depend in large degree on how that history is seen and understood. In late 1993 the Bank proved it knew as much, for as its fiftieth anniversary approached, bracing for a tide of criticism, it hired PR maestro Herb Schmertz, formerly VP of public affairs at Mobil Oil and coauthor of *Goodbye to the Low Profile: The Art of Creative Confrontation*, to assist in its image management.[203] Since his appointment, the Bank has indeed been more aggressive than before, and even creative, and has once again shown itself to be, as Bruce Rich once noted, "an institution where policy pronouncements" are "dissociated from reality."[204]

Rich tells the whole strange story in *Mortgaging the Earth*, his fine history and critique of the Bank, which cites many of its more fantastic flights of "dissociated" rhetoric. The first hails from 1972's UN Conference on the Human Environment, held in Stockholm, the first "UN jamboree" to have an environmental theme. Stockholm was actually more than a typical UN jamboree — it was a sign of things to come. There the UN Environment Program was founded and given a budget of about $40 million a year, smaller than most Bank projects, and far too small to accomplish anything of significance. There Robert McNamara, the technocratic visionary who built the Bank we know today, explained that its environmental office carefully reviewed "each project processed by the Bank," using comprehensive criteria that "encompass the entire spectrum of development." According to McNamara, "While in principle the Bank could refuse a loan on environmental grounds . . . the fact is no such case has yet arisen. Since initiating our environmental review, we have found that in every instance the recommended safeguards can and have been successfully negotiated and implemented."[205]

These must have been reassuring words, and must have echoed proudly through Stockholm's conference chambers. But though the environmental movement of the day heralded them as signs of a new departure, they were simply not true. When, over a decade later, a small group of U.S. researchers finally checked the record, they found that the Bank's 1972 environmental staff, which McNamara said had "negotiated and implemented" safeguards "in every instance," consisted of one person. By 1983 a real "department" existed — it had a staff of six, three of whom were assigned to vaguely defined research, PR, and training functions. That left three people from a staff of six thousand to evaluate the environmental aspects of all new loans, and to monitor the hundreds of projects already in progress.[206]

The Environment Department did its job, which was first of all to exist and be citable as existing. In 1981 Bank president A. W. Clausen — in a speech titled "Sustainable Development: The Global Imperative" — virtually repeated McNamara's words ("For a decade now, the Bank has required . . . that every project it finances be reviewed by a special environmental unit"),[207] as have his successors, dutifully, to this day. Unfortunately, reality is less tractable than appearances. By this time, social and ecological catastrophe had begun regularly to visit Bank-funded projects — in the Amazon, Malaysia, India, and a dozen other places besides. Worse, these catastrophes formed a visible pattern, and were cohering into a serious PR problem.

In 1984, answering activist criticism in Congress, the Bank complained about "a misleading impression that past trends continue," even as it was still funding wildly destructive, uneconomic rain forest colonization schemes in Brazil and Indonesia. Instead of being justified as means of relocating large groups of people, however, these were intended to "develop natural resources that otherwise would be wasted." The Brazilian program, particularly, was "an opportunity to develop sustainable agriculture" in areas with "relatively better soils" where settlement had already occurred. Everything was fine now. The Bank was funding large-scale monocultural eucalyptus plantations, calling them "social forestry." In one case, a massive, near-genocidal "resettlement" plan was actually defended as being "least cost."[208]

Forced resettlement is a particularly dark aspect of the Bank's pursuit of "development." By 1994, according to the Berkeley-based International Rivers Network, the Bank's dam projects alone had displaced more than ten million people,[209] and millions more are threatened by projects in its lending pipeline. Faced with such well-documented numbers, the Bank points eagerly to its resettlement policy, though it cannot name a single instance in which forcibly resettled communities have been fully rehabilitated, as that fourteen-year-old policy requires.[210]

By 1986, when Barber Conable became its new president, the Bank was under heavy attack by a sophisticated international coalition of environmental and human-rights activists. Unlike his predecessors, Conable seemed to engage the real problems, launching reviews of the effects of Bank lending on vulnerable countries, initiating a major effort to fight tropical deforestation through "forest management and protection" (the Tropical Forest Action Plan, or TFAP), and expanding environmental staff to almost one hundred people.[211] All the while the PR department broadcast the good news about the Bank's environmental reforms.

That was the beginning of what Bruce Rich calls the "Emperor's New Clothes" period, for in it the Bank tried to pass greenwash off as reality, and seemed to imagine seriously that its imperial confidence would carry the day. The TFAP, a device by which the Bank hoped to increase sharply its forestry lending, was dubbed an experiment in "sustainable logging." Perhaps a few years earlier this would have flown, but in 1987 Third World green groups — notably Friends of the Earth Brazil and the Malaysia-based World Rainforest Movement — immediately attacked the TFAP as a fraud and launched studies to back up their claims. The case was easy to make. The TFAP would provide small grants for conservation and watershed management, but the bulk of its funds were intended for timber-export operations. In Cameroon TFAP plans called for opening a pristine tropical forest the size of Florida to logging, at a cost of hundreds of millions of dollars. The green sweetener was $4.4 million to address the problem of domestic fuelwood demand. In almost a dozen other countries, events followed a similar course.[212]

"It was so easy in the old days," said Korinna Horta of EDF's International Project, "for the Bank to loan money and tell the borrower to log, log, log. Now, with all the attention on forest conservation they must use elaborate environmental language and objectives to cover their tracks."[213] Bank staffers have gone so far as to argue that the sole alternative to total deforestation is an increase in the number of areas to be logged and in the duration of logging programs. Both these conditions, it seems, are needed to manage logging within "sustainable" limits. Do the Bank's staffers who make such arguments believe them? I do not know. What is certain is that the Bank no longer plays to a uniformly gullible audience. Today lots of people see through even such imaginative casuistry as this.[214]

Unfortunately, there are also lots of people who don't. The greenwash that was pioneered with the TFAP is now standard operating procedure. Production-oriented agricultural and forestry schemes by the dozen now come festooned with green riders and wrapped in "greenspeak," an Orwellian dialect in which environmental destruction is reborn as "sustainable resource management."[215] A late-1980s Brazilian application for a loan intended for natural resource extraction and forest colonization referred instead to "agro-ecological zoning" and "extractive reserves." Chico Mendes, the Brazilian rubber-tapper and socialist activist whose 1988 murder transformed him into an international ecological martyr, spoke against the loan in a letter he sent to Bank president Barber Conable a mere nine weeks before his murder. He argued that the fine claims being made for it, and in particular the claims that it would help the rubber-tappers, were frauds. The "extractive reserves included in Polonoreste II," Mendes said, "only serve to lend the Government's project proposal to the World Bank an ecological tone — which has been very fashionable lately."[216]

The Bank, in the teeth of heavy criticism, had no choice but to announce policy changes. Its new (1991) forestry policy includes environmentally correct terms like "participation," "sustainability," and "conservation," and prohibits the Bank from financing logging in primary moist tropical forests. Unfortunately, the policy was barely in place when a new project — the Forestry and Environment Project in Gabon — came on line to confirm that once again the Bank was financing heavy logging and ignoring its own much-trumpeted environmental rules.[217]

To community-based activists "on the ground," such realities are clear enough. For politicians in conferences and ministerial meetings, they are more abstract, and even crude greenwashing works surprisingly well. The Environment Department, the TFAP, the 1991 forestry policy, the Global Environment Facility — all follow the same logic. The mainline of the Bank's business goes on as usual, but those who wish to believe it has reformed itself, or is trying to do so, are given the material they need to convince themselves. Jimmy Carter, in an article he wrote for the *Earth Summit Times*, praised the GEF for a few unspecified "good projects," then called for reforms designed to democratize its management structure. In words that echoed the professional optimism of politicians around the world, he argued that "with these reforms, the GEF could become the vehicle through which funds are expended much more wisely than in the past."[218]

Yet when the Bank launched the GEF in February 1990, it was as an attempt to head off the founding of any other "green fund" at the Earth Summit. By Rio, the green establishment accepted the GEF as a flawed inevitability. Al Gore made this clear during a Rio press conference, arguing that the United States "should be getting a lot more credit than it has for applying pressure to see that the GEF is more democratic, accountable, and transparent." Asked for evidence that this pressure was making headway against the Bank's antidemocratic and mega-engineering biases, Gore shot back that "World Bank President Lewis Preston says he's going to change that, and I believe him."[219]

Today, Preston too is gone, and his term is known not for any reforms but for being the time in which the Bank's critics finally began to hit their mark. During Preston's term, intense international pressure yielded a few small reforms — the GEF, for example, opened enough to allow a tiny number of NGO observers into its council chambers. At the same time, reporters around the world, echoing the Bank's critics, began to talk of its "midlife crisis." Was this fair? According to Juliette Majot, the editor of *Bankcheck Quarterly*, an extremely well informed

NGO newsletter, the very existence of the GEF marks failure. "The fact that the green fund takes the form of a GEF based in the World Bank is an indictment of the World Bank reform movement. As a movement, we did not oppose the placement of the GEF soon enough or effectively enough, and some NGOs even supported its placement in the World Bank, seeing it as a sign of progress. They couldn't be more wrong."[220]

Optimists see the GEF as a trojan horse that could first force the Bank to learn to carry out proper green projects, and then to reform its mainline policies. But according to EDF's Korinna Horta,

> The GEF is being used in just the opposite way. You have to un-derstand that the GEF gives grants, while the Bank gives loans. Eighty percent of all GEF grants are just tiny little add-ons to regular Bank loans. They are used as bait. For example, a small biodiversity-protection grant will be attached to a big timber loan. That happened in the Congo, though it was canceled. The way it works out is that GEF grants take pressure off the Bank to inter-nalize environmental factors into their development projects, be-cause GEF grants are attached to those projects, and they will "take care of it."[221]

The GEF does its greenwashing simply by doing its job, by being a small but highly visible source of earth-friendly cash. This became al-most impossible to deny after June 29, 1993, when despite the objec-tions of Germany, the United States, and Belgium, the Bank approved a $400 million loan to India for new coal-fired power plants. The loan is only one in a planned series — $2.5 billion has already been spent on related mines and power plants, and $800 million more is projected. As of early 1994, the loan series had displaced 140,000 poor people, and if it goes forward it will displace many more. For what? For 16.6 giga-watts of generating capacity that could be provided more cheaply and more humanely with small-scale, job-creating efficiency measures, and which will dump 120 million tons of carbon dioxide into the air an-nually — about 2.5 percent of *all* increases in global CO_2 emissions pro-jected to occur by the year 2003. Don't worry, though. In an attached grant, the GEF is providing $20 million to India for energy efficiency.[222]

Political scientist and longtime Bank critic Susan George joked in late 1991 that the GEF is "a very small tail wagging a very nasty dog."[223]

At the time, such views were very much the property of a few outside critics, but soon the Bank's troubles began to worsen. In June 1992 an independent investigation of the Sardar Sarovar dam and canal complex in India — a project that the world's green and development activists, and even hundreds of legislators in the United States, Japan, and Scandinavia, had been unable to stop — concluded that it would not only displace more than 100,000 people, impoverish thousands more, and destroy land, forests, and fisheries over vast areas, but that it was also the child of a project-planning process so inept that it could be characterized as grossly delinquent, if not actually corrupt.[224] The Morse Commission, which conducted the investigation, recommended that the Bank "step back" from Sardar Sarovar, but in a decision that would only compound the damage it would suffer from what was becoming a highly visible debacle, the Bank decided to push ahead. The timing could not have been worse. Another special investigatory team, this one assigned by Lewis Preston to review the economic efficiency of the Bank's entire lending portfolio and headed by W. A. Wapenhans, had just concluded that Sardar Sarovar, far from being an aberration, was the child of an "approval culture" in which Bank functionaries systematically construct project appraisals "as marketing devices for securing loan approval (and achieving personal recognition)." This was no longer merely a social or ecological problem. "Major problem loans" were reaching 30 percent of the Bank's portfolio, and its fiscal soundness was becoming an issue. With concise understatement, the Wapenhans team concluded that "there was reason to be concerned."[225]

In 1993 the GEF also started running into some turbulence. Its initial three-year pilot phase was ending, and going permanent required striking an international deal on its terms and governance. The Bank's use of small GEF grants to grease the skids for its mainline lending was no longer a secret, and a sophisticated coalition of reform-minded activists around the world was lobbying to push the emerging institutions of official green grant making out of the Bank's orbit, or at least to democratize their management. The climate negotiations, too, saw the GEF become a major issue, as voices around the world asked why the Bank — a temple of industrial gigantism and structural adjustment — should also be the fiscal agent of the planet's emerging antigreenhouse infrastructure.[226]

As for the claim that the GEF would be an agent of change, the

Bank's own draft "independent" evaluation of the GEF noted "a consistent, biased exaggeration, if not falsification, of the amount of consultation and participation with governments, NGOs, and affected communities."[227] At least, this appeared in the *draft* evaluation — in final printed form, this uncompromising language had been considerably softened.

At the end of 1993, it briefly seemed that the GEF might collapse. Donor (Northern) and recipient (Southern) countries could not agree on "power sharing," and France and then Germany walked out in protest over the G-77's demands for a majority on the GEF's governing council. In the end, all was smoothed over, and the GEF, marginally restructured to be slightly more responsive to Southern concerns, was reauthorized. Still, the GEF's near collapse was revealing in two crucial ways.

First, the flap had little to do with democratizing the Bank or with reforming the GEF. Even the recommendations made in the Bank's own evaluation of GEF's pilot phase were entirely ignored in favor of the baldest sort of North-South power politics. Second, the near-collapse provided proof, if proof was needed, that "democracy" and North-South "power sharing" are not at all the same matter. The G-77 joined the G-7 (the UN's Northern bloc) in objecting to the inclusion of loose words like "transparency" and "community participation" in the GEF's founding documents,[228] and rumor has it that Southern governments even invoked "sovereignty" when arguing against granting NGOs observer status at GEF meetings. This is difficult to verify, since there were no independent observers present when independent observers were discussed.

In all this, "independence" is a constant, contested theme. In late 1993, in reply to a rising tide of criticism, the Bank set up an "independent" office to which even the most powerless communities, feeling themselves the victims of Bank projects, would, so it was said, be able to appeal. According to *Bankcheck's* Juliette Majot:

> Independent of what? Not the World Bank! It will be answerable to both the board and management — and management is quite likely to discourage thorough investigations. It has no budget to speak of. Reports will be made public only after they are presented to the board. The Bank took a fairly well thought-out NGO

idea — independent review — gutted it, reinvented it, and presented it as though it were still credible. And NGOs will, of course, now spend an inordinate amount of time watchdogging the watchdog. It's a masterstroke.[229]

Today the pattern is set. With events — from the Bank's stonewalling on Sardar Sarovar to its refusal to acknowledge the conclusions of its own internal GEF evaluation — piling one on another, the Bank is widely perceived as beyond meaningful reform. Today there are NGO observers in GEF councils, but to what end? The work of those councils is still to manage a small fund, and thus, almost inevitably, to legitimate a larger investment policy that has barely begun to change. There is no shortage of informed critics who believe that the Bank, in its present form, simply cannot be remade into an instrument of sustainability.

The story is changing fast, and in its twistings there will be losses, victories, and no end of lessons in the ways and means of damage control. Without greenwashing, the GEF would never have flown,[230] the appeals office would be only to the good, and the Bank would not have been able to use the ecological crisis to strengthen its hold on world development budgets. But greenwashing, like public relations in general, is only a device, and explains neither the Bank's policies nor the political climate within which it pursues them. This is clear as new threats rise against the Bank, and against the ideology of development, threats that hail not from powerless greens alone, but also from the isolationist budget cutters now threatening the Bank's congressional appropriations.

There has been a convergence between the criticisms leveled against the Bank by development activists and those leveled by the right.[231] It's an old story that took on new life in 1993, when, citing a lack of public accountability and deteriorating loan quality, a U.S. congressional committee tied authorization of Bank funds to calls for specific reforms. At issue was IDA, the Bank's International Development Association, its "soft loan" arm.[232] Looking back, this seems a turning point, for IDA, which offers low-interest loans to only the poorest countries, has long been crucial to the Bank's posture as an antipoverty crusader, a "development bank" rather than a bank as usual. Unfortunately, these claims are seriously distorted — most IDA loans go to impoverished countries that must pay even greater sums back to other

Bank divisions, sums loaned at higher interest to pay for "development" that never came.[233]

In 1995, after its fiftieth anniversary as PR disaster, with right- and left-wing activists both railing against its policies, the Bank made its long flirtation with image manipulation official — it launched its first actual advertising campaign! The theme? "The World Bank: A Good Investment." The budget? Between $3 million and $5 million.[234] The first installment? A defense of IDA. "When we talk about IDA, we are not talking about emergency aid, nor about untied grants to prevent social problems. IDA is an investment, pure and simple. It is not welfare, but, if you like, the international equivalent of welfare reform."[235]

In this strange episode, two points stand out. The first is that in seeking to defend its budget from a reluctant Congress, the Bank is spending a fortune to say that its critics have been right all along, that its "aid" is not aid at all, but an export-promotion fund. The first ad singles out the Johnston Pump Company, a Texas firm that, with the Bank's assistance, made a large sale to Egypt. The second point is that the Bank, far from buffing its image, comes off as desperate and inept. "Development," it is telling the world, was a lie all along, and McNamara's famous "Bank for the Poor" was just a convenient, now obsolete slogan. Visibly laying altruism to rest is a bold new message — Development: What Do *We* Get out of It?

Development as Denial

Harry S. Truman, in his 1949 inaugural address, called for "a bold new program for making the benefits of our scientific advances and industrial progress available for the improvement and growth of underdeveloped areas."[236] This simple exhortation, as clearly as any event or image, marks the distance we have traveled since the birth of the Cold War, when the United States, eager to offer the world's poor an alternative to the communist dream, launched the age of development. This, President Truman took pains to emphasize, would not be like "the old imperialism — exploitation for foreign profit," but rather, "based on the concepts of democratic fair dealing." Almost half a century later, history has not borne out Truman's optimism. The name by which he called the planet's service regions — "underdeveloped areas" — has stuck, but development has failed to win most of them a better role in the world economy. For vast numbers of people within the underdeveloped areas, the conditions of life have gotten worse, sometimes much, much worse.

"Development" still has its supporters, but they are no longer as confident as President Truman was. Their best exhibits — Asia's "newly industrialized countries" — are becoming known as ecological catastrophes, and this greatly diminishes them as signs of a better future. The optimists tell us that "scientific advances and industrial progress" will soon, and more or less of their own account, ameliorate even the ecological crisis now overtaking so much of the South, but a closer look reveals this as an improbable, disingenuous claim. Not all the world's people will find bright futures in exports. Tall tales about the win-win dynamics of "economic growth" no longer soothe, and this despite the fact that the World Bank's poverty-alleviation theory still has "growth" promoting equity by painlessly redistributing wealth.[237] The profits of development are largely appropriated by the rich, in the free-trade zones of Asia and Latin America, as in North America and Europe. The public secret, widely known but rarely discussed, is that "development" implies misery on a grand scale.

Only now, with "environment" and "development" melding together into one overwhelming agenda, are the stakes becoming clear. "Underdevelopment," or rather poverty, will play a major role in the success or failure of the effort to save the living world from destruction. The problem is as easy to state as it is difficult to engage — there will be a way forward that purchases security and dignity for the many, or there will be a long, slow catastrophe. There is no "third way."

The friends of "development" claim that their path promises security and dignity. Thus, while development was long the carrot that Cold War liberals held out to the poor as an alternative to socialism,[238] it is above all poverty itself, and its infamies, that requires a visionary refusal of laissez-faire. Robert McNamara saw this, and spoke out against the evils and irrationality of "absolute poverty," and proposed in its place the virtue of enlightened managerialism. In 1973, setting out his dream of the World Bank as *the* defining global institution, he told its officers, "All the great religions teach the value of each human life. In a way that was never true in the past, we now have the power to create a decent life for all men and women. Should we not make the moral precept our guide to action? The extremes of poverty and deprivation are no longer acceptable. It is development's task to deal with them."[239]

The party of development argues that poverty is the cause of ecological destruction, while green radicals argue that development itself, and all the violence it justifies, and all the destruction it inevitably implies, is an engine of impoverishment. Each side has its wisdom, and each its mindless camp followers, but this is the fundamental faultline of environmental politics.

What is the fundamental cause of rain forest destruction? Some, Bank staffers among them, have not been above blaming "the poor," the "shifting cultivators" who choose from their tiny palette of unsavory options the brutal lives of rain forest pioneers. In fact, as some anonymous activist noted long ago, deforestation is most often caused not by "shifting cultivators" but by "shifted cultivators." Robin Broad and John Cavanagh, movement-based American analysts, write,

> Many of those poor shifting agriculturalists who are blamed for Amazonian deforestation have actually been pushed off their small farms in Southern Brazil by agri-businessmen who are expanding their soybean plantations for a profitable export market. Most end up in urban slums or the Amazon because of a land-distribution system in Brazil that allows 1 percent of the landowners to own 50 percent of the arable land. For most, there is simply no place else to go.[240]

Myths breed more myths, and the assertion that "the poor are the problem" only supports the claims that "the market is the solution," and "aid is the answer." These ideas not only *are* false but are today *seen as false,* and opposed by a global network of activists, analysts, and, indeed, victims. The urban-industrial, export-based models of modernization and social improvement that have been so heavily promoted by the Western political establishment (and its cousins in the old East-bloc development bureaucracy) have caused human suffering and ecological destruction on a grand scale. Moreover, to the chagrin of the development managers, of McNamara's children, the notion that poverty is the principal cause of the destruction and "development" its solution is itself collapsing.

Once certain cover even for the bottomless infamies of colonialism, "development" has itself been delegitimated by all the crimes it has been asked to excuse, and by the efforts of activists on every continent to hold those crimes up to the light of public examination.

The green project is the search for an alternative to "development," one compatible with basic social and ecological realities. This is obviously a complex and difficult project. There's no shortage of good ideas for moving onto more sustainable paths,[241] but who believes that ideas alone can solve the fundamental problems or provoke an easy consensus? Who thinks that Southern activists, schooled in left anticolonial traditions, will see the riddles of sustainability as do Northern environmentalists, who hail from a narrow political culture that still invokes overpopulation as the ultimate explanation of ecological crisis? In fact, they will not. Environmental-justice activists are cousins of Washington eco-technocrats, but they are poor and distant cousins, and rarely sit at the same table. Green-leaning European parliamentarians inhabit the same broad social movement as, say, fire-breathing Brazilian land-rights activists, but it is very broad indeed, and offers them no obvious common program.

Donald Worster, a founder and leading light of American environmental history, once quipped that "sustainability" is a "magic word of consensus." The rhetoric of "sustainable development," he argues, became popular in the mid-1980s *because* it was so vague, because it created an illusory world in which most everyone could "make common cause without much difficulty. Capitalists and socialists, scientists and economists, impoverished masses and urban elites could now all happily march together on a straight and easy path, if they did not ask any potentially divisive questions about where they were going."[242]

"Sustainable development" is only the latest in a long series of comforting incantations. Its many predecessors include "human-centered development," "integrated development," and "endogenous development,"[243] all of which have emerged not from the green movement but the environmental profession, the "executives of the inevitable,"[244] the "development set."[245] The names vary but their logic remains the same — all these models of a new development are risen from the ranks of those who would have everything change, while changing not at all.

What does "sustainable development" mean? The World Bank has taken as its offical post-Rio position that sustainable development is

a blessed condition in which growth can continue indefinitely, ecologically, and profitably. In 1993 it even created an office of Vice President of Environmentally Sustainable Development. The International
Atomic Energy Agency appeals to sustainable development while
pitching its nuclear energy "as a non-CO_2-emitting source of electrical
power."[246] Herman Daly has reviewed the usage of the term "sustainable development" and found reams of apologia for economic
"growth," and even odd phrases like "sustainable increase in the rate
of economic growth."[247] The Bank itself, in an unprecedented and
widely distributed attack on Rich's *Mortgaging the Earth*, capped off a
long series of misleading arguments with what its External Affairs Department seemed to consider a damning, even mortal, blow:

> The book is well removed from current thinking on sustainable
> development. . . . While rightly pointing out the urgent need for
> development practitioners to incorporate environmental concerns
> into policy-making, the book fails to take note of a new under-
> standing in the environmental community of the importance of
> development. . . . [Mr. Rich] falls back on a pre-Brundtland devel-
> opment versus the environment paradigm.[248]

Not only does the Bank here presume to speak for "the environmental community," but it further asserts that its legacy of export-
oriented industrial gigantism and structural adjustment (here known
as "development") is just what is needed to balance the environmental
equation and compute the magic sum of "sustainable development."
Rich, in refusing to recognize this, falls back on "an elite, Northern
perspective."

If such a spin holds, the greens will be seriously hurt, and it is hard
to believe that the many pundits and opinion makers now working to
popularize it don't realize as much. Gregg Easterbrook, author of the
monumentally confusionist *A Moment on the Earth: The Coming Age of
Environmental Optimism,* is a fine example. A clever journalist with a
finger to the wind, Easterbrook has a long history of attacking greens
as purists and elitists.[249] It's an easy brief, for many are, but rather
than seeking their enlightenment, he consistently takes a bad situation
and makes it worse. Easterbrook paints greens as pessimistic, doom-
ridden, "transrational" souls who cannot tolerate good news, dis-

misses "wise use" as a fad (which it is not), speaks for "logic" and "rationalism" while distorting basic science,[250] ignores the many objections to his optimism, and, of course, positions himself as the voice of a "new" environmentalism. His unsurprising conclusion is that development as usual, with some minor green model changes, is the true path of progress and justice.

A piece that appeared in the *New York Times Magazine* in late 1994, before his book came out, illustrates Easterbrook's strategy. "Forget PCB's. Radon. Alar. The World's Greatest Environmental Dangers are Dung Smoke and Dirty Water" could almost win some sort of Oscar for greenwashing. Its foreground is the environmental horror of life in extreme poverty, and thus we are primed, all we good people, to sympathy. But observe where Easterbrook steers us. First comes the introduction, and then the setup: "A large faction within the environmental movement concentrates on the comparatively minor ecological problems of developed nations in order to support the view that Western materialism is the root of all ecological malevolence."[251]

After which we are given a quote from EDF water scientist Deborah Moore — "Issues like African sewage are not sexy, so they always fall to the bottom of the agenda" — and a twisted look back on 1992's Earth Summit — "The prospect of global warming was put above the urgent loss of lives in the third world from water and air pollution." It is as if global warming would not hurt the poor far more than the rich, as if Rio's failure to address poverty could be chalked up to "Western guilt-tripping and America-bashing." From there, the knockout is easy: "What developing nations need to free their populations from death by extreme air pollution is hydroelectric dams, advanced petroleum refining installations, and high-efficiency power stations for the clean combustion of coal."

Deborah Moore, for one, was not convinced. An activist in the global campaign to redefine development and stop large dams, she told me that Easterbrook had deliberately "manipulated" concern for poverty and wretched Third World living conditions into support for a development model that routinely devastates the lives of the poorest and most vulnerable — just the opposite of what he claimed to be doing.[252] What is certain is that he eagerly defends large dams, power plants, and refineries, and sanctimoniously criticizes greens — "How come if small solar is too expensive for the Sierra Club set it's a great idea for peasants in Malawi?"[253] — and is all the while in easy synchrony with a larger antienvironmental backlash in which "development" is claimed, once again and with a new aggressiveness, to be the best way forward for the poor.

Easterbrook, of course, is only a symptom. The question is whether, even now, decades after Truman and McNamara and the early days of "development," we can be won back to big dams and power stations, giant farms, and dreams of progress. The Bank does not seem to think so, for its evolving pitch turns less on development as a means of poverty alleviation, and more on its unique ability to "build tomorrow's markets and prevent tomorrow's wars."[254] Wolfgang Sachs, the German green critic, does not think so either, and confidently told me that "no one really believes in development anymore." Sachs insists, moreover, that "sustainable development" is only a branch of the larger church, and must inevitably share its fate. Appeals to progress and technological optimism are only ritual nods to past beliefs, and

> as far as the Third World is concerned, sustainable development is seen as a security matter, a form of risk prevention, not as progress. In the best of cases, you will try to preserve livelihoods — but you are *not* trying to effect a takeoff. There is more and more a sense of a drift toward a global apartheid. Somalia and Yugoslavia are widely interpreted as signs of the future. The bipolarism of the Cold War is looked on with nostalgia, as an ordering force. Ecology is being redefined within the context of "security."[255]

The subject here is no longer "sustainable development" but "ecological security," the term being auditioned to replace it. And what a peculiar term it is. Darker than its fellow, it is similarly contested, with a similarly uncertain future. Some writers imagine that in "ecological security" they have found the watchword of a hardheaded new green internationalism. Sachs, for his part, thinks "ecological security" will help to draw greens back from the edges of radicalism and into the conservative postures so familiar in the history of "military security." What is certain is that ecological pressure has already brought social instability, and that it will bring much more. What is surprising is that many people imagine that social instability could easily redound to the benefit of hope and international cooperation. It may, but not easily, as was demonstrated by journalist Robert Kaplan in "The Coming Anarchy,"[256] an essay that was for months in 1994 the much-xeroxed, hottest topic of U.S. environmental pessimists.

In "The Coming Anarchy," Kaplan imagined a future in which shortages of food and safe water, overpopulation, soil loss, the easy availability of small but extremely destructive arms, tribalism, poverty, and warlord culture combine to feed a cycle of violence and deterioration that overwhelms the Third World and defeats all efforts at aid or remediation. There was just one serious problem: Kaplan somehow managed to overlook the links between the "coming anarchy" in the South and the institutions of the North. In an image he repeatedly invoked, the people of the North appeared as the passengers of an isolated stretch limousine, wandering the dark and sinister streets of the Third World. Clearly, Kaplan meant to stress the fragility of Northern luxury, but he never even implied that the limo's passengers might have some reponsibility for the cruel conditions on those streets. The transnationals, the global trading system, the policies of the World Bank and the IMF, the fact that the arms flooding the South are manufactured almost exclusively by the permanent members of the Security Council (by 1994 the U.S. share of the international arms trade had risen to an amazing 73 percent)[257] — none of this was even mentioned.

"Eco-security," like "sustainable development," is a suspect but redeemable project. It could become more than a fancy new name for old infamies — but only if its architects face the facts of a world split between rich and poor. "The poor" are not the problem, but the world's division into rich and poor certainly is. This is not simply because the division saddles us with an angry and inequitable society that, facing a darkening future, only promises to become more cynical and fatalistic in its cruelties, but also because, to touch the core of the ecological reckoning, the split society is dysfunctional and inflexible, its dynamics coarse and clumsy, its visions small, confused, timid, and late.[258]

When it comes to policy reform, the split society is a constant obstacle. At both global and domestic levels, the dynamics of wealth and poverty befuddle efforts at environmental reconstruction. Carbon taxes, for example, are among the best instruments available for phasing in a green pricing system,[259] but as a 1992 European Commission study found, they would have their effect, at least in the short term, by reducing consumption not among the rich but among the poor. In Britain and Ireland, "cold wet countries with lots of old houses," carbon taxes would inevitably mean more shivering pensioners, unless special precautions were taken.[260] In a time when safety nets are badly fraying, green taxes — and full-cost pricing in general — would mean suffering for the weak. This is *not* a fatal flaw. A redistribution of wealth would remedy it, and if this is still unrealistic, a serious attempt to reweave the safety nets would move us in the right direction. Unfortunately, such concern with the welfare of the weak is rare in the environmental mainstream, which still avoids the implications of class division, and solaces itself with abstractions like "sustainable development."

A Wavering Edge

As it becomes more difficult to deny environmental deterioration, damage control and image management will become more subtle, more brazen, more baroque. They will become whatever they must in order to reassure and contain, to palm pseudosolutions off as real, to deny that something more than painless adaptation may be necessary.

The fundamental political truth of our time is that the change that is necessary is not "realistic." As Winston Churchill said of the British government in 1936, we go on "in strange paradox, deciding only to be undecided, resolved to be irresolute, adamant for drift," even while "the era of procrastination, of half-measures, of soothing and baffling expedients, of delays, is coming to its close." With words that ring terribly true today, Churchill concluded that "we are entering a period of consequences."[261]

Al Gore, to whose book I owe the Churchill quote above, also referred to the 1938 Munich Pact — an act of "appeasement" that is widely seen as a cowardly denial of the inevitable gathering storm — likening it to our own denials, our own inability to make "the effort to save the environment the central organizing principle of our civilization." Instead, said Gore, we are engaged in "minor shifts in policy, marginal adjustments in ongoing programs, moderate improvements in laws and regulations, rhetoric offered in lieu of genuine change." All are "forms of appeasement, designed to satisfy the public's desire to believe that sacrifice, struggle, and a wrenching transformation of society will not be necessary."[262]

That paragraph today, after the grim disappointments of the Clinton administration, seems to offer a lesson altogether different from what Gore intended. As an author and a senator, he told us that "proposals that are today considered too bold to be politically feasible will soon be derided as woefully inadequate to the task at hand." As vice president he has been prominent among those calling Clinton away from bold departures and into the quicksands of what Americans call "the center," chief among those who practice the art of appeasement until that day when it is seen as "woefully inadequate." But when will that day be?

For now, the "the era of procrastination, of half-measures, of soothing and baffling expedients" continues, and swells of talk assure us that only what is minimally disruptive is actually necessary. And then the circle is closed — since little is done to face the situation, that situation must not be so serious after all. The alternative conclusion, that we are drifting almost unconsciously into a mounting crisis, is not admissible. Things are bad, and even getting worse, and all the suffering "abroad" is terrible, but what can we do? We must take care of our own. We will muddle through.

But if "we are entering a period of consequences," what will it mean if we accept images and good intentions in the place of real change? Let us not forget that the ugliest consequence could be war. Let us not forget that our world, too, with its spreading arsenals and its strained graneries, is the product of earlier optimism, earlier procrastination, earlier lies.

I. F. Stone, a great dissident American journalist of the post–World War II period, once argued, in an essay named "Why SALT Spells Fraud," that "'arms control,' that is, talk about arms control," had become a game "perfected to the point where it may actually be used to cover up a new spiral in the arms race, or indeed to sell the public on the need for new weapons and higher expenditures."[263] It is an essay that deserves rediscovery, for it warns us, clearly and bitterly, that image management does not solve real problems. "Arms control," back when there was a disarmament movement worthy of the name, was what the wizards of "mutually-assured destruction" and "escalation dominance" offered to peace movements to shut them up. So it was with the Atmospheric Test Ban Treaty, and so it was with SALT, the Strategic Arms Limitations Talks. Both played at *managing* the arms race; neither even gestured at stopping it. Certainly they were better than nothing, better than chaos, better than nuclear war, for they left the future (now the present) open to dispute. But they did not begin to face the mad realities of high-technology militarism. "Arms control" solved nothing. It bought time, but it also played a major role in destroying the disarmament movements that, almost alone, were telling hard truths. "Arms control" was the "sustainable development" of its day.

It is tempting, in the face of its agonizingly slow evolution, to wonder if contemporary environmentalism is changing at all. And yet it clearly is. The environmental movement of today is not that of even twenty years ago. A better question is that which 1970s systems theorist and eco-philosopher Gregory Bateson liked to ask: Is it "a difference that makes a difference?" On this question, and on the answer that millions of people find to it, a great deal will turn.

SIX

Realism

We have about 50% of the world's wealth, but only 6.3% of its population. . . . In this situation, we cannot fail to be the object of envy and resentment. Our real task in the coming period is to devise a pattern of relationships which will permit us to maintain this position of disparity without positive detriment to our national security. To do so, we will have to dispense with all sentimentality and day-dreaming; and our attention will have to be concentrated everywhere on our immediate national objectives. We need not deceive ourselves that we can afford today the luxury of altruism and world-benefaction. . . . We should cease to talk about vague and . . . unreal objectives such as human rights, the raising of living standards, and democratization. The day is not far off when we are going to have to deal with straight power concepts. The less we are then hampered by idealistic slogans, the better.

— George Kennan, 1948[1]

In the 1950s American sociologist C. Wright Mills coined the term "crackpot realism" to name the peculiar self-delusions of a "power elite" that, looking forward, could see only the indefinite prolonging of its privileged circumstances of life. Now, years later, at the brink of truly dark possibilities, it is a term worthy of revival.

Crackpot realism is realism gone mad, and crackpot realists are those who "in the name of practicality have projected a utopian image of capitalism." They have information in abundance, but "have replaced a responsible interpretation of events with the disguise of events by a maze of public relations." They have the power to move both money and machines, but have confused "the capacity to elaborate alternatives and gauge their consequences with the executive stance."[2] In a world torn between affluence and poverty, the crackpot realists tell the poor, who must live from day to day, that all will be well in the long run. Amidst deepening ecological crisis, they rush to embrace small, cosmetic adaptations.

Yet Mills called them "realists," for thus they flatter themselves. His sarcasm reveals an important problem — "realism" rings with ironic and cynical overtones. It names a violently contested terrain. Engineers, dictators, and politicians of all kinds have long thought themselves to be the true realists, as, from time to time, have radicals.[3] My claim is simply that, in an age of global ecological crisis, realism must presume a break with denial.

In 1987 the Brundtland Commission announced that ecology and economy had merged "into a seamless net of cause and effect,"[4] and in so doing had demanded a new global bargain between rich and poor. Despite the subsequent collapse of communism and a long series of well-publicized, high-level planetary conclaves — the Earth Summit, the Population Summit, the Social Summit, the Women's Summit, and all the rest — what real progress toward such a bargain have we seen? Almost none. It is time, then, to be blunt about the requirements of a global New Deal, which, if it is to be real, must compel the rich, the major consumers of the planet's resources, to profoundly reform their societies and make room for others. And it must provide the poor with the means to raise their living standards without embarking on a futile effort to copy the Northern model of affluence and development. Above all, it must make "sustainable development" into something more than a cruel slogan.

Condoms, recycling, and energy efficiency can buy time, but they will not ultimately do. A global New Deal must include, according to Robert Goodland, Herman Daly, and Salah El Serafy, a trio of maverick geo-ecologists then writing from within the World Bank, both "population stability" and "income redistribution." Markets, now the defining institutions of public society, must also "learn to function without expansion," and "without wars"; and "economic policy will have to suppress certain activities in order to allow others to expand, so that the sum total remains within the biophysical budget."[5]

It's a tough brief but an honest one. Visions of a better world come hard these days. The world's division into rich and poor is too obvious, and too obviously a wellspring of ecological crisis, to be effectively waved away. As Yale historian Paul Kennedy pointed out in *Preparing for the Twenty-First Century,* the great divide between the rich and the poor is the key to decoding the perpetual sterile pseudodebate between "optimists" and "pessimists." In the end, "the optimists are excited about the world's 'winners' whereas the pessimists worry about the fate of the 'losers.' "[6]

A transition to an ecological society must involve a vast increase in justice and democracy; unfortunately, this does not seem to be the direction of history. Around the world, the welfare state is in deep trouble, and there are many who even say that the dream of equality died in the rubble of the Soviet bloc. Capitalism is triumphant. It has its many variations, but few glorify equity or justice, and few are kind to "the losers." Even this could change, but what good purpose is served by pretending, as today's vogue for optimism demands, such change will be easy?

In 1960, during the heart of the Cold War, Daniel Bell published *The End of Ideology,* a milestone of social-democratic sociology that argued that the failure of communism, its collapse into a Leninist-Stalinist dictatorship, marked not only the end of the dream of socialism but the end of the whole "age of ideology," an age hospitable to large, deterministic social theories, and specifically to "Marxist...dogmatism about the inevitability of a deepening economic crisis and polarized class conflict under capitalism." Capitalist society, according to Bell, was far more adaptable than Marx imagined, and far too adaptable to allow any safe pronouncements about its limits.

The greens think otherwise. Though they seldom name this society as "capitalist," their insistence that "growth" must end is the core of the green challenge to capitalism, and though it is often ignored, it is never effectively refuted. Capitalist economies must expand, but the ecosystem that is their host is finite by nature. It cannot tolerate the indefinite growth of any human economy, least of all one as blindly dynamic as modern capitalism. Murray Bookchin has long argued that capitalism is unreformable, that it must "grow or die."[8] His judgment, if correct, portends almost inconceivable suffering, and so far there are few data to dispute it.

The core question of ecological politics is, Can this society bend, far and fast and deeply enough, and what strategy will maximize its flex-

ion? It's an uncomfortable question that demands our facing the possibility of failure, of death on an enormous scale, and that asks us to
think strategically.

Capitalism has shocked its critics before with its ability to adapt to,
and even thrive under, challenging new conditions. It may be that tomorrow holds wave after wave of green technological breakthroughs,
a planetary New Deal, a revolution of values, massive ecological res-
torations, enlightened and effective forms of global government. It may
even be that "development" can be unlinked from primitive physical
"growth," that capitalism can somehow find a steady state that avoids
both war and economic collapse. We do not know. What we do know,
or should, it that none of this will happen by itself.

Another Realism

We may all be riding on "spaceship Earth," but as German essayist
Hans Magnus Enzensberger pointed out decades ago, some of us ride
first class and some in steerage.[9] Traditional realists see this as a fact of
life, and even extoll the virtues of poverty. In the business section of
the daily newspaper, if not on the editorial page, unemployment is necessary, for it keeps inflation down and bond prices up, just as low environmental and labor standards in the Third World keep prices down.
As American policy analyst George Kennan explained back in 1948, in
days less sensitive to the demands of liberal rhetoric, "Our real task in
the coming period is to devise a pattern of relationships which will
permit us to maintain this position of disparity without positive detriment to our national security."

Such postures have lost any claim to the name of realism. Not all
future Third World regimes, Robert Heilbroner has noted, will "view
the vast difference between first class and cattle class with the forgiving
eyes of their predecessors,"[10] and the same can be said about the losers
in general. Moreover, since weapons proliferation is at all levels unimpeded by any serious efforts at control, we must assume that the
poor of the future will be armed to the teeth. They will be bound to the
rich by the global economy and by planetary TV, but it will be a loose
and unstable coupling. Barring new departures, competition and violence will only increase, as the ecological plunder will continue.

Though it is not a pleasant thought, it seems that we, and our children, will live to see a prematurely discarded theory of 1960s political apocalypticism finally tested. That theory is that things must get worse before they can get better. It posits an ugly futurism, and it has dispiriting consequences, but look hard at the emerging world and say that its day is not coming round at last.

What, then, is realism? Worldwatch's Lester Brown says that we must either "turn things around quickly or the self-reinforcing internal dynamic of the deterioration-and-decline scenario will take over,"[11] and then argues for an "Environmental Revolution" as the best hope. His strategy is to say much that is chilling and yet to remain upbeat and, when it comes to politics, abstract. We have "underestimated what it will take" to reverse the trends now threatening to overcome us, and "can no longer separate the future habability of the planet from the current international distribution of wealth." Large statements, both of these, but they are left to float in warm generality. "Stabilizing the climate" will require "restructuring the world's economy to phase out fossil fuels," but when it comes to how this can be done, there is only anticlimax: vague talk of gradually shifting investments, reforming technologies, and changing values.[12]

Here, too, there is implicit a political theory — large change will come exclusively by small degrees. No need to solve problems like regulating the planetary corporations, halting the spread of nuclear arms, or substantially redistributing land and wealth. We will wake one day to find that incremental reforms have made all the difference. Brown first tells us the environmental revolution is not political, but rather a cousin to the industrial and agricultural revolutions. He then explains that we do not have the kind of time that they required, but even this does not inspire him to discomforting conclusions. If there must be changes that will not come politely, they are best left unremarked.

There is a method here. Worldwatch regales us with fact-laden overviews of ecological deterioration, then leavens its message with a large measure of bright possibilities, from green taxes to windmills. It makes good reading, for it balances pessimism with optimism, and there is nothing to offend. Change makes good rational sense, and change is necessary, so change will come. Even land reform, which once rang throughout the world in calls for "land and liberty" and heroic, bloody peasant uprisings, will come, perhaps easily. First necessity must be established, and this isn't too difficult — the facts are compelling enough. Worldwatch's Holly Brough can therefore review a grim situation and conclude, "If the Earth is to survive and its people prosper, land reform is indispensable." Then comes the optimism: "Donors and developing states now may be less likely to perceive radical land reform as a Communist conspiracy and more as a policy capable of addressing the needs of both the environment and the people."[13]

These are reassuring words, but they contain an optimism that quite overwhelms realism. Meaningful land reform will *not* come easily. Elites have long used anticommunist ideology as an excuse to oppose the redistribution of land, and now they must do without it. But they will find new excuses easily enough. In both the United States and Mexico, "efficiency" is the favorite justification for the destruction of both peasant and family farming.[14]

Herman Daly, in his 1994 farewell lecture to World Bank staff, addressed this crucial problem of narrow self-interest and the refusal to change. Arguing that chronic high unemployment, coupled with the ecological crisis, makes it imperative to shift to policies that promote employment and penalize pollution and the depletion of resources, he invited his listeners to consider the role that a greatly reformed future version of the Bank could play in forcing such policies on the North. "The shift," he suggested, "should be a key part of structural adjustment, but should be pioneered in the North. . . . It is absurd to expect any sacrifice for sustainability in the South if similar measures have not first been taken in the North."[15]

If this is a dream as wild as revolution, if the World Bank, the IMF, and the whole global institutional apparatus must be deeply reformed before a clear path to change can emerge, this at least gives us a metric by which to measure the halting progress of the eco-diplomats, a sieve with which to separate rhetoric and good intentions from meaningful reforms.

The story, of course, does not end here. There are good reasons to believe that change is possible, reasons that range from the green movement itself, to the technological and economic reforms we hear so much about from policy activists, to the obvious fact that greens are hardly alone in seeing the state of the world as intolerable. To see hope in concrete form, one need only pick a subject, from water pollution to family planning to democracy. A few hours of research will generally reveal excellent ideas in profusion, and demonstrate that it is politics, and not any lack of technological or policy alternatives, that holds us in this stasis.

The strongest grounds for hope is this — that time and resources both remain. If, fifty years hence, our children find themselves so in thrall to necessity that they cannot even imagine a better world, it will not be because they met their inexorable fate, but because we failed now, when the broad shape of the future is still open to dispute. Realism lies in acknowledging that change is a practical necessity, that contrived optimism must be rejected, that we cannot always be circumspect about the realities of power. It lies, most of all, in admitting that there is no easy path to a green transition, and perhaps no path at all — for powerful minorities everywhere do not want change.

Last Words

Environmentalism has a peculiar history. As a modern movement, it arose in a century shaped by war, and in particular by the long war — not always cold — against the "reds." Greens have generally remained apart from that war, for real socialism was a pretty unattractive proposition, and it cast a long, dim shadow. No wonder that greens, seeking a new politics, have long claimed to be neither left nor right.

The time for such political innocence is over. This has been a dark century, but the planet is wavering at the edge of even darker possibilities. Given the key role they are fated to play in the politics of an ever-shrinking world, it is past time for environmentalists to face their own history, in which they have too often stood not for justice and freedom, or even for realism, but merely for the comforts and aesthetics of affluent nature lovers. They have no choice. History will judge greens by whether they stand with the world's poor.

Environmentalism emerged in a world where left and even liberal radicalism were lost in the cold corridors of Soviet-style communism. Whatever price the greens paid for their independence from the left tradition, it allowed them to face the world anew, to claim dozens of crucial cultural, political, and technological domains — from safe energy systems to greener cities — for their evolving and fluid agenda. Before environmentalism's rebirth in the late 1960s, even visionary reformers rarely saw such things as transportation systems or diet as intimately linked to the prospect for freedom and dignity. Today millions take it for granted that this is so.

The green movement is reeling under an antienvironmental assault, but there are grounds for hope about its future. Even its long tradition of apolitical, technological pragmatism, its concern with nuts and bolts, has a bright side. Pragmatism can yield results. Greens, often enemies of "free markets," have generally come to their position less by ideologically colored analysis than by observing what most economists still will not admit — that left to their own devices, markets shift ecological and social costs into the "commons," and destroy both nature and human communities in the process.

We find ourselves just now in a strange, strained lull. Our real conditions of life are increasingly visible. There is a pervasive sense that broad change is necessary, and even that it is imminent. Brush aside the charge that ecology is merely a form of nostalgia, and ecology's real lesson is apparent. The past is no guide, the future must be different. Always, other matters force ecology from the front pages, but always it returns, each time more insistently.

The official UNCED treaties prove the point, for there is, in them, little talk of global poverty, of the dark sides of the new economy, of the corporations, of militarism, of democracy. Yet these are the decisive matters, those that will determine our fate. If there was hope in Rio, it was because these subjects, the true agenda of the future, were nevertheless present. They were there in the "alternative treaties" hammered out by thousands of activists from around the world, in excited, staccato conversation, and, most important of all, in the globally shared sense of an emerging common agenda, common movement, common project.

We may be forgiven for being unfamiliar with the alternative treaties. The *New York Times*, in all its reams of Earth Summit coverage, did not mention them at all, while the *Los Angeles Times* graced them with a single snide report, "Strong Treaties Elude Even Activists at Earth Summit," that seemed to delight in the fact of friction, and the necessity of compromise, between Northern and Southern activists.[16]

Whatever the Earth Summit's failures, it broadcast waves of lucid, radical realism around the world. Here is a fragment found soon after Rio on Econet, the North American node of the green movement's semiofficial global computer network.[17] It was entitled "Celebrating the Failure of UNCED," and it captured a mood that has not been altogether forgotten.

> What is needed now is the mobilization of ever larger and more vocal social movements rather than more conversation for conservation. Mainstream Northern NGOs are happy to speak of such movements (and, to a very much lesser degree, support them) when, and only when, the movements are in the South. None of them are building or even supporting true people's movements in the North. They have a membership, usually drawn from liberal professionals, which they encourage to give money, buy T-shirts, and send in lobby cards — but which they actively discourage from taking their own initiative and expressing their rage, horror, or fear over what we are doing to ourselves.[18]

It may be difficult for us to understand that this is not an isolated voice. Change did not come at Rio, but it did announce itself, and the announcement demands blunt repetition — it is long past time to see that the future does not lie with the "already over-emphasized and over-funded national compromise branch of our movement," as it was so precisely called by the grassroots People's Alliance for the Earth Summit.[19]

As awareness of biophysical limits increases, it will become difficult to keep faith with small remedies. It is not impossible that soon ecological deterioration will routinely inspire echoes of William James's call for a "moral equivalent of war,"[20] only this time as a war of cooperation, a war to save the earth. That is what it will take.

Somehow, we must open the future, yet we are haunted by the past, by ghosts of old ideologies, old canards, old dichotomies that obscure the real conditions of our lives. And what are those conditions? That we do not all share the same interests; that it is late — too late for purity, too late for simple utopias,[21] too late for the dream of retreating to "the land," too late for the eco-politician's fantasy of an altogether polite, rationally negotiated global transition. It is *not* too late to act, or to recall the old imperative to "educate, agitate, and organize," or to remember that the deepest springs of hope lie in engagement, in making the choice to make a difference.

We inhabit a paradox. Our age is tragic, and catastrophe does threaten, but though the future is obscure, it does not come to us inexorable and inescapable. Our tragedy lies in the richness of the available alternatives, and in the fact that so few of them are ever seriously explored. It lies in the rigidity of war machines, the legacies of colonialism, the inflexibilities of the industrial tradition, the solaces of consumerism, the cynicism born of long disappointment, the habits of power. No wonder, given all this, that our age seems not merely tragic but tragic in the classical sense, that despite all possibility, we seem trapped in just that remorseless "working of things" that the Greeks saw as the core of tragedy.

Notes

ONE
Where Are We Now?

1. Twilly Cannon, author's interview, summer 1991.
2. Frieder Otto Wolf, author's interview, May 7, 1993.
3. Roger Manser, author's interview, April 27, 1993. Manser's book has been published under two different titles. In Britain it is *Squandered Dividend: The Free Market and the Environment in Eastern Europe* (London: Earthscan, 1993). In the United States it is named *Failed Transitions: The Eastern European Economy and Environment Since the Fall of Communism* (New York: New Press, 1994).
4. Wolfgang Sachs, author's interview, May 5, 1993.
5. Carla Atkinson, "With the Party Over, Green Groups Look Ahead," *Worldwatch*, January/February 1993, p. 35.
6. *O'Dwyer's PR Services Report*, February 1994, quoted in Peter Montague, "PR Firms Promote Cost-Benefit Analysis," *Rachel's Hazardous Waste News*, no. 379 (March 3, 1994). (Environmental Research Foundation, P.O. Box 5036, Annapolis, MD 20403). For overviews of the green PR industry, see Joel Bleifuss, "Covering the Earth with Green PR," *PR Watch: Special Earth Day 25th Anniversary Issue*, first quarter 1995 (Center for Media and Democracy, 3318 Gregory Street, Madison, WI 53711), and, at greater length, John Stauber and Sheldon Rampton, *Toxic Sludge Is Good for You: Lies, Damn Lies, and the Public Relations Industry* (Monroe, Maine: Common Courage Press, 1995). See also Eve Pell, "Buying In: How Corporations Keep an Eye on Environmental Groups That Oppose Them — By Giving Big Wads of Money," *Mother Jones*, April/May 1990, p. 23.
7. Bill Walker, author's interview, spring 1991.
8. David Helvarg, *The War Against the Greens: The Wise-Use Movement, the New Right, and Anti-Environmental Violence* (San Francisco: Sierra Club Books, 1994), p. 300.
9. Bronwen Maddox, "Campaigners All at Sea," *Financial Times*, November 12/13, 1994. See also Keith Schneider, "For the Environment, Compassion Fatigue," *New York Times*, November 6, 1994.
10. Ron Arnold, speaking on ABC-TV's *Nightline*, February 2, 1992.
11. Carl Deal, *The Greenpeace Guide to Anti-Environmental Organizations* (Berkeley: Odonian Press, 1993).
12. John H. Cushman, Jr., "Environmental Lobby Beats Tactical Retreat," *New York Times*, March 30, 1994. John H. Cushman, Jr., "Congress Ends Bid for a Mining Tax," *New York Times*, September 30, 1994. John H. Cushman, Jr., "Few Environmental Laws Emerge from 103d Congress," *New York Times*, October 3, 1994. John H. Cushman, Jr., "Congress Forgoes Its Bid to Speed Cleanup of Dumps," *New York Times*, October 6, 1994.

13. Sam Schuchat, author's interview, March 1994. See also the *1993 Environmental Voting Chart* of the California League of Conservation Voters, 965 Mission Street, Suite 625, San Francisco, CA 94103.

14. David Corn, "Al in the Balance," *The Nation,* April 25, 1994, pp. 545–546.

15. J. T. Houghton, et al., *Climate Change: The IPCC Scientific Assessment* (New York: Cambridge University Press, 1990). For an analysis of the conclusions of the Intergovernmental Panel on Climate Change (IPCC) and their implications, see Peter Hayes and Kirk Smith, eds., *The Global Greenhouse Regime: Who Pays?* (London and New York: Earthscan and UN University Press, 1993), pp. 5–6.

16. Paul Harrison, *The Third Revolution: Environment, Population, and a Sustainable World* (London: I. B. Taurus/Penguin, 1992), p. 282.

17. See Martin Walker, "Global Taxation: Paying for Peace," *World Policy Journal* 10, no. 2, (summer 1993), pp. 7–12.

18. *Agenda Ya Wananchi: Citizens' Action Plan for the 1990s* was adopted at "Roots of the Future, a global NGO conference held in relation to the 1992 Earth Summit," in Paris, France, December 17–20, 1991. It was published by the Environment Liaison Centre International (ELCI) in Nairobi, Kenya (P.O. Box 72461).

19. Noel Brown's keynote speech at David Brower's eightieth birthday celebration, San Francisco, 1992.

20. Dave Henson, then of the Highlander Center, in introductory remarks at the International People's Forum, held in New York City during UNCED's final preparation conference, PrepCom4.

21. World Commission on Environment and Development [the Brundtland Commission], *Our Common Future* (Oxford: Oxford University Press, 1987).

22. James MacNeill, "Honesty, Courage Needed to Save the Summit," *Earth Summit Times,* June 3, 1992, p. 1.

23. Speech on Behalf of the Environment and Development NGOs at the UNCED Plenary, Presented on Their Behalf by Wangari Maathai, June 11, 1992.

24. See, most recently, Wendell Berry, *Sex, Economy, Freedom and Community* (New York: Pantheon, 1993).

25. Christopher Manes, *Green Rage: Radical Environmentalism and the Unmaking of Civilization* (Boston: Little, Brown, 1990).

26. Bill McKibben, *The End of Nature* (New York: Random House, 1989). McKibben's more recent, and more upbeat, effort — *Hope, Human and Wild* (Boston: Little, Brown, 1995) — is, as befits its goal, far more politically specific. It is, unfortunately, less compelling as well.

27. Friedrich Heilman, author's interview, May 1993.

28. Robert Gottlieb, *Forcing the Spring: The Transformation of the American Environmental Movement* (Washington, D.C.: Island Press, 1993), p. 5.

29. Philip Schabecoff, *A Fierce Green Fire: The American Environmental Movement* (New York: Hill and Wang, 1993), p. 251.

30. Alan Durning, "People, Power, and Development," *Foreign Policy,* no. 76 (fall 1989), p. 66. Also, Paul Ekins, *A New World Order: Grassroots Movements for Social Change* (London: Routledge, 1992).

31. For the story of the rise and fall of the Group of Ten, see Gottlieb, *Forcing the Spring*, pp. 117–124.

32. Tani Adams, author's interview, August, 1993.

33. *Beyond UNCED* (Amsterdam: Greenpeace International, 1992), p. 4.

34. Paul Hohnen, author's interview, April 1993.

35. Roger Altman, deputy treasury secretary, quoted in Richard L. Berke, "Group of Governors Supports Trade Accord," *New York Times,* July 17, 1993.

36. Martha Bechler and Angela Gennino, *Southeast Asia Rainforests: A Resource Guide and Directory* (San Francisco: Rainforest Action Network [450 Sansome Street, Suite 700, San Francisco, CA 94111], 1993), p. 3.

37. Bruce Rich, *Mortgaging the Earth: The World Bank, Environmental Impoverishment, and the Crisis of Development* (Boston: Beacon Press, 1994), p. 63.

38. Robert Gottlieb, "An Odd Assortment of Allies: American Environmentalism in the 1990s," in Craige L. LaMay and Everette E. Dennis, eds., *Media and the Environment* (Covelo, Calif.: Island Press, 1993), pp. 44–45.

39. Marcy Darnovsky, "Stories Less Told: Histories of U.S. Environmentalism," *Socialist Review* 92, no. 4 (Duke University Press), p. 28. For much more on "environmental" movements that were not recognized as such, see the fall 1993/winter 1994 issue of *Race, Poverty and the Environment* (c/o Earth Island Institute, 300 Broadway, Suite 28, San Francisco, CA 94133).

40. For the whole story here, and a good deal more about the sanitized official history of environmentalism, see Gottlieb's *Forcing the Spring*.

41. Peter Bahouth, author's interview, June 4, 1992.

42. John H. Cushman, Jr., "A Tug-of-War over Earth Day '95," *New York Times,* October 29, 1994. John H. Cushman, Jr., "25th Earth Day to Have a Political Accent," *New York Times,* April 17, 1995.

43. Environmental Action staff, eds., *Earth Day — The Beginning: A Guide for Survival* (New York: Bantam, 1970), pp. xiii–xv.

44. Murray Bookchin's *Our Synthetic Environment* (New York: Harper and Row, 1974), was first published under the pseudonym Lewis Herber.

45. Council on Environmental Quality, *The Global 2000 Report to the President: Entering the Twenty-First Century* (Washington, D.C.: U.S. Government Printing Office, 1977).

46. Both extinction and forestation are complex matters and are often badly misinterpreted. Reforestation in nothern forests is particularly subject to upbeat reporting that seriously trivializes underlying ecological complexities. For a fair look at the issues here, see Bill McKibben's "An Explosion of Green" in the April 1995 issue of *The Atlantic,* and note the gap between the judiciousness of McKibben's analysis and the feel-good cover of the magazine itself. On the return of eastern U.S. forests, see also William K. Stevens, "The Forest Primeval Isn't What It Used to Be," *New York Times,* September 24, 1995. For an authoritative overview of extinction, see Edward O. Wilson, *The Diversity of Life* (Cambridge: Harvard University Press, 1992).

47. Donella H. Meadows, Dennis L. Meadows, and Jorgen Randers, *Beyond the Lim-*

its: Confronting Global Collapse, Envisioning a Sustainable Future (Post Mills, Vt.: Chelsea Green, 1992), pp. 57–64.

48. Christopher Flavin, author's interview, spring 1991.

49. Celia W. Dugger, "International Disasters Tax America's Compassion," *New York Times*, May 12, 1991. "Compassion fatigue" is also a domestic problem. See Rick Bragg, "Homeless Seeing Less Apathy, More Anger," *New York Times*, February 25, 1994.

50. "El Niño Weather Pattern Surprises Scientists by Length and Strength," *New York Times*, October 24, 1993.

51. "Reading the Patterns," *The Economist*, April 1, 1995. "The Hadley Centre Model — Data Approaches Reality," *Eco Berlin*, no. 9 (April 6, 1995). (*Eco* newsletters have been published by nongovernmental environmental groups at major international conferences since the Stockholm Environment Conference in 1972. *Eco Berlin* was produced by groups attending the first Conference of Parties of the Climate Change Convention in Berlin, March–April, 1995). Odil Tunali, "Climate Models Growing More Accurate," *Worldwatch*, May/June 1995.

52. *The Climate Time Bomb: Signs of Climate Change from the Greenpeace Database* (Amsterdam: Greenpeace International, 1994). William K. Stevens, "Violent Weather Battering Globe in Last 2 Years Baffles Experts," *New York Times*, May 24, 1994. Craig R. Whitney, "Europe Wilts, Records Fall, in Heat Wave," *New York Times*, August 3, 1994. William K. Stevens, "More Extremes Found in Weather, Pointing to Greenhouse Gas Effect," *New York Times*, May 23, 1995. On the U.S. beaches specifically, see William K. Stevens, "Scientists Say Earth's Warming Cloud Could Set Off Wide Disruptions," *New York Times*, September 18, 1995. See also "Global Warming Heats Up," the lead *Times* editorial from the same day.

53. Rachel Carson, *Silent Spring*, (New York: Crest, 1964), p. x.

54. Monica Moore, program director of the Pesticide Action Network, author's interview, May 5, 1994 (PAN, 116 New Montgomery Street, #810, San Francisco, CA 94105).

55. Howard Youth, "Birds Are in Decline," in Lester R. Brown, Hal Kane, and David Malin Roodman, eds., *Vital Signs: 1994* (New York: Norton, 1994), pp. 128–129. For details, see Howard Youth, "Flying into Trouble," *Worldwatch*, January/February 1994.

56. Alexander Cockburn, "Beat the Devil," *The Nation*, June 6, 1994, p. 777.

57. Norman Rush, "What Was Socialism . . . and Why We Will All Miss It So Much," *The Nation*, January 24, 1994, p. 92.

58. Murray Feshbach and Alfred Friendly, Jr., *Ecocide in the USSR: Health and Nature Under Siege* (New York: Basic Books, 1992).

59. Manser, *Failed Transitions*, pp. 37–38.

60. See, for example, Andreas Bernsdorff and Katherine Totten, *Romania: The Toxic Assault. Waste Imports 1986–92* (Hamburg: Greenpeace Germany, August 1992).

61. Frieder Otto Wolf, author's interview, May 7, 1993.

62. B. Drummond Ayers, Jr., "New Border Defense Stems Volume of Illegal Crossings," *New York Times*, October 6, 1994.

63. Mexico's President Carlos Salinas proposed opening the border to migrant workers in the initial NAFTA negotiations, but he did not fight for an "immigration side agreement." In late 1994, after the passage of California's Proposition 187 and just before the end of his term, he again insisted that such an opening was a necessary complement to NAFTA. See Tim Golden, "Salinas Urges Talks on Free Migrant Flow," *New York Times*, November 14, 1994.

64. Joel Simon, "Fabled Frontier," *SF Weekly*, July 7, 1993, p. 10.

65. Stephen Kinzer, "Bonn Parliament Votes Sharp Curb on Asylum Seekers," *New York Times*, May 27, 1993.

66. Sachs, author's interview.

67. Paul Lewis, "Stoked by Ethnic Fighting, Refugee Numbers Grow," *New York Times*, November, 10, 1993. Hal Kane, "Refugees Reach All-Time Record," in Lester R. Brown, Hal Kane, and Ed Ayers, eds., *Vital Signs: 1993* (New York: Norton, 1993), pp. 100–101. Kathleen Newland, "Refugees: The Rising Flood," *Worldwatch*, May/June 1994, pp. 10–20. "The Seekers," *The Nation*, July 26/August 2, 1993, p. 124.

68. Hans Magnus Enzensberger, "The Great Migration," *Granta* 42 (winter 1992), pp. 17–51. See also Matthew Connelly and Paul Kennedy, "Must It Be the Rest Against the West?" *The Atlantic*, December 1994, pp. 61–84.

69. Richard L. Berke, "Politicians Discovering an Issue: Immigration," *New York Times*, March 8, 1994.

70. On the history of the interplay between immigration and population politics, see Gottlieb, *Forcing the Spring*, pp. 253–260. For the situation as it is evolving, see Cathi Tactaquin, "Environmentalists and the Anti-Immigrant Agenda" in the summer 1993 issue of *Race, Poverty and the Environment*, and Betsy Hartman, "Dangerous Intersections," in the summer 1995 issue of *Political Environments* (Committee on Women, Population, and the Environment, c/o Population and Development Program, Hampshire College, P.O. Box 5001, Amherst MA 01002).

71. For example, Tim Weiner, "On the Shores, Immigrants Find a New Wave of Hostility," *New York Times*, June 13, 1993.

72. Globally, 30 percent of the labor force is unemployed. See "Workless: Mass Unemployment in the New World Order," in *Third World Resurgence*, no. 44 (87 Cantonment Road, 10250 Penang, Malaysia).

73. Edward Luttwak, "Why Fascism Is the Wave of the Future," *London Review of Books*, April 7, 1994. See also Doug Henwood's fine analysis of recent U.S. Census data, "Economy Up, People Down," in *Left Business Observer*, no. 66 (October 21, 1994) (LBO, 250 West Eighty-Fifth Street, New York, NY, 10024).

74. For a fine discussion of immigration, one linked to both the structure of the world economy and the environmental crisis, see "The Fifth Boomerang: Immigration," in Susan George's *The Debt Boomerang: How Third World Debt Harms Us All* (London: Pluto Press, 1992).

75. Jacques Attali, *Millennium: Winners and Losers in the Coming World Order* (New York: Random House, 1991) p. 14. This is actually an incomplete accounting of the tale, for it leaves out war, and one of every 130 people on the planet is a refugee from war. See Sadako Ogata, *The State of the World's Refugees: The Challenge of Protection* (New York: Penguin, 1993).

76. See Amartya Sen, "Population: Delusion and Reality," *New York Review of Books,* September 22, 1994.

77. Rik Scarce, *Eco-Warriors: Understanding the Radical Environmental Movement* (Chicago: Nobel Press, 1990), p. 92.

78. Walden Bello, "Population and the Environment: The Food First Perspective," *Food First Action Alert,* Winter 1992–93, p. 2.

79. See John Kenneth Galbraith, *The Culture of Contentment* (Boston: Houghton Mifflin, 1992).

80. Garrett Hardin, June 12, 1993, speaking at Black Oak Books in Berkeley on the occasion of the publication of his *Living Within Limits: Ecology, Economics, and Population Taboos* (New York: Oxford University Press, 1993).

81. Enzensberger, "The Great Migration."

82. Vaclav Havel, "The Power of the Powerless," in *Living in Truth* (London: Faber and Faber, 1986), p. 40.

83. Ibid., pp. 114, 54.

84. Alan Durning, *How Much Is Enough? The Consumer Society and the Future of the Earth* (Norton: New York, 1992), pp. 26–36.

85. See "The Cultivation of Needs," chap. 9 in ibid.

86. Alan Durning, author's interview, June 4, 1993.

87. Al Gore, *Earth in the Balance: Ecology and the Human Spirit* (New York: Houghton Mifflin, 1992). See in particular Part II, "The Search for Balance."

88. Chris Calwell of the Natural Resources Defense Council, original introduction to *Fifty Simple Things You Can Do to Save the Earth* (Berkeley: Earthworks Press, 1989), p. 7.

89. This quote is from an article on the "informal economy" by Craig Cox in the November/December 1994 issue of the *Utne Reader.* See also Alan Durning's celebration of "dumpster diving" in *How Much Is Enough?,* pp. 100–101.

90. Durning, *How Much Is Enough?,* p. 142.

91. *Perspectives of American Voters on the Cairo Agenda: A Report to PrepCom III,* from survey and focus group research conducted for the Pew Global Stewardship Initiative, April 20, 1994, p. 13.

92. Jacob M. Schlesinger and James McGregor, "Buying Friends: Sino-Japanese Trade Soars and 2 Old Foes Cautiously Embrace," *Wall Street Journal Europe,* May 12, 1993, p. 1.

93. See, for example, Michael Ignatieff's *The Needs of Strangers* (New York: Penguin, 1984), especially chap. 4, "The Market and the Republic: Smith and Rousseau."

94. Alan Thein Durning, "World Spending on Ads Skyrockets," in Brown et al., eds., *Vital Signs: 1993* (New York: Norton, 1993), p. 80.

95. Durning, *How Much Is Enough?,* pp. 120, 128.

96. Ibid., p. 119.

97. Thorstein Veblen, *Absentee Ownership and Business Enterprise in Recent Times* (1923), cited in Harry Braverman, *Labor and Monopoly Capital: The Degradation of Work in the Twentieth Century* (New York: Monthly Review, 1974), p. 266.

98. See Durning, *How Much Is Enough?*, p. 131, and also John P. Robinson, "When the Going Gets Tough," *American Demographics* 11, no. 2 (1989), p. 50, cited in Paul Ekins, "The Sustainable Consumer Society: A Contradiction in Terms?" *International Environmental Affairs* 3, no. 4 (fall 1991), p. 245. For an extensive analysis of the issues here, see Juliet B. Schor, *The Overworked American* (New York: Basic, 1992), especially chap. 5, "The Insidious Cycle of Work-and-Spend."

99. Robert Kuttner, *The End of Laissez-Faire: National Purpose and the Global Economy After the Cold War* (New York: Knopf, 1991), p. 53.

100. Ibid., p. 25.

101. Richard Nixon took the lead with an op-ed piece in the *New York Times* — "Save the Peace Dividend," November 19, 1992. This quote, and another snapshot of the situation as it developed, can be found in Edward Balls and John Lloyd, "Much Ado About Lending," *Financial Times*, May 12, 1993.

102. Serge Schmemann, "Yeltsin Calls Vote a Rebuke but Vows to Pursue Reforms," *New York Times*, December 23, 1993.

103. Steven Erlanger, "A 'New' Russia: Yeltsin Needs Consensus and Cash," *New York Times*, December 23, 1993.

104. Lucy Johnson, "IMF Says Only Reform Can Solve Unemployment," Interpress Third World News Service, April 22, 1994. (Interpress is an international news service based in Rome, Italy. Its articles see wide E-mail distribution; this one reached me through Econet, the U.S. affiliate of the Association for Progressive Communications.) Peter Norman, "IMF Calls for Reform of Labour Market to Cut Jobless," *Financial Times*, April 21, 1994.

105. For a fine summary of the issues here, and pointers into the literature, see Walden Bello, with Shea Cunningham and Bill Rau, *Dark Victory: The U.S., Structural Adjustment, and Global Poverty* (Oakland: Food First/The Institute for Food and Development Policy [398 Sixtieth Street, Oakland, CA 94618] with London's Pluto Press and the Transnational Institute, 1994), pp. 56–66.

106. The literature on the Bank is huge and growing. See, first, Bruce Rich, *Mortgaging the Earth*, and also Patricia Adams, *Odious Debts: Loose Lending, Corruption, and the Third World's Environmental Legacy* (London: Earthscan, 1991), especially chap. 6.

107. Thomas L. Friedman, "The World Bank, 50 Years Old, Plots a New Course and Vows to Do Better," *New York Times*, July 24, 1994.

108. For a chilling discussion of the "Bank-Wide Resettlement Review," see Bruce Rich, "Memorandum: Forcible Resettlement in World Bank Projects," Environmental Defense Fund, Washington, D.C., January 1994.

109. See, for example, "Redefining Development," a discussion of Bangladesh's Grameen Bank by one of its founders, Muhammad Yunus, in *Fifty Years Is Enough*, ed. Kevin Danaher (Boston: South End Press, 1994).

110. Susan George and Fabrizio Sabelli, *Faith and Credit: The World Bank's Secular Empire* (Boulder, Colo.: Westview, 1994), p. 164.

111. Rich, *Mortgaging the Earth*, pp. 72–75, 305.

112. Walter Russell Mead, "Why the Deficit Is a Godsend, and Five Other Economic Heresies," *Harper's*, May 1993, p. 61.

113. On nationalism as resistance to "despotic internationalism," see William Pfaff, *The Wrath of Nations: Civilization and the Fury of Nationalism* (New York: Simon and Schuster, 1993). Pfaff had Stalinism and Nazism in mind, but then he was thinking of the past. For a darker view of the new nationalism, see Michael Ignatieff, *Blood and Belonging: Journeys into the New Nationalism* (New York: Farrar, Straus and Giroux, 1993).

114. Herman Daly, "Farewell Lecture to the World Bank," January 14, 1994, in J. Cavanagh, D. Wysham, and M. Arruda, eds., *Beyond Bretton Woods: Alternatives to the Global Economic Order* (London: Pluto Press, TNI and IPS, 1994). For Daly's view that the "free migration" of labor is as destructive as "free trade," see Herman E. Daly and John B. Cobb, Jr., *For the Common Good: Redirecting the Economy Towards Community, the Environment, and a Sustainable Future* (Boston: Beacon Press, 1989), pp. 219, 237.

115. "A former California forestry official," quoted in Deal, *The Greenpeace Guide*, p. 7.

116. For an international view of such repression, see *Defending the Earth: Abuses of Human Rights and the Environment*, published by Human Rights Watch and the Natural Resources Defense Council, June 1992.

117. Mark Dowie, "American Environmentalism: A Movement Courting Irrelevance," *World Policy Journal*, winter 1991–92, p. 69.

118. For an irritating but suggestive history of right-wing currents in ecological thought, see Anna Bramwell's *Ecology in the Twentieth Century* (New Haven: Yale University Press, 1989).

119. Jodi L. Jacobson, "Slavery (Yes, Slavery) Returns," *Worldwatch*, January/February 1992.

120. Thomas L. Friedman, "World's Big Economies Turn to the Jobs Issue," *New York Times*, March 14, 1994.

121. Even *The Economist* agrees, in its fashion. See "A Future for Socialism," June 11–17, 1994.

122. *Human Development Report: 1992*, p. 34. Published for the United Nations Development Program by Oxford University Press. See also Rich, p. 244.

123. Rich, *Mortgaging the Earth*, p. 244.

124. James MacNeill et al., "The West's Shadow Ecologies," *New Perspectives Quarterly*, fall 1991, p. 28 (adapted from *Beyond Interdependence: The Meshing of the World's Economy and the Earth's Economy* [New York: Oxford University Press, 1991]). James Gustave Speth, "A Post-Rio Compact," *Foreign Policy*, no. 88, (fall 1992), p. 149.

125. Paul Bairoch cited in Robert Heilbroner, *Twenty-First Century Capitalism* (New York: Norton, 1993), pp. 55–56.

126. Holly B. Brough, "A New Lay of the Land," *Worldwatch*, January/February 1991, p. 12.

127. Marcus Colchester and Larry Lohmann, eds., *The Struggle for Land and the Fate of the Forests* (London: Zed Books, 1993), p. 141.

128. Nicholas Guppy, "Tropical Deforestation: A Global View," *Foreign Affairs* 62, no. 4, pp. 930–965.

129. Stephen H. Schneider, "The Changing Climate," *Scientific American*, September 1989, p. 79.

TWO

Apocalyptics

1. Susan Sontag, "AIDS and Its Metaphors," *New York Review of Books*, October 27, 1988.

2. Herman Daly interviewed by Steve Lerner, in *Earth Summit: Conversations with Architects of an Ecologically Sustainable Future* (Bolinas, Calif.: Common Knowledge Press, 1991), p. 45.

3. Lester R. Brown, Christopher Flavin, and Sandra Postel, "Picturing a Sustainable Society," in Lester R. Brown et al., *State of the World: 1990* (New York: Norton, 1990) p. 174.

4. Donella H. Meadows, Dennis L. Meadows, and Jorgen Randers, *Beyond the Limits: Confronting Global Collapse, Envisioning a Sustainable Future* (Post Mills, Vt.: Chelsea Green, 1992), pp. xv–xvi.

5. See Anita Gorden and David Suzuki, *It's a Matter of Survival* (Cambridge: Harvard University Press, 1991), "Part 1: Toward the Year 2040."

6. See "Time Is Running Out," *Earth Island Journal*, winter 1992 (Earth Island Institute, 300 Broadway, Suite 28, San Francisco CA, 94133).

7. Mike Roselle, author's interview, February 1990.

8. Philip Shabecoff, "Forty-Year Countdown Is Seen for Environment," *New York Times*, February 11, 1990.

9. Sandra Postel, "Denial in the Decisive Decade," in Lester R. Brown et al., *State of the World: 1992* (New York: Norton, 1992) p. 3.

10. Jane Kay, "Earth Summit Opens on a Profound Note in Rio," *San Francisco Examiner*, June 3, 1992, p. A7.

11. Lester R. Brown, "Launching the Environmental Revolution," in Brown et al., *State of the World: 1992*, p. 176.

12. Randy Hayes, author's interview, 1992.

13. Paul Ehrlich, in a 1967 paper written about the time of *The Population Bomb*. Quoted in Allan Chase, *The Legacy of Malthus: The Social Costs of the New Scientific Racism* (New York: Knopf, 1977), p. 397. See also *The Population Bomb* (New York: Ballantine, 1968), pp. 144 and 148.

14. John F. Burns, "Bangladesh, Still Poor, Cuts Birth Rate Sharply," *New York Times*, September 13, 1994.

15. Bryant Robey, Shea O. Rutstein, and Leo Morris, "The Fertility Decline in Developing Countries," *Scientific American*, December 1993, p 65

16. Donella H. Meadows, Dennis L. Meadows, Jorgen Randers, and William W. Behrens III, *The Limits to Growth* (New York: Universe Books, 1972), p. 24.

17. Sandra Postel and Christopher Flavin, "Reshaping the Global Economy," in Lester R. Brown et al., *State of the World: 1991* (New York: Norton, 1991), p. 186.

18. Brown, "Launching the Environmental Revolution," p. 183.

19. Jessica Tuchman Mathews, "The Case for Reinventing Technology to Promote Sustainable Development," in Lerner, *Earth Summit*, p. 29.

20. Peter M. Vitousek, Paul R. Ehrlich, Anne H. Ehrlich, and Pamela A. Matson, "Human Appropriation of the Products of Photosynthesis," *Bioscience* 36, no. 6, pp. 368–373.

21. Brundtland report cited in Robert Goodland, Herman E. Daly, and Salah El Serafy, editors' introduction to *Population, Technology, and Lifestyle: The Transition to Sustainability* (Washington, D.C.: Island Press, 1992), p. xiii.

22. See Meadows et al., *Beyond the Limits*, pp. 65–66.

23. Donella Meadows, author's interview, January 6, 1994. Also, Meadows et al., *Beyond the Limits*, p. 245.

24. Robert D. Kaplan, "The Coming Anarchy," *The Atlantic*, February 1994, p. 60.

25. Lester Brown, "The New World Order," in Brown et al., *State of the World: 1991*, p. 3.

26. Denis Hayes, "Earth Day 1990: Threshold of the Green Decade," *Natural History*, April 1990.

27. Jack Doyle, *Hold the Applause: A Case Study of Corporate Environmentalism* (Washington: Friends of the Earth U.S. [218 D Street SE, Washington, D.C. 20003], 1991). See especially chap. 6, "The Ozone Game."

28. See, for example, *Selling Science: How the Press Covers Science and Technology*, by Dorothy Nelkin (New York: Freeman, 1987), pp. 55–57.

29. Donella Meadows, author's interview.

30. For telling examples of the optimism, see Meadows et al., *Beyond the Limits*, chap. 5, "Back from Beyond the Limits," and Richard Elliot Benedick, *Ozone Diplomacy: New Directions in Safeguarding the Planet* (Cambridge: Harvard University Press, 1991), especially chap. 14, "Looking Ahead: A New Global Diplomacy."

31. Richard Benedick, *Conservation Foundation Letter*, no. 4, 1989, p. 8. Cited in Rene Bowser et al., *Southern Exposure: Global Climate Change and Developing Countries* (University of Maryland at College Park: Center for Global Change USA, November 1992), p. 25.

32. See *Climbing Out of the Ozone Hole: A Preliminary Survey of Alternatives to Ozone-Depleting Chemicals*, especially chap. 2, "HCFCs and HFCs: Part of the Problem, Not Part of the Solution" (Amsterdam: Greenpeace International, October 1992).

33. Rene Bowser, "History of the Montreal Protocol's Ozone Fund," *Analysis and Perspective* (Bureau of National Affairs, Washington, D.C.), November 20, 1991, p. 637.

34. Bill Walsh, author's interview, December 22, 1993.

35. "Whose World Is It Anyway?" *The Economist*, May 30, 1992, p. "survey 18."

36. For a rare skeptical reading of the significance of the Montreal Protocol and other widely hyped environmental agreements, see Bruce Rich, *Mortgaging the*

Earth: The World Bank, Environmental Impoverishment, and the Crisis of Development (Boston: Beacon Press, 1994), pp. 277–280.

37. *Fossil Fuels in a Changing Climate: How to Protect the World's Climate by Ending the Use of Coal, Oil, and Gas* (Amsterdam: Greenpeace International, 1993).

38. "Current Commitments Won't Stabilize Climate — Bolin," *Eco Geneva*, no. 2 (February 9, 1994). (*Eco Geneva* was a newsletter produced by nongovernmental environmental groups attending the ninth Intergovernmental Negotiating Committee of the Climate Change Convention [INC9], February 1994.) Note also that the worst case is very bad indeed: Walter Sullivan, "New Theory on Ice Sheet Catastrophe Is the Direst One Yet," *New York Times*, May 2, 1995.

39. Andrew Kerr, "Economics of the Madhouse," *Eco Berlin*, no. 3, March 30, 1995. (*Eco Berlin* was a newsletter published by nongovernmental environmental groups attending the first Conference of Parties of the Climate Change Convention in Berlin, March–April, 1995).

40. *The Economist*, June 18, 1994, page 5 of "Power to the People," the energy survey in that issue.

41. Nicholas A. Sundt, "As CO_2 Emissions Soar, Concerns Mount over U.S. Climate Action Plan," *Energy, Economics and Climate Change*, March 1994, pp. 2–6. "U.S. Climate Plan — Hot Air," Greenpeace press release, April 21, 1994.

42. *U.S. Climate Action Report*, August 3 draft, quoted in Nicholas A. Sundt, "U.S. Issues Draft Climate Action Plan," *Energy, Economics and Climate Change*, September 1994. As of this writing, there is talk of a revised plan, but the U.S. administration is unwilling to promise it will meet its emissions target.

43. "From Berlin to Kyoto," *Eco Berlin*, no. 10 (April 7, 1995).

44. Nicholas A. Sundt, "EC Considers, But Does Not Endorse, Another Carbon Tax," *Energy, Economics and Climate Change*, March 1994, pp. 11–12; also, "Commission Finds 'No Guarantee' EU Will Fulfill Year-2000 Commitment," pp. 6–8. For background, see also *Fueling the Fire: EC Policy and the Climate Threat, Briefing on the EC Energy-Carbon Tax Proposal* (Amsterdam: Greenpeace International Climate Campaign, 1993).

45. Nicholas A. Sundt, "Rapid Growth in Energy Use Threatens Japan's CO_2 Commitment," *Energy, Economics and Climate Change*, February 1994, pp. 2–3.

46. "The Elephant in the Room," *Eco Geneva* (INC8), no. 3 (August 18, 1993).

47. Edward A. Gargan, "Shackled by Past, Racked by Unrest, India Lurches Toward Uncertain Future," *New York Times*, February 18, 1994.

48. By some calculations, Southern emissions of carbon dioxide *already* exceeded those of the North. See "Poorer Nations Spew Out the Most Carbon Dioxide," *New York Times*, April 19, 1994. This report is based on U.S. Department of Energy data that are most likely wrong; the trend they indicate, though, is real. For the interpretive issues here, see Susan Subak, "Assessing Emissions: Five Approaches Compared," in Peter Hayes and Kirk Smith, eds., *The Global Greenhouse Regime: Who Pays?* (London and New York: Earthscan and UN University Press, 1993), pp. 51–69. For recent data, see David Malin Roodman, "Carbon Emissions Unchanged," in Lester R. Brown, Hal Kane, and David Malin Roodman, eds., *Vital Signs: 1994* (New York: Norton, 1994), p. 68.

49. Steven Greenhouse, "U.S., After Negotiating Changes, Is Set to Sign Pact on Sea Mining," *New York Times,* March 10, 1994.

50. J. H. Ausubel and D. H. Victor, "Verification of International Environmental Agreements," *Annual Review of Energy and Environment* (Palo Alto, Calif.: Annual Reviews, Inc., 1991).

51. Wolfgang Fischer, "The Verification of International Conventions on Protection of the Environment and Common Resources," Forschungszentrum Julich GmbH, 1991.

52. Peter Weber, "Safeguarding Oceans," in Lester R. Brown et al., *State of the World: 1994* (New York: Norton, 1994), pp. 50–54. For an excellent overview, see *The Ecologist* double issue, "Overfishing: Causes and Consequences," March/April and May/June 1995.

53. Anne Dingwall, author's interview, May 1993.

54. Hilary F. French, "Reconciling Trade and the Environment," in Lester R. Brown et al., *State of the World: 1993* (New York: Norton, 1993) p. 163.

55. Hal Kane, "Off the Scale," *Worldwatch,* May/June 1993, p. 36; "U.S. Seafood Prices Have Climbed,"in Lester R. Brown, Hal Kane, and Ed Ayers, eds., *Vital Signs: 1993* (New York: Norton, 1993), pp. 118–119.

56. Donella Meadows, author's interview. Also, Meadows et al., *Beyond the Limits,* pp. 185–188.

57. Lester R. Brown, "Facing Food Insecurity," in Brown et al., *State of the World: 1994,* pp. 181–182.

58. Jon R. Luoma, "Boon to Anglers Turns Into a Disaster for Lakes and Streams," *New York Times,* November 17, 1992.

59. "Battling the World Bank: An Interview with Nilufar Ahmad," *Multinational Monitor,* October 1992, pp. 21–22. Also, Robin Broad and John Cavanagh, *Plundering Paradise* (Berkeley: University of California Press, 1993), p. 78.

60. Hal Kane, "Fish Catch No Longer Growing," in Brown et al., eds., *Vital Signs: 1993,* pp. 32–33.

61. The best brief overview of all the trends here is probably Lester R. Brown, "Facing Food Scarcity," *Worldwatch,* November/December 1995, pp. 9–20. Brown's pessimism, by the way, has gotten increased attention as grain prices have begun to rise. See, for example, Barnaby J. Feder, "Shortfall in the Grain Fields," *New York Times,* November 19, 1995, and "The Food Crisis That Isn't and the One That Is," *The Economist,* November 25, 1995. *The Economist,* of course, tells us that "market forces will deal with it."

62. For current numbers, see Brown, "Facing Food Insecurity," pp. 190–193.

63. Lester R. Brown, "Meat Production Up Slightly," in Brown et al., eds., *Vital Signs: 1993,* pp. 30–31.

64. Lester R. Brown, "Fertilizer Use Falls Again," in ibid., pp. 42–43.

65. Figures estimated by Dr. H. K. Jain, director of the Indian Agricultural Institute in New Delhi. Cited in C. L. McDougall and Ronnie Hall, *Intellectual Property Rights and the Biodiversity Convention: The Impact of GATT* (London: Friends of the Earth England, Wales and North Ireland, 1995). See also Paul Ehrlich, "The

Loss of Biodiversity: Causes and Consequences," in *Biodiversity*, E. O. Wilson, ed. (Washington, D.C.: National Academy Press, 1988).

66. William K. Stevens, "Feeding a Booming Population Without Destroying the Planet," *New York Times*, April 5, 1994.

67. Royal Society of London and the U.S. National Academy of Sciences, *Population Growth, Resource Consumption, and a Sustainable World* (London and Washington, D.C.: 1992). Such warnings, to be sure, do not impress the "skeptics." As Norman Levitt, coauthor (with Paul R. Gross) of *Higher Superstition: The Academic Left and Its Quarrels with Science* (Baltimore: Johns Hopkins, 1994), once quipped, "Scientists tend to adopt an apocalyptic tone for ceremonial reasons." (Press conference, "The Flight from Science and Reason," June 1, 1995.)

68. See Paul Kennedy, *Preparing for the Twenty-First Century* (New York: Random House, 1993), pp. 65–72, Lester R. Brown, "A Decade of Discontinuity," *Worldwatch*, July/August 1993, p. 19; also, Brown, "Facing Food Insecurity," pp. 177–191.

69. K. Fenelon, *Britain's Food Supplies*, (London: Methuen, 1952), p. 13. Quoted in Tim Lang and Colin Hines, *The New Protectionism: Protecting the Future Against Free Trade* (London: Earthscan, 1993), p. 96.

70. Edward Thompson, "Notes on Exterminism, the Last State of Civilization," in *Exterminism and Cold War* (Verso: London, 1982) p. 20.

71. Seymour M. Hersh, "The Wild East," *The Atlantic*, June 1994, pp. 61–84. See also the three-part, front-page "After the Arms Race" series in the *New York Times*, August 18–20, 1994.

72. R. L. Sivard, *World Social and Military Expenditures 1993* (Washington, D.C.: World Priorities, 1993), p. 10.

73. William Safire, "Optimists Are the Realists," *New York Times*, December 26, 1991.

74. William Safire, "Target: Declinism," *New York Times Magazine*, June 12, 1992.

75. Helen Caldicott, quoted in "Green Guilt and Ecological Overload," by Theodore Roszak, *New York Times*, June 9, 1992. See Roberto Suro, "Rash of Infant Brain Defects Disturbs Border City," *New York Times*, May 31, 1992, and also "Study in South Texas Finds High Birth-Defect Rate," *New York Times*, August 7, 1992.

76. Frank Kermode, *The Sense of an Ending* (New York: Oxford University Press: 1967), p. 93.

77. Lewis H. Lapham, "Notebook," *Harper's*, November 1993, p. 10.

78. Lapham's review — of both McKibben's *The End of Nature* (New York: Random House, 1989) and Francis Fukuyama's "The End of History" (*National Interest*, summer 1989) — was printed as "Endgames" in the November 1989 issue of *Harper's*.

79. Thomas Malthus, *Essay on the Principle of Population* (London: 1798).

80. Ehrlich, *The Population Bomb*, p. 1.

81. Paul R. Ehrlich and Anne E. Ehrlich, *The Population Explosion* (New York: Simon and Schuster, 1990), p. 9.

82. Ehrlich, *The Population Bomb,* pp. 66–67. Cited in Barry Commoner, *The Closing Circle: Nature, Man and Technology* (New York: Bantam, 1971; 1974 ed.), pp. 2–3. Emphasis in original.

83. Jaya Dayal, "U.S. Scientist Relights Fuse to Population Bomb," Interpress Third World News Service, Rome, April 21, 1994.

84. Gerard Piel, writing in *Earth Times* (a newspaper published by nongovernmental groups attending PrepCom3 of 1994's UN Conference on Population and Development), April 10, 1994.

85. Julian Simon, *The Ultimate Resource* (Princeton: Princeton University Press, 1981) p. 5.

86. Ibid., p. 9. See also "The More the Merrier: An Interview with Julian Simon," *Forbes,* April 2, 1990, p. 78.

87. George Orwell, "James Burnham and the Managerial Revolution," in *Collected Essays, Journalism and Letters,* vol. 4 (New York: Harcourt Brace Jovanovich, 1968), pp. 172–173, 174.

88. Julian Simon, "Earth's Doomsayers Are Wrong," *San Francisco Chronicle,* May 12, 1995.

89. Paul Ehrlich, "Call it Brownwash," *Worldwatch,* September/October 1995.

90. Charles C. Mann, "How Many Is Too Many?" *The Atlantic,* February 1993.

91. Barbara Crossette, "Population Debate: The Premises are Changed," *New York Times,* September 14, 1994.

92. For a post-Cairo look at the issues here, see the summer 1995 issue of *Political Environments* (Committee on Women, Population, and the Environment, c/o Population and Development Program, Hampshire College, P.O. Box 5001, Amherst MA 01002), or contact the Women's Environment and Development Organization (WEDO), 845 Third Avenue, Fifteenth Floor, New York, NY 10022. See also Betsy Hartmann's classic *Reproductive Rights and Wrongs: The Global Politics of Population Control and Contraceptive Choice* (New York: Harper and Row, 1987. Rev. ed., Boston: South End Press, 1994).

93. Betsy Hartmann, "Old Maps and New Terrain: The Politics of Women, Population and the Environment in the 1990s," presented to Fifth International Interdisciplinary Congress on Women, San Jose, Costa Rica, February 23, 1993, p. 7.

94. Donella Meadows, author's interview.

95. Walden Bello, "Population and the Environment: The Food First Perspective," *Food First Action Alert,* winter 1992–93, p. 2.

96. "Whose Common Future?" a special issue of *The Ecologist,* 22, no. 4 (July/August 1992), pp. 170–171. *Whose Common Future?* was reprinted in book form by Earthscan in London (1992) and New Society Publishers in Philadelphia (1993).

97. See Karl Polanyi, *The Great Transformation: The Political and Economic Origins of Our Time* (Boston: Beacon Press, 1944), p. 90.

98. Roger Cohen, "Europeans Fear Unemployment Will Not Fade with Recession," *New York Times,* June 13, 1993.

99. Seth Mydans, "A New Tide of Immigration Brings Hostility to the Surface, Poll Finds," *New York Times,* June 27, 1993.

100. Deborah Sontag, "Across the U.S., Immigrants Find the Land of Resentment," *New York Times*, December 11, 1992. Julie Barton, "Circling the Wagons," *San Francisco Bay Guardian*, March 10, 1993. See also *A Statement on Immigrants and the Environment* (National Network for Immigrant and Refugee Rights, 310 Eighth Street, Suite 307, Oakland CA 94607).

101. See Hannah Creighton, "Not Thinking Globally: The Sierra Club Immigration Policy Wars," in "Population and Immigration," the summer 1993 issue of *Race, Poverty and the Environment*.

102. See Mark Dowie, *Losing Ground: American Environmentalism at the Close of the Twentieth Century* (Cambridge: MIT Press, 1995), pp. 162–166.

103. Hans Magnus Enzensberger, "The Great Migration," *Granta* 42 (winter 1992), p. 31.

104. Noam Chomsky, *The Prosperous Few and the Restless Many* (Berkeley: Odonian Press, 1993), p. 66.

105. Paul Ehrlich, "Too Many Rich People: Weighing Relative Burdens on the Planet," UNEP Feature, 1994 UN Conference on Population and Development, posted on Econet "population" conference on August 23, 1994. And see Gretchen C. Daily and Paul Ehrlich, *Socioeconomic Equity, Sustainability, and Earth's Carrying Capacity* (Stanford: Center for Conservation Biology, Stanford University, 1995), or, more accessibly, Daily, Ehrlich, and Ehrlich, *The Stork and the Plow: The Equity Answer to the Human Dilemma* (New York: Putnam's, 1995). This new position, it should be said, is profoundly contradictory. Ehrlich et al. speak now for environmental equity, but he remains a spokesperson for Zero Population Growth, and both he and his wife sit on the board of the Federation for American Immigration Reform, which is foremost among the anti-immigration organizations working to seduce greens by pushing the classically Malthusian theory that the "immigration problem" is rooted in the fecundity of the poor.

106. P. J. O'Rourke, *All the Trouble in the World: The Lighter Side of Overpopulation, Famine, Ecological Disaster, Ethnic Hatred, Plague, and Poverty* (New York: Atlantic, 1994).

107. See, recently, Simon's book-length debate with Norman Myers, *Scarcity or Abundance: A Debate on the Environment* (New York: Norton, 1994).

108. Hartmann, "Old Maps and New Terrain," p. 6.

109. Christopher Flavin and John E. Young, "Shaping the Next Industrial Revolution," in Brown et al., *State of the World: 1993*. John Young, "The New Materialism: A Matter of Policy," *Worldwatch*, September/October 1994. Paul Hawken, *The Ecology of Commerce* (New York: HarperCollins, 1993), pp. 63–65.

110. Paul Ekins, "The Sustainable Consumer Society: A Contradiction in Terms?" *International Environmental Affairs* 3, no. 4, (fall 1991), p. 250.

111. Paul Harrison, *The Third Revolution: Environment, Population, and a Sustainable World* (London: I. B. Taurus/Penguin, 1992), p. 277–278.

112. Meadows et al., *Beyond the Limits*, pp. 78–86.

113. See, for example, John Holdren, "Population and the Energy Problem," *Popula-*

tion and Environment 12, pp. 231–255. And note that while the details of Holdren's analysis differ from the details of Ekins's, their overall thrusts are quite the same.

114. Ekins, "The Sustainable Consumer Society," p. 252.

115. Robey, et al., "The Fertility Decline," p. 65.

116. "The Battle of the Bulge," *The Economist,* September 3, 1994, p. 25. To see this argument and its unpleasant corollaries spelled out, see Virginia Abernethy, "Optimism and Overpopulation," *The Atlantic,* November 1994, pp. 84–91.

117. William K. Stevens, "Third World Gains in Birth Control: Development Isn't Only Answer," *New York Times,* January 2, 1994, p. 4.

118. Alan Cowell, "Is This Abortion? Vatican vrs. U.S.?" *New York Times,* August 11, 1994. Alan Cowell, "Vatican Fights Plan to Bolster Role of Women," *New York Times,* June 14, 1994.

119. Alan Cowell, "Conference on Population Has Hidden Issue: Money," *New York Times,* September 12, 1994. The budgets did not change at Cairo.

120. See *Taking Population Seriously,* by Frances Moore Lappe and Rachel Schurman (Oakland: Food First/The Institute for Food and Development Policy [398 Sixtieth Street, Oakland, CA 94618], 1988).

121. For voices from these countries, see *We Speak for Ourselves: Population and Development* (London: Panos Institute [9 White Lion Street, London N1 9DP], 1994).

122. For current thinking on these matters, see Laurie Ann Mazur, ed., *Beyond the Numbers: A Reader on Population, Consumption and the Environment* (Washington, D.C.: Island Press, 1994).

123. Vandana Shiva, *The Violence of the Green Revolution: Third World Agriculture, Ecology and Politics* (Penang: Third World Network [87 Cantonment Road, 10250 Penang, Malaysia], 1991), pp. 11–12. See also Praful Bidwai, "India's Green Revolution in Crisis," *Science as Culture,* no. 13 (1991) and John Roosa, "Feeding Violence," and Shiva's reply in *Science as Culture,* no. 19 (1993) (London: Free Associations).

124. Peter Rosset, executive director of Food First, author's interview, April 26, 1994. For background, see Miguel A. Altieri, *Agroecology: The Scientific Basis of Alternative Agriculture* (Boulder, Colo.: Westview, 1987).

125. See William K. Stevens, "Green Revolution Is Not Enough, Study Finds," *New York Times,* September 6, 1994. The study itself was coordinated by Robert Repetto at the World Resources Institute. See Repetto, "The 'Second India' Revisited: Population, Poverty, and Environmental Stress over Two Decades," World Resources Institute, September 1994.

126. George Reisman, speaking at the University of California at Berkeley, April 24, 1991. For much more, see Reisman's *The Toxicity of Environmentalism* (Laguna Hills: Jefferson School of Philosophy, Economics, and Psychology [P.O. Box 2934, Laguna Hills, CA 92654], 1990). Ayn Rand herself, incidentally, was an antienvironmental pioneer — her *Environmentalism: The Anti-industrial Revolution,* was first published in 1970.

127. Terry L. Anderson and Donald R. Leal, *Free Market Environmentalism* (Boulder,

Colo.: Westview, 1991), pp. 121, 132, 165, 163. For a critique, see Herman Daly, "Free-Market Environmentalism: Turning a Good Servant Into a Bad Master," *Critical Review* 6, no. 2–3, pp. 171–183.

128. Orwell, "James Burnham and the Managerial Revolution," p. 173.

129. Thomas Homer-Dixon, "On the Threshold: Environmental Changes as Causes of Acute Conflict," *International Studies* 16, no. 2 (fall 1991), pp. 100–104. See also Homer-Dixon's "Destruction and Death," *New York Times*, January 31, 1993, and "Environmental Scarcity and Intergroup conflict," in Michael T. Klare and Daniel C. Thomas, *World Security: Challenges for a New Century* (New York: St. Martin's, 1994).

130. Al Gore, *Earth in the Balance: Ecology and the Human Spirit* (New York: Houghton Mifflin, 1992), p. 313.

131. Richard W. Franke and Barbara H. Chasin, *Kerala: Radical Reform as Development in an Indian State* (Oakland: Institute for Food and Development Policy, 1989), p. 2. See also Franke and Chasin, "Development Without Growth: The Kerala Experiment," *Technology Review*, April, 1990.

132. Susanna Hecht and Alex Cockburn, *The Fate of the Forest: Developers, Destroyers and Defenders of the Amazon* (London: Verso, 1989), p. 207.

133. See "Getting the Future We Deserve," chap. 5 of Andrew Ross's *Strange Weather: Culture, Science and Technology in an Age of Limits* (New York: Verso, 1991).

134. Alvin and Heidi Toffler, *Creating a New Civilization: The Politics of the Third Wave* (Atlanta: Turner Publishing, 1995). See also David Corn's "CyberNewt," *The Nation*, February 6, 1995.

135. The charge that pollution is "altering the nature of the world's clouds," making them "denser and more reflective," and sending "more of the sun's heat back into space" surfaced about 1990. See Tim Tompson, "Where Have All the Clouds Gone?" *Earth Island Journal*, spring 1992.

136. This is a common view among deep green radicals. It first found its canonical form in Jeremy Rifkin's *Algeny: A New Word — A New World* (New York: Viking, 1984), a book Stephen Jay Gould described as "a cleverly constructed piece of anti-intellectual propaganda masquerading as scholarship" ("On the Origin of Specious Critics," *Discover*, January 1985, p. 34).

137. The classic antienvironmental treatment of cancer is Edith Efron's classic *The Apocalyptics: Cancer and the Big Lie* (New York: Simon and Schuster, 1984).

138. Mike Davis, *City of Quartz: Excavating the Future in Los Angeles* (New York: Vintage, 1992), p. 204.

139. Memorandum from C. H. Grennert, Union Carbide Corporation, Public Affairs Group, November 14, 1989.

140. Charles Pillar, *The Fail-Safe Society: Community Defiance and the End of American Technological Optimism* (New York: Basic, 1991). On this point, see pp. 12, 117, 167.

141. Letter to Senator Patrick J. Leahy, by a group of "prominent authorities on risk analysis," April 4, 1995, quoted in William K. Stevens, "Congress Asks, Is Nature Worth More Than a Shopping Mall?" *New York Times*, April 25, 1995. See

also *Rachel's Hazardous Waste News,* no. 379 (March 3, 1994) (Environmental Research Foundation, P.O. Box 5036, Annapolis, MD 20403).

142. Daniel Goleman, "Hidden Rules Often Distort Ideas of Risk," *New York Times,* February 1, 1994.

143. David Kirkpatrick, "Do Cellular Phones Cause Cancer?" *Fortune,* March 8, 1993, p. 89.

144. Keith Schneider, "E.P.A. Moves to Reduce Health Risks from Dioxin," *New York Times,* September 14, 1994. Peter Montague, "Dioxin and Health," *Rachel's Environment and Health Weekly* (formerly *Rachel's Hazardous Waste News*), October 12, 1995.

145. "The Naturalist Digest," KGO Television, San Francisco, April 19, 1992.

146. *UNCED Undermined: Why Free Trade Won't Save the Planet* (Greenpeace International, March 1992), p. 9.

147. Patricia Poore and Bill O'Donnell, "Ozone: Scam or Crisis?" *Garbage,* October 1993, pp. 25, 29.

148. See *The Failure of the Montreal Protocol* (Greenpeace International, June 1990), and *Climbing Out of the Ozone Hole* (Greenpeace International, October 1992).

149. *At the Crossroads: The Multilateral Fund of the Montreal Protocol* (Friends of the Earth International, November 1992).

150. Michael Oppenheimer, "UV-B Increase Observed Over Populated Regions," *Eco Geneva* (INC8), no. 5 (August 20, 1993).

151. For example, Joe Thornton, *The Product Is the Poison: The Case for a Chlorine Phase-out* (Greenpeace USA, 1991). For the traditional spin of the press coverage, see John Holusha, "Greens Pick an Enemy: Chlorine, the Everywhere Element," *New York Times,* December 20, 1992.

152. "The Controversy over Chlorine," in Peter Orris, et al., *New Solutions,* fall 1993, pp. 3–12. Ann Misch, "Chemical Reaction in the Animal Kingdom," *Worldwatch,* July/August 1992, pp. 34–35. *Chlorine, Human Health and the Environment: The Breast Cancer Warning* (Greenpeace USA, 1993). For a brief, excellent overview, see "Turning Point for the Chemical Industry," a set of annotated excerpts from Dr. Barry Commoner's July 30, 1994, speech to the Second Citizen's Conference on Dioxin, in *Rachel's Environment and Health Weekly,* September 1, 1994.

153. Mary S. Wolff et al., "Blood Levels of Organochlorine Residues and Risk of Breast Cancer," *Journal of the National Cancer Institute* 85 (April 21, 1993), pp. 648–652. See also *Rachel's Hazardous Waste News,* no. 334 (April 22, 1993).

154. Bette Hileman, "Environmental Estrogens Linked to Reproductive Abnormalities, Cancer," *Chemical and Engineering News,* January 31, 1994, p. 20.

155. Joe Thornton, *Breast Cancer and the Environment: The Chlorine Connection* (Greenpeace USA, 1992), p. 13.

156. The data are contradictory and obscured by greenwash. See Peter Montague, "Warning on Male Reproductive Health," *Rachel's Environment and Health Weekly,* no. 438 (April 20, 1995), and on the upbeat side, the April 1995 issue of *Fertility and Sterility* (cited in *New York Times Magazine,* May 14, 1995, p. 8).

157. Herman Daly, in Lerner, *Earth Summit,* p. 44.

158. Norman Myers, "The Heat Is On," *Greenpeace*, May/June 1989, p. 11.

159. Jeremy Leggett, *Climate Change and the Insurance Industry: Solidarity in the Risk Community?* (Greenpeace International), p. 3. Also, *Eco Geneva* (INC8), no. 3, (August 18, 1993).

160. Leggett, *Climate Change and the Insurance Industry*, p. 44.

161. Christopher Flavin, "Storm Warmings: Climate Change Hits the Insurance Industry," *Worldwatch*, November/December, 1994. Andrew Fisher, "Munich Re to Cut Exposure as Natural Disasters Increase," *Financial Times*, November 9, 1994.

162. Michael Quint, "Insurers Maneuver to Cut Their Risks from Large Storms," *New York Times*, December 28, 1993. Greg Steinmetz, "Forecasts for an Era of Violent Storms Swings Insurance Industry into Action," *Wall Street Journal*, October 1, 1993.

163. Michael Quint, "New Tools Spread Risks of Insurers," *New York Times*, May 15, 1995.

164. Patrick McCully, "The Age of the Super Cats," unpublished article, 1992. On emerging bailout plans, see, for example, Rebecca Smith, "Federal Disaster Fund Is Proposed," *San Jose Mercury News*, September 27, 1994.

165. *Emerging Impacts of Climate Change?* (Amsterdam: Greenpeace International, 1993), pp. 16–17.

166. Edward O. Wilson quoted in George J. Mitchell and Jack Waugh, *World on Fire: Saving an Endangered Earth* (New York: Scribner's, 1991).

167. Emily Yoffe, "The Silence of the Frogs," *New York Times Magazine*, December 13, 1992, p. 64. Carol Kaesuk Yoon, "Thinning Ozone Layer Implicated in Decline of Frogs and Toads," *New York Times*, March 1, 1994. For a review of the multicausal nature of the decline, see Peter Montague, "New Perspectives on Loss of Species," *Rachel's Environment and Health Weekly*, no. 441 (May 11, 1995).

168. Wolfgang Sachs, "One World Against Many Worlds," *New Internationalist*, no. 232 (June 1992), p. 23.

169. Gary Evans, environmental psychologist at the University of California at Irvine, cited in "L.A. Fights for Breath," *New York Times Magazine*, July 30, 1989.

170. Russell Jacoby, *Social Amnesia: A Critique of Conformist Psychology from Adler to Laing* (Boston: Beacon Press, 1975), p. 4.

171. McKibben, *The End of Nature*, p. 62.

172. Susan Zakin tells this tale well in *Coyotes and Town Dogs: Earth First! and the Environmental Movement* (New York: Viking, 1993), pp. 350–354.

173. Christopher Manes, *Green Rage: Radical Environmentalism and the Unmaking of Civilization* (Boston: Little, Brown, 1990), pp. 237, 235.

174. This quote, cited on p. 92 of *Eco-Warriors: Understanding the Radical Environmental Movement*, by Rik Scarce (Chicago: Nobel Press, 1990), was originally published in an Australian magazine called *Simple Living*. According to Scarce, it was included in the first chapter of Foreman's *Confessions of an Eco-Warrior* (New York: Harmony, 1991), originally entitled *Confessions of an Eco-Brute*. It does not seem to appear in the final edition.

175. Foreman quoted in Manes' *Green Rage*, p. 232.

176. Dave Foreman and Nancy Morton, "Good Luck Darlin', It's Been Great," *Earth First! Journal*, September 1990.

177. See *Defending the Earth: A Dialogue Between Murray Bookchin and Dave Foreman* (Boston: South End Press, 1991).

178. John Young, *Sustaining the Earth* (Cambridge: Harvard University Press, 1990), p. 168.

179. Kennedy, *Preparing for the Twenty-First Century*, p. 28. See also Steven A. Holmes, "Child Death Rate for AIDS Expected to Triple by 2010," *New York Times*, April 4, 1994.

180. Philip Raikes, *Modernizing Hunger: Famine, Food Policy and Farm Policy in the EEC and Africa* (London: Catholic Institute for International Relations, 1988), p. v.

181. William Ophuls, *Ecology and the Politics of Scarcity* (San Francisco: Freeman, 1977), pp. 151–152, 163. See also Langdon Winner's commentary on Ophuls on p. 130 of his *The Whale and the Reactor: A Search for Limits in an Age of High Technology* (Chicago: University of Chicago Press, 1986).

182. Martin W. Lewis, *Green Delusions: An Environmentalist Critique of Radical Environmentalism* (Durham, N.C.: Duke University Press, 1992), pp. 1–2.

183. Thomas Berry quoted in Murray Bookchin, "Will Ecology Become 'the Dismal Science?'" *The Progressive*, December 1991, p. 20. This essay and a few others have been reprinted in *Which Way for the Ecology Movement?* (Edinburgh and San Francisco: AK Press, 1994).

184. The "quote" here is taken from *Chief Seattle Speaks*, a poster published by the Silicon Valley Toxics Coalition (760 North First Street, Second Floor, San Jose, CA 95122). The SVTC is an excellent outfit, but Chief Seattle never spoke these words. There is, indeed, not even a standard version of the words *attributed* to Seattle in this his purported address to President Pierce, which is no doubt why the version Lewis quotes (*Green Delusions*, p. 242) is so different. See Timothy Egan, "Chief's 1854 Warning Tied to 1971 Ecological Script," *New York Times*, April 21, 1992.

185. Richard Preston, *The Hot Zone* (New York, Anchor, 1994), pp. 405, 406.

186. Cornucopians have always considered greens to be doomsters, but the liberal tilt of this subgenre is something new. Its roots trace, I think, to Anna Bramwell's *Ecology in the Twentieth Century* (New Haven: Yale University Press, 1989), an irritating but not unhelpful dark-side history of environmental romanticism. *Green Delusions* came in 1992, and was followed by Paul R. Gross and Norman Levitt's *Higher Superstition: The Academic Left and Its Quarrels with Science*, which demonstrated, in its chapter on environmentalism ("The Gates of Eden"), how easily we can be seduced into carrying water for the right, if only we allow irritation to get the better of us. Gregg Easterbrook's *A Moment on the Earth: The Coming Age of Environmental Optimism* (New York: Viking, 1995) may be the capstone of the whole line. See my "Green Romantics," *The Nation*, May 1, 1995, and also the May 12 issue, in which Easterbrook and I exchange letters.

187. Nicholas Wade, "May This Planet Be Safe from Heretics," *New York Times Book Review*, November 8, 1992.

188. For recent writing on this subject by a close colleague of Bookchin's, see Janet Biehl, "'Ecology' and the Modernization of Fascism in the German Ultra-Right," *Society and Nature* #5 2, no. 2 (1994) (Aigis Publications, 1449 West Littleton Boulevard, Suite 200, Littleton, CO 80120, with the Institute for Social Ecology, P.O. Box 89, Plainfield, VT 05667).

189. Garrett Hardin, "The Tragedy of the Commons," *Science* 162 (December 13, 1968), pp. 1243–1248. See also George Monbiot, "The Real Tragedy of the Commons," *Third World Resurgence,* no. 41 (87 Cantonment Road, 10250 Penang, Malaysia).

190. John Ely, "German Debate on the New Constitution," *Capitalism, Nature, Socialism* 3, no. 1 (March 1992), p. 9.

191. Martin Khor Kok Peng, *The Future of North-South Relations: Conflict or Cooperation?* (Penang: Third World Network [87 Cantonment Road, 10250 Penang, Malaysia], 1992), p. 49.

192. Lyuba Zarsky, author's interview, 1991.

193. Christopher Lasch, *The True and Only Heaven: Progress and Its Critics* (New York: Norton, 1991), pp. 39, 530.

THREE
After the Cold War

1. A. Frohmeyer, European Commission, DG VII, Brussels, quoted in Iza Kruszewska, *Open Borders, Broken Promises. Privatization and Foreign Investment: Protecting the Environment through Contractual Clauses,* A Greenpeace Proposal, Warsaw, June 3, 1993.

2. Quoted in David Lempert, "Soviet Sellout," *Mother Jones,* September/October 1991, p. 21.

3. *Agenda Ya Wananchi: Citizens' Action Plan for the 1990s,* was adopted at "Roots of the Future, a global NGO conference held in relation to the 1992 Earth Summit," in Paris, France, from December 17–20, 1991. It was published by the Environment Liaison Centre International (ELCI) in Nairobi, Kenya (P.O. Box 72461).

4. James Sterngold, "Clinton Discovers That Even Japan Can Go for a Populist," *New York Times,* July 11, 1993.

5. "Forced Labor Logging Russia's Forests," *Taiga News,* no. 6 (June 1993), (Taiga Rescue Network, Storgatan 42, S-666 00 Bengtsfors, Sweden). Report based on information by Alexei Grigoriev of the Russian Socio-Ecological Union. Also, Anjali Acharya, "Plundering the Boreal Forests," *Worldwatch,* May/June 1995.

6. Victor Serge, *Memoirs of a Revolutionary* (London: Writers and Readers, 1984), p. 47.

7. Christopher Slater, author's interview, fall 1992.

8. Steven Erlanger, "Kronstadt Journal; Russia's Great Navy Base: Picture It as Hong Kong," *New York Times,* August 11, 1994.

9. "Harper's Index," *Harper's,* September 1992.

10. Tim Jenkins, "An Introduction to the National Reports," *West Goes East: Na-*

tional Reports on Technology Transfer to Central and Eastern Europe, presented to the Friends of the Earth International West Goes East Conference January 16–18, 1992, Sofia, Bulgaria.

11. Quoted in Stephen Engelberg, "Czechoslovakia's Other Charismatic Vaclav," *New York Times*, May 3, 1992.

12. Alexi Danchev, "The Hard Way to a Sustainable Transition," *Surviving Together*, summer 1992, p. 28 (Institute for Soviet-American Relations, 1601 Connecticut Avenue NW, Suite 301, Washington, DC 20009).

13. "Experts Challenge Jeffery Sachs' Advice to Russian Economists," *Surviving Together*, summer 1992, p. 32.

14. Susan George, *The Debt Boomerang: How Third World Debt Harms Us All* (London: Pluto Press, 1992), p. 107.

15. Roger Manser, p. 9. This book has been published under two different titles. In Britain it is *Squandered Dividend: The Free Market and the Environment in Eastern Europe* (London: Earthscan, 1993). In the United States it is named *Failed Transitions: The Eastern European Economy and Environment Since the Fall of Communism* (New York: New Press, 1994).

16. See, for example, "Russian Capitalism: Under New Management," *The Economist*, October 8, 1994.

17. World Bank, *World Development Report 1992* (Oxford: Oxford University Press, 1992), Table 30. And for a vivid glimpse at the consequences of such extreme polarization, see Diana Jean Schemo, "A Common Bond: Fear of Each Other," *New York Times*, December 24, 1995.

18. See *Ecocide in the USSR* by Murray Feshbach and Alfred Friendly, Jr. (New York: Basic Books, 1992), p. 9, Michael Specter; "Climb in Russia's Death Rate Sets Off Population Implosion," *New York Times*, March 6, 1994; Nicholas Eberstadt, "Marx and Mortality: A Mystery," *New York Times*, April 6, 1994.

19. David Hunter, author's interview, March 22, 1993.

20. On "the second wave of dissidents," see John Feffer's *Shock Waves: Eastern Europe After the Revolutions* (Boston: South End Press, 1992), pp. 160–173.

21. See, for example, Tina Rosenberg, "Meet the New Boss, Same as the Old Boss," *Harper's*, May 1993, and Daniel Singer, "Turncoats and Scapegoats," *The Nation*, August 3/10, 1993.

22. Laurence Weschler, "A Reporter at Large (Poland)," *New Yorker*, May 11, 1992, pp. 41, 59.

23. Andrew Soloman, "Young Russia's Defiant Decadence," *New York Times Magazine*, August 18, 1993, pp. 21, 51.

24. Iza Kruszewska, author's interview, May, 1993.

25. Andre Laletin, author's interview, fall 1992.

26. Tomasz Terlecki, author's interview, September 1992.

27. Zygmunt Fura, author's interview, May 11, 1993.

28. Walter Laqueur, *Black Hundred: The Rise of the Extreme Right in Russia* (New York, HarperCollins, 1993).

29. Michael Renner, "Budgeting for Disarmament," in Lester R. Brown, ed., *State of the World: 1995* (New York: Norton, 1995), p. 164.

30. Manser, *Failed Transitions*, pp. 147–148. Later, as the backlash hit, the press went into damage-control mode. The title of a *New York Times* editorial from September 23, 1993 — "Poland: The Failures of Success" — captured the mood perfectly. Also notable was Anthony Robinson, "'Feel Bad' Factor Threatens Poland's Reformers," *Financial Times*, September 16, 1993.

31. Before the 1993 Polish and Russian elections, there was little but good news about shock therapy. See "Poland's Economic Reforms: If It Works, You've Fixed It," *The Economist*, January 23, 1993, p. 21, and Stephen Engelberg, "21 Months of 'Shock Therapy' Resuscitates Polish Economy," *New York Times*, December 17, 1992. Also notable were more balanced but nevertheless carefully upbeat articles like Steven Erlanger's "Russian Economic Turmoil Persists, But Not Chaos," *New York Times*, November 29, 1992.

32. Peter Passell, "Dr. Jeffrey Sachs, Shock Therapist," *New York Times Magazine*, June 27, 1993, p. 21.

33. Jane Perlez, "Ex-Communists Get Crucial New Role in Polish Election," *New York Times*, September 20, 1993.

34. Maria Guminska, author's interview, May 10, 1993.

35. Darek Sved, author's interview, May 10, 1993.

36. Daniel Singer, "Poland — The Taste of Ashes," *The Nation*, December 7, 1992, p. 696.

37. Dr. Adam Gula, author's interview, May 10, 1993.

38. Manser, *Failed Transitions*, p. 95.

39. "Household Waste Stirs Packaging Debate," *East/West Environment*, April 1993 (158 Buckingham Palace Road, London SW1W 9TR).

40. Marie Haisova, author's interview, May 18, 1993.

41. Manser, *Failed Transitions*, pp. 72–75.

42. Marlise Simons, "Capitalist or Communist, the Air Is Still Bad," *New York Times*, November 3, 1994.

43. Sonni Efron, "Ecological Russian Roulette," *Los Angeles Times*, November 22, 1994.

44. These three stories appeared in the *Boston Globe*, December 18, 1989, the *Christian Science Monitor*, April 18, 1990, and the *New York Times Magazine*, April 29, 1990, respectively.

45. Mark Hertsgaard, "From Here to Chelyabinsk," *Mother Jones*, January/February 1992, p. 71.

46. See Anne H. Ehrlich and John Birks, *Hidden Dangers: Environmental Consequences of Preparing for War* (San Francisco: Sierra Club, 1991).

47. Feshback and Friendly, *Ecocide in the USSR*, pp. 73–75.

48. These quotes are cited in "Cold War Environmentalism: Reporting on Eastern European Pollution," by Miranda Spencer, in the January/February 1991 issue of *Extra!* They are from the *Boston Globe*, December 17, 1990, the *Los Angeles Times*, January 22, 1990, and the *Atlanta Constitution*, February 2, 1990, respectively.

49. Manser's analysis of the communist "pollution economy" is particularly good. See *Failed Transitions*, pp. 27–38.

50. Ibid., p. 31.

51. David Gergen, writing in *U.S. News and World Report*, April 30, 1990. Cited in Spencer, "Cold War Environmentalism." For an excellent look at what the "leaders of Pittsburgh" and their brethren actually did know, and how they tried to avoid that knowledge, see Bill Sells, "What Asbestos Taught Me About Managing Risk," *Harvard Business Review*, March–April 1994, pp. 76–90.

52. See, most significantly, Daniel Ellsberg, *The Pentagon Papers* (New York: Bantam, 1971).

53. Noam Chomsky, *Towards a New Cold War* (New York: Pantheon, 1979). See also "Cold War: Fact and Fancy," chap. 1 of Noam Chomsky's *Deterring Democracy* (London and New York: Verso, 1991).

54. E. P. Thompson, *Exterminism and Cold War* (London: Verso, 1982), and E. P. Thompson et al., *Protest and Survive* (New York: Monthly Review Press, 1981).

55. Andrew Cockburn, *The Threat: Inside the Soviet Military Machine* (New York: Random House, 1983).

56. The General Accounting Office says as much. See Tim Weiner, "Military Is Accused of Lying on Arms for Decade," *New York Times*, June 28, 1993.

57. Quoted in "The Environmental Movement in Central and Eastern Europe," by Duncan Fisher, in the July 1991 issue of *Moving Pictures Bulletin*, p. 16.

58. Manser, *Failed Transitions*, p. 71.

59. Kjell Fornander, "Taiwan: The Grimy Side of the Boom," *Tomorrow* 1, no. 2 (1991), p. 67.

60. See "Sustainable Development in the 1990s," by Robin Broad, John Cavanagh, and Walden Bello, in *Paradigms Lost: The Post–Cold War Era*, edited by Chester Hartman and Pedro Vilanova (London: Pluto Press, 1992), p. 91. See also Walden Bello and Stephanie Rosenfeld, "The Making of an Environmental Nightmare," chap. 12 of their *Dragons in Distress: Asia's Miracle Economies in Crisis* (Oakland, Calif.: Institute for Food and Development Policy, 1990).

61. Fornander, "Taiwan," p. 72.

62. Nicholas D. Kristof, "China Sees 'Market-Leninism' as Way to Future," *New York Times*, September 6, 1993. Patrick E. Tyler, "The Dynamic New China Still Races Against Time," *New York Times*, January 2, 1994.

63. Patrick E. Tyler, "Nature and Economic Boom Devouring China's Farmland," *New York Times*, March 27, 1994. See also Lester R. Brown, *Who Will Feed China?* (New York: Norton, 1995).

64. Patrick E. Tyler, "China Planning People's Car to Put Masses Behind Wheel," *New York Times*, September 22, 1994.

65. Patrick E. Tyler, "A Tide of Pollution Threatens China's Prosperity," *New York Times*, September 25, 1994.

66. Todd Lappin, "Can Green Mix With Red?," *The Nation*, February 14, 1994, pp. 193–195.

67. The Sofia Statement was the result of a January 1992 conference organized by Friends of the Earth International. The conference was entitled West Goes East: Opportunity or Pollution Transfer. (See n. 10, above.)

68. *East/West Environment*, April 1993, p. 9.

69. Gary Cook, author's interview, spring 1993.

70. Michelle Kellman, "Turkmenistan's Wildlife Under the Gun," *Earth Island Journal*, spring 1994, p. 26.

71. Richard Liroff, author's interview, November 1992.

72. R. Dennis Hayes, "Eastern Europe's Nuclear Window," *The Nation*, August 26/September 2, 1991, p. 222.

73. See, in particular, two reports by Friends of the Earth (Washington, D.C.): Tim Jenkins and Simon Roberts, *Dangerous Liaisons: Western Involvement in the Nuclear Power Industry of Central and Eastern Europe* (late 1992), and Jim Barnes, *Russian Roulette: Nuclear Power Reactors in Eastern Europe and the Former Soviet Union* (June 1993).

74. R. Dennis Hayes, "Eastern Europe's Nuclear Window."

75. Zoltan Illes quoted in Feffer, *Shock Waves*, p. 150.

76. Jenkins and Roberts, *Dangerous Liaisons*, p. 23. Letter to the editor from James N. Barnes, director of the International Department of Friends of the Earth U.S., *New York Times*, May 29, 1994.

77. R. Dennis Hayes, "Eastern Europe's Nuclear Window," p. 224.

78. Stewart Boyle and Antony Froggatt, *Shutdown!: Realizing the Low-Cost Option to Phase Out Nuclear Power in Eastern Europe* (Greenpeace International, June 1993).

79. *Nuclear Times*, September 1991, quoted in Jenkins and Roberts, *Dangerous Liaisons*, p. 6.

80. Douglas Frantz, "U.S. Backing Work on Czech Reactors by Westinghouse," *New York Times*, May 22, 1994.

81. Jenkins and Roberts, *Dangerous Liaisons*, p. 16. David Batker, author's interview, August 9, 1993. Maggie Ledford Lawson, "Safety Czech: Trying to Contain Soviet Reactors," *Multinational Monitor*, September 1995.

82. Jenkins and Roberts, *Dangerous Liaisons*, p. 24.

83. *Nuclear Power and Safety in Central and Eastern Europe and the Former Soviet Union*, a confidential March 1993 report by the World Bank and the International Energy Agency.

84. Marlise Simons, "West Is Warned of the High Cost of Fixing Risky Soviet A-Plants," *New York Times*, June 22, 1993.

85. Manser, *Failed Transitions*, pp. 81, 8.

86. Barnes, *Russian Roulette*, p. 7. Marlise Simons, "Major Powers Back a Fund for Soviet-Design Reactors," *New York Times*, January 29, 1993. Keith Schneider, "Energy Designee Plans Russian Aid," *New York Times*, January 19, 1993.

87. Douglas Frantz, "Global Plan on Nuclear Liability," *New York Times*, May 31, 1994.

88. Lydia Popova, "Nuclear Implementation?," *Eco Geneva*, no. 5 (February 16, 1994). (*Eco Geneva* was a newsletter produced by nongovernmental environmental groups attending the ninth Intergovernmental Negotiating Committee of the Climate Change Convention [INC9], February 1994.)

89. Bruce Rich, author's interview, August 23, 1993. The EBRD is also internally

divided on the wisdom of nuclear renovation in the East. See "The EBRD's Nuclear Headache," *The Economist*, February 18, 1995.

90. Peter Hayes, author's interview, August 26, 1993.

91. The *Environmental Action Programme for Central and Eastern Europe* was the focus of the Environment for Europe Ministerial Conference, which took place in Lucerne, Switzerland, April 28–30, 1993.

92. Richard Ackermann, author's interview, July 22, 1993.

93. Rich, author's interview.

94. Barnes, *Russian Roulette*, p. 2.

95. For more on this "pressure to lend," see Bruce Rich, *Mortgaging the Earth: The World Bank, Environmental Impoverishment, and the Crisis of Development* (Boston: Beacon Press, 1994), pp. 72–74. This particular quote is from Rich's article in the September 1993 ("Fifty Years Is Enough") issue of *Bankcheck Quarterly* (International Rivers Network, 1847 Berkeley Way, Berkeley CA 94703).

96. Bheki Maboyi, Gurmit Singh, Karan Capoor, "Consistency Outside the Financial Mechanism," *Eco Geneva*, no. 2 (August 24, 1994).

97. *Power Failure: A Review of the World Bank's Implementation of Its New Energy Policy*, March 1994, published by the Environmental Defense Fund and the Natural Resources Defense Council.

98. " 'Good' Western Nuclear Technology Is No Answer to 'Bad' Soviet Nuclear Plants," a statement by Socio-Ecological Union coordinator Sviatoslav Zabelin and Valery Neminchinsky, an energy expert on the staff of the State Counselor for Ecology and Health. Printed in the summer 1992 issue of *Surviving Together*. For more on energy-efficiency alternatives in the East, see Boyle and Froggatt, *Shutdown!*, pp. 7–11, and Manser, *Failed Transitions*, pp. 139–140.

99. Nicholas Lenssen, "The Right Choice in Eastern Europe," *Worldwatch*, July/August 1992, p. 2.

100. Boyle and Froggatt, *Shutdown!*, p. 2. Also, Jay M. Gould, "Chernobyl Aftermath," *The Nation*, January 3/10, 1993, p. 2.

101. Dr. Alexander Bolsunovsky, "Broken Swords: Military Pollution in Krasnoyarsk," *CIS Environmental Watch*, no. 4 (summer 1993).

102. Stephen F. Cohen, "American Policy and Russia's Future," *The Nation*, April 12, 1993, p. 480. For a fine overview of privatization in Central and Eastern Europe, see "A Capitalist Jumble Sale," in Manser, *Failed Transitions*, pp. 39–69.

103. Peter E. Roderick, *An Appraisal of the European Energy Charter in the Context of Environmental Law and Policy* (Greenpeace International, December 16, 1991).

104. Dr. Jeremy Leggett, *Fossil Fuel Bonanza, Ecological Disaster: The Environmental Costs of the Proposed European Energy Charter* (Atmosphere and Energy Campaign, Greenpeace International, December 1991), p. 1.

105. Linda Himelstein, "Big Oil Plays Big Role Shaping Russia's Energy Laws," excerpted in the spring 1992 issue of ISAR's *Surviving Together*, pp. 23–24.

106. For a fine, easily available overview, see Divish Petrof, "Siberian Forests Under Threat," *The Ecologist* 22, no. 6 (November/December 1992), pp. 267–270.

107. Information about the Weyerhauser and Hyundai deals is via the Siberian Forests Protection Project at the Pacific Environment and Resources Center,

1055 Fort Chronkhite, Sausalito, CA 94965. See also "The Rape of Siberia," *Time*, September 4, 1995.

108. John Vidal, "Poison and Plunder in Russia," *Third World Resurgence*, no. 36, p. 2 (87 Cantonment Road, 10250 Penang, Malaysia).

109. The term is from Charles C. Mann and Mark L. Plummer, "The Butterfly Problem," *The Atlantic*, January 1992.

110. North-West Information Agency, "Green Leader Threatened," *Earth Island Journal*, fall 1991, p. 36.

111. "One Of The Voices," *Eco Madrid*, no. 3 (September 29, 1994). (*Eco Madrid, Alternative Voices of the Planet*, was a newsletter produced by groups attending the Fiftieth Annual Meeting of the World Bank and International Monetary Fund, September–October 1994).

112. Alexei Grigoriev, "Russia's New Forestry Act: Leaving the Door Wide Open for Ruthless Exploitation," *Taiga News*, no. 5 (March 1993), p. 2.

113. Celestine Bohlen, "Russia's New Rich Go on a Giant Buying Spree," *New York Times*, July 31, 1993, p. 1.

114. Manser, *Failed Transitions*, p. 37.

115. R. Dennis Hayes, "Liquidating Libkovice," *Los Angeles Times Magazine*, August 2, 1992, p. 23.

116. Andreas Bernsdorff and Katherine Totten, *Romania: The Toxic Assault, Waste Imports 1986–92* (Hamburg: Greenpeace Germany, August 1992).

117. Andreas Bernsdorff, author's interview, May 6, 1993.

118. Andreas Bernsdorff and Jim Puckett, *Poland: The Waste Invasion, A Greenpeace Dossier* (Amsterdam: Greenpeace International, 1990).

119. Jim Puckett, "Dumping on Our World Neighbors: The International Trade in Hazardous Wastes, and the Case for an Immediate Ban on All Hazardous Waste Exports from Industrialized to Less-Industrialized Countries," in Helga Ole Bergesen et al., eds., *Green Globe Yearbook, 1992* (Fridtjof Nansen Institute, Norway, 1992), p. 93.

120. Ann Leonard, "South Asia: The New Target of International Waste Traders," *Multinational Monitor*, December 1993, pp. 21–24. See also *The Waste Invasion of Asia* (Greenpeace International, 1994).

121. Puckett, "Dumping on Our World Neighbors," pp. 100–102.

122. Manser, *Failed Transitions*, p. 102.

123. Dr. Valentine Katasonov, "The Price of Capitalism: Dumping on the Soviet Union," *Multinational Monitor*, December 1990, p. 30.

124. Robert Bullard, *Dumping in Dixie: Race, Class, and Environmental Quality* (Boulder, Colo.: Westview, 1990).

125. "U.S. Seeks to Undo Basel Waste Ban," *The Ecologist*, January/February 1995.

126. Kruszewska, *Open Borders, Broken Promises*, p. 3.

127. Puckett, "Dumping on Our World Neighbors," p. 94. See also Joel S. Hirschhorn and Kristen U. Oldenburg, *Prosperity Without Pollution: The Prevention Strategy for Industry and Consumers* (New York: Van Nostrand Reinhold, 1991).

128. Terlecki, author's interview.

129. Walter Hook, "Eastern Europe: Paving the Way to Environmental Disaster?"

Sustainable Transport, June 1994. Walter Hook, "The Road Lobby Comes to Hungary," *Sustainable Transport,* winter 1995. (Institute of Transportation and Development Policy, 611 Broadway, Room 616, New York, NY 10012.)

130. Tadeusz Kapta, "Traffic Situation in Central and Eastern Europe Before and After the Political Changes," p. 9, in *Traffic, Transport and Mobility: Ninth East-West Consultation,* December 10–12, 1992, Krakow, Poland (MilieuKontakt Oost-Europa, P.O. Box 18185, 1001 ZB Amsterdam).

131. "Potential New Market of 420M," *Financial Times,* November 9, 1991 (Motor Industry Supplement).

132. Manser, *Failed Transitions,* pp. 96–98, 156.

133. *World Bank Report on Infrastructure on Wrong Track, Campaign Charges,* June 15, 1994 (Development Group for Alternative Policies [Development GAP], 927 Fifteenth Street NW, Fourth Floor, Washington, DC 20005).

134. *Traffic, Transport and Mobility,* p. 13.

135. Bulgarian information from "The World Bank Is Preying on East European Railways," *Eco Madrid,* no. 4 (September 30, 1994). Hungarian information from "Save Our Railway Campaign," E-mail from James Rojas of the Hungarian Traffic Club (relief@osiris.elte.hu), March 1, 1995.

136. *Traffic, Transport and Mobility,* p. 11.

137. Sved, author's interview.

138. Stanislaw Juchnowicz, author's interview, May 12, 1993.

139. *Environmental Action Programme for Central and Eastern Europe,* p. II-5.

140. Grzegorz Peszko, "The *Environmental Action Programme for Central and Eastern Europe:* The Use of Economics to Develop Environmental Policy," p. 3. This was a discussion paper for the Environment for Europe Ministerial Conference in Lucerne. Peszko is with the Green Federation and the Krakow Academy of Economics, Poland.

141. Ibid., p. 11.

142. Bob Hohler, "Cigarette Makers Flock to Eastern Europe," *Boston Globe,* May 26, 1992. See also Richard W. Stevenson, "Tapping a Rich Smoking Frontier," *New York Times,* November 12, 1993.

143. Michael Specter, "Moscow Journal: Freedom Brings Automotive Chaos on the Streets," *New York Times,* March 18, 1995.

144. Bassin quoted in Simons, "Communist or Capitalist, the Air Is Still Bad."

145. Kruszewska, author's interview, April 1993.

146. Kruszewska, *Open Borders, Broken Promises,* p. 6.

147. Roger Manser, author's interview, April 27, 1993.

148. Manser, *Failed Transitions,* pp. 45–46, 93.

149. Craig R. Whitney, "East Europe Still Waits for the Capitalist Push," *New York Times,* May 30, 1993. Craig R. Whitney, "Investment Needs for a New Russia Are Mostly Unmet," *New York Times,* December 14, 1992.

150. Simons, "Communist or Capitalist, the Air Is Still Bad."

151. Richard W. Stevenson, "East Europe's Low Wages Luring Manufacturers from West Europe," *New York Times,* May 11, 1993. Richard W. Stevenson, "Foreign

Capitalists Brush Aside Risks to Invest in Russia," *New York Times*, October 11, 1994.

152. The term is from Robert Reich, the U.S. labor secretary, who argues that "ominous forces" are dividing the country (and the world) into an "overclass" safe in elite suburbs, an "underclass quarantined in surroundings that are unspeakably bleak, and often violent," and an "anxious class" trapped "in the frenzy of effort it takes to preserve their standing." See Catherine S. Manegold, "Reich Urges Executives to Aid Labor," *New York Times*, September 25, 1994.

153. Marc Fisher, "Why Are German Workers Striking? To Preserve Their Soft Life," WP service, *International Herald Tribune*, May 4, 1992.

154. Jane Perlez, "Czechs Thrive Under Capitalism, Unlike Some of Their Neighbors," *New York Times*, January 31, 1994. "Trade Union Protest in Prague," Radio Free Europe/Radio Liberty daily report, March 23, 1994.

155. Jacques Attali, "A Poor and Ghastly Europe is Dangerously Close," *Volkskrant*, September 9, 1992. Quoted in John Hontelez and Bram van der Lek, *New Items for Central and Eastern Europe, Volume 2. The European Community and Environment: With or Without Maastricht* (Brussels: Friends of the Earth European Coordination [rue Blanche 29, 1050 Brussels, Belgium], December 1992).

156. Hontelez and van der Lek, *New Items for Central and Eastern Europe*, p. 62.

157. For background, see Richard W. Stevenson, "East Europe Says Barriers to Trade Hurt Its Economies," *New York Times*, January 25, 1993, and also Manser, *Failed Transitions*, pp. 154–155.

158. Michael Specter, "Siberia Awaits the Onslaught," *New York Times*, September 4, 1994.

159. Manser, *Failed Transitions*, pp. 98–100. See also Peter Gowan, "Old Medicine, New Bottles: Western Policy Toward East Central Europe," *World Policy Journal*, winter 1991–92.

160. "Walesa Looks for Way to Keep the Reform Going," *The Guardian*, February 7, 1992. Quoted in Kruszewska, *Open Borders, Broken Promises*, p. 12.

161. Christian Koth, "East German States," a regional report in *West Goes East* (see n. 10, above), p. 86.

162. Roger Cohen, "An Empty Feeling is Infecting Eastern Europe," *New York Times*, March 21, 1993.

163. *Environmental Business Opportunities in Poland*, Prospectus Publications, Canada, cited in Manser, *Failed Transitions*, p. 92.

164. "Hard Times for Russian Greens," *Ecosocialist Review*, spring 1993, p. 15 (608 North Milwaukee, #403, Chicago, IL 60647).

165. Duncan Fisher, *Paradise Deferred: Environmental Policymaking in Central and Eastern Europe* (London: Royal Institute of International Affairs, 1992), pp. 14–15.

166. See Robert Gottlieb, *Forcing the Spring: The Transformation of the American Environmental Movement* (Washington: Island Press, 1993), pp. 290–292, for a short history of Environmentalists for Full Employment.

167. For a contemporary exposition of the argument, see Tom Lent, *Energy for Employment* (Greenpeace USA, July 1992).

168. Andrej Kassenberg, author's interview, July 1992.

169. Margaret Bowman and David Hunter, "Environmental Reforms in Post-Communist Central Europe: From High Hopes to Hard Realities," *Michigan Journal of International Law*, summer 1992, p. 980.

170. *West Goes East* (see n. 10, above), p. 37.

171. Quoted in Weschler, "A Reporter at Large (Poland)," p. 66.

172. This list owes much to Susan George and Fabrizio Sabelli, *Faith and Credit: The World Bank's Secular Empire* (Boulder, Colo.: Westview, 1994), pp. 18–19. See also Ross Hammond and Lisa A. McGowan, *The Other Side of the Story: The Real Impact of World Bank and IMF Structural Adjustment Programs* Washington, D.C.: Development GAP, 1993. For a view of SAPs as seen by activists in the South, see "Medicine that Kills: World Bank-IMF Policies in Third World," a special issue of *Third World Resurgence*, no. 17.

173. Cited in Walden Bello with Shea Cunningham and Bill Rau, *Dark Victory: The U.S., Structural Adjustment, and Global Poverty* (Oakland: Food First/The Institute for Food and Development Policy [398 Sixtieth Street, Oakland, CA 94618], with London's Pluto Press and the Transnational Institute, 1994), p. 36. *Dark Victory* is an excellent overview and critique of structural adjustment and related matters.

174. Walden Bello, author's interview, April 12, 1994.

175. Giovanni Andrea Cornia, Richard Jolly, and Frances Stewart "Protecting the Vulnerable and Promoting Growth," *Adjustment with a Human Face*, vol. 1 (Oxford: Clarendon Press, 1987).

176. Theodore Panayotou and Chalongphob Sussangkarn, *The Debt Crisis, Structural Adjustment and the Environment: The Case of Thailand* (Bangkok: Thailand Development Research Institute, October 1991). Cited in Lyuba Zarsky, *Lessons of Liberalization in Asia: From Structural Adjustment to Sustainable Development* (Berkeley: Nautilus Institute for Security and Sustainable Development [746 Ensenada, Berkeley, CA 94707], April 1993), p. 30.

177. David Reed, ed., *Structural Adjustment and the Environment* (Boulder, Colo.: Westview, 1992).

178. Maria Concepcion Cruz, Carrie A. Meyer, Robert Repetto, *The Environmental Effects of Stabilization and Structural Adjustment Programs: The Philippines Case* (Washington, D.C.: World Resources Institute, September 1992).

179. *Ghana: The Illusion of Success*, a Development GAP paper for the 1992 International NGO Forum on World Bank and IMF Adjustment Lending, Washington, D.C.

180. Ross Hammond, author's interview, August 15, 1993.

181. The term is from "Reorganizing the Bank: An Opportunity for Renewal, Report to the President from the Steering Committee on Reorganization of the World Bank," April 1987. Quoted in George and Fabrizio, *Faith and Credit*, p. 126.

182. Structural adjustment lending is now between 17 and 22 percent of the Bank's new loan disbursements, varying with whom you talk to. Different sources, even within the Bank, cite different figures, and making sense of the situation is not easy. There is, for one thing, an irreducible bit of semantics involved. As

Ross Hammond of Development GAP noted, "You can argue that *all* World Bank loans that are oriented toward neoliberal reconstruction, including sector loans, are actually SAP-related." Author's interview, September 14, 1994.

183. Smitu Kothari, author's interview, November 24, 1992.

184. Rich, *Mortgaging the Earth,* especially chap. 3, "Brave New World at Bretton Woods."

185. "Neo-Bolsheviks of the I.M.F.," Georgy A. Arbatov of Yeltsin's Consulative Council, *New York Times* op-ed page, April 7, 1992. See also "IMF's 'Lunatic Scheme' for Russia," an interview with Tatian Koryagina, deputy of the Russian Federation, in the June 10, 1992, issue of *The* (American) *Guardian.*

186. Stephen Greenhouse, "US Asks IMF to Increase Aid to Russia and to Ease Conditions," *New York Times,* March 27, 1993.

187. Steven Erlanger, "New Yeltsin Steps on Economy Hint Easing of Reforms," *New York Times,* December 18, 1993. Finally, a few days later, came Elaine Sciolino, "U.S. Is Abandoning 'Shock Therapy' for the Russians," *New York Times,* December 21, 1993.

188. Rich, *Mortgaging the Earth,* pp. 301–315, gives an excellent overview of that debate.

189. See *Environmental Reforms of the Multilateral Development Banks,* a report to the U.S. Charles Stewart Mott Foundation by David A. Worth, April 6, 1992, p. 16.

190. Lauri Udall, speaking at the International Rivers Network offices, April 1993.

191. Alex Hittle, *New Items for Central and Eastern Europe, Volume 1: The World Bank* (Brussels: Friends of the Earth European Coordination, May/June 1992), p. 2.

192. Quoted in "Promoting Sustainable Development and Democracy in Central and Eastern Europe: The Role of the European Bank for Reconstruction and Development," by Chris A. Wold and Durwood Zaelke in the spring 1992 issue of *American University Journal of International Law and Policy,* p. 560. See also Donald M. Goldberg and David B. Hunter, "EBRD's Environmental Promise: A Bounced Check?" *CIEL Brief,* no. 3 (December 1994) (Center for International Environmental Law, 1621 Connecticut Avenue NW, Washington, DC 20009).

193. Hunter, author's interview.

194. John Hontelez, author's interview, May 4, 1993.

195. Bob Wilkenson, author's interview, March 1993.

196. Richard Ackerman, author's interview, August 22, 1993.

197. Margaret Bowman, author's interview, June 1993.

198. Simons, "Communist or Capitalist, the Air Is Still Bad."

199. "Flight of Fancy," *The Economist,* April 8, 1995.

200. Stephen Cohen, author's interview, October 1992.

201. Richard Nixon, "Clinton's Greatest Challenge," *New York Times,* March 5, 1993.

202. See "Rio Summit Indicates Former East Bloc Hasn't Defined Role in New World Order," *Wall Street Journal,* June 11, 1992, and "Negotiators in Rio Agree to Increase Aid to Third World," *New York Times,* June 14, 1992.

203. David Runnalls, "Summit Recap: No Cash, More G-77," *Earth Summit Times,* June 14, 1992.

204. Kassenberg, author's interview.

205. Bowman, author's interview.

206. "Africa, Out in the Cold," *New York Times,* January 4, 1994.

207. Martin Khor, "Months After Rio Pledges, Aid Fatigue Hits the North," Third World Network Briefing Paper, June 20, 1993.

208. John Tanner, "IMF Policies a Fiasco Says Oxfam," *Third World Resurgence,* no. 33, p. 30.

209. Steven Greenhouse, "Republicans Plan to Guide Foreign Policy by Purse Strings," *New York Times,* November 13, 1994.

210. World Bank Annual Report, 1993, pp. 80–82.

211. Statement of Susan B. Levine, Deputy Assistant Secretary of the Treasury, International Development, Debt and Environment, Before the Committee on Banking, Finance, Trade and Monetary Policy, U.S. House of Representatives, November 18, 1993.

212. "Foreign-Aid Chief Asserts Sen. Helms Is Out of Touch," *San Francisco Chronicle,* November 22, 1994. See also *New York Times* editorial "Linking Exports to Aid" (October 19, 1994), which notes that such links do not serve the interests of "development."

213. *Yen Aid Watch: News and NGO Opinions About Japan and Development Finance* (Tokyo: Friends of the Earth Japan [4-8-15 Nakameguro, Meguro-ku, Tokyo 153, Japan], August 1994), p. 4.

214. R. A. Forrest, "Japanese Aid and the Environment," *The Ecologist,* January/February 1991, p. 26. Quoted in "Whose Common Future?" *The Ecologist,* July/August 1992, p. 193. "Whose Common Future?" was reprinted in book form by Earthscan in London (1992) and New Society Publishers in Philadelphia (1993).

215. *Aid as Obstacle: Twenty Questions About Our Foreign Aid and the Hungry* (Oakland: Institute for Food and Development Policy, 1980 and forthcoming revision); Patricia Adams, *Odious Debts: Loose Lending, Corruption, and the Third World's Environmental Legacy* (London: Earthscan, 1991); Cheryl Payer, *Lent and Lost: Foreign Credit and Third World Development* (London: Zed, 1991); Graham Hancock, *Lords of Poverty: The Power, Prestige, and Corruption of the International Aid Business* (New York: Atlantic Monthly Press, 1989).

216. Kristin Dawkins, *Balancing: Policies for Just and Sustainable Trade* (Minneapolis: Institute for Agriculture and Trade Policy [1313 Fifth Street SE, #303, Minneapolis, MN 55414], January 1994).

217. The term was popularized by Chakravarthi Raghavan, *Recolonization: GATT, The Uruguay Round, and the Third World* (London: Zed, 1990).

218. An admirable exception is Celestine Bohlen, "One Year Later, Russians Doubt West's Aid Total," *New York Times,* April 4, 1993.

219. "A Classic Case of Economic Tragedy," *Sydney Morning Herald,* October 21, 1991.

220. Ackermann, author's interview, July 22, 1993.

221. Francis Fukuyama, "The End of History," *National Interest,* summer 1989, p. 3.

222. Frieder Otto Wolf, author's interview, May 7, 1993.

223. George Sessions, author's interview, February 1991.

224. George Reisman, speaking at the University of California at Berkeley, April 24, 1991.

225. George F. Kennan, "The G.O.P. Won the Cold War? Ridiculous," *New York Times,* op-ed page, October 28, 1992. Also, Kennan, "The Failure of Our Success," *New York Times,* March 14, 1994.

FOUR
New World Orders?

1. "A fruit farmer," in both the UK and Brazil, National Farmers Union Annual General Meeting, London, 1993. David Richardson, "UK Agriculture Faces Up to the Necessity of Change," *Financial Times,* February 16, 1993; quoted in Tim Lang and Colin Hines, *The New Protectionism: Protecting the Future Against Free Trade,* (London: Earthscan, 1993), p. 80.

2. FDR, 1937 message to Congress on the Fair Labor Standards Act, quoted in "Making Trade Fair" by George E. Brown, Jr., J. William Goold, and John Cavanagh, in *World Policy Journal,* spring 1992, p. 318.

3. *Hutchinson Encyclopedia,* first electronic edition (Camberly, Surrey: 1991).

4. Warren E. Leary, "New Fungus Blight Is Threatening Potato Crops Around the World," *New York Times,* October 24, 1993.

5. Al Gore, *Earth in the Balance: Ecology and the Human Spirit* (New York: Houghton Mifflin, 1992), pp. 68–70.

6. Cecil Woodham-Smith, *The Great Hunger: Ireland 1845–1849* (London, Penguin, 1962), pp. 75–77.

7. Ibid., p. 123.

8. See Mark Ritchie, "Free Trade Versus Sustainable Agriculture: The Implications of NAFTA," *The Ecologist* 22, no. 5 (September/October, 1992).

9. Lang and Hines, *The New Protectionism,* p. 117.

10. *Forbes* magazine figures, as cited in "America's Summit Ignores Hemisphere's Realities," December 8, 1994, press release by Washington's Development GAP (Development Group for Alternative Policies). See also the "Worsening Income Distribution" graph in "Mexico: How the Election Will Reshape the Economy," *Business Week,* August 22, 1994, p. 43.

11. Richard Rothstein, "Free Trade Scam," in John Cavanagh, John Gershman, Karen Baker, and Gretchen Helmke, eds., *Trading Freedom: How Free Trade Affects Our Lives, Work, and Environment* (Oakland, Calif.: Food First, 1992), p. 59. This figure reflects overall trends in Latin America that, contrary to those who believe that the "lost decade" of the 1980s was an anomaly, have only continued. According to the UN Economic Commission for Latin America, the number of poor in the region could grow to 192 million out of a population of 440 million by the year 2000 if economic policies are not changed.

12. Sanford J. Lewis, Marco Kaltofan, and Gregory Ormsby, "Border Rivers in Peril," in Cavanagh et al., *Trading Freedom*, p. 69.

13. Walden Bello, "Population and the Environment: The Food First Perspective," *Food First Action Alert*, winter 1992–93, p. 4.

14. L.A. Times Bureau story, cited in Kristin Dawkins, *Balancing: Policies for Just and Sustainable Trade* (Minneapolis: Institute for Agriculture and Trade Policy [1313 Fifth Street SE, #303, Minneapolis, MN 55414], January 1994), p. 12.

15. John Tanner, "Somalis Failing to Catch Rich Fish Harvest," Interpress Third World News Service, Rome, February 17, 1993.

16. Herman Daly and Robert Goodland, *An Ecological-Economic Assessment of Deregulation of International Commerce Under GATT* (Washington, D.C.: Environment Department, World Bank, September 25, 1992).

17. See "Dancing Round GATT," *The Economist*, November 26, 1994, pp. 25–26; David E. Sanger, "Trade Accord Ensnares Dole in Crosscurrent," *New York Times*, November 11, 1994.

18. See *Trade Secrets: Transparency and Accountability in International Trade* (London: Friends of the Earth England, Wales and North Ireland, December 14, 1993).

19. Bob Davis, "Fighting 'Nafta': Free-Trade Pact Spurs a Diverse Coalition of Grass-Roots Foes," *Wall Street Journal*, December 23, 1992.

20. Mark Ritchie, "Free Trade Agreements and the Environment — Look for the Devil in the Details," *International Society for Ecological Economics* 4, no. 3 (July, 1993), p. 9.

21. "Surprise, Surprise," *The Economist*, December 18, 1993, p. 13.

22. "GATT Will Build America," *The Economist*, June 27, 1992, p. 14.

23. "GATT Comes Right . . . ," *The Economist*, December 18, 1993, p. 14.

24. *A Report to Greenpeace on the Proposed North American Free Trade Agreement — A View from the US*, prepared by Joshua Karliner of Greenpeace International, June 3, 1991, p. 21.

25. Steven Shrybman, "Trading Away the Environment," *World Policy Journal*, winter 1991–92, p. 105.

26. Lori Wallach, at the Cowell Theater in San Francisco, 1993.

27. Natalie Avery, Martine Drake, and Tim Lang, "Codex Alimentarius: Who Is Allowed In? Who Is Left Out?," *The Ecologist* 23, no. 3 (May/June 1993).

28. *1994 Report on US Barriers to Trade and Investment* (Brussels: Services of the European Commission, April 1994), (Doc. no. I/194/94).

29. Hilary F. French, "The GATT: Menace or Ally?," *Worldwatch*, September/October 1993, p. 14.

30. Daly and Goodland, *An Ecological-Economic Assessment*, p. 30.

31. Shrybman, "Trading Away the Environment," p. 108.

32. *Everything You Always Wanted to Know About GATT, But Were Afraid to Ask* (Washington, D.C.: Public Citizen's Congress Watch, November 1991).

33. Anthony DePalma, "Law Protects Mexico's Workers But Its Enforcement Is Often Lax," *New York Times*, August 15, 1993.

34. Ricardo quoted in Doug Henwood, "The Philanthropy of Financiers," *Left Business Observer*, no. 61 (December 13, 1993), p. 3.

35. Adam Smith, *Wealth of Nations*, 1776. Quoted in Herman E. Daly and John B. Cobb, Jr., *For the Common Good: Redirecting The Economy Towards Community, the Environment, and a Sustainable Future* (Boston: Beacon Press, 1989), p. 215.

36. James Brooke, "America — Environmental Dictator?" *New York Times*, May 3, 1992.

37. Dave Phillips, author's interview, November 24, 1992.

38. Shrybman, "Trading Away the Environment," p. 102.

39. Carla Hills quoted in *GATT: The Environment and the Third World, An Overview*, part 5, "GATT and Labor" (Manzanita: Environmental News Network [P.O. Box 680, Manzanita, OR 97130], 1991).

40. Rod Leonard, author's interview, August 10, 1993.

41. *Dolphins Aren't the Only Sacrifice: The Impacts of Commercial Tuna Fishing on Oceans, Marine Life and Human Communities* (Greenpeace International, August 1993), p. 18.

42. Kristin Dawkins, *NAFTA: The New Rules of Corporate Conquest* (*Open Magazine Pamphlet Series*, P.O. Box 2726, Westfield, NJ 07091), p. 11.

43. David Dodwell, "Gatt Issues Warning Against Environmental Imperialism," *Financial Times*, February 12, 1993.

44. Karl Marx, "The Fetishism of Commodities and the Secret Thereof," *Capital, Volume One: A Critical Analysis of Capitalist Production* (New York: International Publishers, 1967), p. 71.

45. Phillips, author's interview.

46. U.S. Office of Technology Assessment, "Competing Economies: America, Europe, and the Pacific Rim" (Washington, D.C.: Government Printing Office, 1992). Cited in Brown et al., "Making Trade Fair," pp. 311–312.

47. The situation has not improved. See, for example, Dean Baker, "Trade Reporting's Information Deficit," in the November/December 1994 issue of *EXTRA!*, the magazine of FAIR, Fairness and Accuracy in Reporting.

48. Keith Bradsher, "Buchanan Joins the Foes of Trade Pact," *New York Times*, August 27, 1993.

49. Tim Golden, "A History of Pollution in Mexico Casts Clouds over Trade Accord," *New York Times*, August 16, 1993.

50. H. Jeffrey Leonard, *Pollution and the Struggle for the World Product* (Cambridge, Mass.: Cambridge University Press, 1988). Cited in "Strengthing Global Environmental Governance," in Lester R. Brown et al., *State of the World: Report 1992* (New York: Norton, 1992), p. 167.

51. See Stephen Baker, Geri Smith, and Elizabeth Weimer, "The Mexican Worker," *Business Week*, April 19, 1993; Louis Uchitelle, "Those High-Tech Jobs Can Cross the Border, Too," *New York Times*, March 28, 1993; and Harley Shaiken, "Two Myths About Mexico," *New York Times*, August 22, 1993.

52. Jim Stanford, *Going South: Cheap Labor as an Unfair Subsidy in North American Free Trade* (Ottawa: Canadian Centre for Policy Alternatives, December 1991).

53. Elaine Sciolino, "Pressures Rise over China's Trade Status," *New York Times*, May 20, 1994.

54. Daly and Goodland, *An Ecological-Economic Assessment*, p. 9.

55. Ibid., p. 13.

56. José Lutzenberger's letter to Lawrence Summers, written in February 1992, is cited in Bruce Rich, *Mortgaging the Earth: The World Bank, Environmental Impoverishment, and the Crisis of Development* (Boston: Beacon Press, 1994), p. 246. The best discussion of the whole episode is almost certainly "A Fundamentalist Freedom Fighter," chap. 5 of Susan George and Fabrizio Sabelli, *Faith and Credit: The World Bank's Secular Empire* (Boulder, Colo.: Westview, 1994).

57. Summers's memo was published, in abridged form, under the title "Let Them Eat Pollution," *The Economist*, February 8, 1992.

58. "Whose World Is It Anyway?" *The Economist*, May 30, 1992, p. "survey 7."

59. "World Climate Body Colonized by OECD Economists," *Third World Resurgence*, no. 49. For details on what promises to be a long, evolving controversy, contact the Global Commons Institute, 42 Windsor Road, London NW2 5DS. See also Daphne Wysham, "Ten-to-One Against Costing People's Lives for Climate Change," *The Ecologist*, January/February 1995, and the exchange of letters in *The Ecologist*, July/August 1995.

60. Robert Goodland and Herman Daly, "Ten Reasons Why Northern Income Growth Is Not the Solution to Southern Poverty," in Robert Goodland, Herman E. Daly, Salah El Serafy, eds., *Population, Technology, and Lifestyle: The Transition to Sustainability* (Washington, D.C.: Island Press, 1992), p. 128.

61. *Trade and the Environment* was released in February 1992 and included in the subsequent *International Trade, 1990–91*, published by the GATT Secretariat (Geneva, March 1992). This quote is from p. 2.

62. See, for example, Kaushik Basu, "The Poor Need Child Labor," an op-ed piece run in the *New York Times* on November 29, 1994, just before the congressional vote on GATT's ratification. Tom Harkin, the senator from Iowa, replied on the letters page on December 4, 1994.

63. Robin Broad and John Cavanagh, "Beyond the Myths of Rio: A New American Agenda for the Environment," *World Policy Journal* 10, no. 1 (spring 1993), p. 67.

64. The seminal study of growing affluence and the "environmental transition" that is said to accompany it focused on the relationship between per capita income and air pollution in Mexico City. (See G. M. Grossman and A. B. Krueger, "Environmental Impacts of a North American Free Trade Agreement," Discussion Paper 158, Woodrow Wilson School of Public and International Affairs, Princeton University, 1991.) It found that air quality, which had of course worsened considerably since the beginning of the "development" process, began to improve as per capita income reached about $5,000. Mainstream thinking has it that this is the general case, that environmental quality across the board improves with affluence, but such a conclusion is quite unjustified. More likely, richer middle-class consumers simply switched to cleaner American cars. Before we can know if "growth" in general is good for "the environment" in general, a good deal of research is necessary, research that concentrates not simply on pollution, but on broader measures of general environmental health such as biodiversity loss, greenhouse gas emissions, forest health, coastlines, wetlands, etc.

65. *Trade and the Environment,* pp. 17, 19.

66. "Pollution and the Poor," *The Economist,* February 15, 1992, p. 19.

67. Smitu Kothari, author's interview, November 24, 1992.

68. James K. Boyce, "NAFTA: Wiping out 7000 Years of Biodiversity," *Nautilus Bulletin,* December 1993, p. 10. David Bacon, "After NAFTA," *Environmental Action,* fall 1995 (Environmental Action Foundation, 6930 Carroll Avenue, Suite 600, Takoma Park, MD 20912).

69. "NAFTA Fact Check," in "The Case Against NAFTA," a special issue of *Multinational Monitor,* October 1993, p. 8.

70. Tim Golden, "Mexican Rebels Are Retreating; Issues Are Not," *New York Times,* January 5, 1994.

71. See Jonathan Tasini, "A Tale of Two Cities: How NAFTA Will Hurt Workers on Both Sides of the Border," *Multinational Monitor,* October 1993, for a view from before the Mexican collapse. For later views from the fair-trade camp, see Andrew Wheat, "The Fall of the Peso and the Mexican 'Miracle,' " *Multinational Monitor,* April 1995. Incidentally, the minimum daily wage in Mexican border factories was about $5.00 in 1993, before NAFTA. As of late 1995 it had fallen to about $2.20. (David Corn, "Grading Free Trade," *The Nation,* January 1, 1996.)

72. Walter Russell Mead, "Bushism Found: A Second-Term Agenda Hidden in Trade Agreements," *Harper's,* September 1992, p. 33.

73. Anthony DePalma, "The Mexicans Fear for Corn, in Danger from Free Trade," *New York Times,* July 12, 1993.

74. William D. Nordhaus, "Reflections on the Economics of Climate Change," *Journal of Economic Perspectives* 7, no. 4 (fall 1993), p. 17.

75. Donella Meadows, author's interview, January 6, 1994.

76. Mark Dowie, "American Environmentalism: A Movement Courting Irrelevance," *World Policy Journal,* winter 1991–92, pp. 87–88. For the larger story here, see Mark Dowie, *Losing Ground: American Environmentalism at the Close of the Twentieth Century* (Cambridge, Mass.: MIT Press, 1995).

77. Alexander Cockburn, "NAFTA and the Shameful Seven," *The Nation,* June 28, 1993, p. 894. Also, Mark Dowie, "NAFTA Friends," *The Nation,* April 18, 1994, p. 516.

78. Allen R. Myerson, "Trade Pact's Environmental Efforts Falter," *New York Times,* October 17, 1994; "Border Health Hazards," *Multinational Monitor,* April 1995; Sarah Anderson and John Cavanagh, eds., *NAFTA's First Year: Lessons for the Hemisphere* (December 6, 1994; available from the Institute for Policy Studies, 1601 Connecticut Avenue NW, Washington, DC 20009); Bacon, "After NAFTA."

79. *NAFTA and the Northern American Agreement on Environmental Cooperation (CAAEC): Side-Stepping the Environment,* a Greenpeace Policy Brief, Summer 1993.

80. "American Survey," *The Economist,* September 18, 1993, p. 28.

81. Keith Schneider, "Environmentalists Fight Each Other over Trade Dispute," *New York Times,* September 16, 1993.

82. Al Meyerhof, author's interview, November 1993.

83. David Rosenbaum, "Good Economics Meet Protective Politics," *New York Times,* September 19, 1993.

84. Sarah Anderson and Ken Silverstein, "Oink Oink," *The Nation,* December 20, 1993.

85. "The Discreet Charm of the Multicultural Multinational," *The Economist,* July 30, 1994. "Multinationals," *The Economist,* March 27, 1993, p. 5.

86. You may observe this silence in, for example, Gareth Porter and Janet Welsh Brown, *Global Environmental Politics* (Boulder, Colo.: Westview, 1991), or in just about anything from Washington's World Resources Institute.

87. These statistics are from *Ongoing and Future Research: Transnational Corporations and Issues Relating to the Environment,* United Nations Centre on Transnational Corporations (UNCTC), April 5–14, 1989, p. 6. Cited in *The Greenpeace Book of Greenwash* (Washington: Greenpeace USA [1436 U Street NW, Washington, DC 20009], 1992).

88. "The Power of the Transnationals," in "Whose Common Future?" *The Ecologist,* July/August 1992, p. 159. "Whose Common Future?" was reprinted in book form by Earthscan in London (1992) and New Society Publishers in Philadelphia (1993).

89. Dr. Arjun Makhijani, Dr. A. van Buren, A. Bickel, and S. Saleska, *Climate Change and Transnational Corporations, Analysis and Trends,* UNCTC Environment Series, no. 2 (New York: United Nations, 1992), p. 47. Cited in *The Greenpeace Book of Greenwash.*

90. *Ongoing and Future Research,* p. 77.

91. Makhijani et al., *Climate Change and Transnational Corporations,* p. 77.

92. *Ongoing and Future Research.* See also chap. 6 in *Shattering: Food, Politics, and the Loss of Genetic Diversity,* by Cary Fowler and Pat Mooney (Tucson: University of Arizona Press, 1990), and Michael Pollan, "The Seed Conspiracy," *New York Times Magazine,* March 20, 1994, pp. 49–50.

93. *World Investment Report 1993: Transnational Corporations and Integrated International Production* (Geneva: UN Conference on Trade and Development, 1993). Also, "TNCs Securing More Rights Without Obligations, Says UN Report," Chakravarthi Raghavan, *Third World Resurgence,* no. 40, pp. 30–33.

94. Frederic Clairmont and John Cavanagh, "The World's Top 200 Corporations," *Third World Resurgence,* no. 42/43, pp. 29–31.

95. Jeremy Brecher, "After NAFTA: Global Village or Global Pillage?" *The Nation,* December 6, 1993, p. 685.

96. *World Investment Report 1991: The Triad in Foreign Direct Investment* (New York: UN Centre on Transnational Corporations, 1991). *World Investment Report: 1992* (New York: UN Transnational Corporations and Management Division, 1992). See also "Multinationals," *The Economist,* March 27, 1993, p. 18.

97. "Global Economic Prospects and the Developing Countries," an April 1992 World Bank publication. Also David Dodwell, "Multinationals' Cross-Border Trade Surges," *Financial Times,* June 12, 1992.

98. Jan Knippers Black, "The No World Order," *In These Times* 16, no. 41 (November 11–29, 1992).

99. Alfred P. Sloan, Jr., "Business Bigness," a letter to General Motors stockholders, July 11, 1935.

100. "Mitsubishi Corporation and the Tropical Timber Trade," *Mori No Koe* (a Japanese timber-issues newsletter), October 1992, pp. 12–13. Michael Marks, author's interview, December 7, 1993.

101. Karl Polanyi, *The Great Transformation: The Political and Economic Origins of Our Time* (Boston: Beacon Press, 1944), pp. 3, 80, 117.

102. "Help Wanted: A New Secretary General for the United Nations," *Heritage Backgrounder Update*, no. 157 (April 8, 1991).

103. Ian Williams, "Why the Right Loves the U.N.," *The Nation*, April 13, 1992.

104. "Multinationals," *The Economist*, March 27, 1993, p. 5.

105. John Cavanagh, Robin Broad, and Peter Weiss, "The Need for a Global New Deal," *The Nation*, December 27, 1993, p. 797.

106. Lang and Hines, *The New Protectionism*, p. 37.

107. *Transnational Corporations and Sustainable Development: Recommendations of the Executive Director* (New York: UN Centre on Transnational Corporations, December 16, 1991).

108. Harris Gleckman, author's interview, September 7, 1993.

109. "Whose Common Future?" p. 163.

110. Martin Khor, "Regulating Transnational Corporations: The Biggest Gap in UNCED's Agenda," *Third World Economics*, April 16–30, 1992, p. 18.

111. Peter Hansen, author's interview, summer 1992.

112. Chakravarthi Raghavan's comment was made at Trade, Environment and Development, a conference organized by the Institute for Agriculture and Trade Policy during PrepCom4 in New York.

113. Bill Pace, author's interview, November 1992.

114. Hansen, author's interview.

115. William K. Stevens, "Gore Promises U.S. Leadership on Sustainable Development Path," *New York Times*, June 15, 1993.

116. Martin Khor, "A Year After Rio, the CSD Inches Forward," *Third World Resurgence*, no. 36, pp. 12–13.

117. See *Renewing the United Nations System*, a July 1994 Ford Foundation study by Sir Brian Urquhart and Erskine Childers, and Boutros-Ghali's own proposals, made in his *Agenda for Development*, a draft version of which was circulated in September 1994. The common theme of these and other initiatives is restoring the UN's control over the World Bank and International Monetary Fund.

118. Harris Gleckman, author's interview.

119. James Brooke, "U.S. Has Starring Role at Rio Summit as Villain," *New York Times*, June 1, 1992.

120. "Summit Watch," *San Francisco Examiner*, June 11, 1992.

121. One excellent overview of the UNCED negotiations, including details of who nixed what, is *The Final Effort: A Progress Report on Preparatory Negotiations for the UNCED*. It was written at the end of PrepCom4 by Angela Harkavy for CAPE '92, an UNCED coalition that consisted of the National Audubon Society, Environmental Defense Fund, Friends of the Earth, Natural Resources Defense

Council, National Wildlife Federation, and the Sierra Club. See also Rich, *Mortgaging the Earth*, pp. 256–269.

122. Mark Valentine, "PrepCom4: The Road to Rio is Paved with Good Intentions," *Earth Island Journal*, June 1992, p. 2.

123. "Atmosphere Debate Running Out of Steam," *Earth Summit Times*, June 13, 1992.

124. Chris Bowers, "Europe's Motorways: The Drive for Mobility," *The Ecologist* 23, no. 4 (July/August 1993), p. 125. There is as well increasing resistance to the road-building campaign. See Alan Riding, "Swiss Give New Meaning to the World Roadblock," *New York Times*, February 28, 1994, and "The Classless Society," *The Economist*, February 19, 1994.

125. "EC Still Sluggish on Ratification," in *Eco Geneva*, no. 1 (August 16, 1993). (*Eco Geneva* is a newsletter produced by nongovernmental environmental groups attending the eighth Intergovernmental Negotiating Committee of the Climate Change Convention [INC8], August 1993.) Also, Timm Kraegenow of Germanwatch, "Figures Speak Louder Than Word," *Eco Geneva*, no. 10 (August 27, 1993).

126. David Lascelles and Christina Lamb, "A Game of Missed Opportunities," *Financial Times*, June 15, 1992, p. 14.

127. Walden Bello, author's interview, April 12, 1994.

128. Quig Heng and Li Jan, "Public Safety and Security in the Three Gorges Area," *Research in Crime and Reform* 2 (1993), a monthly "internal" journal received by Human Rights Watch/Asia and translated by Canada's Probe International.

129. *The Final Effort*, p. 15. See also Peter Hayes and Kirk Smith, eds., *The Global Greenhouse Regime: Who Pays?* (London: Earthscan and UN University Press, 1993), p. 345.

130. "The Two Faces of the EU," *Eco Berlin*, no. 9 (April 6, 1995). (*Eco Berlin* is a newsletter produced by nongovernmental environmental groups attending the first Conference of Parties of the Climate Change Convention in Berlin, March–April, 1995.)

131. Christopher Flavin, "Showdown in Berlin," *Worldwatch*, July/August 1995.

132. For a roundup, see William K. Stevens, "Climate Talks Enter Harder Phase of Cutting Back Emissions," *New York Times*, April 11, 1995. Also, "Climate Summit Fails to Combat Climate Change," Greenpeace press release, Berlin, April 7, 1995.

133. Peter Padbury, author's interview, July 1992.

134. Lascelles and Lamb, "A Game of Missed Opportunities."

135. Beth Burrows, "Intellectual Property Rights and Biopiracy," *Global Pesticide Campaigner* 4, no. 2, (June 1994). (Published by the Pesticide Action Campaign, 116 New Montgomery Street, #810, San Francisco, CA 94105.)

136. On the activist challenge, led by the Rural Advancement Foundation International, see "Agracetus 'Species' Patent Update," *Global Pesticide Campaigner*, June 1994, and also November 1993. RAFI is at 71 Bank Street, #504, Ottawa, Ontario K1P 5N2, Canada. In late 1994 the U.S. Patent Office issued a prelimi-

nary ruling against Grace. See Teresa Riordan, "U.S. Revokes Cotton Patents After Outcry from Industry," *New York Times*, December 8, 1994.

137. "Patenting Indigenous Peoples," *Earth Island Journal*, fall 1993, p. 13. See also Chris Bright, "Who Owns Indigenous People's DNA?" *Worldwatch*, November/December 1994, p. 8.

138. Vandana Shiva, "Violating Peoples' Rights, Protecting Corporate Profits — The U.S. Interpretation of the Biodiversity Convention," *Third World Resurgence*, no. 34, p. 2. See also Vandana Shiva, *Monocultures of the Mind: Perspectives on Biodiversity and Biotechnology* (London: Zed Books, 1993).

139. Lascelles and Lamb, "A Game of Missed Opportunities."

140. Marc Cooper, "The White House Effect," *Village Voice*, June 16, 1992, p. 29.

141. The private-property card may be the strongest held by antienvironmentalists. See Linda Greenhouse, "High Court Limits the Public Power on Private Land," *New York Times*, June 25, 1994. See also, for context, David Helvarg, *The War Against the Greens: The Wise-Use Movement, the New Right, and Anti-Environmental Violence* (San Francisco: Sierra Club Books, 1994) and, for a discussion of the backlash against the antienvironmental backlash, Timothy Egan, "Unlikely Alliances Attack Property Rights Measures," *New York Times*, May 15, 1995.

142. "AmBushing the Environment," *Friends of the Earth*, March 1992, p. 8.

143. Henk Hobbelink, "Biodiversity at Rio: Conservations or Access?" *Capitalism, Nature, Socialism* 3, no. 4 (December 1992), p. 120. On the Bank's relationship to the CGIAR gene banks, see "World Bank's Attempted Coup over Genetic Resources" and related articles in *Third World Resurgence*, no. 48.

144. Pat Mooney, speaking at *Citizen's Dialogue: Biodiversity, Biotechnology and Intellectual Property Rights*, September 19, 1994, San Francisco. The Dialogue was organized by the Institute for Agriculture and Trade Policy in Minneapolis.

145. Darrell Posey, "Protecting Biocultural Diversity," in Steve Lerner, *Beyond the Earth Summit: Conversations with Advocates of Sustainable Development* (Bolinas, Calif.: Common Knowledge Press, 1992), pp. 136, 142.

146. In 1993 Indian peasant farmers revolted against the control of their seed stocks by Cargill and other planetary corporations. For information on this revolt, see "The Seed Satyagraha: Indian Farmers and Global Capital Face Off," *Dollars and Sense*, September/October 1994.

147. Mark Valentine, author's interview, June 1992.

148. Russ Hoyle, "Biotech Helps Salvage Biodiversity Treaty," *Biotechnology* 11 (August 1993), p. 878.

149. See Shiva, "Violating Peoples' Rights," and Hoyle, "Biotech Helps Salvage Biodiversity Treaty," for two very different views of this industry-NGO alliance.

150. U.S. Government Letter of Submittal, Convention on Biological Diversity, November 16, 1993, p. xii.

151. William J. Clinton, Letter of Transmittal, Convention on Biological Diversity, November 20, 1993, p. iv.

152. Deth Durrows, author's interview, October 1993.

153. Martin Khor Kok Peng, *The Future of North-South Relations: Conflict or Coopera-*

tion? (Penang: Third World Network [87 Cantonment Road, 10250 Penang, Malaysia]), pp. 31, 49.

154. Ibid., pp. 44–45.

155. Xabier Gorostiaga, "Complementarity or Confrontation Between East and South: From the Crisis of Civilization to the New World Community," *Worlds Apart — Worlds Together, Conference of Papers* (Peace Research Center [Nijmegen, Pax Christi Netherlands, Utrecht], 1992), p. 31.

156. Bello, author's interview.

157. Rich, *Mortgaging the Earth*, p. 245.

158. See, for example, R. L. Sivard's annual *World Social and Military Expenditures 1992* (Washington, D.C.: World Priorities, 1992); Norman Myers, *Ultimate Security: The Environmental Basis of Political Stability* (New York: Norton, 1993); and J. P. Holdren and R. K. Pachauri, *An Agenda of Science for Environment and Development into the 21st Century* (Cambridge, England: Cambridge University Press, 1992), chap. 4, "Energy."

159. Note on secretary-general's *Financial Report and Mechanisms for Sustainable Development*, prepared by the Secretariat for the Commission on Sustainable Development's Ad Hoc Working Group on Finance in preparation for the May 1994 CSD conference, paragraph 60.

160. Richard Ackermann, author's interview, July 22, 1993.

161. "No More Than a Dream in Rio," *Bankcheck Quarterly*, July 1992.

162. Paul Lewis, "Negotiators in Rio Agree to Increase Aid to Third World," *New York Times*, June 13, 1992. The charade is incessantly repeated. See, for example, "The Social Summit: Worlds Apart," *The Economist*, March 11, 1995.

163. Paul Lewis, "U.N. Panel Finds Action on Environment Lagging," *New York Times*, May 29, 1994. "New Commission Is Told That Funding of UNCED Follow-Ups Is 'Not Encouraging,'" *International Documents Review*, June 7–18, 1994, reported in *Multilateral News* (Institute for Agriculture and Trade Policy), June 21, 1994.

164. Susan George, *The Debt Boomerang: How Third World Debt Harms Us All* (London: Pluto Press, 1992), pp. xv–xvi.

165. Fiona Goldee, "Third World Debt Drains Third World Health," *Third World Resurgence*, no. 41. For the details, see *Africa Make or Break: Action for Recovery* (Oxford, England: Oxfam, 1993).

166. Daly and Goodland, *An Ecological-Economic Assessment*, p. 16. See also Rich, *Mortgaging the Earth*, p. 309.

167. Charles Arden-Clarke, *South-North Terms of Trade, Environmental Protection and Sustainable Development*. World Wildlife Fund discussion paper, Gland, Switzerland, 1992. Cited in Daly and Goodland, *An Ecological-Economic Assessment*, p. 16.

168. Ross Hammond, author's interview, August 15, 1993.

169. Hal Kane, "Third World Debt Still Rising," in Brown et al., eds., *Vital Signs: 1994* (New York: Norton, 1994), p. 74.

170. For a rare attempt at a comprehensive reckoning of South-North resource flows, see Martin Khor's "South-North Resource Flows and Their Implications for Sus-

tainable Development," *Third World Resurgence,* no. 46, pp. 14–25. Khor estimates the net flow at half a trillion dollars a year!

171. "The Divide at the Summit," *Greenpeace,* July/September 1992, p. 2.

172. Angela Gennino and Sara Colm, "The Killing Forests," *San Francisco Weekly,* June 24, 1992.

173. Martha Bechler and Angela Gennino, *Southeast Asia Rainforests: A Resource Guide and Directory* (San Francisco: Rainforest Action Network [450 Sansome Street, Suite 700, San Francisco, CA 94111], 1993), p. 25.

174. "Earth Summit: Mahathir Defends His Country's Logging Practices," Interpress Third World News Service, Rome, June 17, 1992.

175. David E. Pitt, "Rich and Poor Countries Negotiate Accord on Preservation of Forests," *New York Times,* January 23, 1994.

176. Derek Dennison, "The Temperate Rainforest: Canada's Clear-Cut Secret," *Worldwatch,* July/August 1993, p. 9. Aybrey Diem, "Clearcutting British Columbia," *The Ecologist* 22, no. 6 (November/December 1992).

177. Martin Khor, speaking at the World Affairs Council in San Francisco, October 1991.

178. Angela Gennino, author's interview, August 21, 1993.

179. Joe Kane, "With Spears from All Sides," *New Yorker,* September 27, 1993. See also the exchange of letters between Kane and the NRDC's Robert F. Kennedy, Jr., in the issue of October 25, 1993. The whole story is in Joe Kane, *Savages* (New York: Knopf, 1995).

180. After the establishment of the World Trade Organization, this issue began to heat up. There is in particular a disagreement between Southern activists — notably the Malaysia-based Third World Network — who oppose international labor standards as a form of Northern protectionism, and the "charterists," who see such standards as a valuable, even indispensable, organizing tool. The debate is hard to follow, for it is not really public, but signs surface from time to time on "trade.strategy" and other Econet conferences. For a bit of background, see John Cavanagh, "Strategies to Advance Labor and Environmental Standards: A North-South Dialogue," *Capitalism, Nature, Socialism* 4, no. 3 (September, 1993), pp. 1–6.

181. "G-77 Chairman Criticizes Uruguay Round Outcome as Against the South," posted on Econet's "trade.strategy" conference on March 1, 1994.

182. John Maynard Keynes's "National Self-Sufficiency" was first published in Britain's *New Statesman* in 1933.

183. Lang and Hines, *The New Protectionism,* p. 3. See also Lang and Hines, "GATT: The Pitfalls Amid the Promise," *New York Times,* April 17, 1994.

184. Herman E. Daly, "The Perils of Free Trade," *Scientific American,* November 1993, p. 50.

185. "Workers Beaten at Sony Maquiladora." April 19, 1994, press release from Committee for Justice in the Maquiladoras.

186. Barbara Crossette, "Human Rights Group Urges Stronger U.N. Action," *New York Times,* December 11, 1994.

187. Thomas L. Friedman, "Profit Motive Gets the Nod," *New York Times*, May 27, 1994.
188. For a long and fascinating discussion of this and related points, see Ben Barber, *Jihad vs. McWorld* (New York: Random House, 1995).
189. Mead, "Bushism Found," *Harper's*, p. 42.
190. Walter Russell Mead, "An American Grand Strategy: The Quest for Order in a Disordered World," *World Policy Journal* 10, no. 1 (spring 1993), p. 18.
191. Josh Karliner, "Confronting Transnational Corporations at the Global Level," unpublished manuscript, March 1993.
192. Steven Shrybman, author's interview, September 7, 1993.
193. Cited in Daly and Goodland, "An Ecological-Economic Assessment," p. 1.
194. Brown et al., "Making Trade Fair," pp. 311–312. See also *A Just and Sustainable Trade and Development Initiative for North America*, by The Alliance for Responsible Trade, Citizens Trade Campaign, and The Mexican Action Network on Free Trade (and endorsed by the Action Canada Network), September 1993.
195. See David E. Sanger, "Trade Agreement Ends Long Debate, but Not Conflicts," *New York Times*, December 4, 1994.
196. Keith Bradsher, "The G.O.P. Looks Homeward on Trade," *New York Times*, October 16, 1994.
197. Rod Leonard, author's interview, December 8, 1992.
198. Mead, "An American Grand Strategy." Also, author's interview, December 8, 1992.
199. Myerson, "Trade Pact's Environmental Efforts Falter."
200. Pratap Chatterjee, "'Green Trade' Workplan Is the Opposite of What Activists Want," Interpress Third World News Service, Rome, April 11, 1994.
201. Angela Gennino, author's interview.
202. Frances Williams, "Aid Agency Challenges GATT Chief over 'Winner' Claim," *Financial Times*, April 13, 1994. Alison Maltland, "Agriculture Accord Could Leave Poorest Worst Off," *Financial Times*, April 14, 1994. "The Third World GATT Trap" and "South Africa's Rude Awakening," *Multinational Monitor*, May 1994. Nathaniel C. Nash, "Latin Economic Speedup Leaves Poor in the Dust," *New York Times*, September 7, 1994. Paul Krugman, "Fantasy Economics," *New York Times*, September 26, 1994.

FIVE

The Age of Greenwashing

1. George Orwell, *1984* (New York: New American Library, 1984), pp. 174–175.
2. Michael Kelly, "David Gergen, Master of the Game," *New York Times Magazine*, October 31, 1993, p. 64.
3. The details of this well-known episode come from Martin Litton, a fierce opponent of the Diablo Canyon nuke, who was on the board of directors of the Sierra Club at the time. Author's interview, February 1993.
4. O'Dwyer's PR Services, April 1995. Quoted in Joel Bleifuss, "Covering the Earth

with Green PR," *PR Watch: Special Earth Day 25th Anniversary Issue*, first quarter 1995 (Center for Media and Democracy, 3318 Gregory Street, Madison, WI 53711).

5. Dorothy Nelkin, *Selling Science: How the Press Covers Science and Technology* (New York: Freeman, 1987), p. 144.

6. Mark Dowie, "Could PR Have Saved Exxon's Image?" *San Francisco Weekly*, February 20, 1991, p. 9.

7. Bill Walker, "Green Like Me," *Greenpeace*, May/June 1991.

8. Bleifuss, "Covering the Earth," p. 3. There's no really good estimate, for corporations simply do not release the numbers. See also John Stauber and Sheldon Rampton, *Toxic Sludge Is Good for You: Lies, Damn Lies, and the Public Relations Industry* (Monroe, Maine: Common Courage Press, 1995).

9. David Kirkpatrick, "Environmentalism: The New Crusade," *Fortune*, February 12, 1990, p. 52.

10. Greider quoted in Charles Lewis and Margaret Ebrahim, "Can Mexico and Big Business USA Buy NAFTA?" *The Nation*, June 14, 1993, p. 839.

11. Burson quoted in Joyce Nelson, "The Great Global Greenwash: Burson-Marsteller vrs. the Environment," *Covert Action Quarterly*, no. 44 (spring 1993) (1500 Massachusetts Avenue NW, Washington, DC 20005).

12. Ronald Smothers, "Study Concludes That Environmental and Economic Health Are Compatible," *New York Times*, October 19, 1994. Paul Rauber, "Beyond Greenwash," *Sierra*, July/August 1994.

13. Justine Lowe, "Chevron's Fish Stories," *San Francisco Bay Guardian*, July 18, 1990, p. 43.

14. Peter Grinspoon, "Atom and Eve — A Love Story," *The Nation*, December 23, 1992. On postfeminism and green marketing, see Marcy Darnovsky, " 'New Traditionalism' Repackaging Ms. Consumer," *Social Text*, no. 29 (vol. 9, no. 4, 1991), pp. 72–94.

15. Joan Hamilton, "Saving Energy for Fanfare and Profit," *Sierra*, September/October 1991, p. 36.

16. Nazli Choucri, "The Global Environment and Multinational Corporations," *Technology Review*, April 1991, p. 58.

17. Philip M. Klasky, "Countdown to Contamination," *San Francisco Examiner*, October 28, 1992, p. A19; and Bill Walker, "Greenwashing America," *SF Weekly*, November 6, 1991, p. 17.

18. Joel S. Hirschhorn and Kristen U. Oldenburg, *Prosperity Without Pollution: The Prevention Strategy for Industry and Consumers* (New York: Van Nostrand Reinhold, 1991).

19. Robert Gottlieb, *Forcing the Spring: The Transformation of the American Environmental Movement* (Washington, D.C.: Island Press, 1993), pp. 303–304.

20. Jack Doyle, *Hold the Applause: A Case Study of Corporate Environmentalism* (Washington: Friends of the Earth U.S. [218 D Street SE, Washington, DC 20003], 1991). See especially chap. 6, "The Ozone Game."

21. Peter Schwartz, speaking at 1991's ECO/TECH conference in Monterey, California. *The Art of the Long View* (New York: Doubleday/Currency, 1991).

22. John Holusha, "Ed Woolard Walks Du Pont's Tightrope," *New York Times*, October 14, 1990. Doyle, *Hold the Applause*, p. 2.

23. John Elkington cited in Roger Milne, "Painting the Board Rooms Green," *Tomorrow* 1, no. 2 (1991), pp. 32, 33.

24. Jon Entine, "Shattered Image," *Business Ethics*, September/October 1994, pp. 23–28.

25. "Outfront," *Mother Jones*, November/December 1992, p. 16. Mary Scott and Howard Rothman, *Companies with a Conscience: Intimate Portraits of Twelve Firms That Make a Difference* (Secaucus, N.J.: Carol Publishing Group, 1992).

26. Harden Tibbs, *Industrial Ecology: An Environmental Agenda for Industry* (Emeryville: Global Business Network [5900-X Hollis Street, Emeryville, CA 94608], 1993), pp. 5, 22. For more of this sort of optimism, see Christopher Flavin and John E. Young, "Shaping the Next Industrial Revolution," in Lester R. Brown et al., *State of the World: 1993* (New York: Norton, 1993), p. 180.

27. Jim Donahue, "Mischief, Misdeeds and Mendacity: The Real 3M," *Multinational Monitor*, May 1991, p. 29. See also Peter Sinsheimer and Robert Gottlieb, "Pollution Prevention Voluntarism: The Example of 3M," in Robert Gottlieb, ed., *Reducing Toxics: A New Approach to Policy and Industry Devision Making* (Washington, D.C.: Island Press, 1995).

28. See Barry Commoner, *Making Peace with the Planet* (New York: Pantheon, 1990). Also Commoner, "Why We Have Failed," *Greenpeace*, September/October 1989, pp. 12–13.

29. John Holusha, "Hutchinson No Longer Holds Its Nose," *New York Times*, February 3, 1991.

30. Art Kleiner, "The Three Faces of Dow," *Garbage*, July/August 1991, p. 53.

31. Joel Hirschhorn in response to a question, ECO/TECH 1991, discussion session.

32. Donahue, "Mischief, Misdeeds and Mendacity," p. 30.

33. Dick Russell and Owen deLong, "Can Business Save the Environment?" *E Magazine*, November/December 1991, p. 35.

34. See n. 31, above.

35. Tibbs, *Industrial Ecology*.

36. Ibid.

37. For more on industrial ecology, see Robert A. Frosch and Nicholas E. Gallopoulos, "Strategies for Manufacturing," *Scientific American*, September 1989, pp. 144–152.

38. Tibbs, *Industrial Ecology*, pp. 6, 7. See also Paul Hawken, *The Ecology of Commerce* (New York: HarperCollins, 1993), pp. 61–64.

39. Marcy Darnovsky, *The Green Go to Market: Environmentalists Confront Consumer Culture*, Ph.D. dissertation, University of California, Santa Cruz, 1996.

40. Barry Commoner, author's interview, March 3, 1993.

41. Mike Kieschnick at ECO/TECH 1991. See also Paul Rauber, "The Stockholder's Smile," *Sierra*, July/August, 1990, p. 18, and Mark Dowie's "Clean, Green and Guilt-Free Funds," *The Nation*, April 26, 1993, p. 550, as well as the letters that followed (*The Nation*, June 21, 1993).

42. The Atmosphere Alliance has done a brief, useful "Who's Who" of the "skeptics," front groups, and right-wing foundations working to confuse climate politics. See *Life Support: A Citizen's Guide to Solving the Atmospheric Crisis (1995)*, pp. 15–19. (Atmosphere Alliance, P.O. Box 10346, Olympia, WA 98502.)

43. David Beers and Catherine Capellaro, "Greenwash!" *Mother Jones*, March/April 1991, p. 88.

44. Chip Berlet and William K. Burke, "Corporate Fronts: Inside the Anti-Environmental Movement," *Greenpeace*, January/February 1991, p. 8. See also Carl Deal, *The Greenpeace Guide to Anti-Environmental Organizations* (Berkeley: Odonian Press, 1993).

45. "Why Do You Want to Know?" *Mother Jones*, March/April 1992, p. 18.

46. Stephan Schmidheiny with the Business Council for Sustainable Development, *Changing Course: A Global Business Perspective on Development and the Environment* (Cambridge, Mass.: MIT Press, 1992), p. xxii.

47. Ibid., pp. 16–18.

48. Ibid., p. 15.

49. *The Greenpeace Book of Greenwash* (Washington: Greenpeace USA [1436 U Street NW, Washington, DC 20009], 1992), p. 1.

50. See "Global Leader in Greenwash: Asea Brown Boveri and the Environment," chap. 2 in Iza Kruszewska's *Open Borders, Broken Promises. Privatization and Foreign Investment: Protecting the Environment Through Contractual Clauses*, A Greenpeace Proposal, Warsaw, June 3, 1993.

51. *The Greenpeace Book of Greenwash*, p. 7.

52. Noah Walley and Bradley Whitehead, "It's Not Easy Being Green," *Harvard Business Review*, May/June 1994, pp. 46–52.

53. Josh Mailman, author's interview, late 1993.

54. Langdon Winner, *The Whale and the Reactor: A Search for Limits in an Age of High Technology* (Chicago: University of Chicago Press, 1986), pp. 3–18.

55. Alternative technology has a vast classic literature. *The Whole Earth Catalog* best exemplifies the apolitical U.S. origins of the idea, but *Radical Technology*, Godfrey Boyle and Peter Harper, eds., (New York: Pantheon, 1975) shows that not all the early catalogers buried the political implications of their experiments. "Towards a Liberatory Technology," in Murray Bookchin, *Post-Scarcity Anarchism* (Montreal: Black Rose, 1986), David Dickson, *The Politics of Alternative Technology* (New York: Universe, 1975), Ivan Illich, *Tools for Conviviality* (New York: Harper Colophon, 1973), and E. F. Schumacher, *Small Is Beautiful: Economics as if People Mattered* (London: Blond and Briggs, 1973), were all key texts. For an interesting analysis of the whole school, see "Building a Better Mousetrap" in Winner's *The Whale and the Reactor*.

56. See, for example, "Developing and Sharing Appropriate Technologies," in Al Gore, *Earth in the Balance: Ecology and the Human Spirit* (New York: Houghton Mifflin, 1992), pp. 317–337.

57. Dilan Johnson, Office of Environmental Quality, author's interview, November 1993.

58. Allen R. Myerson, "Solar Power, for Earthly Prices," *New York Times*, November 15, 1994. Matthew L. Wald, "Thirsty New Solar Cells Drink In the Sun's Energy," *New York Times*, December 4, 1994.

59. Hardin Tibbs, author's interview, December 21, 1993.

60. Timothy Egan, "New York Mob Views Recycling and Turns Green," *New York Times*, November 29, 1990.

61. A. Treneman, "Green Brigades Go Naked into Battle," *The Observer*, March 8, 1992, p. 54. Quoted in Simon Fairlie, "Long Distance, Short Life: Why Big Business Favours Recycling," *The Ecologist* 22, no. 6 (November/December 1992), p. 276.

62. Fairlie, "Long Distance, Short Life," p. 277–278.

63. Ann Leonard, "Plastics: Trashing the Third World," *Multinational Monitor*, June 1992, p. 26. Also, author's interview, March 31, 1993.

64. Susan Diesenhouse, "Polyester Becomes Environmentally Correct," *New York Times*, February 20, 1994.

65. Leonard, "Plastics: Trashing the Third World," p. 26.

66. Madeleine Cobbing and Simon Divecha, "Battery Assault: The Recycling Myth," *Multinational Monitor*, January/February 1994, pp. 35–36.

67. "Ban on Exports Would Promote Justice, Congressmen, Diplomats, Greenpeace Say," *BNA International Environment Daily*, Washington, March 1, 1994.

68. Alan Durning, *How Much Is Enough? The Consumer Society and the Future of the Earth* (Norton: New York, 1992), p. 73.

69. See, for example, *Biopolymers: Making Materials Nature's Way*, U.S. Congressional Office of Technology Assessment (OTA-BP-E-102), September 1993.

70. Deal, *The Greenpeace Guide to Anti-Environmental Organizations*, p. 9.

71. Hydrogen has virtues that brilliantly complement those of solar, as has been known for a long time. Murray Bookchin called in 1962 for "non-polluting energy sources such as solar and wind power, methane generators, and possibly liquid hydrogen" (*Our Synthetic Environment* [New York: Colophon, 1974], p. xix.) Twelve years later, Barry Commoner made the case in more detail, in *The Politics of Energy* (New York: Knopf, 1979). The standard reference on solar-hydrogen is Joan M. Ogden and Robert H. Williams, *Solar Hydrogen: Moving Beyond Fossil Fuels* (Washington: World Resources Institute, 1989). See also the excellent *Fossil Fuels in a Changing Climate: How to Protect the World's Climate by Ending the Use of Coal, Oil, and Gas* (Amsterdam: Greenpeace International, 1993).

72. The oil-price connection is from a July 1991 report on Luz on U.S. National Public Radio. Also, Julie Gozan, "Solar Eclipsed," *Multinational Monitor*, April 1992, p. 9. On the low price of oil, and fossil fuels in general, as an ecological catastrophe, see a long series of reports by *New York Times* reporter Matthew L. Wald, for example: "An Energy Glut in the Ground Imperils Ecological Hopes" (October 15, 1989), "Gulf Victory: An Energy Defeat?" (June 18, 1991), "Cheap Fuel Hurts Goal for Climate" (May 25, 1992), "Carbon Tax: Green Twist on Oil Price" (June 6, 1992).

73. Louis Uchitelle, "The 'Right' Price for Oil in the U.S.," *New York Times*, March 12, 1991.

74. Articles and ads arguing that nuclear power can combat global warming, and singing the praises of "passively safe" reactor designs, were particularly thick during the greenhouse scare of the late 1980s. See William J. Broad, "Experts Call Reactor Design 'Immune' to Disaster," *New York Times*, November 15, 1988; Matthew L. Wald, "The Nuclear Industry Tries again," *New York Times*, November 26, 1989; Matthew L. Wald, "New Ideas Changing Nuclear Debate," *New York Times*, July 22, 1990, and, for a wrap-up, Harvey Wasserman, "Nuclear Power's Desert Mirage," *E Magazine*, July/August 1991.

75. Stephen H. Schneider, *Global Warming: Are We Entering the Greenhouse Century?* (San Francisco: Sierra Club, 1989), p. 245.

76. John Greenwald, "Time to Choose," *Time*, April 29, 1991.

77. David Malin Roodman, "U.S. Nuclear Budget Grows," *Worldwatch*, January/February 1994, p. 6.

78. "Signs of the Times," *Worldwatch*, October/November 1993, p. 9. See Nicholas Lenssen, "Nuclear Power at a Virtual Standstill," in Brown et al., eds., *Vital Signs: 1993* (New York: Norton, 1993), p. 50. Philip Shenon, "Energy-Hungry, Asia Embraces Nuclear Power," *New York Times*, April 23, 1995.

79. Note that "true cost" is no merely rhetorical issue. The "attempted internalization of environmental impacts" hits nuclear power hard by forcing safety measures and other elaborations that radically increase construction costs. (John P. Holdren, "Energy in Transition," *Scientific American*, September 1990, p. 159.)

80. "Nuclear Energy Means Cleaner Air," a magazine ad that appeared just about everywhere in early 1993.

81. Megan Ryan, "Power Move: The Nuclear Salesmen Target the Third World," *Worldwatch*, March/April, 1994.

82. Harvey Wasserman, "Last Stand on Prairie Island," *The Nation*, March 7, 1994, p. 305.

83. Mike Mariotte of NIRS (Nuclear Information Research Service, in Washington, D.C.), author's interview, November 30, 1993.

84. Gore, *Earth in the Balance*, p. 327.

85. John Newhouse, "The Diplomatic Round: Earth Summit," *New Yorker*, June 1, 1992, p. 69.

86. Al Gore, preface to the paperback edition of *Earth in the Balance* (New York: Plume, 1993), p. xvii.

87. New Earth 21 plan, quoted in Kjell Fornander, "Japan, Inc., Gets into the Environment Business," *Tomorrow* 1, no. 1 (1991), p. 38. Also, "Promotion of the New Earth 21," provided by the Japanese Embassy, Washington, D.C.

88. Tadashi Ogura, "Japanese Nuclear Power and Joint Implementation," *Eco Geneva*, no. 4 (February 14, 1994). (*Eco Geneva* is a newsletter produced by nongovernmental environmental groups attending the ninth Intergovernmental Negotiating Committee of the Climate Change Convention [INC9], February 1994.) German industry has the same plans — Anke Herold and Robin Wood, "Ger-

many Goes Nuclear on JI," *Eco Berlin,* no. 8 (April 5, 1995). (*Eco Berlin* was published at the first Conference of Parties of the Climate Change Convention in Berlin, March–April, 1995.)

89. Beth Burrows, "Ethics and Other Irrational Considerations," *Boycott Quarterly,* spring 1993.

90. Quoted in Les Levidow, "Cleaning Up on the Farm," *Science as Culture, No. 13* (London: Free Association Books, 1991), p. 547.

91. Bill R. Baumgardt and Marshall A. Martin, "The Origins of Biotechnology and Its Potential for Agriculture," in *Agricultural Biotechnology: Issues and Choices,* Purdue University Agricultural Experiment Station, 1991, p. 3.

92. For a straight dose of this sort of optimism, see Dennis Avery, "Saving the Planet with Pesticides," *The True State of the Planet,* Ronald Bailey, ed., (New York: Free Press, 1995).

93. Industrial agriculture is no clear winner over the best forms of traditional agro-ecology, even in narrow productivity terms. In the first place, it is unsustainable. For example, even the Food and Agricultural Organization is concerned that green-revolution yields are dropping in Asia. See Martin Khor, "Move Away from Green Revolution," *Third World Resurgence,* no. 39, pp. 2–3) (87 Cantonment Road, 10250 Penang, Malaysia).

94. Beth Burrows, "Brave New Food," *PCC Sound Consumer,* September 1992.

95. Jane Rissler and Margaret Mellon, *Perils Amidst the Promise: Ecological Risks of Transgenic Crops in a Global Market* (Cambridge: Union of Concerned Scientists [26 Church Street, Cambridge, MA 02238], December 1993), p. 1.

96. Ibid., pp. 2–3. Also, Keith Schneider, "Science Group Urges a Delay in Selling Gene-Altered Food," *New York Times,* December 21, 1993.

97. See Lawrence Busch et al., *Plants, Power, and Profit: Social, Economic, and Ethical Consequences of the New Biotechnologies* (Cambridge, Mass: Basil Blackwell, 1991), or Jack Kloppenberg, *First the Seed: The Political Economy of Plant Biotechnology* (New York: Cambridge University Press, 1988).

98. For both scientific and political details on herbicide tolerance, see *Biotechnology's Bitter Harvest: Herbicide-Tolerant Crops and the Threat to Sustainable Agriculture,* a March 1990 report of the Biotechnology Working Group (Rebecca Goldburg, Environmental Defense Fund; Jane Rissler, National Wildlife Federation; Hope Shand, Rural Advancement Fund International; Chuck Hassebrook, Center for Rural Affairs).

99. Walter Truett Anderson, *To Govern Evolution: Further Adventures of the Political Animal* (New York: Harcourt Brace Jovanovich, 1987).

100. The Third National Agricultural Biotechnology Conference was held in Sacramento, California, in May 1991. Anderson's keynote was delivered on May 30.

101. Bill Liebhardt, author's interview, February 25, 1993.

102. Richard Hindmarsh, "The Flawed 'Sustainable' Promise of Genetic Engineering," *The Ecologist* 21, no. 5 (September/October 1991), and Tracey Clunies-Ross and Nicholas Hildyard, "The Politics of Industrial Agriculture," *The Ecologist* 22, no. 2 (March/April 1992).

103. Bill Liebhardt, "BGH, Rotational Grazing and Land Grants," *Sustainable Agriculture* 5, no. 2 (winter 1993) (the newsletter of the University of California's Sustainable Agriculture Research and Education Program).

104. William C. Liebhardt, *The Dairy Debate* (Oakland: ANR Publications [a division of the University of California Department of Agriculture and Natural Resources], 1993).

105. Margaret Mellon, May 30, 1991, speaking at NABC-3 (National Agricultural Biotechnology Conference: Biological, Social, and Institutional Concerns; sponsored by the NAB Council in cooperation with the University of California Agricultural Issues Center).

106. Ibid. See also Frederick H. Buttel, "Social Relations and the Growth of Modern Agriculture," in C. R. Carroll et al., *Agroecology* (New York: McGraw Hill, 1990), p. 139.

107. Jack Kloppenberg, author's interview, March 17, 1993.

108. Edward Goldsmith speaking at Black Oak Books in Berkeley, February 1, 1993.

109. Paul Kennedy, *Preparing for the Twenty-First Century* (New York: Random House, 1993), p. 80. For a further discussion of the likely impact of biotech synthesis on Third World economies, see *Genewatch* (the newsletter of the Council for Responsible Genetics, 5 Upland Road, Cambridge, MA 02140) 6, nos. 2–3, and Martin Khor, "Third World Farmers' Livelihood May Be Wiped Out by Biotech-Produced Crops," *Third World Resurgence*, no. 44, pp. 25–26.

110. Mercio Gomes, et al., *A Vision from the South: How Wealth Degrades the Environment: Sustainability in the Netherlands* (Utrecht: International Books, Uitgeverij Jan van Arkel, 1992), p. 62. See also Sandra Postel, "Carrying Capacity: Earth's Bottom Line," in Lester R. Brown et al., *State of the World: 1994* (New York: Norton, 1994), pp. 16–17.

111. The "social studies of science" literature is vast and fascinating, and some of its stars would consider this statement naive. I do not think that it is. In any case, for good entries into the literature, see Bob Young, "Introduction," in Les Levidow, ed., *Radical Science Essays* (London: Free Association Books, 1986); Bruno Latour, *Laboratory Life* (Princeton: Princeton University Press, 1979), especially chap. 4 on "fact constructions"; Donna Haraway, *Primate Visions* (New York: Routledge, 1989); and Sandra Harding, *The Science Question in Feminism* (Ithaca, N.Y.: Cornell University Press, 1986). For a more classical perspective, see Thomas Kuhn, *The Structure of Scientific Revolutions* (Chicago: University of Chicago Press, 1970), or Imre Lakatos and Alan Musgrave, *Criticism and the Growth of Knowledge* (New York: Cambridge University Press, 1970). On the uses of "nature," see Winner, "The State of Nature Revisited," in *The Whale and the Reactor.*

112. "Bush Asks Cautious Response to Threat of Global Warming," *New York Times*, February 6, 1990, p. 1.

113. William K. Stevens, "Skeptics are Challenging Dire 'Greenhouse' Views," *New York Times*, December 13, 1989, p. 1.

114. On Lindzen's continued quotability as chief skeptic, see William K. Stevens,

"Experts Confirm Human Role in Global Warming," *New York Times*, September 10, 1995.

115. Richard A. Kerr, "Greenhouse Skeptic Out in the Cold," *Science*, December 1, 1989, pp. 1118–1119. Lindzen publicly withdrew his cloud hypothesis, so central to earlier greenhouse denials, in October 1991, though he continues to believe, contrary to most other scientists, that water vapor will have a cooling effect (see Gore, *Earth in the Balance*, p. 380).

116. "Bush Denies Delaying Action on Averting Shift in Climate," *New York Times*, April 19, 1990.

117. William K. Stevens, "Estimates of Warming Gain More Precision and Warn of Disaster," *New York Times*, December 15, 1992. Walter Sullivan, "Study of Greenland Ice Finds Rapid Change in Past Climate," *New York Times*, July 15, 1993.

118. From the IPCC's October 1990 report, cited in R. A. Kerr, "New Greenhouse Report Puts Down Dissenters," *Science* 249 (August 3, 1990), pp. 481–82.

119. William K. Stevens, "Scientists Confront Renewed Backlash on Global Warming," *New York Times*, September 14, 1993.

120. Jeffrey Salmon, "Greenhouse Anxiety," *Commentary* 96, no. 1 (July 1993), p. 25.

121. Ben W. Bolch and Robert D. McCallum, *Apocalypse Not: Science, Economics and Environmentalism* (Washington, D.C.: Cato Institute, 1993).

122. Dixy Lee Ray, *Environmental Overkill: Whatever Happened to Common Sense?* (New York: Harper Perennial, 1994).

123. Dixy Lee Ray and Lou Guzzo, *Trashing the Planet: How Science Can Help Us Deal with Acid Rain, Depletion of the Ozone, and Nuclear Waste (Among Other Things)* (New York: Harper Perennial, 1992).

124. Stephens, "Scientists Confront Renewed Backlash."

125. For a history of the long years it took to get the ozone crisis taken seriously, see Sharon L. Roan, *Ozone Crisis: The 15-Year Evolution of a Sudden Global Emergency* (New York: Wiley, 1989).

126. Gary Taubes, "The Ozone Backlash," *Science* 260 (June 11, 1993), pp. 1580–1583. The essential text here, the one which fed Limbaugh's campaign and to which almost all "ozone scare" science traces, is Rogelio A. Maduro and Ralf Schauerhammer, *The Holes in the Ozone Scare: The Scientific Evidence That the Sky Isn't Falling* (Washington, D.C.: Scientific Associates, 1992). To place it on the political spectrum, note that the publicity for *The Ozone Scare* urges the "overthrow of the murderous environmentalist regime now ruling our schools, governing institutions, and the media." See John Passacantando and Andre Carothers, "Crisis? What Crisis? The Ozone Backlash," *The Ecologist* 25, no. 1 (January/February 1995), and also David Helvarg, *The War Against the Greens: The Wise-Use Movement, the New Right, and Anti-Environmental Violence* (San Francisco: Sierra Club Books, 1994), pp. 232, 285–286. In late 1995, the inevitable finally occurred — see William K. Stevens, "G.O.P. Seeks to Delay Ban on Chemical Harming Ozone," *New York Times*, September 21, 1995.

127. Peter Huber introduced the term into the rhetoric of denial. See his *Galileo's*

Revenge: Junk Science in the Courtroom (New York: Basic, 1991) or "Junk Science in the Courtroom," *Forbes*, July 8, 1991, p. 68.

128. See Matthew L. Wald, "Pioneer in Radiation Sees Risk Even in Small Doses," *New York Times*, December 8, 1992, and Jay M. Gould, "Chernobyl — The Hidden Tragedy," *The Nation*, March 15, 1993, p. 331. For more detail, see Jay M. Gould and Benjamin A. Goldman, *Deadly Deceit: Low-Level Radiation, High-Level Cover-up* (New York: Four Walls Eight Windows, 1990).

129. See Paul Brodeur, *The Great Power-line Cover-up: How the Utilities and the Government Are Trying to Hide the Cancer Hazards Posed by Electromagnetic Fields* (Boston: Little, Brown, 1993).

130. Liane Casten, "The Dioxin File: Anatomy of a Cover-up," *The Nation*, November 30, 1992, p. 658. "Dioxin Charade Poisons the Press," *Extra!*, January/ February 1992, p. 12. Ann Misch, "Chemical Reaction," *Worldwatch*, March/ April, 1993.

131. Julian L. Simon and Aaron Wildavsky, "Facts, Not Species, Are Periled," *New York Times*, May 13, 1993.

132. See letters by Norman Myers and E. O. Wilson in "Before Skies Become Entirely Barren of Birds," *New York Times*, May 25, 1993.

133. Charles C. Mann, "Extinction: Are Ecologists Crying Wolf?" *Science* 253 (August 16, 1991). Charles C. Mann and Mark. L. Plummer, "The Butterfly Problem," *The Atlantic*, January 1992, and *Noah's Choice: The Future of Endangered Species* (New York: Knopf, 1995). Also, Carol Kaesuk Yoon, "Boom and Bust May Be the Norm in Nature, Study Suggests," *New York Times*, March 15, 1994.

134. Daniel B. Botkin, *Discordant Harmonies: A New Ecology for the Twenty-First Century* (New York: Oxford, 1990), pp. 10, 62. For a discussion of Botkin, and some suggestions of the politics of this paradigm shift, see Donald Worster, *The Wealth of Nature* (New York: Oxford, 1993), pp. 150–153.

135. Donald Ludwig, Ray Hilborn, Carl Walters, "Uncertainty, Resource Exploitation, and Conservation: Lessons from History," *Science* 260 (April 2, 1993), and William K. Stevens, "Biologists Fear Sustainable Yield Is Unsustainable Idea," *New York Times*, April 20, 1993.

136. Emily Yoffe, "The Silence of the Frogs," *New York Times Magazine*, December 12, 1992, p. 66. Kathryn Phillips, *Tracking the Vanishing Frogs: An Ecological Mystery* (New York: St. Martin's, 1994).

137. John Maynard Keynes, *The General Theory of Employment, Interest and Money*, 1936.

138. Michael Rothschild, *Bionomics: The Inevitability of Capitalism* (New York: Henry Holt, 1990).

139. For a discussion of abstraction in modern economics, and its tendency to entirely abstract itself from empirical research in the real social and physical worlds, see Hawken, *The Ecology of Commerce*, p. 59. Also, Doug Henwood, "Intellectual Bankrupcy," *Left Business Observer*, no. 57, p. 5.

140. "California Air Show," *Wall Street Journal* editorial, October 8, 1990.

141. Keith Schneider's five-part series ran between March 21 and March 26, 1993.

These particular quotes are from the first article in that series, "New View Calls Environmental Policy Misguided." Schneider once wrote that dioxin is "considered no more risky than spending a week sunbathing," and later admitted making it up (David Moberg, "Dioxin Clouding the Press?," *Mother Jones,* July/August 1994). For a running critique of the series, see *Rachel's Hazardous Waste News,* nos. 330, 331, 332, 333, and 379 (Environmental Research Foundation, P.O. Box 5036, Annapolis, MD 20403).

142. See Thomas Michael Powers and Paul Rauber, "The Price of Everything," *Sierra,* November/December 1993, pp. 87–96.

143. World Bank, *World Development Report 1992: Development and the Environment* (New York: Oxford University Press, 1992), p. 67.

144. "Environmental Protection in the 1990s: A Time for New Approaches." Address by Gus Speth to the New England Environmental Conference of March 16, 1991.

145. Paul Hawken, "A Declaration of Sustainability," *Utne Reader,* September/October 1993, p. 57.

146. *A New Generation of Environmental Leadership: Action for the Environment and the Economy* (Washington: World Resources Institute, 1993), p. 6.

147. For an open-minded review of the issues here, see Frances Cairncross, *Costing the Earth: The Challenge for Governments, the Opportunities for Business* (Boston: Harvard Business School Press, 1992).

148. Ibid., p. 63.

149. Roger Manser, pp. 33, 80. This book has been published under two different titles. In Britain it is *Squandered Dividend: The Free Market and the Environment in Eastern Europe* (London: Earthscan, 1993). In the United States it is named *Failed Transitions: The Eastern European Economy and Environment Since the Fall of Communism* (New York: New Press, 1994).

150. *The Environmental Impact of the Car* (Amsterdam: Greenpeace International, 1991), p. 13. *Fossil Fuels in a Changing Climate* (Amsterdam: Greenpeace International, 1993), p. 18.

151. See James J. MacKenzie, Roger C. Dower, and Don Chen, *The Going Rate: What It Really Costs to Drive* (Washington: World Resources Institute, 1993), or Harold M. Hubbard, "The Real Cost of Energy," *Scientific American,* April 1991, pp. 36–42. If "externalities" and not direct subsidies are the issue, the figure may be even larger: a 1993 report by the Natural Resources Defense Council estimates them as between $380 billion and $660 billion (John Millar and John Moffet, *The Price of Mobility: Uncovering the Hidden Costs of Transportation,* 1993). In Europe, much higher gasoline prices still do not internalize the full costs of transportation. The European Federation of Transport and the Environment estimates the externality at $120 billion a year (Pre Kageson, *Getting the Prices Right — A European Scheme for Making Transportation Pay Its True Cost* [Rue de la Victoire 26, 1060 Brussels, Belgium], 1993).

152. Jeremy Rifkin, *Beyond Beef: The Rise and Fall of Cattle Culture* (New York: Plume, 1993), and John Robbins, *Diet for a New America* (Walpole, Mass.: Stillpoint, 1987).

153. The classic text here is Marc Reisner's *Cadillac Desert: The American West and Its Disappearing Water* (New York: Penguin, 1987).

154. Peter Passell, "Greening California," *New York Times*, February 27, 1991.

155. Robert Cullen, "The True Cost of Coal," *The Atlantic*, December 1993, pp. 38–52.

156. *Fiscal Fission: The Economic Failure of Nuclear Power*, by Komanoff Energy Associates, December 1992. Available from Greenpeace USA.

157. Stephen Shrybman, author's interview, May 18, 1994.

158. Speth, "Environmental Protection in the 1990s."

159. W. D. Nordhaus, "Global Warming: Slowing the Greenhouse Express," in H. Aaron, ed., *Setting National Priorities* (Washington, D.C.: Brookings Institution, 1990), quoted in David W. Orr, "Pascal's Wager and Economics in a Hotter Time," *The Ecologist* 22, no. 2 (March/April 1992), p. 42. See also Nordhaus, "Reflections on the Economics of Climate Change," *Journal of Economic Perspectives* 7, no. 4 (fall 1993), pp. 11–25.

160. W. D. Nordhaus, "Greenhouse Economics: Count Before You Leap," *The Economist*, July 7, 1990.

161. Nordhaus, "Global Warming."

162. See Peter Passell, "A Study Says Global Warming May Help U.S. Agriculture," *New York Times*, September 8, 1994.

163. Jon R. Louma, "Generate 'Nega Watts,' Says Fossil Fuel Foe," *New York Times*, April 20, 1993.

164. Peter Passell, "Cure for Greenhouse Effect: The Costs Will Be Staggering," *New York Times*, November 19, 1989.

165. Stephen H. Schneider, *Global Warming*, p. 256.

166. See Amory B. Lovins, John W. Barnett, and L. Hunter-Lovins, *Supercars: The Coming Light-Vehicle Revolution* (Snowmass, Colo.: Rocky Mountain Institute [1739 Snowmass Creek Road, Snowmass, CO 81654], 1993).

167. Amory Lovins, speaking at Hackers/93. Hackers is an annual conference of the U.S. techno-bohemian elite.

168. For a critique of "clean" cars, see "'Clean' Cars Still Kill — Message to Bill and Al," *Paving Moratorium Updata and Auto-Free Times*, summer 1993. (Alliance for a Paving Moratorium, P.O. Box 4347, Arcata, CA 95521). Also Marcia D. Lowe, "Reinventing Transport," *State of the World: 1994*, pp. 87–90.

169. Amory Lovins, "Abating Global Warming," *Earth Island Journal*, winter 1990, p. 20. See also Amory Lovins, "Does Abating Global Warming Cost or Save Money?" *Rocky Mountain Institute* 6, no. 3 (1990).

170. John Holdren, author's interview, November 19, 1993.

171. Lovins, "Abating Global Warming," p. 21. For more detail, see Amory B. Lovins, L. Hunter-Lovins, Florentine Krause, and Wilfrid Bach, *Least-Cost Energy: Solving the CO$_2$ Problem* (Snowmass, Colo.: Rocky Mountain Institute, 1981, reprinted with a new preface in 1989). A followup is presented in Florentine Krause's "Least-Cost Insurance Against Climate Risks: The Cost of Cutting Carbon Emissions," in the fall 1992 issue of *Earth Island Journal*. (The study is available from the International Project for Sustainable Energy Paths in El

Cerrito, California.) See also Michael Phillips, *The Least-Cost Energy Path for Developing Countries* (Washington, D.C.: International Institute for Energy Conservation, 1991).

172. Herman Daly, author's interview, July 26, 1993.

173. Andrew Stirling, "Environmental Valuation: How Much Is the Emperor Wearing?" *The Ecologist* 23, no. 3 (May/June 1993), p. 97.

174. Peter Passell, "Polls May Help Government Decide the Worth of Nature," *New York Times*, September 6, 1993, p. 1.

175. "The Ivory Paradox," *The Economist*, March 2, 1991, p. 16. For more detail, see Cairncross, *Costing the Earth*, pp. 136–141.

176. Raymond Bonner, "Crying Wolf Over Elephants," *New York Times Magazine*, February 7, 1993, p. 16. For details on this point, see Raymond Bonner, *At the Hand of Man: Peril and Hope for Africa's Wildlife* (New York: Random House, 1993).

177. Ann Misch, "Can Wildlife Traffic Be Stopped?" *Worldwatch*, September/October 1992, p. 26. And see Peter Matthiessen, *African Silences* (New York: Random House, 1991).

178. Garth Owen-Smith, April 21, 1993, at the 1993 Goldman Awards press conference, San Francisco, California.

179. Peter Korn, "The Case for Preservation," *The Nation*, March 30, 1992, p. 415. William K. Stevens, "Battle Looms on Plans for Endangered Species," *New York Times*, November 16, 1993.

180. "Our First 150 Years," *The Economist*, September 4–10, 1993.

181. "Whose Common Future?" *The Ecologist*, July/August 1992, pp. 173–179. Reprinted in book form by Earthscan in London (1992) and New Society Publishers in Philadelphia (1993).

182. For an intriguing notion of what might actually be necessary, see Michael Albert and Robin Hahnel, *Looking Forward: Participatory Economics for the Twenty-First Century* (Boston: South End Press, 1991).

183. Mark Sagoff, *The Economy of the Earth* (New York: Cambridge University Press, 1988), p. 88.

184. Cairncross, *Costing the Earth*, p. 100.

185. Joseph Goffman, "Learning to Love Emissions Trading," *E Magazine*, January/February 1993, p. 54.

186. Jeffrey Taylor, "CBOT Plan for Pollution-Rights Market Is Encouraging Plenty of Competition," *Wall Street Journal*, August 24, 1993.

187. "Massachusetts Plan Aims for Pollution-Credit Trade," *Wall Street Journal*, September 29, 1993.

188. Fred Munson, "Free Market Environmentalism: Selling Our Right to Clean Air," *Greenpeace*, summer 1993.

189. At the climate convention's 1995 Berlin Conference of Parties, it was decided that in the "pilot phase" of the evolving joint implementation program, rich countries would not actually be allowed to earn "credits" by financing cleanups in poorer regions. Rich countries, that is, will not simply be able to buy pollution rights from poor ones and in so doing avoid the need to reform their con-

sumption patterns and their economies. It was a victory for international environmental justice, but a pretty small one — it's likely that such credits, and therefore true pollution trading, will be allowed when the pilot is declared completed, which will be no later than 1999.

190. Sandor quoted in *Futures: The Magazine of Commodities and Options* (October 1991). Cited by Eric Nelson, "Pollution Trading," *Z Magazine*, September 1993, p. 50. To see his vision coming true, see Michael Quint, "New Tools Spread Risks of Insurers," *New York Times*, May 15, 1995.

191. Alex Farrell, author's interview, January 18, 1994.

192. For an authoritative version of the standard defense of SO_2 trading, see "Testimony on Title IV of the Clean Air Act before the Senate Committee on Environment and Public Works Subcommittee on Clean Air and Nuclear Regulation," October 21, 1993, by John Goffman, senior attorney, Environmental Defense Fund.

193. Mark A. Bernstein, Alexander E. Farrell, James J. Winebrake, *The Clean Air Act's SO_2 Emissions Market: An Estimate of Regulator Restrictions and Market Uncertainty*, Energy Management and Policy Program, University of Pennsylvania, February 16, 1993. Also, Powers and Rauber, "The Price of Everything," pp. 89–90.

194. Benjamin A. Goldman, *The Truth About Where You Live* (New York: Random House, 1991). See also, Goldman, "Polluting the Poor," *The Nation*, October 5, 1992.

195. James Dao, "A New, Unregulated Market: Selling the Right to Pollute," *New York Times*, February 6, 1993, p. 1. See also Peter Passell, "Economic Scene," *New York Times*, April 8, 1993.

196. Herman E. Daly and John B. Cobb, Jr., *For the Common Good: Redirecting the Economy Towards Community, the Environment, and a Sustainable Future* (Boston: Beacon Press, 1989), pp. 244–245. This particular idea for enforcing limits by way of tradable rights was first floated by Kenneth Boulding (*The Meaning of the Twentieth Century: The Great Transition* [New York: Harper and Row, 1964]).

197. Thomas F. Homer-Dixon, "On the Threshold: Environmental Changes as Causes of Acute Conflict," *International Security* 16, no. 2 (fall 1991), p. 101.

198. National Public Radio "Marketplace," March 17, 1995. The tale is told more sedately, in more detail, by Peter Weber, "Protecting Ocean Fisheries and Jobs," in Lester R. Brown, ed., *State of the World: 1995* (New York: Norton, 1995), pp. 32–33.

199. John Ruskin, *Unto This Last* (Lincoln: University of Nebraska Press, 1967; orig. ed., 1860), p. 30. Quoted in C. Douglas Lummis, "Equality," in Wolfgang Sachs, ed., *The Development Dictionary: A Guide to Knowledge as Power* (London: Zed Books, 1992), p. 44.

200. Bruce Rich, *Mortgaging the Earth: The World Bank, Environmental Impoverishment, and the Crisis of Development* (Boston: Beacon Press, 1994), p. ix.

201. Interpress Third World News Service release, Rome, October 14, 1991.

202. Bruce Rich, "Memorandum: Forcible Resettlement in World Bank Projects," Environmental Defense Fund, Washington, D.C., January 1994, p. 1.

203. Natalie Avery and Ross Hammond, "Bank Hires PR Maestro," *Bankcheck Quarterly* (International Rivers Network, 1847 Berkeley Way, Berkeley, CA 94703), January 1994, p. 1. Ross Hammond, "Bank Adjusts Image," *Bankcheck Quarterly*, June 1994, p. 5. Herb Schmertz with William Novak, *Goodbye to the Low Profile: The Art of Creative Confrontation* (Boston: Little, Brown, 1986).

204. Rich, *Mortgaging the Earth*, p. 102.

205. Ibid., p. 82.

206. Ibid., p. 111–112.

207. A. W. Clausen, "Sustainable Development: The Global Imperative," Fairfield Osborn Memorial Lecture in Environmental Science, Washington, D.C., November 12, 1981, in World Bank, *The Development Challenge of the Eighties: A. W. Clausen at The World Bank, Major Policy Addresses 1981–86* (Washington, D.C.: World Bank, 1986), pp. 29–30. Cited in Rich, *Mortgaging the Earth*, p. 111.

208. Rich, *Mortgaging the Earth*, pp. 118, 135, 160.

209. Leonard Sklar, *Damming the Rivers: The World Bank's Lending for Large Dams, 1994* (Berkeley: International Rivers Network, 1994).

210. Rich, "Memorandum," pp. 1–2.

211. Rich, *Mortgaging the Earth*, p. 146.

212. Ibid., pp. 162–164.

213. Angela Gennino, "Forest Policy Undermined in Gabon," *Bankcheck Quarterly*, November 1992, p. 5.

214. Pratap Chatterjee, "World Bank Forestry Policy Under Attack by Its Economists," Interpress Third World News Service, May 13, 1994.

215. Rich, *Mortgaging the Earth*, p. 153.

216. Ibid., p. 167.

217. *A Clear Cut Above: A Fact Sheet on Forestry and the World Bank*, by Korinna Horta and Mimi Keliner of EDF and Sean Clark of Greenpeace, 1994.

218. Jimmy Carter, "UNCED's Challenge Not Impossible," *Earth Summit Times*, June 8, 1992, p. 6.

219. Juliette Majot, "For Your Eyes Only," *Bankcheck Quarterly*, July 1992, p. 5.

220. Juliette Majot, author's interview, March, 1992.

221. Korinna Horta, author's interview, March 30, 1993.

222. Todd Goldman and Karan Capoor, "Soot in the Pipeline," *Eco Geneva* (INC8), no. 8, (August 25, 1993). Bruce Rich, author's interview, August 23, 1993. To gauge the extent of the irrationality here, note the vast potential for energy-efficiency improvements in India. According to the U.S. Agency for International Development, efficiency measures could save as much as $13 billion and reduce peak-power demands by as much as 36 gigawatts by 2005 (Hilary F. French, "Rebuilding the World Bank," in Lester R. Brown et al., *State of the World: 1994*, p. 167).

223. Susan George, author's interview, December 22, 1991.

224. See Rich, *Mortgaging the Earth*, pp. 249–254, and Barbara Crossette, "Movement Fights Harm to Poorer Nations," *New York Times*, June 23, 1992.

225. "Lies, Fantasy and Cynicism," *The Ecologist* 22, no. 6 (November/December

1992), p. 259. Rich, *Mortgaging the Earth*, pp. 254–256. Also, see the exchange of letters in the *New York Times* between Environmental Defense Fund staff (January 6, 1993) and Willi Wapenhans (January 23, 1993).

226. "The Funding Mechanism: Hostage to the World Bank?" *Eco Geneva* (INC8), no. 8 (August 23, 1993). For background, see "The World Bank's Energy Sector Contributes to Global Warming," in *The World Bank's Greenwash: Touting Environmentalism While Trashing the Planet* (Greenpeace International, April 1992), p. 6.

227. World Bank, "Interim Report of the Independent Evaluation of the Global Environment Facility — Pilot Phase," August 26, 1993, p. 63.

228. Korinna Horta and Scott Hajost, "Cartagena Meeting," posted to "gef.forum" on Econet, December 22, 1993.

229. Juliette Majot, author's interview, October 19, 1993. For the evolving story of the appeals office and related developments, see Jonathan Fox and L. David Brown, eds., *The Struggle for Accountability: The World Bank, NGOs, and Grassroots Movements* (Cambridge, Mass.: MIT Press, 1996).

230. See Rich, *Mortgaging the Earth*, pp. 302, 312. In late 1994, the GEF's structure finally set. Years of international struggle for democracy and transparency resulted in a final arrangement in which a small number of elite NGOs could observe the GEF's nonexecutive meetings. It could have been worse.

231. In 1994 the Cato Institute, a radical free-market think tank in Washington, D.C., released *Perpetuating Poverty: The World Bank, the IMF, and the Developing World*, a book that echoes the environmentalists' critique of the Bank in significant ways. The big difference in perspective comes on the nature of large corporations — the last chapter of *Perpetuating Poverty* is "The Liberating Potential of Multinational Corporations."

232. "U.S. Congress Puts World Bank on Short Leash," EDF press release, October 1, 1993.

233. Exact figures available in Thomas Fues and Barbara Unmuessig, *IDA Replenishment and Multilateral Debt: Net Transfers of IMF and World Bank Towards Severely Indebted Low-Income Countries* (Bonn: World Economy, Ecology and Development, March 28, 1995).

234. Stuart Elliot, "The Media Business. Advertising: Sensing a Need to Polish Its Image, the World Bank Gets Ready for Its First Campaign," *New York Times*, May 17, 1995.

235. World Bank press release no. B95/S93; "World Bank Launches Major Campaign to Show . . . Real Benefits to America of Helping the Poorest Countries," May 16, 1995.

236. Harry S. Truman, Inaugural Address, January 20, 1949, in *Documents on American Foreign Relations* (Princeton: Princeton University Press, 1967). Cited by Gustavo Esteva in Sachs, ed., *The Development Dictionary*.

237. Rich, *Mortgaging the Earth*, p. 84.

238. On "containment liberalism," see Walden Bello with Shea Cunningham and Bill Rau, *Dark Victory: The U.S., Structural Adjustment, and Global Poverty* (Oakland:

Food First [398 Sixtieth Street, Oakland, CA 94618] with London's Pluto Press and the Transnational Institute, 1994), pp. 10–17.

239. McNamara cited in Rich, *Mortgaging the Earth*, p. 84.

240. Robin Broad and John Cavanagh, "Beyond the Myths of Rio: A New American Agenda of the Environment," *World Policy Journal* 10, no. 2 (spring 1993), p. 67. See also "Landlessness, Land Insecurity, and Deforestation: The Plight of Third World Farmers," *Third World Resurgence*, no. 26, p. 4.

241. Good discussions of alternatives to development as usual are becoming easy to find. See "What on Earth Is to Be Done?" in Bruce Rich's *Mortgaging the Earth;* Hilary F. French's "Rebuilding the World Bank" in Brown et al., *State of the World: 1994;* Jim Barnes, *Bankrolling Success* (Washington: Friends of the Earth, 1994); John Cavanagh, Daphne Wysham, and Marcos Aruda, *Beyond Bretton Woods* (London: Pluto, 1994); and Michael Shuman, *Towards a Global Village,* (Washington, D.C.: Institute for Policy Studies, 1994).

242. Donald Worster, "The Shaky Ground of Sustainable Development," in *The Wealth of Nature*, pp. 143–144.

243. Gustavo Esteva in Sachs, ed., *The Developmental Dictionary*, p. 16.

244. W. R. Arney, *Experts in the Age of Systems* (Albuquerque: University of New Mexico Press, 1991), quoted in "Whose Common Future?" p. 181.

245. "The Development Set" is a poem by Ross Coggins, found in the front matter of *Lords of Poverty: The Power, Prestige, and Corruption of the International Aid Business* by Graham Hancock (New York: Atlantic Monthly Press, 1989).

246. Presentation of the International Atomic Energy Agency to the Commission on Sustainable Development, First Session, June 14–25, 1993.

247. Herman Daly in *Earth Summit: Conversations with Architects of an Ecologically Sustainable Future,* by Steve Lerner (Bolinas, Calif.: Common Knowledge Press, 1991), p. 40.

248. "Setting the Record Straight . . . ," World Bank External Affairs Department, March 1994, p. 3. Rich wrote a detailed response to the Bank in a April 7 memo to "Interested NGOs."

249. See Easterbrook's contribution to misunderstanding greenhouse politics on the *New York Times* op-ed page, August 13, 1993, or, even farther back, his defense of "passively safe" nukes in *Newsweek*'s "Special Report" on the environment, July 24, 1989, p. 42.

250. For specifically scientific critiques of Easterbrook, see *Rachel's Environment and Health Weekly*, no. 437 (April 13, 1995), and, at far greater length, the Environmental Defense Fund's excellent, point-by-point *A Moment of Truth: Correcting the Scientific Errors in Gregg Easterbrook's A Moment on the Earth* (EDF, 257 Park Avenue South, New York, NY 10010).

251. Gregg Easterbrook, "Forget PCB's. Radon. Alar. The World's Greatest Environmental Dangers Are Dung Smoke and Dirty Water," *New York Times Magazine*, September 11, 1994. The same argument, in more diffuse form, can be found on pages 577–585 of *A Moment on the Earth*. Easterbrook, by the way, is particularly misleading in matters relating to development and the Third World.

252. Deborah Moore, author's interview, September 1994.
253. Easterbrook, "Forget PCB's. Radon. Alar." Also, *A Moment on the Earth*, p. 584.
254. World Bank press release no. B95/S93, p. 2.
255. Wolfgang Sachs, author's interview, May 5, 1993. See as well Wolfgang Sachs, ed., *Global Ecology: A New Arena of Political Conflict* (London: Zed Books, 1993).
256. Robert D. Kaplan, "The Coming Anarchy," *Atlantic Monthly*, February 1994.
257. William D. Hartung, *And Weapons for All* (New York: HarperCollins, 1994), p. 291. See the most recent SIPRI yearbook for the situation, as it evolves. (Stockholm International Peace Research Institute, Oxford University Press). On the U.S. share, in 1994, see Eric Schmitt, "U.S. Arms Merchants Fatten Share of Sales to Third World," *New York Times*, August 2, 1994.
258. For a fine discussion of this and related points, see Christopher Lasch, *The Revolt of the Elites and the Betrayal of Democracy* (New York: Norton, 1994).
259. Lester R. Brown, "A New Era Unfolds," *State of the World: 1993*, p. 21.
260. "The Distributional Consequences of Taxes on Energy and the Carbon Content of Fuels," in *European Economy, 1992*, published by the European Commission. Cited in "Greenery and Poverty," *The Economist*, September 18, 1993, p. 80.
261. Cited by Gore, *Earth in the Balance*, p. 196.
262. Ibid., pp. 273–274.
263. I. F. Stone. "Why SALT Spells Fraud," in *Polemics and Prophecies, 1967–1970: A Nonconformist History of Our Times* (Boston: Little, Brown, 1989), p. 241.

SIX

Realism

1. George Kennan, "Policy Planning Study No. 23," written for the U.S. State Department in February 1948, cited in Noam Chomsky, *What Uncle Sam Really Wants* (Berkeley, Calif.: Odonian Press, 1993), p. 9.
2. C. Wright Mills, *The Power Elite* (Oxford, 1956), p. 356.
3. See "The Realist School and Its Critics: Interpreting the Postwar World," chap. 10 of Richard Falk's *Explorations at the Edge of Time* (Philadelphia: Temple University Press, 1992).
4. World Commission on Environment and Development, *Our Common Future* (Oxford: Oxford University Press, 1987), p. 5.
5. Robert Goodland, Herman E. Daly, Salah El Serafy, eds., *Population, Technology, and Lifestyle: The Transition to Sustainability* (Washington, D.C.: Island Press, 1992), p. xiii.
6. Paul Kennedy, *Preparing for the Twenty-First Century* (New York: Random House, 1993), p. 334.
7. Daniel Bell, "Afterword, 1988: The End of Ideology Revisited," in *The End of Ideology: On the Exhaustion of Political Ideas in the Fifties* (Cambridge: Harvard University Press, 1988), p. 421.
8. See, for example, Murray Bookchin, "Toward an Ecological Society," in *Toward an Ecological Society* (Montreal: Black Rose Books, 1980), p. 65. The essay was

originally written in March 1974. More recently, see his "Death of a Small Planet," in *The Progressive*, August, 1989.

9. Hans Magnus Enzensberger, "A Critique of Political Ecology," in *Dreamers of the Absolute* (London: Radius, 1988).

10. Heilbroner quoted in Homer-Dixon, "On the Threshold," pp. 113–114.

11. Lester R. Brown, "Launching the Environmental Revolution," in Brown et al., *State of the World: 1992* (New York: Norton, 1992), p. 174.

12. Lester R. Brown, "The Earth Summit," *Worldwatch*, May/June 1992, p. 2.

13. Holly B. Brough, "A New Lay of the Land," *Worldwatch*, January/February 1991, pp. 12, 19.

14. See, for example, Antonio Ma. Nieva, "Land Scam: Agrarian 'Reform,' Ramos Style," *Multinational Monitor*, January/February 1994, pp. 19–24, and Anthony DePalma, "Rage Builds in Chiapas Village Where Land Is Life," *New York Times*, February 27, 1994.

15. Herman Daly, "Farewell Lecture to the World Bank," January 14, 1994, in J. Cavanagh, D. Wysham, and M. Arruda, eds., *Beyond Bretton Woods: Alternatives to the Global Economic Order* (London: Pluto Press, TNI and IPS, 1994).

16. Maura Dolan, "Strong Treaties Elude Even Activists at Earth Summit," *Los Angeles Times*, June 11, 1992, p. 1.

17. For information about Econet, contact the Institute for Global Communications, 18 De Boom Street, San Francisco, CA 94107.

18. George Marshall, "Celebrating the Failure of UNCED," *Peace News*, July 1992 (Peace News and War Resisters International, 55 Dawes Street, London, SE17 1EL).

19. "Draft Proposal from People's Alliance for What to Do with the Post-Rio U.S. Citizen's Network on UNCED," written by some of the more grassroots-oriented members of the Citizen's Network Steering Committee, August 5, 1992.

20. William James, "The Moral Equivalent of War," *Essays on Faith and Morals* (New York and London: Longmans Green, 1949). Also, see Christopher Lasch, *The True and Only Heaven: Progress and Its Critics* (New York: Norton, 1991), pp. 300–302.

21. See Falk, *Explorations at the Edge of Time*, especially chap. 5, "Transition to Peace and Justice: The Challenge of Transcendence Without Utopia."

Index

About the Author

Tom Athanasiou has been active in environmental and technology politics for more than two decades. He has written for *The Nation,* the *San Francisco Chronicle,* the *Ecologist, Worldwatch Magazine,* and scores of other publications. As a day job, he runs an electronic publishing group at Sun Microsystems.